Improving Your Splunk Skills

Leverage the operational intelligence capabilities of Splunk to unlock new hidden business insights

James D. Miller
Paul R. Johnson
Josh Diakun
Derek Mock

BIRMINGHAM - MUMBAI

Improving Your Splunk Skills

First published: August 2019

Production reference: 1140819

Published by Packt Publishing Ltd.
Livery Place
35 Livery Street
Birmingham
B3 2PB, UK.

ISBN 978-1-83898-174-7

www.packtpub.com

`mapt.io`

Mapt is an online digital library that gives you full access to over 5,000 books and videos, as well as industry leading tools to help you plan your personal development and advance your career. For more information, please visit our website.

Why subscribe?

- Spend less time learning and more time coding with practical eBooks and Videos from over 4,000 industry professionals

- Improve your learning with Skill Plans built especially for you

- Get a free eBook or video every month

- Mapt is fully searchable

- Copy and paste, print, and bookmark content

Packt.com

Did you know that Packt offers eBook versions of every book published, with PDF and ePub files available? You can upgrade to the eBook version at `www.packt.com` and as a print book customer, you are entitled to a discount on the eBook copy. Get in touch with us at `customercare@packtpub.com` for more details.

At `www.packt.com`, you can also read a collection of free technical articles, sign up for a range of free newsletters, and receive exclusive discounts and offers on Packt books and eBooks.

Contributors

About the authors

James D. Miller is an innovator and accomplished Sr. Project Lead and Solution Architect with 37 years of experience of extensive design and development across multiple platforms and technologies. His roles include leveraging his consulting experience to provide hands-on leadership in all phases of advanced analytics and related technology projects, as well as providing recommendations for process improvement, report accuracy, adoption of disruptive technologies, and insight identification.

Paul R. Johnson has over 10 years of data intelligence experience in the areas of information security, operations, and compliance. He is a partner at Discovered Intelligence, a company specializing in data intelligence services and solutions. Paul previously worked for a Fortune 10 company, leading IT risk intelligence initiatives and managing a global Splunk deployment. Paul co-founded the Splunk Toronto User Group and lives and works in Toronto, Canada.

Josh Diakun is an IT operation and security specialist with a focus on creating data-driven operational processes. He has over 10 years of experience managing and architecting enterprise-grade IT environments. For the past 7 years, he has been architecting, deploying and developing on Splunk as the core platform for organizations to gain security and operational intelligence. Josh is a founding partner at Discovered Intelligence, a company specializing in data intelligence services and solutions. He is also a co-founder of the Splunk Toronto User Group.

Derek Mock is a software developer and big data architect who specializes in IT operations, information security, and cloud technologies. He has 15 years' experience developing and operating large enterprise-grade deployments and SaaS applications. He is a founding partner at Discovered Intelligence, a company specializing in data intelligence services and solutions. For the past 6 years, he has been leveraging Splunk as the core tool to deliver key operational intelligence. Derek is based in Toronto, Canada, and is a co-founder of the Splunk Toronto User Group.

Packt is searching for authors like you

If you're interested in becoming an author for Packt, please visit authors.packtpub.com and apply today. We have worked with thousands of developers and tech professionals, just like you, to help them share their insight with the global tech community. You can make a general application, apply for a specific hot topic that we are recruiting an author for, or submit your own idea.

Table of Contents

Preface

Splunk makes it easy for you to take control of your data and drive your business with the cutting edge of operational intelligence and business analytics. Through this Learning Path, you'll implement new services and utilize them to quickly and efficiently process machine-generated big data.

You'll begin with an introduction to the new features, improvements, and offerings of Splunk 7. You'll learn to efficiently use wildcards and modify your search to make it faster. You'll learn how to enhance your applications by using XML dashboards and configuring and extending Splunk. You'll also find step-by-step demonstrations that'll walk you through building an operational intelligence application. As you progress, you'll explore data models and pivots to extend your intelligence capabilities.

By the end of this Learning Path, you'll have the skills and confidence to implement various Splunk services in your projects.

This Learning Path includes content from the following Packt products:

- Implementing Splunk 7 – Third Edition by James D. Miller
- Splunk Operational Intelligence Cookbook – Third Edition by Paul R. Johnson, Josh Diakun, and Derek Mock

Who this book is for

This Learning Path is designed for data analysts, business analysts, and IT administrators who want to leverage the Splunk enterprise platform as a valuable operational intelligence tool. Existing users of Splunk who want to upgrade and get up and running with Splunk 7.x will also find this Learning Path to be of great value. Some knowledge of Splunk services will help you get the most out of this Learning Path.

What this book covers

Chapter 1, *The Splunk Interface*, walks you through the most common elements in the Splunk interface.

Chapter 2, *Understanding Search*, dives into the nuts and bolts of how searching works so that you can make efficient searches to populate cool reports.

Chapter 3, *Tables, Charts, and Fields*, starts using fields for more than searches; we'll build tables and graphs. Then we'll learn how to make our own fields.

Chapter 4, *Data Models and Pivots*, covers data models and pivots, the pivot editor, pivot elements and filters, and sparklines.

Chapter 5, *Simple XML Dashboards*, demonstrates simple XML dashboards; their purpose; using wizards to build, schedule the generation of, and edit XML directly; and building forms.

Chapter 6, *Extending Search*, uses more advanced features of Splunk to help extend the search language and enrich data at search time.

Chapter 7, *Working with Apps*, explores what makes up a Splunk app, as well as the latest *self-service* app management (originally introduced in version 6.6) updated in version 7.0.

Chapter 8, *Building Advanced Dashboards*, covers module nesting, layoutPanel, intentions, and an alternative to intentions with SideView Utils.

Chapter 9, *Summary Indexes and CSV Files*, explores the use of summary indexes and the commands surrounding them.

Chapter 10, *Configuring Splunk*, overviews how configurations work and gives a commentary on the most common aspects of Splunk configuration.

Chapter 11, *Play Time – Getting Data In*, introduces you to the many ways in which you can get data into Splunk. This chapter will play a key role in highlighting what data to consider and how to efficiently and effectively get that data into Splunk.

Chapter 12, *Building an Operational Intelligence Application,* builds on the understanding of visualizations that you gained as a result of the previous chapter to now introduce the concept of dashboards.

Chapter 13, *Diving Deeper – Advanced Searching, Machine Learning and Predictive Analytics,* helps you harness the ability to converge data from different sources and understand or build relationships between the events.

Chapter 14, *Speed Up Intelligence – Data Summarization,* provides you with a short introduction to common situations where summary indexing can be leveraged to speed up reports or preserve focused statistics over long periods of time.

Chapter 15, *Above and Beyond – Customization, Web Framework, HTTP Event Collector, REST API, and SDKs,* introduces you to four very powerful features of Splunk. These features provide the ability to create a very rich and powerful interactive experience with Splunk.

To get the most out of this book

To start with the book, you will first need to download Splunk from https://www.splunk.com/en_us/download.html.

You can find the official installation manual at http://docs.splunk.com/Documentation/Splunk/latest/Installation/Systemrequirements.

 The codes in this book use a data generator which can be used to test the queries given in the book. However, since the data is randomly generated, not all queries will work as expected and you may have to modify them accordingly.

Download the example code files

You can download the example code files for this book from your account at www.packt.com. If you purchased this book elsewhere, you can visit www.packt.com/support and register to have the files emailed directly to you.

You can download the code files by following these steps:

1. Log in or register at `www.packt.com`.
2. Select the **SUPPORT** tab.
3. Click on **Code Downloads & Errata**.
4. Enter the name of the book in the **Search** box and follow the onscreen instructions.

Once the file is downloaded, please make sure that you unzip or extract the folder using the latest version of:

- WinRAR/7-Zip for Windows
- Zipeg/iZip/UnRarX for Mac
- 7-Zip/PeaZip for Linux

The code bundle for the book is also hosted on GitHub at `https://github.com/PacktPublishing/Improving-your-Splunk-skills`. In case there's an update to the code, it will be updated on the existing GitHub repository.

We also have other code bundles from our rich catalog of books and videos available at `https://github.com/PacktPublishing/`. Check them out!

Conventions used

There are a number of text conventions used throughout this book.

`CodeInText`: Indicates code words in text, database table names, folder names, filenames, file extensions, pathnames, dummy URLs, user input, and Twitter handles. Here is an example: "The events must have a `_time` field."

A block of code is set as follows:

```
sourcetype="impl_splunk_gen" ip="*"
| rex "ip=(?P<subnet>\d+\.\d+\.\d+)\.\d+"
| table ip subnet
```

Bold: Indicates a new term, an important word, or words that you see onscreen. For example, words in menus or dialog boxes appear in the text like this. Here is an example: "There are several ways to define a field. Let's start by using the **Extract Fields** interface."

Warnings or important notes appear like this.

 Tips and tricks appear like this.

Get in touch

Feedback from our readers is always welcome.

General feedback: If you have questions about any aspect of this book, mention the book title in the subject of your message and email us at customercare@packtpub.com.

Errata: Although we have taken every care to ensure the accuracy of our content, mistakes do happen. If you have found a mistake in this book, we would be grateful if you would report this to us. Please visit www.packt.com/submit-errata, selecting your book, clicking on the Errata Submission Form link, and entering the details.

Piracy: If you come across any illegal copies of our works in any form on the Internet, we would be grateful if you would provide us with the location address or website name. Please contact us at copyright@packt.com with a link to the material.

If you are interested in becoming an author: If there is a topic that you have expertise in and you are interested in either writing or contributing to a book, please visit authors.packtpub.com.

Reviews

Please leave a review. Once you have read and used this book, why not leave a review on the site that you purchased it from? Potential readers can then see and use your unbiased opinion to make purchase decisions, we at Packt can understand what you think about our products, and our authors can see your feedback on their book. Thank you!

For more information about Packt, please visit packt.com.

1
The Splunk Interface

This chapter will walk you through the most common elements in the Splunk interface, and will touch upon concepts that are covered in greater detail in later chapters. You may want to dive right into them, but an overview of the user interface elements might save you some frustration later. We will cover the following topics in this chapter:

- Logging in and app selection
- A detailed explanation of the search interface widgets
- A quick overview of the admin interface

Logging in to Splunk

The Splunk GUI (Splunk is also accessible through its **command-line interface** (**CLI**) and REST API) is web-based, which means that no client needs to be installed. Newer browsers with fast JavaScript engines, such as Chrome, Firefox, and Safari, work better with the interface. As of Splunk Version 6.2.0 (and version 7.0 is no different), no browser extensions are required.

The default port (which can be changed) for a Splunk installation is still `8000`. The address will look like `http://mysplunkserver:8000` or `http://mysplunkserver.mycompany.com:8000`:

The Splunk interface

If you have installed Splunk on your local machine, the address can be some variant of `http://localhost:8000`, `http://127.0.0.1:8000`, `http://machinename:8000`, or `http://machinename.local:8000`.

Once you determine the address, the first page you will see is the login screen. The default username is *admin* with the password *changeme*. The first time you log in, you will be prompted to change the password for the admin user. It is a *good idea* to change this password to prevent unwanted changes to your deployment.

By default, accounts are configured and stored within Splunk. Authentication can be configured to use another system, for instance, **Lightweight Directory Access Protocol (LDAP)**. By default, Splunk authenticates locally. If LDAP is set up, the order is as follows: `LDAP / Local`.

The home app

After logging in, the default app is the **Launcher** app (some refer to it as **Home**). This app is a launching pad for apps and tutorials.

Note that with your first login, Splunk will present a popup displaying **Help us improve Splunk software** that will ask you permission (Splunk) to collect information about your Splunk usage. It is up to you how to respond.

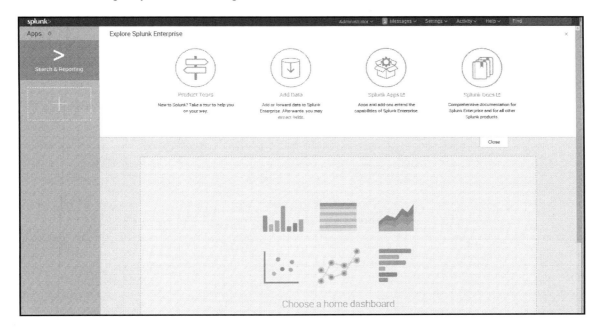

In earlier versions of Splunk, the **Welcome** tab provided two important shortcuts, **Add data** and **Launch search** app. In version 6.2.0, the **Home** app was divided into distinct areas or panes that provided easy access to **Explore Splunk Enterprise** (**Add Data, Splunk Apps, Splunk Docs,** and **Splunk Answers**) as well as **Apps** (the app management page), **Search & Reporting** (the link to the **Search** app), and an area where you can set your default dashboard (choose a home dashboard).

In version 7.0, the *main page* has not been changed very much, although you may notice some difference in the graphics. But the general layout remains the same, with the same panes and access to the same functionalities.

We'll cover apps and dashboards in later chapters of this book:

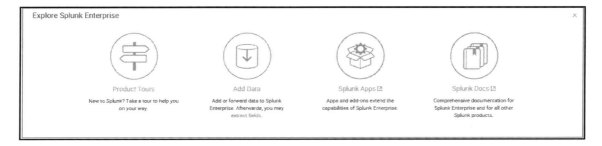

The **Explore Splunk Enterprise** pane shows the following links:

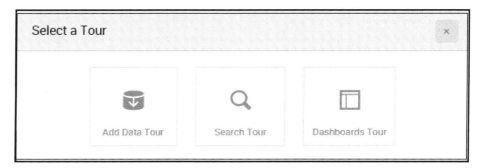

- **Product Tours** (a change in 7.0): When you click here, you can select a specific tour for your review (**Add Data Tour**, **Search Tour** and **Dashboards Tour**).

 Note: for first-timers, when you first click on any of the following links, Splunk will ask whether you'd like to pause and view a tour based on the link you chose. Of course, you always have the opportunity to go back at any time to the **Product Tours** link to review a tour.

- **Add Data**: This links **Add Data** to the Splunk page. This interface is a great start for getting local data flowing into Splunk (making it available to Splunk users). The **Preview data** interface takes an enormous amount of complexity out of configuring dates and line breaking. We won't go through those interfaces here, but we will go through the configuration files that these wizards produce in Chapter 10, *Configuring Splunk*.

- **Splunk Apps**: This allows you to find and install more apps from the Splunk Apps Marketplace (`https://splunkbase.splunk.com`). This marketplace is a useful resource where Splunk users and employees post Splunk apps, mostly free but some premium ones as well. Note that you will need to have a `splunk.com` user ID.

- **Splunk Docs**: This is one of your links to the wide amount of Splunk documentation available, specifically `https://answers.splunk.com`, to come on board with the Splunk community on Splunkbase (`https://splunkbase.splunk.com/`) and get the best out of your Splunk deployment. In addition, this is where you can access `http://docs.splunk.com/Documentation/Splunk` for the very latest updates to documentation on (almost) any version of Splunk.

The **Apps** section shows the apps that have GUI elements on your instance of Splunk. App is an overloaded term in Splunk. An app doesn't necessarily have a GUI; it is simply a collection of configurations wrapped into a directory structure that means something to Splunk. We will discuss apps in a more detailed manner in `Chapter 7`, *Working with Apps*.

Search & Reporting is the link to the Splunk **Search & Reporting** app:

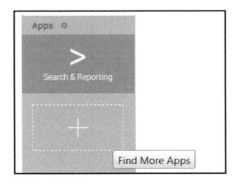

Beneath the **Search & Reporting** link, Splunk provides an outline that, when you hover over it, displays a **Find More Apps** balloon tip. Clicking on the link opens the (same) **Browse more apps** page as the **Splunk Apps** link mentioned earlier:

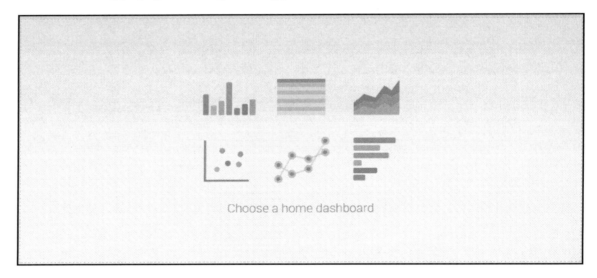

Choose a home dashboard provides an intuitive way to select an existing (simple XML) dashboard and set it as part of your Splunk **Welcome** or **Home** page. This sets you at a familiar starting point each time you enter Splunk. The following screenshot displays the **Choose Default Dashboard** dialog:

Once you select (from the drop-down list) an existing dashboard, it will be a part of your welcome screen every time you log in to Splunk—until you change it. There are no dashboards installed by default after installing Splunk, except the **Search & Reporting** app. Once you have created additional dashboards, they can be selected as the default.

The top bar

The bar *across the top* of the window contains information about where you are as well as quick links to preferences, other apps, and administration.

The current app is specified in the upper-left corner. The following screenshot shows the upper-left Splunk bar when using the **Search & Reporting** app:

Clicking on the text takes you to the default page for that app. In most apps, the text next to the logo is simply changed, but the whole block can be customized with logos and alternate text by modifying the app's CSS. We will cover this in Chapter 7, *Working with Apps*:

The upper-right corner of the window, as seen in the previous screenshot, contains action links that are almost always available:

- The name of the user who is currently logged in appears first. In this case, the user is **Administrator**. Previously, clicking on the username allowed you to select **Edit Account** (which would take you to the **Your account** page) or **Logout** (of Splunk). In version 7.0, it's a bit different. The first option is now listed as **Account Settings**, which opens a settings page similar to prior versions (below is the 7.0 page). **Logout** is the other option, and, like prior versions, it ends the session and forces the user to log in again.

The following screenshot shows what the your account page looks like:

This form presents the global preferences that a user is allowed to change. Other settings that affect users are configured through permissions on objects and settings on roles. (Note that preferences can also be configured using the command-line interface or by modifying specific Splunk configuration files.) Preferences include the following:

- **Full name** and **Email address** are stored for the administrator's convenience.
- **Set password** allows you to change your password. This is relevant only if Splunk is configured to use internal authentication. For instance, if the system is configured to use Windows Active Directory via LDAP (a very common configuration), users must change their password in Windows.
- **Global/Time zone** can be changed for the logged-in user.

 Setting the time zone only affects the time zone used to display the data. It is very important that the date is parsed properly when events are indexed. We will discuss this in detail in >Chapter 2, *Understanding Search*.

- **Default application** controls where you first land after login. Most users will want to change this to search.
- **Restart backgrounded jobs** controls whether unfinished queries should run again if Splunk is restarted.
- **Search/Search assistant/Syntax highlighting/auto-format and Show line numbers**: these properties are used for assistance with command syntax, including examples, autocomplete syntax, or to turn off search assistance. Syntax highlighting displays search string components in different colors.

- **Messages** allows you to view any system-level error messages you may have pending. When there is a new message for you to review, a notification displays as a count next to the **Messages** menu. You can click on the **X** to remove a message.

- The **Settings** link presents the user with the configuration pages for all Splunk **Knowledge** objects, **Distributed environment**, **System** and **Licensing**, **Data**, and **Users and Authentication** settings. For any option that you are unable to see, you do not have the permissions to view or edit it:

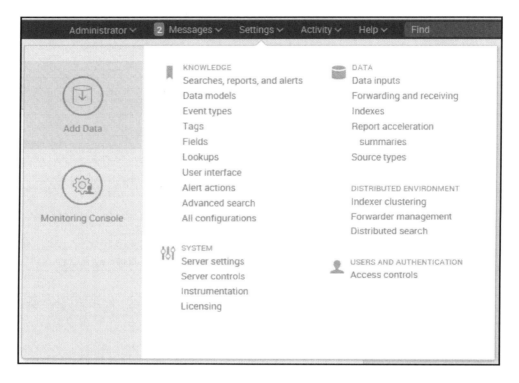

- The **Activity** menu lists shortcuts to Splunk **Jobs**, **Triggered Alerts**, and (in previous versions **System Activity)** views.
- You can click on **Jobs** (to open the search jobs manager window, where you can view and manage currently running searches) or **Triggered Alerts** (to view scheduled alerts that are triggered).

Note: In version 7.0, **System Activity** (to see dashboards about user activity and status of the system) has been removed from under Activity. You can actually access all of this detailed information in Search!

- **Help** lists links to video tutorials, **Splunk Answers**, the Splunk **Contact Support** portal, and online **Documentation**:

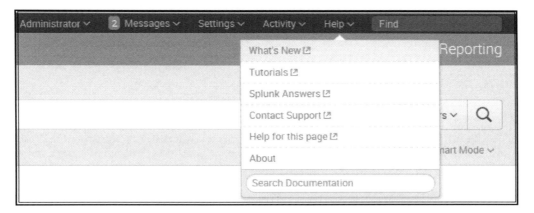

- **Find** can be used to search for objects within your Splunk Enterprise instance. These saved objects include **Reports**, **Dashboards**, **Alerts**, and so on. Errors can be searched with the **Search & Reporting** app by clicking on **Open error** in search.

The Search & Reporting app

The **Search & Reporting** app (or just the search app) is where most actions in Splunk start. This app is a dashboard where you will begin your searching.

Data generator

If you want to follow the examples that appear in the next few chapters, install the `ImplementingSplunkDataGenerator` demo app by following these steps:

1. Download `ImplementingSplunkDataGenerator.tar.gz` from the code bundle available at `http://www.packtpub.com/support`
2. Choose **Manage apps...** from the **Apps** menu
3. Click on the button labeled **Install app** from the file
4. Click on **Choose File**, select the file, and then click on **Upload**

This data generator app will produce about 16 megabytes of output per day. The app can be disabled so that it stops producing data by using **Manage apps...** under the **App** menu.

The Summary view

Within the **Search & Reporting** app, the user is presented with the **Summary** view, which contains information about the data that the user searches by default. This is an important distinction; in a mature Splunk installation, not all users will always search all data by default. But if this is your first trip into **Search & Reporting**, you'll see the following:

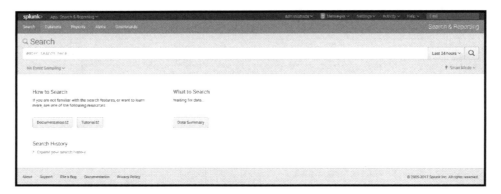

From the screen depicted in the previous screenshot, you can access the Splunk documentation related to **What to Search** and **How to Search**. Once you have at least *some data* indexed (a topic we'll discuss later), Splunk will provide some statistics on the available data under **What to Search**.

Remember that this reflects only the indexes that this particular user searches by default; there are other events that are indexed by Splunk, including events that Splunk indexes about itself. We will discuss indexes in Chapter 8, *Building Advanced Dashboards*.

What to Search is shown in the following screenshot:

In previous versions of Splunk, *panels* such as the **All indexed data** panel provided statistics for a user's indexed data. Other panels gave a breakdown of data using three important pieces of metadata—**Source, Sourcetype**, and **Hosts**. In the current version, 7.0.0, you access this information by clicking on the button labeled **Data Summary**, which presents the following to the user:

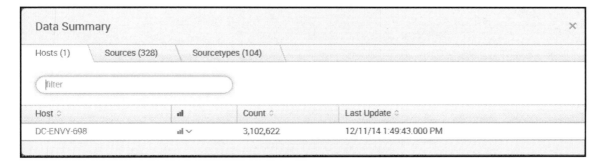

This dialog splits the information into three tabs—**Hosts, Sources** and **Sourcetypes**:

- A host is a captured hostname for an event. The majority of cases, the host field is set to the name of the machine where the data originated. There are cases where this is not known, so the host can also be configured arbitrarily.

- A source in Splunk is a unique path or name. In a large installation, there may be thousands of machines submitting data, but all data on the same path across these machines counts as one source. When the data source is not a file, the value of the source can be arbitrary. For instance, the name of a script or network port.
- A source type is an arbitrary categorization of events. There may be many sources across many hosts in the same source type. For instance, given the sources `/var/log/access.2012-03-01.log` and `/var/log/access.2012-03-02.log` on the hosts `fred` and `wilma`, you could reference all these logs with source type access or any other name that you like.

Let's move on now and discuss each of the Splunk widgets (just below the app name). The first widget is the navigation bar:

As a general rule, within Splunk, items with downward triangles are menus. Items without a downward triangle are links.

We will cover customizing the navigation bar in Chapter 7, *Working with Apps*.

Next, we find the **Search** bar. This is where the magic starts. We'll go into great detail shortly:

Search

Okay, we've finally made it to search. This is where the real power of Splunk lies.

For our first search, we will search for the word (not case-specific) error. Click in the search bar, type the word error, and then either press *Enter* or click on the magnifying glass to the right of the bar:

Upon initiating the search, we are taken to the search results page (which hasn't really changed in version 7.0):

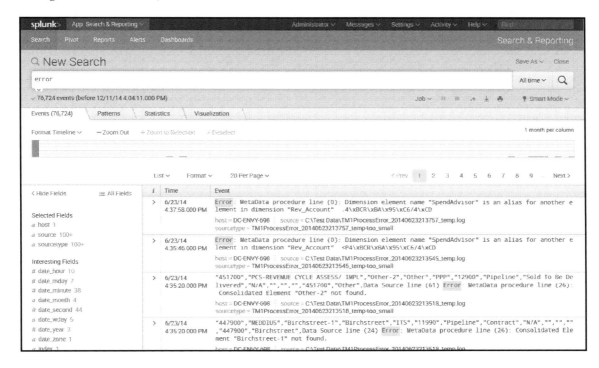

Note that the search we just executed was across **All time** (by default); to change the search time, you can utilize the Splunk time picker.

However, since the data is randomly generated, not all queries will work as expected and you may have to modify them accordingly.

You can find the steps to upload the datasets in the previous Data generator section.

Refer to the *Using the time picker* section for details on changing the time frame of your search.

Actions

Let's inspect the elements on this page. Below the **Search** bar, we have the event count, action icons, and menus:

76,724 events (before 12/11/14 4:04:11.000 PM)   Job ∨ ‖ ■ ↗ ↓ ⦿   ♥ Smart Mode ∨

Starting from the left, we have the following:

- The **number of events** matched by the base search. Technically, this may not be the number of results pulled from disk, depending on your search. Also, if your query uses commands, this number may not match what is shown in the event listing.
- **Job**: It opens the **Search job inspector** window, which provides very detailed information about the query that was run.
- **Pause**: It causes the current search to stop locating events but keeps the job open. This is useful if you want to inspect the current results to determine whether you want to continue a long-running search.
- **Stop**: This stops the execution of the current search but keeps the results generated so far. This is useful when you have found enough and want to inspect or share the results found so far.
- **Share**: It shares the search job. This option extends the job's lifetime to seven days and sets the read permissions to everyone.
- **Print**: This formats the page for printing and instructs the browser to print.
- **Export**: It exports the results. Select this option to output to CSV, raw events, XML, or **JavaScript Object Notation (JSON)** and specify the number of results to export.
- **Smart mode**: This controls the search experience. You can set it to speed up searches by cutting down on the event data it returns and additionally by reducing the number of fields that Splunk will extract by default from the data (*Fast mode*). You can otherwise set it to return as much event information as possible (*Verbose mode*). In Smart mode (the default setting), it toggles search behavior based on the type of search you're running.

Timeline

Now we'll skip to the timeline below the action icons:

Along with providing a quick overview of the event distribution over a period of time, the timeline is also a very useful tool for selecting sections of time. Placing the pointer over the timeline displays a popup for the number of events in that slice of time. Clicking on the timeline selects the events for a particular slice of time.

Clicking and dragging selects a range of time:

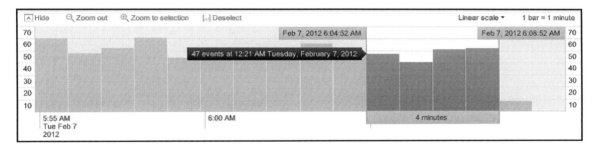

Once you have selected a period of time, clicking on **Zoom to selection** changes the time frame and reruns the search for that specific slice of time. Repeating this process is an effective way to drill down to specific events.

Deselect shows all events for the time range selected in the time picker.

Zoom out changes the window of time to a larger period around the events in the current time frame.

The field picker

To the left of the search results, we find the *field picker*. This is a great tool for discovering patterns and filtering search results:

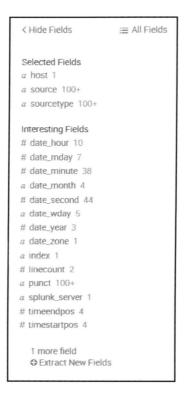

Fields

The field list contains two lists.

- **Selected Fields**, which have their values displayed under the search event in the search results
- **Interesting Fields**, which are other fields that Splunk has picked out for you

Above the field list are two links, **Hide Fields** and **All Fields**:

- **Hide Fields**: Hides the field list area from the view
- **All Fields**: Takes you to the **Selected Fields** window:

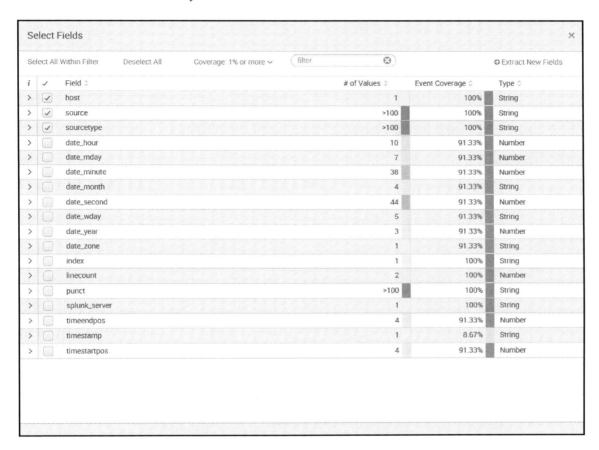

Search results

We are almost through with all the widgets on the page. We still have a number of items to cover in the search results section, though, just to be thorough:

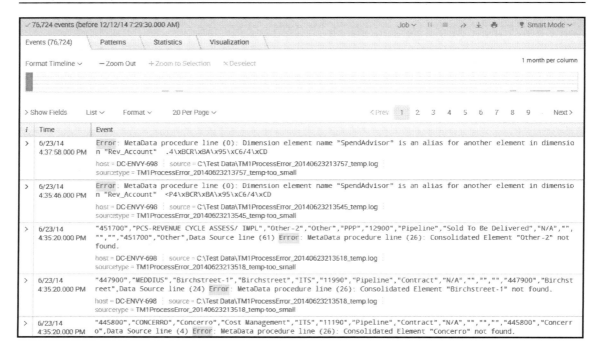

As you can see in the previous screenshot, at the top of this section, we have the number of events displayed. When viewing all results in their raw form, this number will match the number above the timeline. This value can be changed either by making a selection on the timeline or by using other search commands.

Next, we have the action icons (described earlier) that affect these particular results.

Under the action icons, we have four results tabs:

- **Events** list, which will show the raw events. This is the default view when running a simple search, as we have done so far.
- **Patterns** streamlines event pattern detection. A list of the most common patterns among the set of events is returned by your search. A number of events that share a similar structure are represented by these patterns.
- **Statistics** populates when you run a search with transforming commands such as stats, top, chart, and so on. The previous keyword search for *error* does not display any results in this tab because it does not have any transforming commands.

- **Visualization** transforms searches and also populates the **Visualization** tab. The results area of the **Visualization** tab includes a chart and the statistics table used to generate the chart. Not all searches are eligible for visualization—a concept which will be covered later in this book.

Under the previously described tabs, is the timeline that we will cover in more detail later in this chapter.

Options

Beneath the timeline (starting from the left) is a row of option links, including:

- **Show Fields**: Shows the **Selected Fields** screen
- **List**: Allows you to select an output option (**Raw, List,** or **Table**) for displaying the search result
- **Format**: Provides the ability to set **Result display options**, such as **Show row numbers**, **Wrap results**, the **Max lines** (to display) and **Drilldown** as *on* or *off*
- **NN Per Page**: This is where you can indicate the number of results to show per page (**10, 20,** or **50**)

To the right are options that you can use to choose a page of results, and to change the number of events per page.

 In older versions of Splunk (prior to 4.3), these options were available from the **Results display options** popup dialog.

Events viewer

Finally, we make it to the actual events. Let's examine a single event:

```
>   1   6/23/14         Error: MetaData procedure line (0): Dimension element name "SpendAdvisor" is an alias for another element in
        4:37:58.000 PM  dimension "Rev_Account"   .4\xBCR\xBA\x95\xC6/4\xCD
                        host = DC-ENVY-698   source = C:\Test Data\TM1ProcessError_20140623213757_temp.log
                        sourcetype = TM1ProcessError_20140623213757_temp-too_small
```

Starting from the left, we have:

- **Event Details**: Clicking here (indicated by the *right facing arrow*) opens the selected event, provides specific information about the event by type, field, and value, and allows you the ability to perform specific actions on a particular event field. In addition, Splunk offers a button labeled **Event Actions** to access workflow actions, a few of which are always available.
- **Build Event Type**: Event types are a way to name events that match a certain query. We will dive into event types in Chapter 6, *Extending Search*.
- **Extract Fields**: This launches an interface for creating custom field extractions. We will cover field extraction in Chapter 3, *Tables, Charts, and Fields*.
- **Show Source**: This pops up a window with a simulated view of the original source.
- **The event number**: Raw search results are always returned in the order *most recent first*.
- Next appear any workflow actions that have been configured. Workflow actions let you create new searches or links to other sites, using data from an event. We will discuss workflow actions in Chapter 6, *Extending Search*.
- Next comes the parsed date from this event, displayed in the time zone selected by the user. This is an important and often confusing distinction. In most installations, everything is in one time zone—the servers, the user, and the events. When one of these three things is not in the same time zone as the others, things can get confusing. We will discuss time in great detail in Chapter 2, *Understanding Search*.
- Next, we see the raw event itself. This is what Splunk saw as an event. With no help, Splunk can do a good job finding the date and breaking lines appropriately; but as we will see later, with a little help, event parsing can be more reliable and more efficient.
- Below the event are the fields that were selected in the field picker. Clicking on the value adds the field value to the search.

Using the time picker

Now that we've looked through all the widgets, let's use them to modify our search. First, we will change our time. The default setting of **All time** is fine when there are few events, but when Splunk has been gathering events over a period of time (perhaps for weeks or months), this is less than optimal. Let's change our search time to one hour:

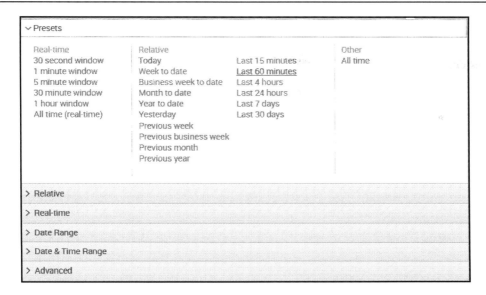

The search will run again, and now we see results for the last hour only. Let's try a custom time. **Date Range** is an option:

If you know specifically when an event happened, you can drill down to whatever time range you want here. We will examine the other options in Chapter 2, *Understanding Search*.

The time zone used in **Custom Time Range** is the time zone selected in the user's preferences, which is, by default, the time zone of the Splunk server.

Using the field picker

The field picker is very useful for investigating and navigating data. Clicking on any field in the field picker pops open a panel with a wealth of information about that field in the results of your search:

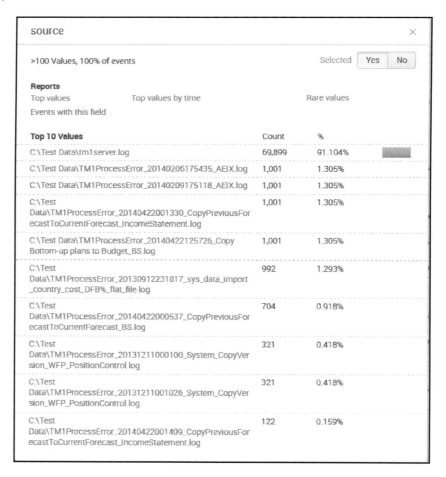

Looking through the information, we observe the following:

- *Number (of) values, appears in X% of results* tells you how many events contain a value for this field.
- **Selected** indicates if the field is a selected field.
- **Top values** and **Top values by time** (allows referring to the **Top 10 Values** returned in the search) present graphs about the data in this search. This is a great way to dive into reporting and graphing. We will use this as a launching point later.
- **Rare values** displays the least common values of a field.
- **Events with this field** will modify the query to show only those events that have this field defined.
- The links are actually a quick representation of the top values overall. Clicking on a link adds that value to the query. Let's click on `c:\\Test Data\\tm1server.log`:

```
error source="C:\\Test Data\\tm1server.log"
```

This will rerun the search, now looking for errors that affect only the source value `c:\\Test Data\\tm1server.log`.

The settings section

The **Settings** section, in a nutshell, is an interface for managing configuration files. The number of files and options in these configuration files is truly daunting, so the web interface concentrates on the most commonly used options across the different configuration types.

Splunk is controlled exclusively by plain text configuration files. Feel free to take a look at the configuration files that are being modified as you make changes in the admin interface. You will find them by hitting the following locations:

```
$SPLUNK_HOME/etc/system/local/
$SPLUNK_HOME/etc/apps/
$SPLUNK_HOME/etc/users/<user>/<app>/local
```

You may notice configuration files with the same name at different locations. We will cover in detail the different configuration files, their purposes, and how these configurations merge together in Chapter 10, *Configuring Splunk*. Don't start modifying the configurations directly until you understand what they do and how they merge.

Clicking on **Settings** on the top bar takes you to the **Settings** page:

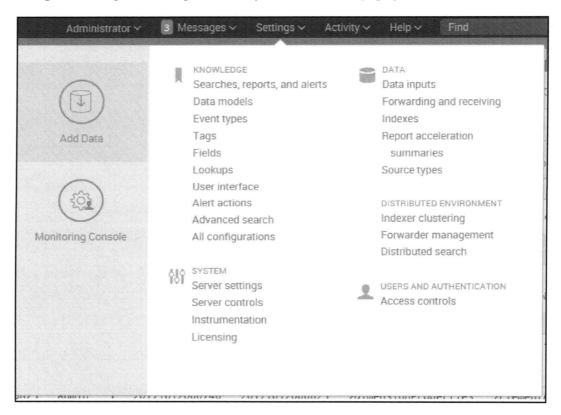

The reader will note that the layout of the setting page has changed a bit in version 7.0, but it is generally the same as prior versions. We'll point out the differences here. First, there have been some name changes (**Distributed Management Console** is now **Monitoring Console**) and a few extra links added (under **SYSTEM** we see **Instrumentation**, and **DATA** has added **Source Types**).

The options are organized into logical groupings, as follows:

- **KNOWLEDGE**: Each of the links under **KNOWLEDGE** allows you to control one of the many object types that are used at search time. The following screenshot shows an example of one object type, workflow actions: **Searches, reports, and alerts**:

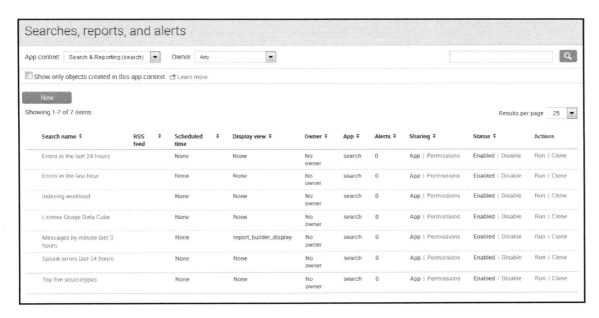

- **System**: The options under this section control system-wide settings:
    - **System settings** covers network settings, the default location to store indexes, outbound email server settings, and how much data Splunk logs about itself
    - **Server controls** contains a single page that lets you restart Splunk from the web interface
    - **Licensing** lets you add license files or configure Splunk as a slave to a Splunk license server
    - **Instrumentation** (new to version 7.0) lets you configure automated reporting settings, view collected data, export data to a file, or send data to Splunk

- **Data**: This section is where you manage the data flow:
    - **Data Inputs**: Splunk can receive data by reading files (either in batch mode or in real time), listening to network ports, or running scripts.
    - **Forwarding and receiving**: Splunk instances don't typically stand alone. Most installations consist of at least one Splunk indexer and many Splunk forwarders. Using this interface, you can configure each side of this relationship and more complicated setups .
    - **Indexes**: An index is essentially a data store. Under the covers, it is simply a set of directories, created and managed by Splunk. For small installations, a single index is usually acceptable. For larger installations, using multiple indexes allows flexibility in security, retention, and performance tuning, as well as better use of hardware. We will discuss this further in Chapter 10, *Configuring Splunk*.
    - **Report acceleration summaries**: Accesses automatically-created summaries to speed up completion times for certain kinds of reports.
    - **Source Types**: Allows access to the source types page. Source types are used to assign configurations like timestamp recognition, event breaking, and field extractions to data indexed by Splunk.

- **Distributed environment**: The three options here relate to distributed deployments :
    - **Indexer clustering**: Access to enabling and configuring Splunk **Indexer clustering**, which we will discuss later in this book.
    - **Forwarder management**: Access to the forwarder management UI distributes deployment apps to Splunk clients.
    - **Distributed search**: Any Splunk instance running searches can utilize itself and other Splunk instances to retrieve results. This interface allows you to configure access to other Splunk instances.

- **Users and authentication**: This section provides authentication controls and an account link:
    - **Access controls**: This section is for controlling how Splunk authenticates users and what users are allowed to see and do. We will discuss this further in Chapter 10, *Configuring Splunk*.

In addition to the links, the **Settings** page also presents a panel on the left-hand side of the page. This panel includes two icons, **Add Data** and (previously) **Distributed Management Console**, now **Monitoring Console**:

- **Add Data** links to the **Add Data** page. This page presents you with three options for getting data into your Splunk Enterprise instance: **Upload**, **Monitor**, and **Forward**.
- **Monitoring Console** is where you can view detailed performance information about your Splunk Enterprise deployment.

Splunk Cloud

An exciting new option for Splunk is *Splunk Cloud*. This option offers *almost* all of Splunk's features and functionalities *along with* the convenience of being on a real cloud platform:

- Readily available online, Splunk lists the following statement as per `http://docs.splunk.com/Documentation/SplunkCloud/6.6.3/User/WelcometoSplunkCloud`:

"Splunk Cloud provides a layer of security and operational control that causes it to differ from Splunk Enterprise".

In my experience, moving any software or service to the cloud typically will have some implications. With Splunk Cloud, you can expect the following differences (from Splunk Enterprise):

- There is no CLI (Splunk's command-line interface) support. This means that some (administrative) tasks can be achieved through the web browser but most will require Splunk support.
- Only apps that have been assessed (on security and stability) and accepted by Splunk support are allowed to be installed and run in Splunk Cloud.
- If you selected a *managed* Splunk Cloud, Splunk support must install and configure all apps (self-service Splunk Cloud still allows you to install apps yourself).
- Direct monitoring of TCP, UDP, file, and syslog inputs. Unlike Splunk Enterprise, these data types cannot be sent straight to Splunk Cloud (an on-premises forwarder must be used).
- Scripted Alerts are supported only in approved apps.

- License pooling is not available in Splunk Cloud. The license manager is not internet-accessible to the Splunk Cloud customers.
- Again, for *managed* Splunk Cloud deployments, the **HTTP event collector** (HEC) must be set up for you by Splunk.
- Access to the Splunk API is initially turned off (for Splunk Clusters) but can be turned on by Splunk support. To enable API access to Splunk Cloud sandbox(es) and trials, and single instance deployments, you must file a Support ticket (not recommended due to the short duration of trials).

Try before you buy

It's worth giving Splunk Cloud a try (even if you are not seriously considering its usage in the near future). If you have a valid Splunk ID, you can *test-drive* Splunk Cloud for free (for 15 days):

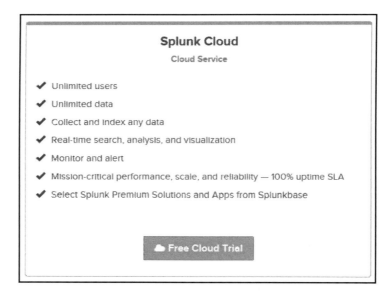

To use your Splunk ID to test drive Splunk Cloud, all you need to do is register and agree to the conditions and terms. This is the **Terms of Service** acceptance page:

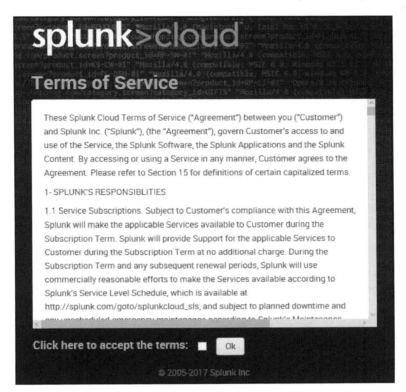

Once you check the box (and then click on the button labeled **Ok**), you will be sent an instructional email, and you are ready to go!

A quick cloud tour

Let's start with accessing your instance. Once you've received the acknowledgement that your Splunk Cloud (trial) instance is ready, you can point your browser to the provided URL. You will notice that the web address for Splunk Cloud is prefixed with a unique identifier that qualifies your particular instance (this is actually the server name where your instance resides):

And the **Log In** page is a bit different in appearance (from Splunk Enterprise):

Once you are authenticated, we see the Splunk Cloud main page:

First things first. Looking across the task bar (at the top of the page), if you click on **Support & Services** and then **About**, you will notice that the Splunk Cloud version is 6.6.3.2, which is NOT the latest on-premise or locally installed version:

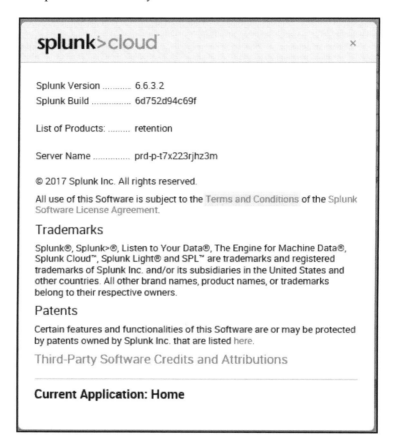

The top bar in Splunk Cloud

The top bar in Splunk Cloud is relatively the same but shifts the locally installed Splunk right-located links (**Messages**, **Settings**, **Activity**, and **Find**) to the left:

While on the right, there is **My Splunk**:

The **My Splunk** link sends you to the **Instances** page, where you can view and edit information about the Splunk instances you have access to. You can also use this page as a portal to access all of your instances by clicking on the button labeled **Access Instance** next to the instance you which to log in to. This is the **Instances** page:

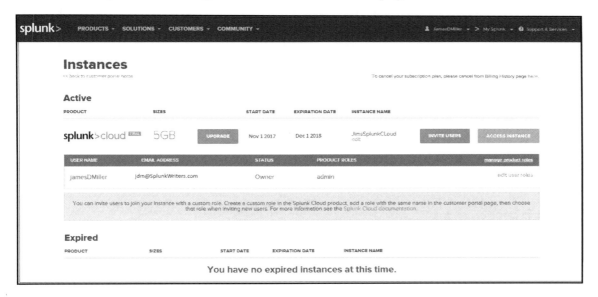

On the app list (left of the home app page) in Splunk Cloud, you will notice three apps preloaded for you: *Splunk Reference App-PAS, Universal Forwarder,* and *eventgen* (as follows):

Splunk reference app – PAS

Splunk's **Pluggable Auditing System (PAS)** (originally available as version 1.0 back in January 2015) is a Splunk App designed to describe how to develop Splunk apps. It is intended to present *recommended practices* in addition to the Splunk developer platform.

PAS also:

- Enables you to monitor countless document repositories to track who has viewed, modified, deleted, or downloaded documents or other artifacts from numerous sources
- Detects suspicious activities
- Analyzes trends

Universal forwarder

The Splunk *universal forwarder* is a no-license-required app that is not unique to Splunk Cloud or even new to Splunk 7.0; in fact, it has been available and in use for quite some time and several releases.

Since it's a *cloud-specific* app, we'll not spend much time on it here. But, as a reminder, **UF** is a dedicated, lightweight form of Splunk Enterprise containing only the vital components required to forward data and is intended to run on production servers, requiring minimal CPU and memory. It has the slightest effect possible on other software, making it ideal for Splunk Cloud.

eventgen

eventgen is also *not new* nor Splunk Cloud-specific. eventgen permits you create *dummy* events to randomly generate, allowing you to get events into Splunk for testing their applications.

Note: since eventgen is used by the internal Splunk team for developing its numerous applications and demos, it is probably a good use of the reader's time to become familiar with its almost infinite amount of configurability to simulate real data.

Next steps

As mentioned at the beginning of this section, when you sign up for Splunk Cloud, an email will be sent to your registered email ID to let you log in to your Splunk Cloud account. You will also receive an app unique to you to help you configure your forwarded to send data to your Cloud as shown in the Cloud documentation:

```
http://docs.splunk.com/Documentation/SplunkCloud/latest/User/
GetstartedwithSplunkCloud
```

 Note: https://splunkbase.splunk.com/apps/#/product/cloud is a great place to see what apps are Cloud-compatible or what apps are available specifically for Splunk Cloud.

Understanding Search 2

To successfully use Splunk, it is vital that you write effective searches. Using the index efficiently will make your initial discoveries faster, and the reports you create will run faster for you and for others. In this chapter, we will cover the following topics:

- How to write effective searches
- How to search using fields
- Understanding time
- Saving and sharing searches
- Event annotation

Using search terms effectively

The key to creating an effective search is to take advantage of the index. The Splunk index is effectively a huge word index, sliced by time. One of the most important factors for the performance of your searches is how many events are pulled from the disk. The following few key points should be committed to memory:

- **Search terms are case insensitive**: Searches for error, Error, ERROR, and ErRoR are all the same.
- **Search terms are additive**: Given the search item *mary error*, only events that contain both words will be found. There are Boolean and grouping operators to change this behavior; we will discuss these later.
- **Only the time frame specified is queried**: This may seem obvious, but it's very different from a database, which would always have a single index across all events in a table. Since each index is sliced into new buckets over time, only the buckets that contain events for the time frame in question need to be queried.
- **Search terms are words, including parts of words**: A search for *foo* will also match *foobar*.

With just these concepts, you can write fairly effective searches. Let's dig a little deeper, though:

- **A word is anything surrounded by whitespace or punctuation (and sometimes a split of words)**: For instance, given the log line `2012-02-07T01:03:31.104-0600 INFO AuthClass Hello world. [user=Bobby, ip=1.2.3.3]`, the words indexed are `2012`, `02`, `07T01`, `03`, `31`, `104`, `0600`, `INFO`, `AuthClass`, `Hello`, `world`, `user`, `Bobby`, `ip`, `1`, `2`, `3`, and `3`. This may seem strange, and possibly a bit wasteful, but this is what Splunk's index is really, really good at—dealing with huge numbers of words across huge numbers of events.

- **Splunk is not grep with an interface**: One of the most common questions is whether Splunk uses regular expressions for your searches. Technically, the answer is no. Splunk does use regex internally to extract fields, including autogenerated fields, but most of what you would do with regular expressions is available in other ways. Using the index as it is designed is the best way to build fast searches. Regular expressions can then be used to further filter results or extract fields.

- **Numbers are not numbers until after they have been parsed at search time**: This means that searching for `foo>5` will not use the index, as the value of `foo` is not known until it has been parsed out of the event at search time. There are different ways to deal with this behavior depending on the question you're trying to answer.

- **Field names are case sensitive**: When searching for `host=myhost`, `host` must be lowercase. Likewise, any extracted or configured fields have case-sensitive field names, but the values are case insensitive:
  - `Host=myhost` will not work
  - `host=myhost` will work
  - `host=MyHost` will work

- **Fields do not have to be defined before indexing data**: An indexed field is a field that is added to the metadata of an event at index time. There are legitimate reasons to define indexed fields, but in the vast majority of cases, it is unnecessary and is actually wasteful. We will discuss this in `Chapter 3`, *Tables, Charts, and Fields*.

Boolean and grouping operators

There are a few operators that you can use to refine your searches (note that these operators must be in uppercase so as not to be considered search terms):

- **AND** is implied between terms. For instance, `error mary` (two words separated by a space) is the same as `error AND mary`.
- **OR** allows you to specify multiple values. For instance, `error OR mary` means find any event that contains either word.
- **NOT** applies to the next term or group. For example, `error NOT mary` would find events that contain `error` but do not contain `mary`.
- **The quote marks ("")** identify a phrase. For example, `"Out of this world"` will find this exact sequence of words. `Out of this world` will find any event that contains all of these words, but not necessarily in that order.
- **Parentheses (( ))** are used for grouping terms. Parentheses can help avoid confusion in logic. For instance, these two statements are equivalent:
    - `bob error OR warn NOT debug`
    - `(bob AND (error OR warn)) AND NOT debug`
- **The equal sign (=)** is reserved for specifying fields. Searching for an equal to sign can be accomplished by wrapping it in quotes. You can also escape characters to search for them. `\=` is the same as `=`.
- **Brackets ([ ])** are used to perform a subsearch.

You can use these operators in fairly complicated ways if you want to be very specific, or even to find multiple sets of events in a single query. The following are a few examples:

- `error mary NOT jacky`
- `error NOT (mary warn) NOT (jacky error)`
- `index=myapplicationindex ( sourcetype=sourcetype1 AND ( (bob NOT error) OR (mary AND warn) ) ) OR ( sourcetype=sourcetype2 (jacky info) )`

This can also be written with some whitespace for clarity:

```
index=myapplicationindex
(
sourcetype=security
AND
(
(bob NOT error)
OR
(mary AND warn)
)
)
OR
(
sourcetype=application
(jacky info)
)
```

Clicking to modify your search

Though you can probably figure it out by just clicking around, it is worth discussing the behavior of the GUI when moving your mouse around and clicking:

- Clicking on any word or field value will give you the option to **Add to search** or **Exclude from search** the existing search or create a **New search**, as shown in the following screenshot:

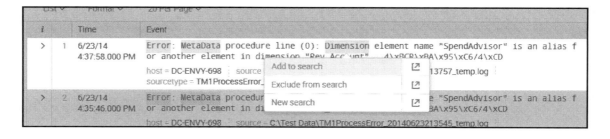

- Clicking on a word or a field value that is already in the query will give you the option to *remove it* from the existing query or, as previously, create a *new* search, as shown in the following screenshot:

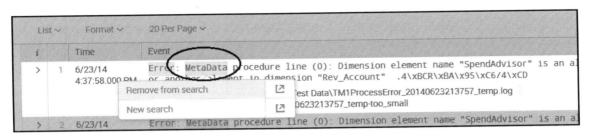

Event segmentation

In prior versions of Splunk, event segmentation was configurable through a setting in the **Options** dialog. In version 6.2, the options dialog is not present; although segmentation (discussed later in this chapter) is still an important concept, it is not accessible through the web interface/options dialog in this version.

Field widgets

Clicking on values in the **Select Fields** dialog (the *field picker*) or in the field value widgets underneath an event will again give us an option to append (add to) or exclude (remove from) our search, or as shown before, to start a new search.

For instance, if `source=C:\Test Data\TM1ProcessError_20140623213757_temp.log` appears under your event, clicking on that value and selecting **Add to search** will append `source=C:\Test Data\TM1ProcessError_20140623213757_temp.log` to your search:

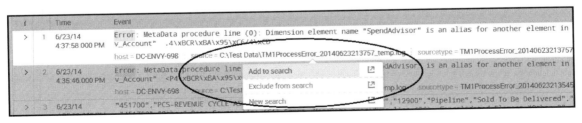

To use the field picker, you can click on the **All Fields** link (see the following screenshot):

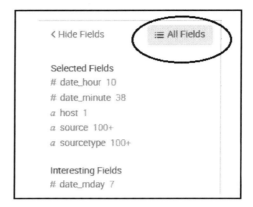

Expand the results window by clicking on > in the far-left column. Clicking on a result will append that item to the current search:

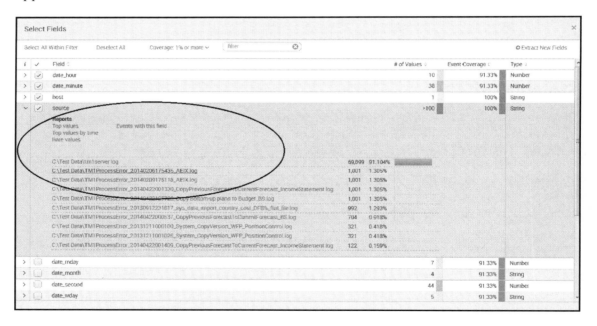

If a field value looks like `key=value` in the text of an event, you will want to use one of the field widgets instead of clicking on the raw text of the event. Depending on your event segmentation setting, clicking on the word will either add the value or `key=value`.

The former will not take advantage of the field definition; instead, it will simply search for the word. The latter will work for events that contain the exact quoted text, but not for other events that actually contain the same field value extracted in a different way.

Time

Clicking on the time next to an event will open the **_time** dialog (shown in the following screenshot), allowing you to change the search to select **Events Before or After** a particular time period, and it will also have the following choices:

- **Before this time**
- **After this time**
- **At this time**

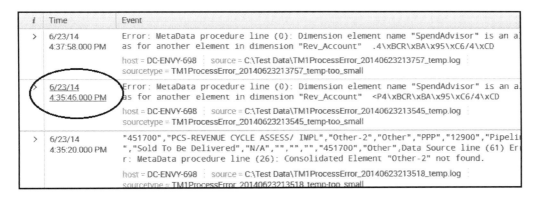

In addition, you can select **Nearby Events** within *plus*, *minus*, or *plus or minus* a number of seconds (the default), *milliseconds*, *minutes*, *hours*, *days*, or *weeks*:

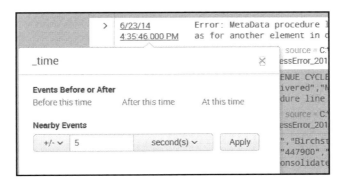

One search trick is to click on the time of an event, select **At this time**, and then use **Zoom out** (above the timeline) until the appropriate time frame is reached.

Using fields to search

When we explored the GUI in Chapter 1, *The Splunk Interface*, you probably noticed fields everywhere. Fields appear in the field picker on the left and under every event. Where fields actually come from is transparent to the user, who simply searches for key=value. We will discuss adding new fields in Chapter 3, *Tables, Charts, and Fields*, and in Chapter 10, *Configuring Splunk*.

Using the field picker

The field picker gives us easy access to the fields (currently defined) for the results of our query. Splunk will extract some fields from event data without your help such as: **host**, **source**, and **sourcetype** values, timestamps, and others. Additional fields to be extracted can be defined by you. Clicking on any field presents us with the details about that field in our current search results:

As we go through the following items in this widget, we see a wealth of information right away:

- *N Value, X% of events* is a good indication of whether we are getting the results we think we're getting. If every event in your results should contain this field, and this is not 100%, either your search can be made more specific or a field definition needs to be modified. In addition, N Value indicates the number of unique values that this field contains.

- **Selected**-**Yes** or **No** indicates whether the field is selected (is part of the search query results) or not (simply listed as interesting additional fields found by Splunk within the data).
- **Reports**-**Top Values**, **Top Values by time**, **Rare values**, and **Events with this field:**
  - **Top values** (overall) shows a table of the most common values for this field for the time frame searched.
  - **Top values by time** shows a graph of the most common values occurring in the time frame searched.
  - **Rare values** show a table of the most unique values for this field for the time frame searched.
  - **Events with this field** adds `fieldname="*"` to your existing search to make sure you only get the events that have this field. If the events you are searching for always contain the name of the field (in this case, network), your query will be more efficient provided you also add the field name to the query. In this case, the query would look like this: `sourcetype="impl_splunk_gen" network="*" network`.
- **Values** shows a very useful snapshot of the top ten most common values, **Count** is the number found for each of these values, and % is the percentage that the value is found in this field in the results of the search.

Using wildcards efficiently

Though the index is based on words, it is possible to use wildcards when necessary, albeit a little carefully. Take a look at some interesting facts about wildcards:

- Only trailing wildcards are efficient: Stated simply, `bob*` will find events containing `Bobby` efficiently, but `*by` or `*ob*` will not. The latter cases will scan all events in the time frame specified.
- Wildcards are tested last: Wildcards are tested after all other terms. Given the search `authclass *ob* hello world`, all other terms besides `*ob*` will be searched first. The more you can limit the results using full words and fields, the better your search will perform.

Supplementing wildcards in fields

Given the following events, a search for `world` would return both events:

```
2012-02-07T01:04:31.102-0600 INFO AuthClass Hello world. [user=Bobby,
ip=1.2.3.3]
2012-02-07T01:23:34.204-0600 INFO BarClass Goodbye. [user=Bobby,
ip=1.2.3.3, message="Out of this world"]
```

What if you only wanted the second event but all you know is that the event contains `world` somewhere in the field message? The query `message="*world*"` would work but it is very inefficient, because Splunk must scan every event looking for `*world`, and then determine whether `world` is present in the field message.

You can take advantage of the behavior mentioned earlier—wildcards are tested last. Rewriting the query as `world message="*world*"` gives Splunk a chance to find all the records with `world`, and then inspect those events for the more specific wildcard condition.

All about time

Time is an important and confusing topic in Splunk. If you want to skip this section, absorb one concept: time must be parsed properly on the way into the index, as it cannot be changed later without indexing the raw data again.

How Splunk parses time

Given the date `11-03-04`, how would you interpret this date? Your answer probably depends on where you live. In the United States, you would probably read this as November 3, 2004. In Europe, you would probably read this as March 11, 2004. It would also be reasonable to read this as March 4, 2011.

Luckily, most dates are not this ambiguous, and Splunk makes a good effort to find and extract them, but it is absolutely worth the trouble to give Splunk a little help by configuring the time format. We'll discuss the relevant configurations in `Chapter 10`, *Configuring Splunk*.

How Splunk stores time

Once the date is parsed, the date stored in Splunk is always stored as a GMT epoch. Epoch time is the number of seconds since January 1, 1970. By storing all events using a single time zone, there is never a problem lining up events that happen in different time zones. This, of course, only works properly if the time zone of the event can be determined when it is indexed. This numeric value is stored in the field _time.

How Splunk displays time

The text of the original event, and the date it contains, is never modified. It is always displayed as it was received. The date displayed to the left of the event is determined by the time zone of the Splunk instance or the user's preference, as specified in your account:

How time zones are determined and why it matters

Since all events are stored according to their GMT time, the time zone of event only matters at parse time, but it is vital to get it right. Once the event is written into the index, it cannot be changed without reindexing the raw data.

The time zone can come from a number of places, in the following order of precedence:

- The time zone specified in the log. For instance, the date 2012-02-07T01:03:23.575-0600, -0600 indicates that the zone is 6 hours behind GMT. Likewise, Tue 02 Feb, 01:03:23 CST 2012 represents the same date.
- The configuration associated with a source, host, or sourcetype, in that order. This is specified in props.conf. This can actually be used to override the time zone listed in the log itself, if necessary. We will discuss this in Chapter 10, *Configuring Splunk*.

- The time zone of the Splunk instance forwarding the events. The time zone is relayed along with the events, just in case it is not specified elsewhere. This is usually an acceptable default. The exception is when different logs are written with different time zones on the same host, without the time zone in the logs. In that case, it needs to be specified in `props.conf`.
- The time zone of the Splunk instance parsing the events. This is sometimes acceptable and can be used in interesting ways in distributed environments.
- The important takeaway, again, is that the time zone needs to be known at the time of parsing and indexing the event.

Different ways to search against time

Now that we have our time indexed properly, how do we search against time? The **Date & Time Range** picker provides a neat set of options for dealing with search times:

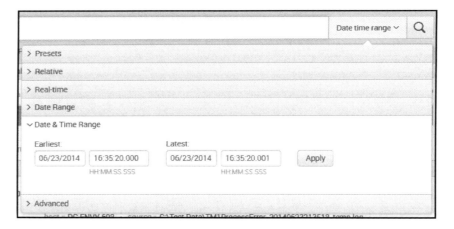

This picker widget is organized by:

- **Presets**
- **Relative**
- **Real-time**
- **Data Range**
- **Date & Time Range**
- **Advanced**

Let's take a look at each of these.

Presets

Presets are time ranges that are predefined for you in Splunk Enterprise. You should be aware, though, that if you are searching potentially large amounts of data, the results will return faster if you run the search over a smaller time period (rather than **All time (real-time)**):

∨ Presets			
Real-time	Relative		Other
30 second window	Today	Last 15 minutes	All time
1 minute window	Week to date	Last 60 minutes	
5 minute window	Business week to date	Last 4 hours	
30 minute window	Month to date	Last 24 hours	
1 hour window	Year to date	Last 7 days	
All time (real-time)	Yesterday	Last 30 days	
	Previous week		
	Previous business week		
	Previous month		
	Previous year		

> Relative
> Real-time
> Date Range
> Date & Time Range
> Advanced

Relative

If the **Relative** presets are not what you need, you can use the custom **Relative** time range options to specify a time range for your search that is relative to Now. You can select from the list of time range units, **Seconds Ago**, **Minutes Ago**, and so on:

Splunk also provides the ability to use **Beginning of second** (the default) or a **No Snap-to** time unit to indicate the nearest or latest time to which your time amount rounds up. If you don't specify a *snap-to* time unit, Splunk snaps automatically to the second. Unlike the **Presets**, to actually apply your (**Relative**) selections to the search, you need to click on the **Apply** button.

Real-time

The custom **Real-time** option gives you the ability to set the start time for your real-time time range window. Keep in mind that the search time ranges for historical searches are set at the time at which the search runs. With real-time searches, the time ranges are constantly updating and the results accumulate from the beginning of your search.

You can also specify a time range that represents a sliding window of data, for example, the last 30 seconds.

When you specify a sliding window, Splunk takes that amount of time to accumulate data. For example, if your sliding window is 5 minutes, you will not start to see data until after the first 5 minutes have passed:

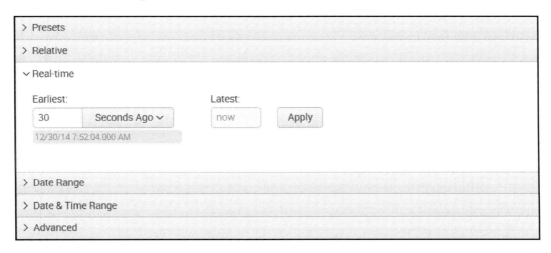

Windowed real-time versus all-time real-time searches

When designing your searches, it's important to keep in mind that there is a difference between Splunk real-time searches that take place within a set window (like **30** seconds or 1 minute) and real-time searches that are set to **All time**.

In windowed real-time searches, the events in the search can disappear as they fall outside of the window, and events that are newer than the time the search job was created can appear in the window when they occur.

In all-time real-time searches, the window spans all of your events, so events do not disappear once they appear in the window. But events that are newer than the time the search job was created can appear in the window as they occur.

In comparison, in historical searches, events never disappear from within the set range of time that you are searching and the latest event is always earlier than the job creation time (with the exception of searches that include events that have future-dated timestamps).

Date range

You can use the custom **Date Range** option to add calendar dates to your search. You can choose among options to return events: **Between** a beginning and end date, **Before** a date, and **Since** a date (for these fields, you can either type the date in the textbox or select the date from a calendar):

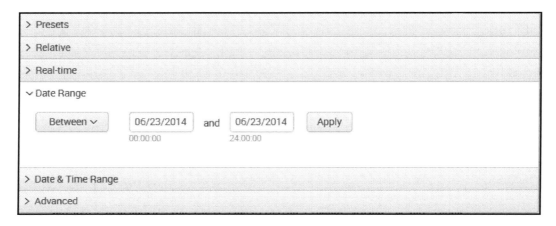

Date and time range

Use the custom **Date & Time Range** option to specify calendar dates and times for the beginning and ending of your search. Again, you can type the date into the textbox or select the date from a calendar:

Advanced

Use the **Advanced** option to specify the earliest and latest search times. You can write the times in Unix (epoch) time or relative time notation. The epoch time value that you enter is converted to local time. This timestamp is displayed under the text field so that you can verify your entry:

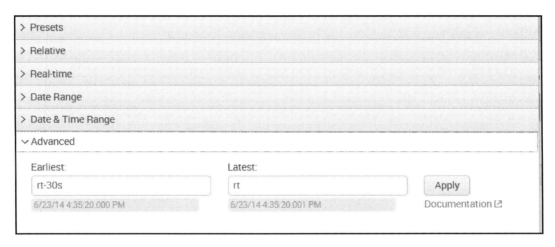

Specifying time in-line in your search

You can also directly use relative and exact times in your searches. For instance, given the search item `bob error`, you can specify the time frame you want to use directly in the search, using the fields **Earliest** and **Latest**:

- To search for errors affecting `bob` in the last 60 minutes, use `earliest=-60m bob error`
- To search for errors affecting `bob` in the last 3 hours, snap to the beginning of the hour using `earliest=-3h@h bob error`
- To search for errors affecting `bob` yesterday, use `earliest=-1d@d latest=-0d@d bob error`
- To search for errors affecting `bob` since midnight on Monday, use `earliest=-0@w1 bob error`

You cannot use different time ranges in the same query; for instance, in a Boolean search, (`earliest=-1d@d latest=-0d@d bob error`) OR (`earliest=-2d@d latest=-1d@d mary error`) will not work. The `append` command provides a way of accomplishing this (union will work as well).

_indextime versus _time

It is important to note that events are generally not received at the same time as stated in the event. In most installations, the discrepancy is usually of a few seconds, but if logs arrive in batches, the latency can be much larger. The time at which an event is actually written in the Splunk index is kept in the internal field `_indextime`.

The time that is parsed out of the event is stored in `_time`.

You will probably never search against `_indextime`, but you should understand that the time you are searching against is the time parsed from the event, not the time at which the event was indexed.

Making searches faster

We have talked about using the index to make searches faster. When starting a new investigation, following a few steps will help you get results faster:

1. Set the time to the minimum time that you believe will be required to locate relevant events. For a chatty log, this may be as little as a minute. If you don't know when the events occurred, you might search a larger time frame and then zoom in by clicking on the timeline while the search is running.
2. Specify the index if you have multiple indexes. It's good to get into the habit of starting your queries with the index name. For example, `index=myapplicationindex error bob`.
3. Specify other fields that are relevant. The most common fields to specify are `sourcetype` and `host`. For example, `index=myapplicationindex sourcetype="impl_splunk_gen" error bob`. If you find yourself specifying the field source on a regular basis, you could probably benefit from defining more source types. Avoid using the `sourcetype` field to capture other information, for instance, data center or environment. You would be better off using a lookup against host or creating another indexed field for those cases.

4. Add more words from the relevant messages as and when you find them. This can be done simply by clicking on words or field values in events, or field values in the field picker. For example, `index=myapplicationindex sourcetype="impl_splunk_gen" error bob authclass OR fooclass`.

5. Expand your time range once you have found the events that you need, and then refine the search further.

6. To disable **Field discovery** in earlier versions of Splunk; there was a toggle at the top of the field picker. In version 6.2 (and newer), the feature is a bit different. You can simply open the field picker and use the **Select All Within Filter** or **Deselect All** checkbox to remove any unnecessary fields from the list that Splunk will extract. This can greatly improve speed, particularly if your query retrieves a lot of events. Extracting all the fields from events simply takes a lot of computing time, and disabling this option prevents Splunk from doing all that work when not necessary. Take a look at the following screenshot:

If the query you are running is taking a long time to run, and you will be running this query on a regular basis—perhaps for an alert or a dashboard—using a summary index may be appropriate. We will discuss this in `Chapter 9`, *Summary Indexes and CSV Files*.

Sharing results with others

It is often convenient to share a specific set of results with another user. You could always export the results to a CSV file and share it, but this is cumbersome. In earlier versions of Splunk, a URL could be saved and shared; in version 6.2, things were changed a bit (although you still can save your search as a bookmarked URL), and this remains the same now in version 7.0.

The URL

To share your search as a bookmarked URL, you can click on the share icon to view the **Share Job** dialog:

From here, you can simply right-click on the share icon and bookmark your search for later use:

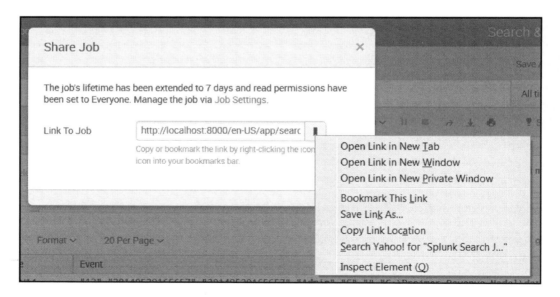

You can also share your search and search results in a variety of other ways, starting by clicking on the **Save As** link.

This lists your options for saving the search and search results. Your choices are the following:

- **Report**
- **Dashboard Panel**
- **Alert**
- **Event Type**

Save As Report

To save your search as a report, click on the **Report** link. This opens the **Save As Report** dialog:

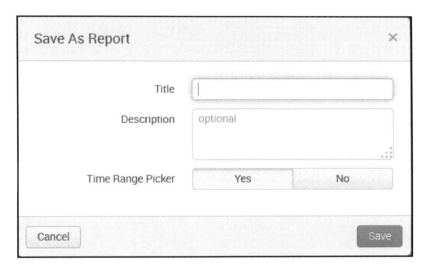

From here, you need to do the following:

1. Enter a **Title** (or name) for your report
2. Enter an optional **Description** to remind users what your report does
3. Indicate if you'd like to include the Splunk **Time Range Picker** as a part of your report

Once you click on **Save**, Splunk prompts you to either review **Additional Settings** for your newly-created report (**Permissions, Schedule, Acceleration,** and **Embed**), **Add** (the report) **to Dashboard** (we will talk more about dashboards in `Chapter 5`, *Simple XML Dashboards*), **View** the report, or **Continue Editing** the search:

In my example, I named my report **My Error Report**, added a description (**a simple example of a save as report**), and included **Time Range Picker**. The following screenshot displays the saved report after clicking on **View**:

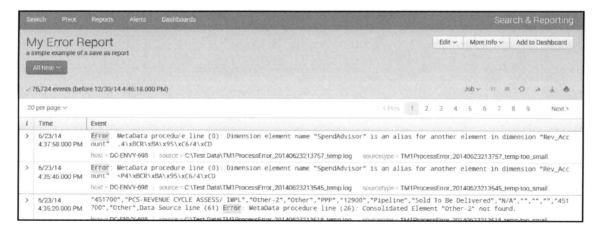

The additional settings that can be made to the report are as follows:

- **Permissions**: Allows you to set how the saved report is displayed: by owner, by app, or for all apps. In addition, you can make the report read-only or writable (can be edited).
- **Schedule**: Allows you to schedule the report (for Splunk to run/refresh it based upon your schedule. For example, an interval like every week, on Monday at 6:00, and for a particular time range (as described earlier).
- **Acceleration**: Not all saved reports qualify for acceleration, and not all users (not even admins) have the ability to accelerate reports. Generally speaking, Splunk Enterprise will build a report acceleration summary for the report if it determines that the report would benefit from summarization (acceleration). More on this topic later.
- **Embed**: Report embedding lets you bring the results of your reports to large numbers of report stakeholders. With report embedding, you can embed scheduled reports in external (non-Splunk) websites, dashboards, and portals. Embedded reports can display results in the form of event views, tables, charts, maps, single values, or any other visualization type. They use the same formatting as the originating report. When you embed a saved report, you do this by copying a Splunk-generated URL into an HTML-based web page:

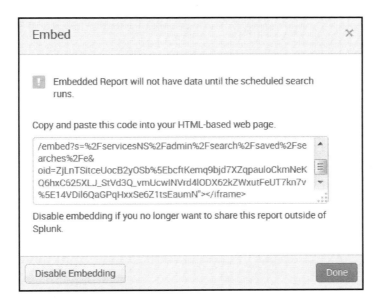

Save As Dashboard Panel

We'll be discussing dashboards in Chapter 5, *Simple XML Dashboards*, but for now, you should know that you can save your search as a new dashboard or as a new panel in an existing one. Permissions can also be set:

Save As Alert

An alert is an action that a saved search triggers based on specified results of the search. When creating an alert, you specify a condition that triggers the alert (basically, a saved search with trigger conditions). When you select **Save as Alert**, the following dialog is provided to configure search as an alert:

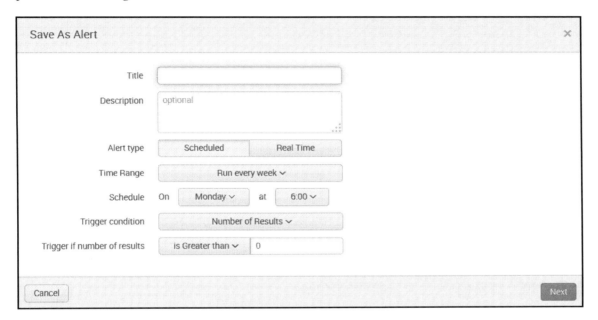

Save As Event Type

Event types are a categorization system to help you make sense of your user-defined data fields. It simplifies searches by letting you categorize events. Event types let you classify events that have common characteristics. When your search results come back, they're checked against known event types. An event type is applied to an event at search time if that event matches the event type definition.

The simplest way to create a new event type is through Splunk Web. After you run a search that would make a good event type, click on `Save As` and select `Event Type`. This opens the `Save as Event Type` dialog, where you can provide the event type name and optionally apply tags to it:

Searching job settings

Once you run a search, you can access and manage information about the search job (an individual instance of a running or completed search, pivot, or report, along with its related output) without leaving the **Search** page. This is done by clicking on **Job** and choosing among the available options:

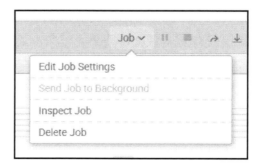

You can also perform the following tasks:

- **Edit Job Settings**: Select this to open the **Job Settings** dialog, where you can change the job's read permissions, extend the job's lifespan, and get a URL for the job which you can use to share the job with others. You can also put a link to the job in your browser's bookmark bar.
- **Send Job to Background**: Select this if the search job is slow to complete and you would like to run the job in the background while you work on other Splunk Enterprise activities (including running a new search job).
- **Inspect Job**: Opens a separate window and displays information and metrics for the search job via the **Search Job Inspector**.
- **Delete Job**: Use this to delete a job that is currently running, is paused, or has finalized. After you have deleted the job, you can still save the search as a report.

Saving searches for reuse

As an example, let's build a search query, save it (as a report), and then make an alert out of it. First, let's find errors that affect `mary`, one of our most important users. This can simply be the query `mary error`. Looking at some sample log messages that match this query, we see that some of these events probably don't matter (the dates have been removed to shorten the lines):

```
ERROR LogoutClass error, ERROR, Error! [user=mary, ip=3.2.4.5]
WARN AuthClass error, ERROR, Error! [user=mary, ip=1.2.3.3]
ERROR BarCLass Hello world. [user=mary, ip=4.3.2.1]
WARN LogoutClass error, ERROR, Error! [user=mary, ip=1.2.3.4]
DEBUG FooClass error, ERROR, Error! [user=mary, ip=3.2.4.5]
ERROR AuthClass Nothing happened. This is worthless. Don't log this.
[user=mary, ip=1.2.3.3]
```

We can probably skip the `DEBUG` messages; the `LogoutClass` messages look harmless and the last message actually says that it's worthless. `mary error NOT debug NOT worthless NOT logoutclass` limits the results to:

```
WARN AuthClass error, ERROR, Error! [user=mary, ip=1.2.3.3]
ERROR BarCLass Hello world. [user=mary, ip=4.3.2.1]
```

For good measure, let's add the sourcetype field and some parentheses:

```
sourcetype="impl_splunk_gen" (mary AND error) NOT debug NOT worthless NOT
logoutclass
```

Another way of writing the same thing is as follows:

```
sourcetype="impl_splunk_gen" mary error NOT (debug OR worthless OR
logoutclass)
```

In order that we don't have to type our query every time, let's go ahead and save it as a report for quick retrieval.

First choose **Save As...** and then **Report**.

The **Save As Report** window appears:

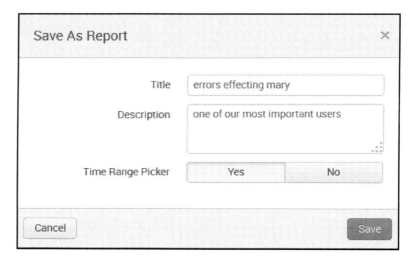

Enter a value for **Title**, in our case, errors affecting `mary`. Optionally, we can add a short description of the search. The time range is filled in based on what was selected in the time picker, and we decide to include the **Time Range Picker** in the saved report. Click on **Save**:

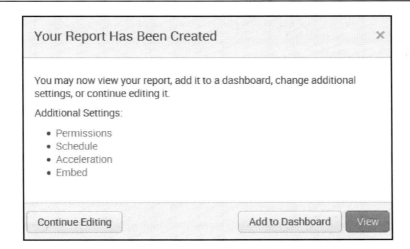

Once we see the preceding window (**Your Report Has Been Created**), we click on **Permissions** and see the **Edit Permissions** window:

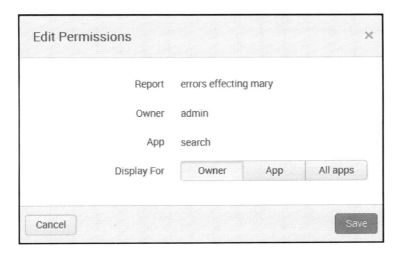

For **Display For**, let's click on **App** (rather than the default **Owner** shown in the preceding screenshot):

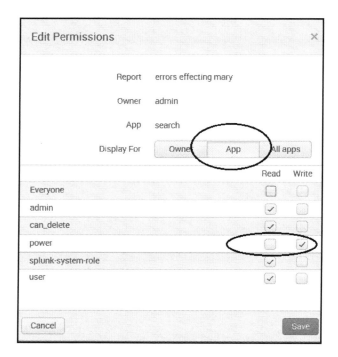

Next, we'll check **Read** for all user roles except **power**, since we know that certain users in our Splunk environment are members of this group (including our friend mary). Finally, we can click on **Save**.

The search report is then available under **Reports**:

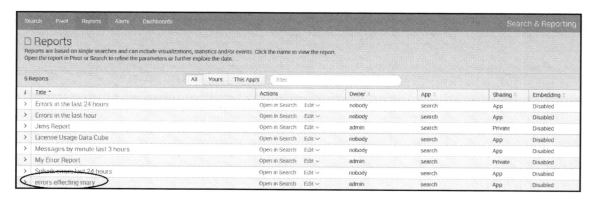

Selecting search/report from the menu runs the search using the latest data available.

Creating alerts from searches

Let's continue with our example. We want to take our original search query, schedule it, and then set a triggered response.

Any saved search can also be run on a schedule. One use for scheduled searches is firing alerts. Let's get started with our example. Go to the **Reports** page (shown in the previous screenshot) and click on **Open in Search** for our report (errors affecting mary). This opens our saved report not as a report but as a search query (it also runs the search). From there, we can click on Save As and choose Alert.

Using the **Save As Alert** window (shown in the next screenshot), we can fill in the appropriate details for our alert:

The fields can be filled as follows:

- **Title**: I kept the original search title (`errors affecting mary`) but added the word `alert`
- **Description**: I kept this the same, but in reality, we'd want to add more of a description
- **Alert Type**: I selected **Scheduled**, since I want this alert search to be run every day
- **Time Range**: I selected the preset **Run every day**
- **Schedule At**: Here, I selected the preset **12:00**
- **Trigger condition**: I selected the preset **Number of Results,** since I'd like to trigger an event if my search finds any errors generated by our favorite user, `mary`
- **Trigger if number of results**: I selected the preset **is Greater than** and filled in zero (this means that I am interested in any errors that are found by my search)

After filling in all this, we can click on **Next** and we see that we have more information to provide:

This time, the window is divided into the following areas: **Enable Actions**, **Action Options**, and **Sharing**.

Enable Actions

The fields are as follows:

- **List in Triggered Alerts**: You can check this if you want to display your triggered alert in the Splunk Alert Manager, which lists details of triggered alerts for 24 hours or a specified duration
- **Send Email**: You can configure your alert to send an email to specified users when the alert gets triggered
- **Run a Script**: You can have Splunk run a script when your alert gets triggered

Action Options

The fields for **Action Options** are as follows:

- **When triggered, execute actions**: **Once** or **For each result**. For example, should the alert trigger for each error that `mary` receives or once for all errors within a time range?
- **Throttle?**: You can use throttling (usually based on time and/or event count) to reduce the frequency at which an alert triggers, since an alert can trigger frequently based on similar results that the search returns or the schedule to run the alert.

Sharing

Should the alert **Permissions-Private** or **Shared in App** be shared with other users?

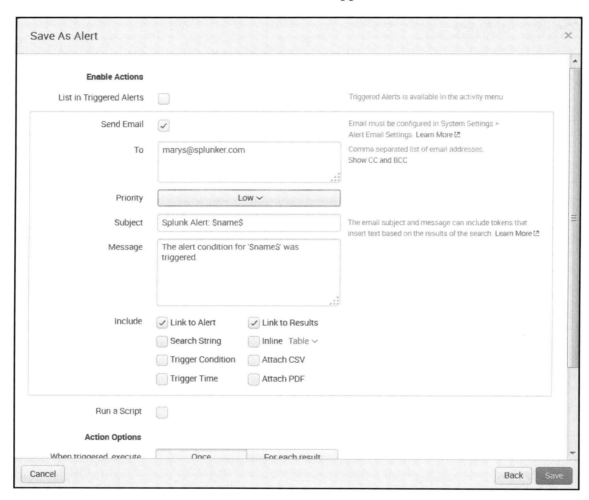

For our example, I've elected to trigger an email to `mary` (`marys@splunker.com`), with a link to both the alert and the alert results within the email so that she can review her errors. In addition (as shown in the next screenshot), I have decided to send an email **Once** (for all events/errors within the time range, not for each one) and leave the alert as **Private**:

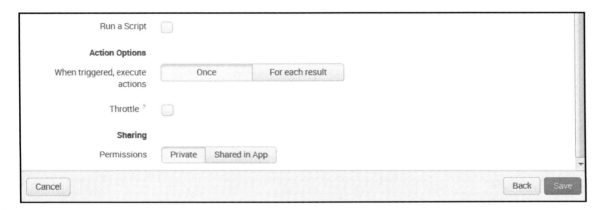

After hitting **Save**, our alert is ready to go:

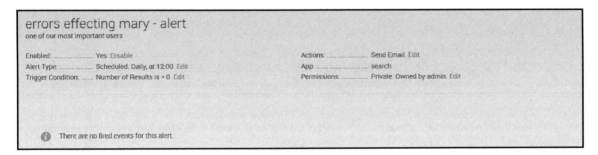

Event annotations

An annotation is generally defined as an explanation or comment; *event annotations* are new in Splunk version 7.0. With the implementation of this feature, you can now add explanations or context to trends returned by Splunk (time) charts. Splunk event annotations are presented as *colored flags* that display time stamp information and custom descriptions in labels when you hover your mouse over them, as shown in the example in the following screenshot:

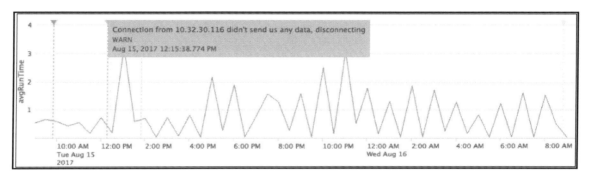

To illustrate how an event annotation could be used, Splunk offers an example where administrators are monitoring machine logs looking for user login errors. There is a Splunk chart that has been created to show login errors over time, and an *event annotation* has been added to flag the times when the servers are down for maintenance (during that time period).

With the server downtimes annotated, it can easily be concluded that the two events (servers down and login errors) are related. Using event annotations in this way gives you the ability to correlate or associate discrete datasets.

Event annotations are created using simple XML using the Splunk command `search type="annotation"` and are supported only for line charts, column charts, and area charts.

An illustration

To illustrate a simple example, we can consider a `timecount` query within a Splunk dashboard. Opening an existing dashboard, we see the following query that counts the occurrences of the text `error` within machine logs that are indexed in source type's names starting with `tm1`:

```
sourcetype="tm1*" error | timechart count
```

Suppose we know that there are times when various ETL processes are inactive and want to correlate these events with the count of errors occurring. We can create the following event annotation query:

```
<query>sourcetype="tm1*" error | timechart count</query>
        <earliest>-30week</earliest>
      <latest>-1weeks</latest>
          <sampleRatio>1</sampleRatio>
```

We then add it to the XML of our dashboard (using `search type="annotation"`):

```
<!--- main search -->
<search type="annotation">
  <query>sourcetype="tm1*" Process | eval annotation_label = "Processes Offline"</query>
  <earliest>-30week</earliest>
  <latest>-15weeks</latest>
</search>
<search>
  <!-- Secondary search that drives the annotations -->
  <query>sourcetype="tm1*" error | timechart count</query>
    <earliest>-30week</earliest>
  <latest>-1weeks</latest>
      <sampleRatio>1</sampleRatio>
</search>
```

When we save our dashboard, we can see our results:

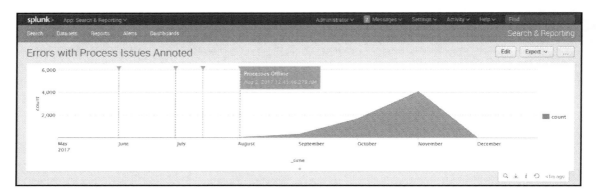

You can get event context for any time chart (line, column, or area), and event annotation markers and labels can be pulled from sources such as log data, lookup files, or external sources. All together in single view!

3
Tables, Charts, and Fields

Up to this point, we have learned how to search for and retrieve raw events, but you will most likely want to create tables and charts to expose useful patterns. Thankfully, the reporting commands in Splunk make short work of most reporting tasks. We will step through a few common use cases in this chapter. Later in the chapter, we will learn how to create custom fields for even more custom reports.

Specifically, in this chapter, we will cover the following topics:

- The pipe symbol
- Using top to show common field values
- Using stats to aggregate values
- Using chart to turn data
- Using timechart to show values over time
- Working with fields
- Acceleration
- Chart enhancements in version 7.0

About the pipe symbol

Before we dive into the actual commands, it is important to understand what the pipe symbol (|) is used for in Splunk. In a command line, the pipe symbol is used to represent the sending of data from one process to another. For example, in a Unix-style operating system, you might say:

```
grep foo access.log | grep bar
```

The first command finds, in the file `access.log`, lines that contain `foo`. Its output is taken and piped to the input of the next `grep` command, which finds lines that contain `bar`. The final output goes wherever it was destined to go, usually to the Terminal window.

The pipe symbol is different in Splunk in a few important ways:

- Unlike the command line, events are not simply text, but rather each of them is a set of key/value pairs. You can think of each event as a database row, Python dictionary, JavaScript object, Java map, or Perl associative array. Some fields are hidden from the user but are available for use. Many of these hidden fields are prefixed with an underscore, for instance, `_raw`, which contains the original event text, and `_time`, which contains the parsed time in UTC epoch form. Unlike a database, events do not adhere to a schema and fields are created dynamically.
- Commands can do anything to the events that they are handed. Usually, a command does one of the following:
  - Modifies or creates fields, for example, `eval` and `rex`
  - Filters events, such as `head` and `where`
  - Replaces events with a report, for example, `top` and `stats`
  - Sorts the results of a search using `sort`
- Some commands can act as generators, which produce what you might call synthetic events, such as `|metadata` and `|inputcsv`.

We will get to know the pipe symbol very well through examples.

Using top to show common field values

A very common question that may often arise is: "Which values are the most common?" When looking for errors, you are probably interested in figuring out what piece of code has the most errors. The `top` command provides a very simple way to answer this question.

Let's step through a few examples.

First, run a search for errors:

```
sourcetype="tm1" error
```

The preceding example searches for the word `error` in all source types starting with the character string `"tm1*"` (with the asterisk being the wildcard character).

In my data, it finds events containing the word `error`, a sample of which is listed in the following screenshot:

i	Event
>	Error: MetaData procedure line (0): Dimension element name "SpendAdvisor" is an alias for another element in dimens ount" .4\xBCR\xBA\x95\xC6/4\xCD
>	Error: MetaData procedure line (0): Dimension element name "SpendAdvisor" is an alias for another element in dimens ount" <P4\xBCR\xBA\x95\xC6/4\xCD
>	"451700","PCS-REVENUE CYCLE ASSESS/ IMPL","Other-2","Other","PPP","12900","Pipeline","Sold To Be Delivered","N/A", 700","Other",Data Source line (61) Error: MetaData procedure line (26): Consolidated Element "Other-2" not found.
>	"447900","MEDDIUS","Birchstreet-1","Birchstreet","ITS","11990","Pipeline","Contract","N/A","","","","447900","Birch Source line (24) Error: MetaData procedure line (26): Consolidated Element "Birchstreet-1" not found.
>	"445800","CONCERRO","Concerro","Cost Management","ITS","11190","Pipeline","Contract","N/A","","","","445800","Conce urce line (4) Error: MetaData procedure line (26): Consolidated Element "Concerro" not found.
>	"446700","SPEND ADVISOR","SpendAdvisor","Cost Management","ITS","11190","Pipeline","Contract","N/A","","","","44670 isor",Data Source line (3) Error: MetaData procedure line (26): Consolidated Element "SpendAdvisor" not found.
>	Error: MetaData procedure line (0): Dimension element name "SpendAdvisor" is an alias for another element in dimens ount" %4\xBCR\xBA\x95\xC6/4\xCD

Since I happen to know that the data I am searching is made up of application log files generated throughout the year, it might be interesting to see the month that had the most errors logged. To do that, we can simply add `| top date_month` to our search, like so:

```
sourcetype="tm1*" error | top date_month
```

The results are transformed by `top` into a table like the following one:

date_month ⌄	count ⌄	percent ⌄
october	69899	99.757382
december	165	0.235482
june	5	0.007136

From these results, we see that **october** is logging significantly more errors than any other month. We should probably take a closer look at the activity that occurred during that month.

Next, perhaps we would like to determine whether there is a particular day of the week when these errors are happening. Adding another field name to the end of the command instructs `top` to slice the data again. For example, let's add `date_wday` to the end of our previous query, like so:

```
sourcetype="tm1*" error | top date_month date_wday
```

The results might look like the following screenshot:

date_month	date_wday	count	percent
october	wednesday	69889	99.743110
december	wednesday	98	0.139862
december	tuesday	67	0.095620
october	tuesday	9	0.012844
june	friday	3	0.004281
october	thursday	1	0.001427
june	thursday	1	0.001427
june	monday	1	0.001427

In these results, we see that **wednesday** is logging the most errors from the month of **october**. If we simply want to see the distribution of errors by **date_wday**, we specify only the user field, like so:

```
sourcetype=tm1* error | top date_wday
```

Controlling the output of top

The default behavior for `top` is to show the 10 largest counts. The possible row count is the product of all fields specified, in this case, `date_month` and `date_wday`. Using our data in this example, there are eight possible combinations. If you would like to see less than ten rows (or, in our example, less than eight), add the argument `limit`, like so:

```
sourcetype=tm1* error | top limit=4 date_month date_wday
```

Arguments change the behavior of a command; they take the form of `name=value`. Many commands require the arguments to immediately follow the command name, so it's a good idea to always follow this structure.

Each command has different arguments, as appropriate. As you type in the search bar, a drop-down help box will appear for the last command in your search, as shown in the following screenshot:

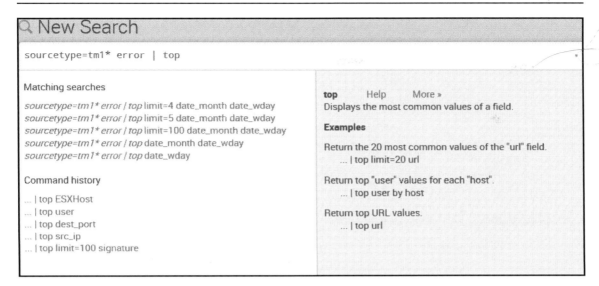

The preceding screenshot lists **Matching searches** in the upper-left corner; if there are no matching searches, this section will not be displayed.

The **Help** option takes you to the documentation for that command at http://www.splunk.com, and **More >>** provides concise inline documentation.

Let's use a few arguments to make a shorter list but also roll all other results into another line:

```
sourcetype=tm1* error
| top
limit=4
useother=true otherstr=everything else
date_month date_wday
```

This produces results like what is shown in the following screenshot:

date_month	date_wday	count	percent
october	wednesday	69889	99.743110
december	wednesday	98	0.139862
december	tuesday	67	0.095620
october	tuesday	9	0.012844
everything else	everything else	6	0.008563

The last line represents everything that didn't fit into the top four. The
top option useother enables this last row, while the option otherstr controls the value
printed instead of the default value other.

The reader may review the Splunk documentation for additional information on the top
command and options at:

http://docs.splunk.com/Documentation/Splunk/7.0.0/SearchReference/Top

For the opposite of top, see the rare command.

Using stats to aggregate values

While top is very convenient, stats is extremely versatile. The basic structure of a stats
statement is:

```
stats functions by fields
```

Many of the functions available in stats mimic similar functions in SQL or Excel, but there
are many functions unique to Splunk too. The simplest stats function is count. Given the
following query, the results will contain exactly one row, with a value for the field count:

```
sourcetype=tm1* error | stats count
```

Using the by clause, stats will produce one row per unique value for each field listed,
which is similar to the behavior of top. Run the following query:

```
sourcetype=tm1* error | stats count by date_month date_wday
```

It will produce a table like this:

date_month ≎	date_wday ≎		count ≎
december	tuesday		67
december	wednesday		98
june	friday		3
june	monday		1
june	thursday		1
october	thursday		1
october	tuesday		9
october	wednesday		69889

There are a few things to note about these results:

- The results are sorted against the values of the *by* fields, in this case, **date_month** followed by **date_wday**. Unlike `top`, the largest value will not necessarily be at the top of the list. You can sort in the GUI simply by clicking on the field names at the `top` of the table, or by using the `sort` command.
- There is no limit to the number of rows produced. The number of rows will equal all possible combinations of field values.
- The function results are displayed last. In the next example, we will add a few more functions, and this will become more obvious.

Using `stats`, you can add as many `by` fields or functions as you want into a single statement. Let's run this query:

```
sourcetype=tm1* error | stats count avg(linecount) max(linecount)
as "Slowest Time" by date_month date_wday
```

The results look like those in the following screenshot:

date_month	date_wday	count	avg(linecount)	Slowest Time
april	tuesday	3	1.000000	1
december	friday	16	257.000000	257
december	monday	13	257.000000	257
december	saturday	15	239.933333	257
december	sunday	10	257.000000	257
december	thursday	20	257.000000	257
december	tuesday	69	8.420290	257
december	wednesday	116	38.603448	257
february	friday	5	257.000000	257
february	monday	12	257.000000	257
february	saturday	10	257.000000	257

Let's step through every part of this query, just to be clear:

- `sourcetype=tm1* error` is the query itself
- `| stats` starts the `stats` command
- `count` will return the number of events
- `avg(linecount)` produces an average value of the `linecount` field
- `max(linecount) as Slowest Time` finds the maximum value of the `linecount` field and places the value in a field called `Slowest Time`

The quotes are necessary ("Slowest Time") because the field name contains a space:

- `by` indicates that we are done listing functions and want to list the fields to slice the data by. If the data does not need to be sliced, `by` and the fields following it can be omitted.
- `date_month` and `date_wday` are our fields for slicing the data. All functions are actually run against each set of data produced for every possible combination of `date_month` and `date_user`.

If an event is missing a field that is referenced in a `stats` command, you may not see the results you are expecting. For instance, when computing an average, you may wish for events missing a field to count as zeros in the average. Also, for events that do not contain a field listed in the `by` fields, the event will simply be ignored.

To deal with both of these cases, you can use the `fillnull` command to make sure that the fields you want exist.

Let's look at another example, using a time-based function and a little trick. Let's say we want to know the most recent time at which a particular user saw an error each day.

We can use the following query:

```
sourcetype=tm1* Error TheUser="Admin" | stats count
  first(date_wday) max(_time) as _time by source
```

This query produces the following table:

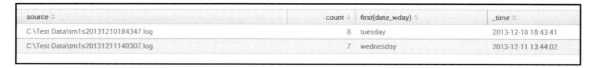

source	count	first(date_wday)	_time
C:\Test Data\tm1s20131210184347.log	8	tuesday	2013-12-10 18:43:41
C:\Test Data\tm1s20131211140307.log	7	wednesday	2013-12-11 13:44:02

Let's step through this example:

- `sourcetype=tm1* Error TheUser="Admin"` is the query that will find all errors logged by the user `"Admin"`.
- `| stats` is our command.
- `count` shows how many times this user saw an error each day.
- `first(date_wday)` gives us the weekday that was most recently logged for this user. This will be the most recent event, since results are returned in the order of the most recent first.

- `max(_time)` as `_time` returns the time at which the user most recently saw an error that day. This takes advantage of three aspects of time in Splunk:
  - `_time` is always present in raw events. As discussed in `Chapter 2`, *Understanding Search*, the value is the number of seconds since January 1, 1970, UTC.
  - `_time` is stored as a number and can be treated as such.
  - If there is a field called `_time` in the results, Splunk will always display the value as the first column of a table in the time zone selected by the user.
- `by source` is our field to split the results against, and in this example, it is done by data `source` or the error log file where the error(s) were found.

We have only seen a few functions in `stats`. There are dozens of functions and some advanced syntax that we will touch upon in later chapters. The simplest way to find the full listing is to search with your favorite search engine for the Splunk `stats` functions.

Using chart to turn data

The `chart` command is useful for turning data across two dimensions. It is useful for both tables and charts. Let's start with one of our examples from `stats`:

```
sourcetype="tm1*" error | chart count over date_month by date_wday
```

The resultant table looks like this:

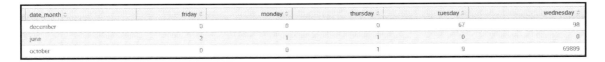

date_month	friday	monday	thursday	tuesday	wednesday
december	0	0	0	67	98
june	2	1	1	0	0
october	0	0	1	9	69889

If you look back at the results from `stats`, the data is presented as one row per combination. Instead of a row per combination, `chart` generates the intersection of the two fields. You can specify multiple functions, but you may only specify one field each for `over` and `by`.

Switching the fields (by rearranging our search statement a bit) turns the data the other way:

date_wday	december	june	october
friday	0	3	0
monday	0	1	0
thursday	0	1	1
tuesday	67	0	9
wednesday	98	0	69889

By simply clicking on the **Visualization** tab (to the right of the **Statistics** tab), we can see these results in a chart:

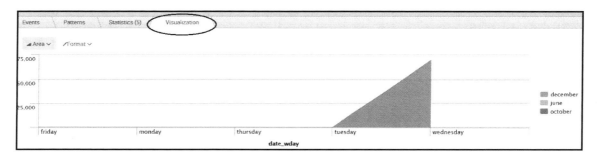

This is an **Area** chart, with particular format options set. Within the chart area, you can click on **Area** to change the chart type (**Line**, **Area**, **Column**, **Bar**, and so on) or **Format** to change the format options (**Stack**, **Null Values**, **Multi-series Mode**, and **Drilldown**).

The chart types are pretty self-explanatory, so let's go ahead and take a look at the (chart) **Format** options. These options are grouped as:

- **General**: Under **General**, you have the option to set the **Stack Model** (which indicates how Splunk will display your chart columns for different series alongside each other or as a single column) determine how to handle **Null Values** (you can leave gaps for null data points, connect to zero data points, or just connect to the next positive data point), set the **Multi-series mode** (**Yes** or **No**), and turn **Drilldown** (active or inactive) on or off.
- **X-Axis**: Is mostly visual. You can set a custom title, allow truncation of label captions, and set the rotation of the text for your chart labels.
- **Y-Axis**: Here you can set not only a custom title but also the scale (linear or log), interval, and min and max values.

- **Chart Overlay**: Here you can set the following options:
    - **Overlay**: Select a field to show as an overlay.
    - **View as Axis**: Select **On** to map the overlay to a second *y* axis.
    - **Title**: Specify a title for the overlay.
    - **Scale**: Select **Inherit**, **Linear**, or **Log**. **Inherit** uses the scale for the base chart. **Log** provides a logarithmic scale, useful for minimizing the display of large peak values.
    - **Interval**: Enter the units between tick marks in the axis.
    - **Min Value**: The minimum value to display. Values less than the **Min Value** do not appear on the chart.
    - **Max Value**: The maximum value to display. Values greater than the **Max Value** do not appear on the chart.
- **Legend**: Finally, under **Legend**, you can set **Position** (where to place the legend in the visualization or whether to exclude the legend), and setting **Truncation** decides how to represent names that are too long to display. Keep in mind that, depending on your search results and the visualization options that you select, you may or may not get a usable result. Some experimentation with the various options is recommended.

Using timechart to show values over time

The `timechart` option lets us show numerical values over time. It is similar to the `chart` command, except that time is always plotted on the *x* axis. Here are a couple of things to note:

- The events must have a `_time` field. If you are simply sending the results of a search to the timechart, this will always be true. If you are using interim commands, you will need to be mindful of this requirement.
- Time is always bucketed, meaning that there is no way to draw a point per event.

Let's see how many errors have been occurring:

```
sourcetype="tm1*" error | timechart count
```

The default chart will look something like this:

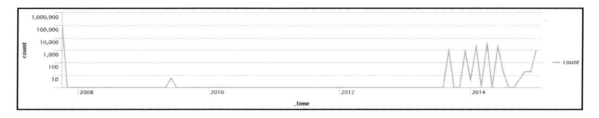

Now let's see how many errors have occurred per weekday over the same time period.

We simply need to add `by user` to the query:

```
sourcetype="tm1*" error | timechart count by date_wday
```

This produces the following chart:

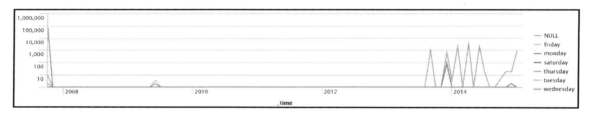

As we stated earlier, the *x* axis is always time. The *y* axis can be:

- One or more functions.
- A single function with a `by` clause.
- Multiple functions with a `by` clause (a new feature in Splunk 4.3). An example of a timechart with multiple functions might be as follows:

```
sourcetype="tm1*" error | timechart count as "Error Count"
count(sourcetype) as "Source Count"
```

This would produce a graph as follows:

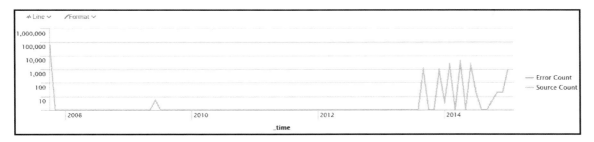

The timechart options

Timechart has many arguments and formatting options. We'll touch upon a few examples of formatting, but they are too numerous to cover in detail. We will use other chart types in later chapters. Let's throw a few options in (to a simple search) and see what they do:

```
sourcetype="*" GET | timechart bins=100 limit=3 useother=false
    usenull=false count as "Error count" by user
```

Let's step through each of these arguments:

- `sourcetype="*"` `GET` is our search query.
- `bins` defines how many bins to slice time into. The number of bins will probably not be exactly 100, as the time will be sliced into logical units. In our example, this comes to 10 minutes per bin. To be more exact, you can use `span` (for example, `span=1h`) for hourly slices, but note that if your `span` value creates too many time slices, the chart will be truncated.
- `limit` changes the number of series returned. The series with the largest values are returned, much like in `top`. In this case, the most common values of a user will be returned.
- `useother` instructs timechart whether to group all series beyond the limit into another bucket. The default value is `true`.
- `usenull` instructs timechart whether to bucket, into the group `NULL`, events that do not have a value for the fields in the `by` clause. The default value is `true`.

This combination of arguments produces a graph similar to this:

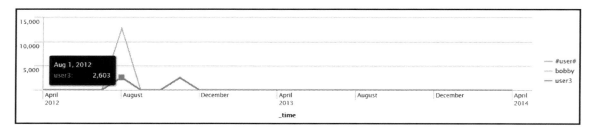

As mentioned earlier in this chapter, Splunk offers us a variety of **Formatting options** for our visualizations. Clicking on the drop-down selector on the **Visualization** tab in the following graph gives us quite a few options to work with:

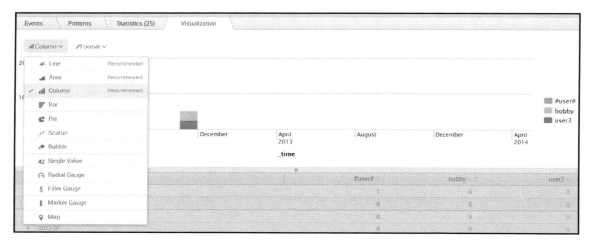

The preceding graph shows a common chart style, the stacked column. This graph is useful for showing how many events of a certain kind occurred, but with colors to give us an idea of the distribution. Some great examples of all of the available chart styles are available at http://www.splunk.com/, and we will touch upon more styles in later chapters.

Working with fields

All the fields that we have used so far were either indexed fields (such as `host`, `sourcetype`, and `_time`) or fields that were automatically extracted from `key=value` pairs. Unfortunately, most logs don't follow this format, especially for the first few values in each event. New fields can be created either using inline commands or through configuration.

A regular expression primer

Most of the ways to create new fields in Splunk involve regular expressions (sometimes referred to as regex). As mentioned in the Splunk documentation:

> *"Regex is a powerful part of the Splunk search interface, and understanding it is an essential component of Splunk search best practices"*

There are many books and sites dedicated to regular expressions, so we will only touch upon the subject here. The following examples are really provided for completeness; the Splunk web interface may suffice for most users.

Given the `log snippet ip=1.2.3.4`, let's pull out the `subnet` (`1.2.3`) into a new field called `subnet`. The simplest pattern would be the following literal string:

```
ip=(?P<subnet>1.2.3).4
```

This is not terribly useful as it will only find the subnet of that one IP address. Let's try a slightly more complicated example:

```
ip=(?P<subnet>\d+\.\d+\.\d+)\.\d+
```

Let's step through this pattern:

- `ip=` simply looks for the raw string `ip=`.
- `(` starts a *capture buffer*. Everything until the closing parenthesis is part of this capture buffer.
- `?P<subnet>`, immediately inside the parentheses, says *create a field called subnet from the results of this capture buffer*.
- `\d` matches any single digit, from 0 to 9.
- `+` says *one or more of the item immediately before*.
- `\.` matches a literal period. A period without the backslash matches any character.

- `\d+\.\d+` matches the next two parts of the IP address.
- `)` ends our capture buffer.
- `\.d\+` matches the last part of the IP address. Since it is outside the capture buffer, it will be discarded.

Now, let's step through an overly complicated pattern to illustrate a few more concepts:

```
ip=(?P<subnet>\d+.\d*\.[01234-9]+)\.\d+
```

Let's step through this pattern:

- `ip=` simply looks for the raw string `ip=`.
- `(?P<subnet>` starts our capture buffer and defines our field name.
- `\d` means digit. This is one of the many backslash character combinations that represent some sets of characters.
- `+` says *one or more of what came before*, in this case `d`.
- `.` matches a single character. This will match the period after the first set of digits, though it would match any single character.
- `\d*` means zero or more digits.
- `\.` matches a literal period. The backslash negates the special meaning of any special punctuation character. Not all punctuation marks have a special meaning, but so many do that there is no harm adding a backslash before a punctuation mark that you want to literally match.
- `[` starts a character set. Anything inside the brackets will match a single character in the character set.
- `01234-9` means the characters 0, 1, 2, 3, and the range 4-9.
- `]` closes the character set.
- `+` says *one or more of what came before*, in this case, the character set.
- `)` ends our capture buffer.
- • `\.\d+` is the final part of the IP address that we are throwing away. It is not actually necessary to include this, but it ensures that we only match if there were, in fact, four sets of numbers.

There are a number of different ways to accomplish the task at hand. Here are a few examples that will work:

- `ip=(?P<subnet>\d+\.\d+\.\d+)\.\d+`
- `ip=(?P<subnet>(\d+\.){2}\d+)\.\d+`
- `ip=(?P<subnet>[\d\.]+)\.\d`
- `ip=(?P<subnet>.*?\..*?\..*?)\.`
- `ip=(?P<subnet>\S+)\.`

For more information about regular expressions, consult the manual pages for **Perl Compatible Regular Expressions (PCRE)**, which can be found online at `http://www.pcre.org/pcre.txt`, or one of the many regular expression books or websites dedicated to the subject. We will build more expressions as we work through different configurations and searches, but it's definitely worthwhile to have a reference handy.

Commands that create fields

In Splunk, fields are extracted from the event data; to fully leverage the power of Splunk, you have the ability to create additional fields or to have Splunk extract additional fields that you define. This allows you to capture and track information that is important to your needs, but which is not automatically discovered and extracted by Splunk.

There are a number of commands that create new fields, but the most commonly used ones are `eval` and `rex`.

eval

The `eval` command allows you to use functions to build new fields, much like how you build a formula column in Excel, for example:

```
sourcetype="impl_splunk_gen" | eval
  req_time_seconds=date_second/1000 | stats avg(req_time_seconds)
```

This creates a new field called `req_time_seconds` on every event that has a value for `date_second`. Commands after this statement see the field as if it were part of the original event. The `stats` command then creates a table of the average value of our newly-created field:

avg(req_time_seconds) ⌄
0.029819

There are a huge number of functions available for use with `eval`. The simplest way to find the full listing is to search Google for *Splunk eval functions*. I would suggest bookmarking this page, as you will find yourself referring to it often.

rex

The `rex` command lets you use regular expressions to create fields. It can work against any existing field but, by default, will use the field `_raw`. Let's try one of the patterns that we wrote in our short regular expression primer:

```
sourcetype="impl_splunk_gen" | rex
"ip=(?P<subnet>\d+\.\d+\.\d+)\.\d+" | chart values(subnet) by
date_minute
```

This would create a table like this:

	date_minute ⌄	values(subnet) ⌄
	0	118.192.35
		123.125.67
		173.174.50
		208.115.113
		209.85.238
		220.181.51
		27.159.200
		27.159.213
		31.3.244
		46.17.97
		65.60.148
	1	173.174.50
		188.230.91
		208.115.111
		209.85.238

20 Per Page ⌄   Format ⌄   Preview ⌄

With the addition of the `field` argument, we can work against the `ip` field that is already being created automatically from the `name=value` pair in the event:

```
sourcetype="impl_splunk_gen" | rex field=ip "(?P<subnet>.*)\."|
  chart values(subnet) by date_minute
```

This will create exactly the same result as the previous example.

Extracting loglevel

In some of our examples, we searched for the raw word *error*. You may have noticed that many of the events weren't actually errors, but simply contained the word error somewhere in the message. For example, given the following events, we probably only care about the second event:

```
2012-03-21T18:59:55.472-0500 INFO This is not an error
2012-03-21T18:59:42.907-0500 ERROR Something bad happened
```

Using an extracted field, we can easily create fields in our data without reindexing that allow you to search for values that occur at a specific location in your events.

Using the extract fields interface

There are several ways to define a field. Let's start by using the **Extract Fields** interface. To access this interface, choose **Extract Fields** from the workflow actions menu next to any event:

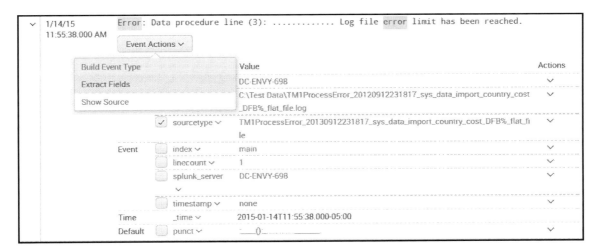

This menu launches the **Extract Fields** view:

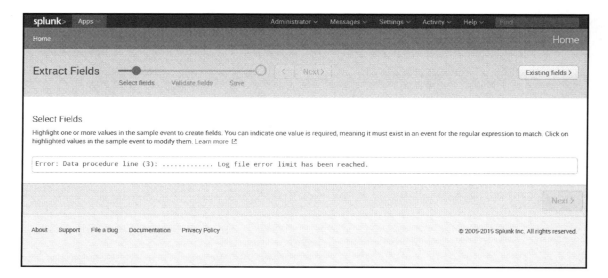

In Splunk version 6.2, we have access to a wizard which helps us provide the information required for Splunk to attempt building a regular expression that matches.

Although you may choose multiple fields, in this case, we specify **Error**:

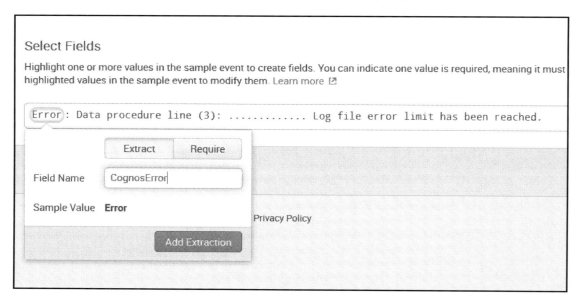

In the popup, you can provide a custom **Field Name** (I chose `CognosError`) and then click the button labeled **Add Extraction**.

Under **Preview,** you can see two tabs—**Events**, and our new field **CognosError**:

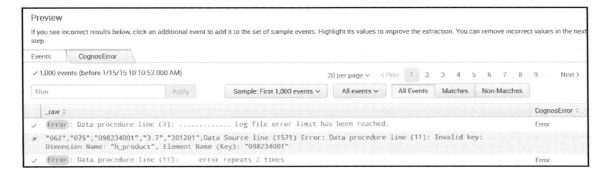

Under **Events**, we get a preview of what data was matched in context, and under **CognosError** we can see our new field.

Finally, under **Show Regular Pattern**, we see the regular expression that Splunk generated, which is as follows:

```
^(?P<CognosError>\w+)
```

You can step through the pattern and, if you are so inclined, make edits to it:

Clicking on the button labeled **Edit the Regular Expression** (shown in the preceding screenshot) presents a dialog to let you modify the pattern manually:

Once you make any edits to the pattern, **Preview** will be enabled and will launch a new search with the pattern loaded into a very useful query that shows the most common values extracted.

Save prompts you for a name for your new field. Assuming that you modified the originally-generated pattern string, you can enter a new name (rather than `CognosError`), and then select the desired permissions for accessing this new field:

Now that we've defined our field, we can use it in a number of ways, as follows:

- We can search for the value using the field name, for instance, `loglevel=CognosError`.
- When searching for values by field name, the field name is case-sensitive, but the value is not case-sensitive. In this case, `loglevel=CognosError` will work just fine, but `LogLevel=cognoserror` will not.
- We can report on the field, whether we searched for it or not. For instance, `sourcetype="impl_splunk_gen" user=mary | top loglevel`.
- We can search for only those events that contain our field: `sourcetype="impl_splunk_gen" user=mary loglevel="*"`.

Using rex to prototype a field

When defining fields, it is often convenient to build the pattern directly in the query and then copy the pattern into the configuration. You might have noticed that the test in the **Extract Fields** workflow used rex.

Let's turn the subnet pattern we built earlier into a field. First, we build the query with the rex statement:

```
sourcetype="impl_splunk_gen" ip="*"
| rex "ip=(?P<subnet>\d\.\d\.\d+)\.\d+"
| table ip subnet
```

Since we know there will be an ip field in the events which we care about, we can use ip="*" to limit the results only to events that have a value for that field.

The table command takes a list of fields and displays a table, one row per event:

ip ≎	subnet ≎
64.134.155.137	
64.134.155.137	
64.134.155.137	
64.134.155.137	
64.134.155.137	
64.134.155.137	
64.134.155.137	
64.134.155.137	
64.134.155.137	
64.134.155.137	
64.134.155.137	

As we can see, the `rex` statement doesn't always work. Looking at the pattern again, you may notice that the first two instances of `\d` are now missing their trailing `+`. Without the plus sign, only addresses with a single digit in both their first and second sections will match. After adding the missing plus signs to our pattern, all rows will have a subnet:

```
sourcetype="impl_splunk_gen" ip="*"
| rex "ip=(?P<subnet>\d+\.\d+\.\d+)\.\d+"
| table ip subnet
```

ip ⇕	subnet ⇕
64.134.155.137	64.134.155
64.134.155.137	64.134.155
64.134.155.137	64.134.155
64.134.155.137	64.134.155
64.134.155.137	64.134.155
64.134.155.137	64.134.155
64.134.155.137	64.134.155
64.134.155.137	64.134.155
64.134.155.137	64.134.155
64.134.155.137	64.134.155
64.134.155.137	64.134.155
64.134.155.137	64.134.155
173.174.50.156	173.174.50

We can now take the pattern from the `rex` statement and use it to build a configuration.

Using the admin interface to build a field

Taking our pattern from the previous example, we can build the configuration to wire up this extract.

First, click on **Settings** in the upper menu bar. From there, select `Fields`. The `Fields` section contains everything, funnily enough, about fields.

Here you can view, edit, and set permissions on field extractions. Define event workflow actions, field aliases, and even rename source types.

For now, we're interested in **Field extractions**.

After clicking on **Add new** to the right of **Field extractions**, or on the **New** button after clicking on **Field extractions**, we are presented with the interface for creating a new field:

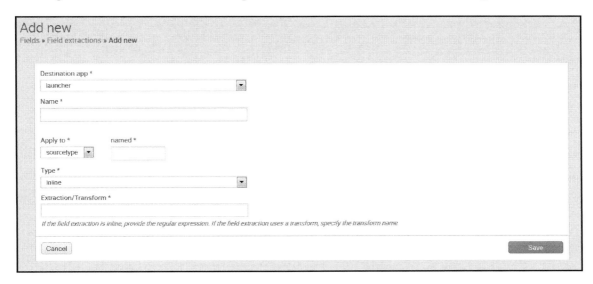

Now, we step through the fields:

- **Destination app** lets us choose the app where this extraction will live and where it will take effect, by default. We will discuss the scope of configurations in `Chapter 10`, *Configuring Splunk*.
- **Name** is simply a display name for the extraction. Make it as descriptive as you like.
- **Apply to** lets you choose what to bind this extraction to. Your choices are **sourcetype**, **source**, and **host**. The usual choice is **sourcetype**.
- **named** is the name of the item we are binding our extraction to.
- **Type** lets us choose either **Inline**, which means specifying the regular expression here, or **Uses transform**, which means we will specify a named transform that exists already in the configuration.
- **Extraction/Transform** is where we place our pattern if we chose a **Type** option of **Inline**, or else the name of a **Transform** object.

Once you click on **Save**, you will return to the listing of extractions. By default, your extraction will be private to you and will only function in the application it was created in. If you have the rights to do so, you can share the extraction with other users and change the scope of where it runs. Click on **Permissions** in the listing to see the permissions page, which most objects in Splunk use:

Object should appear in		
⦿ Keep private ◯ This app only (search) ◯ All apps		

Permissions

Roles	Read	Write
Everyone	☐	☐
admin	☐	☐
can_delete	☐	☐
power	☐	☐
user	☐	☐

The top section controls the context in which this extraction will run. Think about when the field would be useful, and limit the extractions accordingly. An excessive number of extractions can affect performance, so it is a good idea to limit the extracts to a specific app when appropriate. We will talk more about creating apps in Chapter 7, *Working with Apps*.

The second section controls what roles can read or write this configuration. The usual selections are the **Read** option for the **Everyone** parameter and the **Write** option for the admin parameter. As you build objects going forward, you will become very familiar with this dialog. Permissions and security, in general, can be complex and affect where an app will eventually be visible—the reader is advised to take time to review whether the permissions set for apps are actually what is expected.

Indexed fields versus extracted fields

When an event is written to an index, the raw text of the event is captured along with a set of indexed fields. The default indexed fields include host, sourcetype, source, and _time. There are distinct advantages and a few serious disadvantages to using indexed fields.

First, let's look at the advantages of an indexed field (we will actually discuss configuring indexed fields in `Chapter 10`, *Configuring Splunk*):

- As an indexed field is stored in the index with the event itself, it is only calculated at index time, and in fact, can only be calculated once at index time.
- It can make finding specific instances of common terms efficient. See the *Indexed field case 1 - rare instances of a common term* section as an example.
- You can create new words to search against those which simply don't exist in the raw text or are embedded inside a word. See from the *Indexed field case 2 - splitting words* section to the *Indexed field case 4 - slow requests* section.
- You can efficiently search for words in other indexed fields. See the *Indexed field case 3 - application from source* section.

Now for the disadvantages of an indexed field:

- It is not retroactive. This is different from extracted fields where all events, past and present, will gain the newly-defined field if the pattern matches. This is the biggest disadvantage of indexed fields and has a few implications, as follows:
    - Only newly-indexed events will gain a newly-defined indexed field. If the pattern is wrong in certain cases, there is no practical way to apply the field to already-indexed events.
    - Likewise, if the log format changes, the indexed field may not be generated (or may be generated incorrectly).
- It adds to the size of your index on disk.
- It counts against your license.
- Any changes will require a restart to be applied and disrupt data flow temporarily.
- In most cases, the value of the field is already an indexed word, in which case creating an indexed field will likely have no benefit, except in the rare cases where that value is very common.

With the disadvantages out of our way, let's look at a few cases where an indexed field would improve search performances and then at one case where it would probably make no difference.

Indexed field case 1 - rare instances of a common term

Let's say your log captures process exit codes. If `1` represents a failure, you probably want to be able to search for this efficiently. Consider a log that looks something like this:

```
4/1/12 6:35:50.000 PM process=important_process.sh, exitcode=1
```

It would be easy to search for this log entry using `exitcode=1`. The problem is that, when working with extracted fields, the search is effectively reduced to this:

```
1 | search exitcode="1"
```

Since the date contains `1`, this search would find every event for the entire day and then filter the events to the few that we are looking for. In contrast, if `exitcode` were defined as an indexed field, the query would immediately find the events, only retrieving the appropriate events from the disk. Please note that binding an indexed field to any time (stamp) is risky. This wreaks havoc on data integrity and is not considered best practice.

Indexed field case 2 - splitting words

In some log formats, multiple pieces of information may be encoded into a single word without whitespace or punctuation to separate the useful pieces of information. For instance, consider a log message such as this:

```
4/2/12 6:35:50.000 PM kernel: abc5s2: 0xc014 (UNDEFINED).
```

Let's pretend that `5s2` (a made-up string of characters for an example) is an important piece of information that we need to be able to search for efficiently. The query `*5s2` would find the events but would be a very inefficient search (in essence, a full table scan). By defining an indexed field, you can very efficiently search for this instance of the string `5s2`, because essentially, we create a new word in the metadata of this event.

Defining an indexed field only makes sense if you know the format of the logs before indexing, if you believe the field will actually make the query more efficient, (see previous section), and if you will be searching for the field value. If you will only be reporting on the values of this field, an extracted field will be sufficient, except in the most extreme performance cases.

Indexed field case 3 - application from source

A common requirement is to be able to search for events from a particular web application. Often, the only easy way to determine the application that created the logs is by inspecting the path to the logs, which Splunk stores in the indexed field source. For example, given the following path, the application name is `app_one`:

```
/opt/instance19/apps/app_one/logs/important.log
```

You can search for this instance using `source="*/app_one/*"`, but this effectively initiates a full table scan. You can define an extracted field and then search for `app="app_one"`, but unfortunately, this approach will also be no more efficient because the word we're looking for is not contained in the field `_raw`. If we define this field as an indexed field, `app="app_one"` will be an efficient search.

Once again, if you only need this field for reporting, the extracted field is just fine.

Indexed field case 4 - slow requests

Consider a web access log with a trailing request time in microseconds:

```
[31/Jan/2012:18:18:07 +0000] "GET / HTTP/1.1" 200 7918 ""
"Mozilla/5.0..." 11/11033255
```

Let's say we want to find all requests that took longer than 10 seconds. We can easily extract the value into a field, perhaps `request_ms`. We could then run the search `request_ms>10000000`. This query will work, but it requires scanning every event in the given time frame. Whether the field is extracted or indexed, we would face the same problem, as Splunk has to convert the field value to a number before it can test the value.

What if we could define a field and instead search for `slow_request=1`? To do this, we can take advantage of the fact that, when defining an indexed field, the value can be a static value. Having Splunk search for a static value—rather than examining the value of every event and then trying to match it—would improve the efficiency of the search. This can be accomplished with a transform, like so:

```
REGEX = .*/(\d{7,})$
FORMAT = slow_request::1
```

We will cover transforms, and the configurations involved, in `Chapter 10`, *Configuring Splunk*.

Once again, this is only worth the trouble if you need to efficiently search for these events and not simply report on the value of `request_ms`.

Indexed field case 5 - unneeded work

Once you learn to make indexed fields, it may be tempting to convert all your important fields into indexed fields. In most cases, it is essentially a wasted effort and ends up using extra disk space, wasting license, and adding no performance boost.

For example, consider this log message:

```
4/2/12 6:35:50.000 PM [vincentbumgarner] [893783] sudo bash
```

Assuming that the layout of this message is as follows, it might be tempting to put both `userid` and `pid` into indexed fields:

```
date [userid] [pid] action
```

Since the values are uncommon, and are unlikely to occur in unrelated locations, defining these fields as indexed fields is most likely wasteful. It is much simpler to define these fields as extracted fields and shield ourselves from the disadvantages of indexed fields.

Chart enhancements in version 7.0

Splunk provides a fine collection of charting resources to be used for creating dashboards. You can check the full *Chart configuration reference* in the documentation found at:

```
https://docs.splunk.com/Documentation/Splunk/latest/Viz/ChartConfigurationRefer
ence
```

In version 7.0, they've gone on and expanded the charting collection by adding some cool, new **chart enhancements** that increase the selection of *visual styles* and *chart options*, all geared to improving the visualization of metrics and multi-series monitoring use cases.

Line width, line style, and a new series comparison option in the legend are included in these enhancements, and all are editable by **SimpleXML**.

Let's take a look at a few of these new options.

charting.lineWidth

This charting option gives you the chance to set a chart's line width in pixels (px). There are no special instructions for the use of this new option. You simply include it as part of your chart definition:

```
<option name-"charting.linewidth">2px</option>
```

In the given XML, we've added the `linewidth` option to the XML that was used to show an *Event Annotation* in `Chapter 2`, *Understanding Search*:

```xml
<dashboard>
  <label>Errors with Process Issues Annoted</label>
  <row>
    <panel>
      <chart>
        <search>
          <!-- Secondary search that drives the annotations -->
          <query>sourcetype="tm1*" error | timechart count</query>
          <earliest>-30week</earliest>
          <latest>-1weeks</latest>
          <sampleRatio>1</sampleRatio>
        </search>
        <search type="annotation">
          <query>sourcetype="tm1*" Process | eval annotation_label =
"Processes Offline"</query>
          <earliest>-30week</earliest>
          <latest>-15weeks</latest>
        </search>
        <!--- main search -->
        <option
name="charting.axisLabelsX.majorLabelStyle.overflowMode">ellipsisNone</opti
on>
        <option
name="charting.axisLabelsX.majorLabelStyle.rotation">0</option>
        <option name="charting.axisTitleX.visibility">visible</option>
        <option name="charting.axisTitleY.visibility">visible</option>
        <option name="charting.axisTitleY2.visibility">visible</option>
        <option name="charting.axisX.abbreviation">none</option>
        <option name="charting.axisX.scale">linear</option>
        <option name="charting.axisY.abbreviation">none</option>
        <option name="charting.axisY.scale">linear</option>
        <option name="charting.axisY2.abbreviation">none</option>
        <option name="charting.axisY2.enabled">0</option>
        <option name="charting.axisY2.scale">inherit</option>
        <option name="charting.chart">line</option>
        <option name="charting.chart.bubbleMaximumSize">50</option>
```

```
                <option name="charting.chart.bubbleMinimumSize">10</option>
                <option name="charting.chart.bubbleSizeBy">area</option>
                <option name="charting.chart.nullValueMode">gaps</option>
                <option name="charting.chart.showDataLabels">none</option>
                <option
name="charting.chart.sliceCollapsingThreshold">0.01</option>
                <option name="charting.chart.stackMode">default</option>
                <option name="charting.chart.style">shiny</option>
                <option name="charting.drilldown">none</option>
                <option name="charting.layout.splitSeries">0</option>
                <option
name="charting.layout.splitSeries.allowIndependentYRanges">0</option>
                <option
name="charting.legend.labelStyle.overflowMode">ellipsisMiddle</option>
                <option name="charting.legend.mode">standard</option>
                <option name="charting.legend.placement">right</option>
                <option name="charting.lineWidth">9px</option>
                <option name="trellis.enabled">0</option>
                <option name="trellis.scales.shared">1</option>
                <option name="trellis.size">medium</option>
            </chart>
        </panel>
    </row>
</dashboard>
```

We can see the results of increasing the line width to 9px as follows:

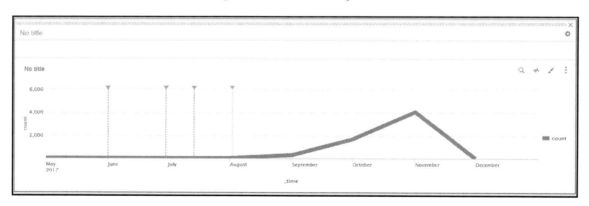

charting.data.fieldHideList

With this option, you can hide the search fields from appearing in a chart to make the chart clearer or to accentuate a particular data point. For example, this visualization shows both the *host* and *count* fields:

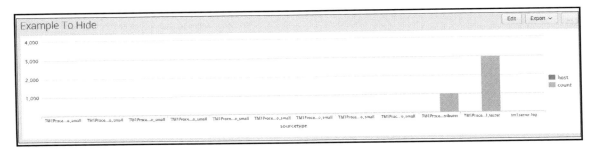

By editing the dashboard XML and adding the following option:

```
<option name="charting.data.fieldHidelList">["host"]</otion>
```

We can hide the **host** field from the chart:

charting.legend.mode

This new charting option is super when comparing *different data series* on a chart. The default argument is "standard" which is what is used in previous releases for charting multi-series data:

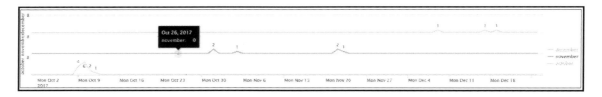

The new `seriesCompare` option now populates the values for *each data series* on the legend, making it easier to compare values at different points on the chart:

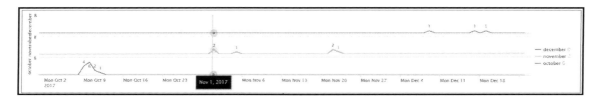

charting.fieldDashStyles

With the new charting option `fieldDashStyles`, you can experiment with various dash styles (`dash`, `dashDot`, `dot`, `longDash`, `longDashDot`, `longDashDotDot`, `shortDash`, `shortDot`, `shortDashDot`, `shortDashDotDot`, `solid`) for each of your charts fields.

Like the other charting options, you can apply a style within the XML:

```
<option name="charting.fieldDashStyles">{count":"shortDashDotDot"}</option>
```

In the following example, we used the preceding `shortDashDotDot` style:

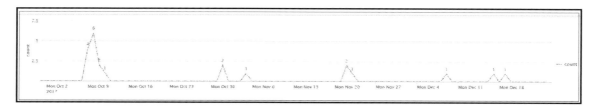

charting.axis Y.abbreviation

Finally, depending upon the chart type, using the following new charting options:

```
charting.axisX.abbreviation
charting.axisX.abbreviation
charting.axisY.abbreviation
charting.axisY2.abbreviation
```

You can add abbreviations to the X or Y values using the closest SI prefix.

That wraps up our review of the latest 7.0 charting enhancements. Feel free to experiment.

Data Models and Pivots

4

In Splunk version 7.0, Splunk has implemented various key optimizations in its core search technology in an effort to reduce the time and resources required to run data model accelerations and accelerated searches. To this end, we have added a section on this topic.

In this chapter, we will introduce the following:

- Data models
- Pivots (along with pivot elements and filters)
- Sparklines

Also in Splunk, data models and pivots should be discussed together because data models drive (Splunk) pivots. So, let's start by defining data models.

What is a data model?

The Splunk product documentation (2015-2017) defines a data model as:

"a hierarchically structured, search-time mapping of semantic knowledge about one or more datasets (that encode the domain knowledge necessary to generate specialized searches of those datasets) so that Splunk can use these specialized searches to generate reports and charts for pivot users."

Data models enable you to create Splunk reports and dashboards without having to develop Splunk searches (required to create those reports and dashboards), and can play a big part in Splunk app development. You can create your own data models, but before you do, you should review the data models that your organization may have already developed. Typically, data models are designed by those that understand the specifics around the format, the semantics of certain data, and the manner in which users may expect to work with that data. In building a typical data model, knowledge managers use knowledge object types (such as lookups, transactions, search-time field extractions, and calculated fields).

Another way to perhaps understand data models, if you are familiar with relational databases, is to think of a Splunk data model as a sort of database schema. Using the **Splunk Pivot Editor**, data models let you generate statistical tables, charts, and visualizations based on column and row configurations that you select.

What does a data model search?

Splunk data models are really a group or set of specific information (referred to as objects) pulled together to create specific Splunk search strings, each used to generate a search that returns a particular dataset. That dataset, returned by the object you select, is governed by particular object constraints and attributes.

Data model objects

As I mentioned, data models are constructed from a series of objects and these objects will be one of four types—event, search, transaction, or child. They are arranged hierarchically, with child objects inheriting from the parent objects they are associated with:

- *Event objects* are the most common data model objects, broadly representing a type of event. Event objects are typically defined by a constraint (which we will discuss next).
- *Transaction objects* enable you to create data models that represent transactions (groups of related events that span time) using fields that have already been added to the model via an event or search object. This means that you can't create data models that are composed only of transaction objects and their child objects. Before you create a transaction object, you must already have some event or search object trees in your model.

- *Search objects* use an arbitrary Splunk search that includes transforming commands to define the dataset that they represent.
- The most top-level objects in a data model are referred to as *root objects* and each can be a parent object to many child objects. Splunk calls the relationship of a parent and child object an *object tree*. The data that this object tree represents is first selected by the root and then refined by each of its child objects.

Object constraining

All data model objects are defined by sets of constraints that will filter out information that is not pertinent to the object. A constraint may be a simple Splunk search (with no pipes or additional commands), a more complex search, or even a transaction. Constraints are inherited by child objects. Constraint inheritance ensures that each child object represents a subset of the data represented by its parent objects. So, for example, a data model may have a root object that defines a particular indexed source (`sourcetype=speciallogs_*`), while a child object of that root might narrow down that search to only the errors that appear in that `datasource (error*)`. You might use this data model if you know that you only want to report on *errors* within the events that belong to the `speciallogs` sourcetype.

Attributes

Data model objects also include attributes, which are simply fields (exposed for use in reporting) associated with the dataset that the object represents. There are five types of object attributes: auto-extracted (fields that Splunk derives at search time), `eval` expressions (field derived from an `eval` expression that you enter in the attribute definition), lookups (they add fields from external data sources such as CSV files and scripts), regular expressions (a field that is extracted from the object event data using a regular expression) and GeoIP (of a lookup that adds geographical attributes, such as latitude, longitude, country, and city to events in the object dataset).

Attributes fall into one of three categories: *inherited attributes* (from the object's parent), *extracted attributes* (that you add to an object), or *calculated* (attributes that are the result of a calculation or a lookup).

When you define data model attributes, you can define (for each object in the data model) whether it is *visible* or *hidden*. Attributes are visible by default. This is particularly important if each object in your data model has many attributes but only a few are essential for your user's needs. Determining which attributes to include in a Splunk data model and which attributes to expose is a critical part of the overall design of the model. Typically, it's often helpful if each object exposes only the data that is relevant to that object, making it easier to understand and use for your average Splunk user.

In addition to attribute visibility, it is also possible to make any attribute required or optional. Indicating that an attribute is required means that every event represented by the object must have that attribute. When you define an attribute as optional, it means that the object may have events that do not have that attribute at all.

Acceleration in version 7.0

Prior to and along with the release of version 7.0, Splunk posted material that touted *"optimizations to core search technology,"* promising decreases in the time and resources required to run data model accelerations as well as *accelerated searches* with faster search and DMA performance.

From reported experiences, Splunk Enterprise users appear to be constantly gaining threefold improvements on their data model acceleration time.

 Note: For other types of searches, search performance improvements of two to ten times have been reported.

Splunk indicates that version 7.0 uses **supplementary parallelization** to convert sequential processing into multi-threaded processing in order to utilize multiple processors simultaneously in a shared-memory. And it uses improved **refactored techniques** to improve search performance for some types of searches or (at minimal) achieve the same performance using one-third of the previously required resources.

To be clear, these improvements were mostly reported when moving from version 5.0, and, for those environments, these gains make the upgrade worthwhile as the same hardware can gain significant performance improvements and/or reduce the footprint required.

Creating a data model

So now that we have a general idea of what a Splunk data model is, let's go ahead and create one. Before we can get started, we need to verify that our user ID is set up with the proper access required to create a data model. By default, only users with an admin or power role can create data models. For other users, the ability to create a data model depends on whether their roles have write access to an app.

To begin (once you have verified that you do have access to create a data model), you can click on **Settings** and then on **Data models** (under **KNOWLEDGE**):

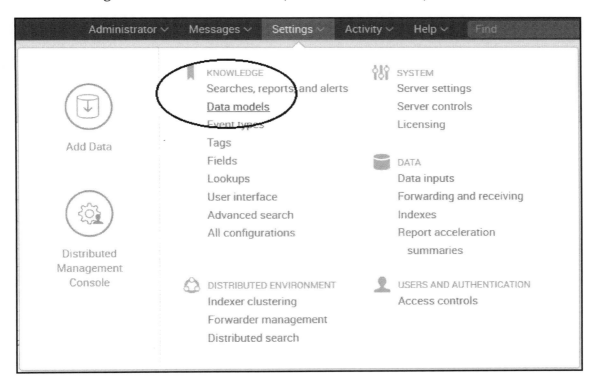

This takes you to the **Data Models** (management) page, shown in the next screenshot. This is where a list of data models is displayed. From here, you can manage the permissions, acceleration, cloning, and removal of existing data models. You can also use this page to upload a data model or create new data models, using the **Upload Data Model** and **New Data Model** buttons on the upper-right corner, respectively.

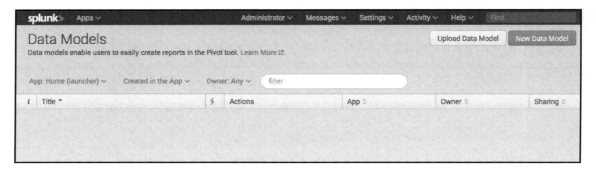

Since this is a new data model, you can click on the button labeled **New Data Model**. This will open the **New Data Model** dialog box (shown in the following image). We can fill in the required information in this dialog box:

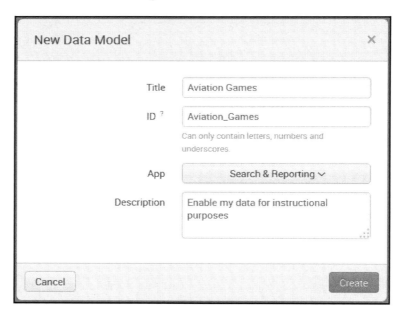

Filling in the new data model dialog

You have four fields to fill in order to describe your new Splunk data model (**Title, ID, App,** and **Description**):

- **Title**: Here you must enter a **Title** for your data model. This field accepts any character, as well as spaces. The value you enter here is what will appear on the data model listing page.
- **ID**: This is an optional field. It gets prepopulated with what you entered for your data model title (with any spaces replaced with underscores. Take a minute to make sure you have a good one, since once you enter the data model **ID**, you can't change it.
- **App**: Here you select (from a drop-down list) the Splunk app that your data model will serve.
- **Description**: The description is also an optional field, but I recommend adding something descriptive to later identify your data model.

Once you have filled in these fields, you can click on the button labeled **Create**. This opens the data model (in our example, **Aviation Games**) in the Splunk **Edit Objects** page as shown in the following screenshot:

The next step in defining a data model is to add the first object. As we have already stated, data models are typically composed of object hierarchies built on root event objects. Each root event object represents a set of data that is defined by a constraint, which is a simple search that filters out events that are not relevant to the object.

Getting back to our example, let's create an object for our data model to track purchase requests on our **Aviation Games** website.

To define our first event-based object, click on **Add Dataset** (as shown in the following screenshot):

Our data model's first object can either be a **Root Event,** or **Root Search**. We're going to add a **Root Event**, so select **Root Event**. This will take you to the **Add Event Dataset** editor:

Our example event will expose events that contain the phrase `error`, which represents processing errors that have occurred within our data source. So, for **Dataset Name,** we will enter `Processing Errors`.

The **Dataset ID** will automatically populate when you type in the **Dataset Name** (you can edit it if you want to change it). For our object's constraint, we'll enter `sourcetype=tm1* error`. This constraint defines the events that will be reported on (all events that contain the phrase `error` that are indexed in the data sources starting with `tml`). After providing **Constraints** for the event-based object, you can click on **Preview** to test whether the constraints you've supplied return the kind of events that you want.

The following screenshot depicts the preview of the constraints given in this example:

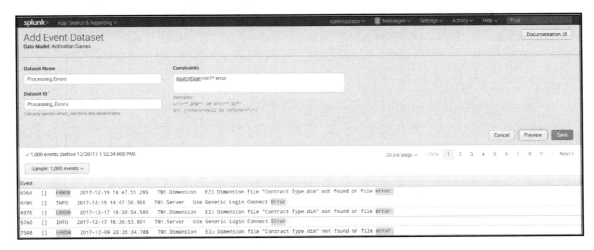

After reviewing the output, click on **Save**. The list of attributes for our root object is displayed: **host**, **source**, **sourcetype**, and **_time**. If you want to add child objects to client and server errors, you need to edit the attributes list to include additional attributes:

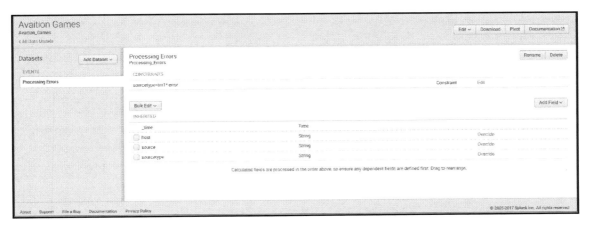

Editing fields (attributes)

Let's add an auto-extracted attribute, as mentioned earlier in this chapter, to our data model. Remember, auto-extracted attributes are derived by Splunk at search time. To start, click on **Add Field**:

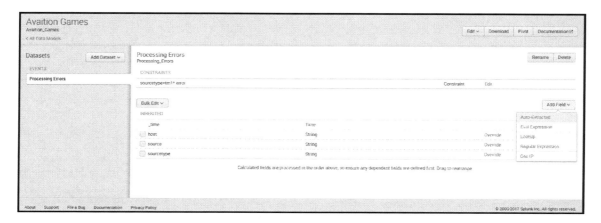

Next, select **Auto-Extracted**. The **Add Auto-Extracted Field** window opens:

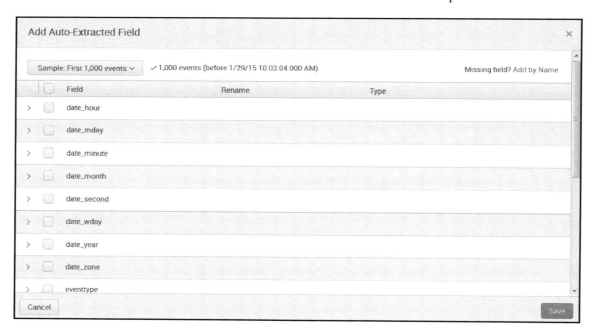

You can scroll through the list of automatically extracted fields and check the fields that you want to include. Since my data model example deals with errors that occurred, I've selected **date_mday**, **date_month**, and **date_year**.

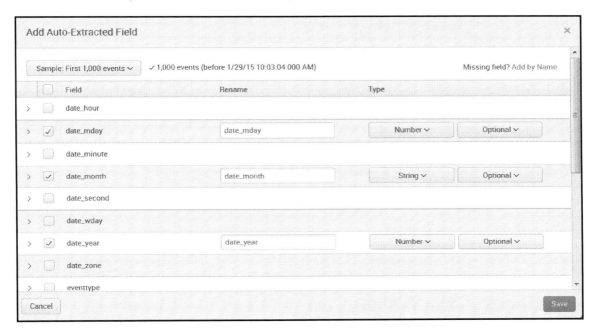

Notice that to the right of the field list, you have the opportunity to rename and type set each of the fields that you selected. **Rename** is self-explanatory, but for **Type**, Splunk allows you to select **String**, **Number**, **Boolean**, or **IPV$** and indicate if the attribute is **Required**, **Optional**, **Hidden**, or **Hidden & Required**. **Optional** means that the attribute doesn't have to appear in every event represented by the object. The attribute may appear in some of the object events and not others.

Once you have reviewed your selected field types, click on **Save**:

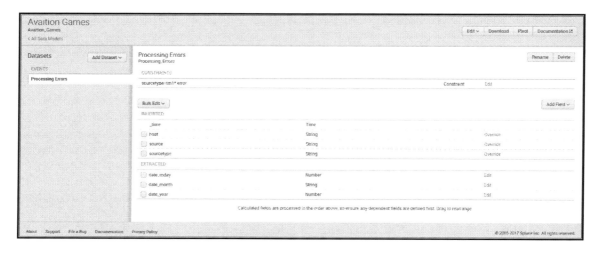

Lookup attributes

Let's discuss lookup attributes now. Splunk can use the existing lookup definitions to match the values of an attribute that you select to values of a field in the specified lookup table. It then returns the corresponding field/value combinations and applies them to your object as (lookup) attributes.

Once again, if you click on **Add Field** and select **Lookup**, Splunk opens the **Add Fields with a Lookup** page (shown in the following screenshot) where you can select from your currently defined lookup definitions. For this example, we select **dnslookup**:

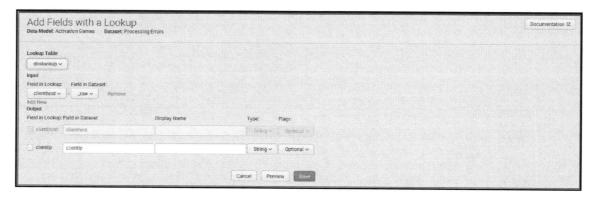

The **dnslookup** converts **clienthost** to **clientip**. We can configure a lookup attribute using this lookup to add that result to the processing errors objects.

Under **Input**, select **clienthost** for **Field in Lookup** and **Field in Dataset**. **Field in Lookup** is the field to be used in the lookup table. **Field in Dataset** is the name of the field used in the event data. In our simple example, Splunk will match the field **clienthost** with the field **host**:

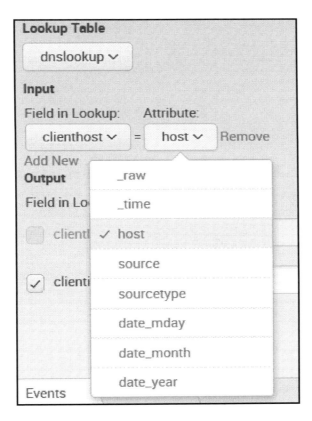

Under **Output**, I have selected **host** as the output field to be matched with the lookup. You can provide a **Display Name** for the selected field. This display name is the name used for the field in your events. I simply typed `AviationLookupName` for my display name (see the following screenshot):

Again, Splunk allows you to click on **Preview** to review the fields that you want to add. You can use the tabs to view the **Events** in a table, or view the values of each of the fields that you selected in **Output**. For example, the following screenshot shows the values of **AviationLookupName**:

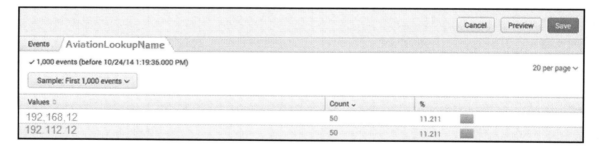

Finally, we can click on **Save**:

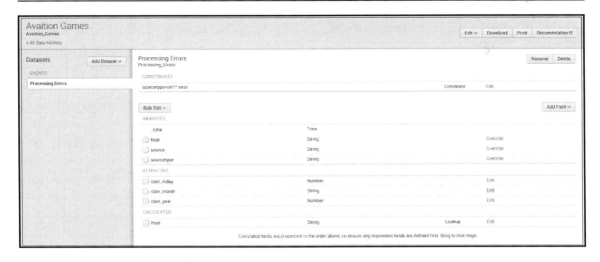

Children

We have just added a root (or parent) object to our data model. The next step is to add some children. Although a child object inherits all the constraints and attributes from its parent, when you create a child, you will give it additional constraints with the intention of further filtering the dataset that the object represents.

To add a child object to our data model, click on **Add Field** and select **Child**:

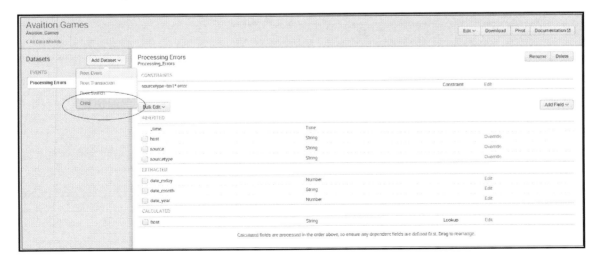

Splunk then opens the editor window, **Add Child Dataset** (shown in the following screenshot):

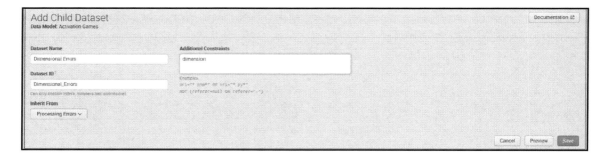

On this page, follow these steps:

- Enter the **Object Name**: Dimensional Errors.
- Leave the **Object ID** as it is: Dimensional_Errors.
- Under **Inherit From**, select **Processing Errors**. This means that this child object will inherit all the attributes from the parent object, **Processing Errors**.
- Add the **Additional Constraints**, dimension, which means that the data models search for the events in this object; when expanded, it will look something like sourcetype=tm1* error dimension.
- Finally, click on **Save** to save your changes:

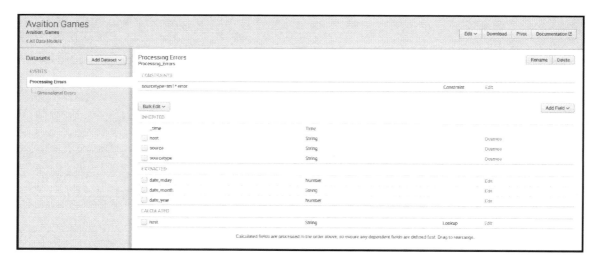

Following the previously outlined steps, you can add more objects, each continuing to filter the results until you have the results that you need.

At this point, the next step in implementing a Splunk data model is to use it. So let's continue and determine how.

What is a pivot?

As we stated earlier in this chapter, data models drive (Splunk) pivots. So what is a pivot? A pivot is created by using the Splunk Pivot Editor and can be a simple (or complex) table, chart, or dashboard. You use the Pivot Editor to map fields of data that you have defined in a data model to a specific data visualization without having to deal with the Splunk Enterprise Search Processing Language.

The Splunk pivot is a simple *drag-and-drop* interface that uses your (predefined) data models and data model objects. These data models (designed by the knowledge managers in your organization using the method that we outlined in the previous sections) are used by the pivot tool to define and subdivide, and to set attributes for the event data that you are interested in.

In earlier versions of Splunk, one could begin the creation of a Pivot from the home page and selecting **Pivot**. In version 7.0, it's a bit different.

You can create a Splunk pivot table by following these steps:

1. Go to the Splunk **Home** page and click on **Settings**; then select **Data Models**.
2. Next, select a data model to pivot (we'll use the previously created **Aviation Games**):

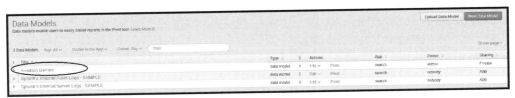

3. Once you select your data model, the **Datasets Editor** page will open, where you can select **Pivot**:

4. Next, from the **Select a Dataset** page, you can indicate a specific dataset (identifying which dataset to work with):

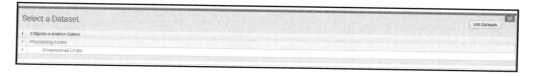

5. Once you select a dataset, you can select from the list of objects (which can be an event, transaction, search, or child type of object, and represent a specific view or slice of a Splunk search result) within that dataset to work with (or click on **Edit Datasets** to edit or add to the objects within the data model):

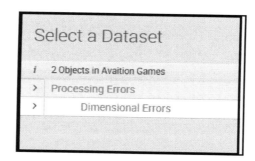

6. After you select a specific object, Splunk will take you to the Pivot Editor, where you can create your pivot:

The Pivot Editor

Splunk will start the Pivot Editor in what is referred to as *pivot table mode*.

In pivot table mode, the editor displays only one row that represents the object's total result count over all time, based on the type of object you've selected:

- **Event type**: The total number of events (selected by the object)
- **Transaction type**: The total number of transactions (identified by the object)
- **Search type**: The total number of table rows (returned by the base search in the object)

Pivot tables are defined by you using Splunk pivot elements, which are of four basic pivot element categories: **Filters**, **Split Rows**, **Split Columns**, and **Column Values**.

Only two pivot elements will be defined when you start: a filter element (always set to **All time**) and a column values element (always set to **Count_of**, which is based on the object type of your selected object, as shown in the following screenshot:).

Using the editor, you can add, define, and remove multiple pivot elements from each pivot element category to define your pivot table:

- **Filters**: To reduce the result count for the object
- **Split rows**: To split out the pivot results by rows
- **Split columns**: To break up field values by columns
- **Column values**: To show aggregate results such as counts, sums, and averages

Working with pivot elements

Within the Pivot Editor, all pivot element categories can be managed in the same way:

- Click on the + icon to open up the element dialog, where you choose an attribute, and then define how the element uses that attribute
- Click on the pencil icon on the element to open the element dialog and edit how a pivot element is defined
- Drag and drop elements within its pivot element category to reorder them
- Drag and drop the elements between pivot element categories to transfer the element to the desired pivot category (there are some restrictions on what can and cannot be transferred by drag and drop)
- Click on the pencil icon on the element to open the element dialog and click on **Remove** to remove the element (or you can click on the element and shake it up and down until it turns red, then drop it—my favorite method)

The management of the pivot elements is done using the pivot element dialog. The element dialog is broken up into two steps: Choose (or change) the element, and configure the element (configuration). Let's look at each category.

Filtering pivots

Splunk Pivots can be filtered using filter elements.

Splunk supports three kinds of filter elements for use with pivots. It's important to understand each and they are explained as follows:

- **Time**: Always present and cannot be removed. Time defines the time range for which your pivot will return results.
- **Match**: Enables the ability to set up matching for strings, numbers, timestamps, Booleans, and IPv4 addresses (although currently only as AND, not OR, matches).
- **Limit**: Enables you to restrict the number of results returned by your pivot.

 Configuration options for the match and limit filter elements depend on the type of attribute that you've chosen for the element.

Split (row or column)

The Splunk configuration options that are available for split (row and column) depend on the type of attribute you choose for them.

 Some split configuration options are specific to either row or column elements while others are available for either element type.

Those configuration options, regardless of attribute type, are:

- Both split row and split column:
    - **Max rows and max columns**: This is the maximum number of rows or columns that can appear in the results table
    - **Totals**: Indicates whether to include a row or column that represents the total of all the others in an attribute called ALL
- Only split row elements:
    - **Label**: Is used to override the attribute name with a different text or character string
    - **Sort**: Used to reorder the split rows

- Only split column:
    - **Group Others**: Indicates whether to group any results excluded by the *max columns limit* into a separate OTHER column

Configuration options dependent upon attribute type are:

- String attributes:
    - There are no configuration options specific to string attributes that are common to both split row and split column elements
- Numeric attributes:
    - **Create ranges**: Indicates whether you want your numeric values represented as ranges (yes) or listed separately (no)
- Boolean attributes:
    - You can provide alternate labels for true and false values
- Timestamp attributes:
    - **Period**: Use this to bucket your timestamp results by year, month, day, hour, minute, or second

Column values

You will find a column value element providing the total results returned by a selected object over all time. You have the option to keep this element, change its label, or remove it. In addition, you can add new column value elements such as:

- List distinct values
- First/last value
- Count/distinct count
- Sum
- Average
- Max/min
- Standard deviation
- List distinct values
- Duration
- Earliest/latest

Pivot table formatting

You can format the results of your pivot in many ways. You can set the number of results displayed per page (10, 20, or 50) by using the pagination dropdown.

If you use **Format dropdown,** you can even control table wrapping and the display of row numbers, and determine drill-down and data overlay behavior. Pivot table drill-down is set to *cell mode* by default and works similar to Splunk table drill-down (discussed earlier in this chapter).

A quick example

Let's try a quick example. Once we have selected a data model (in our case, **Aviation Games**), from the **Select a Dataset** page, we can choose **Processing Errors**, which will land us on the **New Pivot** (Pivot Editor):

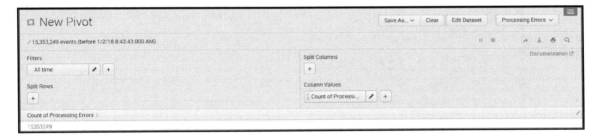

To build a simple pivot, we can do the following quick steps:

1. Add/Verify the filters:

   Remember, **All time** is the default; this will include all results found over all time. You can click on the pencil and amend this filter to be based upon any of Splunk's **Presets** or a specific **Date Range**:

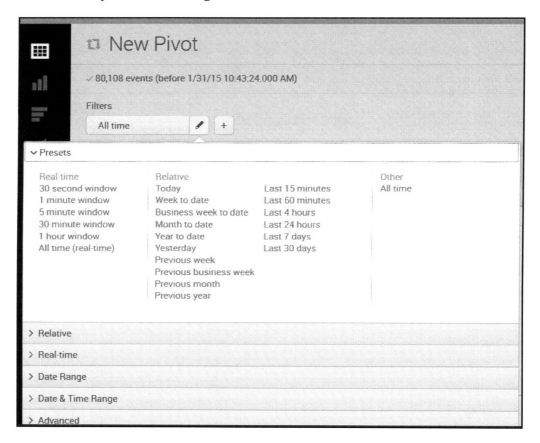

For this example, we'll just leave the default selection.

2. Configure the **Split Rows**.

   Directly under **Filters** is **Split Rows**. For **Split Rows**, I've selected **date_month**:

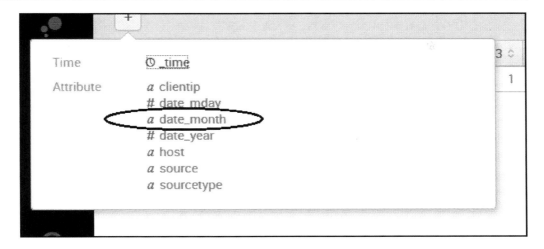

3. After making the selection, you are able to provide additional settings for the selected row:

I've provided a new name (**Label**) for the row (my_Month) and left the defaults for **Sort**, **Max Rows** (to display), and **Totals**.

4. Configure the **Split Columns.**

Moving to the upper-right side of the **Pivot** page, we have **Split Columns**. For **Split Columns**, I've selected **date_mday**:

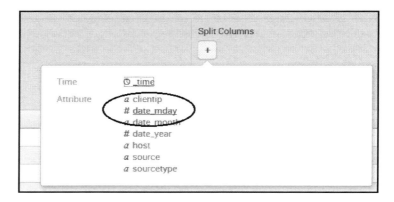

Once you select **date_mday**, you are given the opportunity to set some additional values:

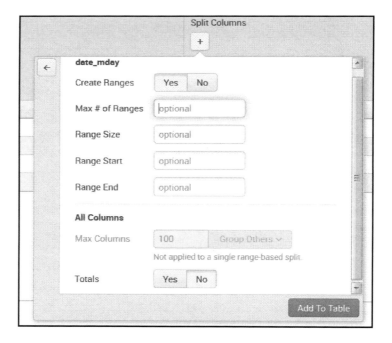

We'll leave the defaults again and click on the button labelled **Add To Table**.

5. Configure the **Column Values.** Finally, for the **Column Values**, (by clicking on the pencil) you can see that Splunk defaulted to providing a **count** (of processing errors) found in the indexed data (shown in the following screenshot). You can click on the button labeled **Update**:

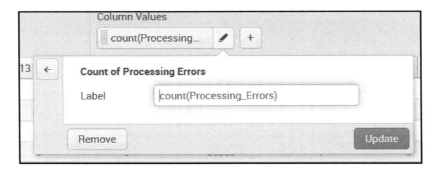

6. View the results of our sample pivot in the following screenshot:

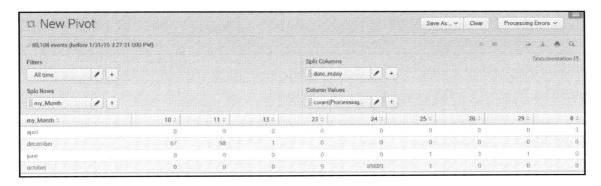

From here, you have the option to **Clear the Pivot** (and start over), or click on **Save As** and save the pivot as a Splunk report or as a dashboard panel for later use.

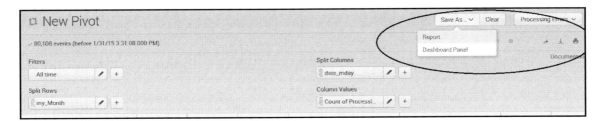

Sparklines

Growing in popularity as a data visualization option, sparklines are inline charts that represent the general shape of a variation (typically over time) in some measurement (such as miles per gallon or home value), in a simple and highly condensed way. Splunk provides you the ability to add sparklines to stats and chart searches, improving their usefulness and overall information density.

Let's look at a simple Splunk search example like the following:

```
sourcetype=csv "0001" "USD" | chart AVG(Jan) by PERIOD
```

It creates the following results table:

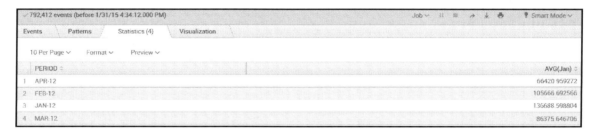

As you can see, the preceding example of search generates a table that shows average amounts by the field **PERIOD**—just two columns.

If you add the keyword `sparkline` to the search pipeline, you can have Splunk include sparklines with the results:

> The sparklines feature is always used in conjunction with chart and stats because it is a function (of those two search commands) and not a command by itself.
>
> ```
> sourcetype=csv "0001" "USD" | chart sparkline AVG(Jan) by
> PERIOD
> ```

If we run this Splunk search, it generates a table similar to the previous one, except that now for each row you have a sparkline chart:

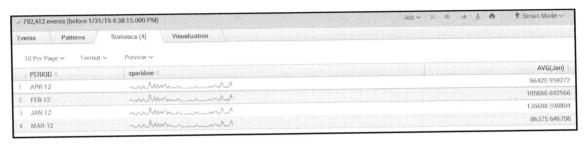

Here is an additional example—using sparklines to view the variations of an amount (the rounded value of **Jan**) by **COMPANY**:

```
sourcetype=csv "0001" "USD" | eval RJan= round(Jan) | chart
  sparkline Sum(RJan) by COMPANY
```

The results are shown in the following screenshot:

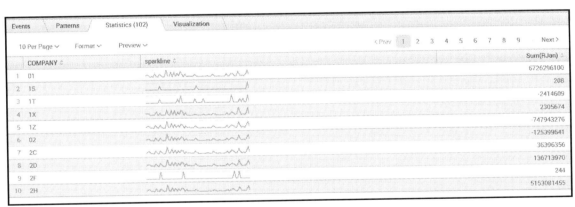

Now you can more easily see patterns in the data that may have been unseen before.

 The Splunk sparkline displays information in relation to the events represented in that sparkline but not in relation to other sparklines.

Simple XML Dashboards

5

Dashboards are a way for you to capture, group, and automate tables and charts into useful and informative views.

In this chapter, we will quickly cover the wizards provided in Splunk 7.0 and then dig into the underlying XML. With XML, you can easily build interactive forms, further customize panels, and use the same query for multiple panels, among other things.

XML—an industry-standard meta language—is a powerful tool. It is suggested that the reader have some knowledge of its fundamentals. A variety of sources are currently available other than this book.

We will also cover how and when to schedule the generation of dashboards to reduce both the wait time for users and the load on the server. This chapter will cover the following topics:

- The purpose of dashboards
- Using wizards to build dashboards
- Scheduling the generation of dashboards
- Editing the XML directly
- UI examples app
- Building forms

The purpose of dashboards

Any search, table, or chart that you create can be saved and made to appear in menus for other users to see. With that power, why would you bother creating a dashboard?

Here are a few reasons:

- A dashboard can contain multiple panels, each running a different query.
- Every dashboard has a unique URL, which is easy to share.
- Dashboards are more customizable than an individual query.
- The search bar is removed, making it less intimidating to many users.
- Forms allow you to present the user with a custom search interface that only requires specific values.
- Dashboards look great. Many organizations place dashboards on projectors and monitors for at-a-glance information about their environment.
- Dashboards can be scheduled for PDF delivery by email. This feature is not the most robust, but, with some consideration, it can be used effectively. With all that said, if a saved search is working well the way it is, there is no strong reason to turn it into a dashboard.

Using wizards to build dashboards

Since the goal of this chapter is understanding Splunk dashboards (and not the fundamentals of searching), we'll utilize several new simple search strings as well as some of the queries from previous chapters to illustrate certain points. So, let's start by making an operational dashboard for showing **Forecast Events** within our indexed data. The following is a simple search string to begin our exercise:

```
sourcetype="*" Forecast | timechart count as "Forecast Events" by
date_month
```

This is shown in the following screenshot:

In addition to our search string, I've selected **Previous Year** from the Splunk presets (see the preceding screenshot).

This will produce a graph like this one:

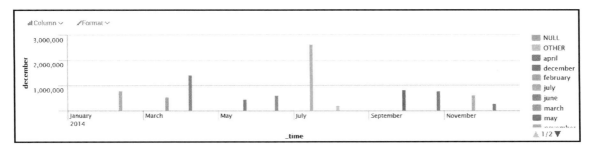

To add this to a dashboard, we can perform the following steps:

1. Click on **Save As** and then choose **Dashboard Panel**:

2. This opens a dialog that guides you through saving the query as a dashboard:

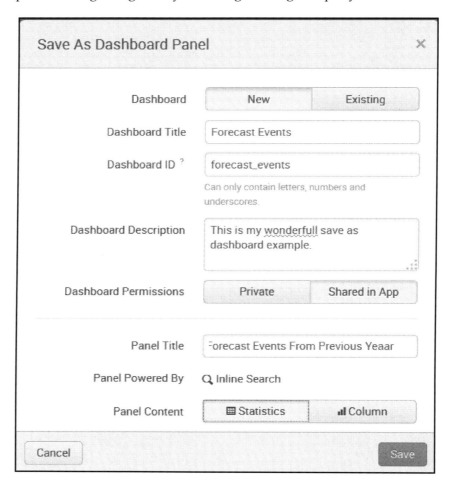

3. Enter the following details and click on the **Save** button:
   - **Dashboard-New/Existing**: This allows you to indicate whether your search is to be saved as part of an existing dashboard or as a new one. In our example, I've selected **New**.
   - **Dashboard Title**: Simply provide a title for your dashboard to display.
   - **Dashboard ID**: This is the Splunk dashboard ID, which defaults to whatever you have entered for your title, with special characters (such as spaces) replaced.

- **Dashboard Description**: This is where you can provide a short note about what your dashboard does.
- **Dashboard Permissions**: Select whether your dashboard will be private (not accessible to other users) or shared within an app.
- **Panel Title**: This is a sort of subtitle, which means that it will be the title/caption displayed for the dashboard panel (where your search runs).
- **Panel Powered By**: This is set by Splunk. Our example is powered by an inline search string.
- **Panel Content**: This is where you indicate a format for the search results.

4. You should now receive the following message:

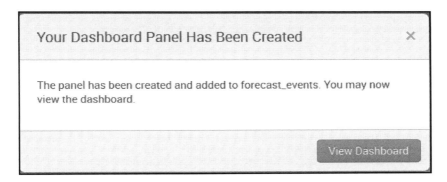

Your new dashboard is ready to use. It is that simple.

As you create more dashboards, you will end up creating a lot of searches. A naming convention will help you keep track of which search belongs to which dashboard. Here is one possible approach:

```
Dashboard - [dashboard name] - [search name and panel type]
```

When the number of dashboards and searches becomes large, apps can be used to group dashboards and searches together, providing yet another way to organize and share assets.

After saving our dashboard, it will be available under the **Dashboards** menu (see the following screenshot):

On the **Dashboards** page, if we click on our dashboard name (**Forecast Events**), Splunk displays our single panel dashboard:

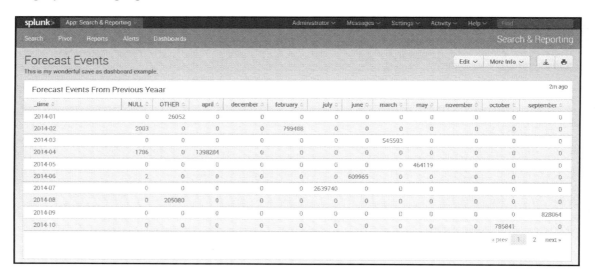

Forecast Events From Previous Yeaar

_time	NULL	OTHER	april	december	february	july	june	march	may	november	october	september
2014-01	0	26052	0	0	0	0	0	0	0	0	0	0
2014-02	2003	0	0	0	799486	0	0	0	0	0	0	0
2014-03	0	0	0	0	0	0	0	545593	0	0	0	0
2014-04	1796	0	1398284	0	0	0	0	0	0	0	0	0
2014-05	0	0	0	0	0	0	0	0	464119	0	0	0
2014-06	2	0	0	0	0	0	609965	0	0	0	0	0
2014-07	0	0	0	0	0	2639740	0	0	0	0	0	0
2014-08	0	205080	0	0	0	0	0	0	0	0	0	0
2014-09	0	0	0	0	0	0	0	0	0	0	0	828064
2014-10	0	0	0	0	0	0	0	0	0	0	785841	0

Adding another panel

Perhaps we would like to add a second panel to our dashboard. To do that, we can open the dashboard and click on **Edit**:

In version 7.0, clicking on Edit opens the **Edit Dashboard** page:

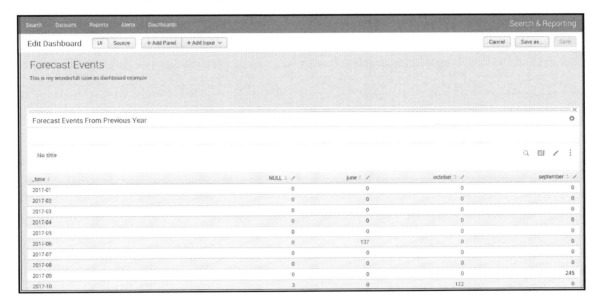

Splunk now gives us the following selections (where we will—for now—select **Add Panel**):

The following options are displayed:

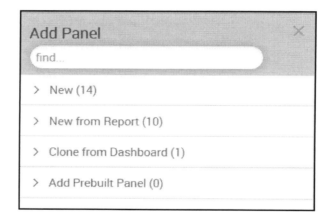

Here, we have the ability to add a new panel to our dashboard from a variety of sources:

- **New**: Creates one from scratch
- **New from Report**: Creates a panel from an existing report
- **Clone from Dashboard**: Creates a panel from an existing dashboard
- **Add Prebuilt Panel**: As the name says, it adds a prebuilt panel to our dashboard

So, for our example, let's select **New**:

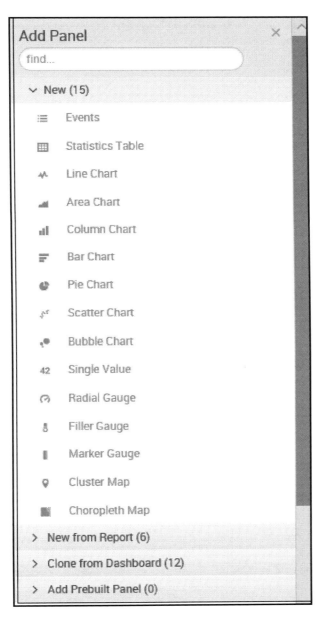

Again, various options are displayed. For illustrative purposes, let's select **Pie Chart** and fill in the **New Pie Chart** options (shown in the following screenshot). I simply plugged in the original time preset (**Previous year**), added a **Content Title,** and provided the same search string. The idea here is to present the same information as our initial dashboard panel but in a different format:

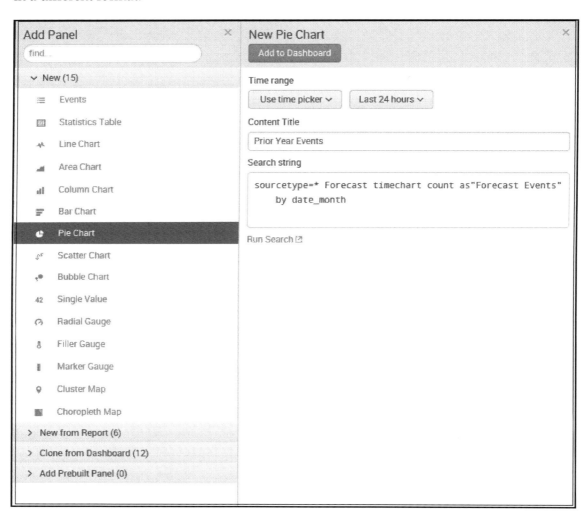

Next, click on the button labeled **Add to Dashboard**:

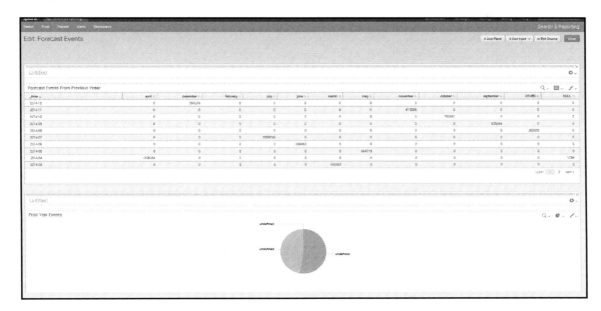

The preceding screenshot is what our new, *two-panel* dashboard looks like. To be sure, the pie chart isn't very interesting, so let's make a change. You'll notice *four* icons in the upper-right corner of the lower panel. If you click on one second icon from the left (which looks like a tiny pie chart), you'll see that you have the option of changing the visualization type, and that Splunk has looked at your data and made some recommendations.

You can try out the different choices; I selected an **Area**:

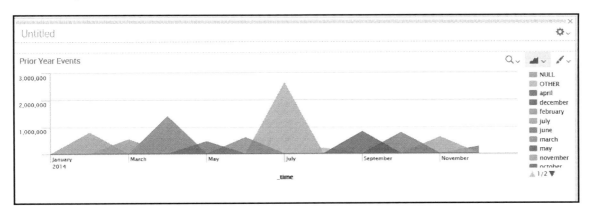

Note that, in version 7.0, the visualization selector is more type more sophisticated, as shown in the following screenshot:

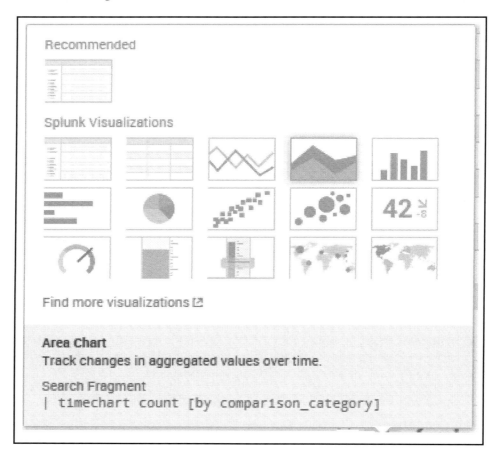

A cool trick

By default, each new panel is added to the bottom of the dashboard as you see in the preceding screenshot. You can rearrange your dashboard panels anyway you like; typically, page space allows you to have up to three panels distributed horizontally (but you are not limited to three), which is a great way to show visualizations. If you click on the upper border of your panel, you can drag panels around the page, like so:

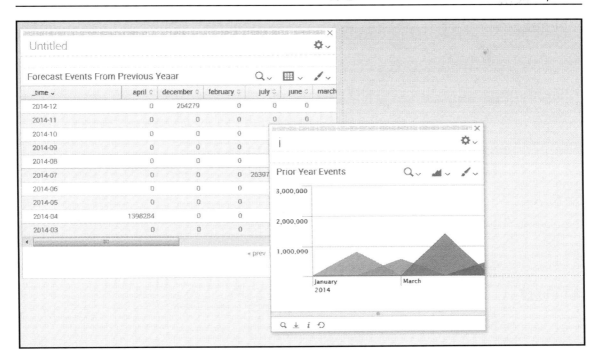

Let's get back to those four icons on our dashboard panels:

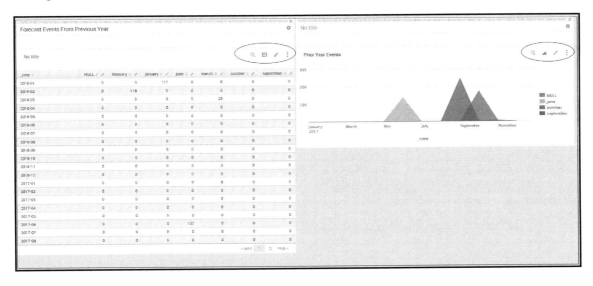

Let's click on the first (leftmost) icon that looks like a magnifying glass. Now, in version 7.0, the **Edit Search** screen appears:

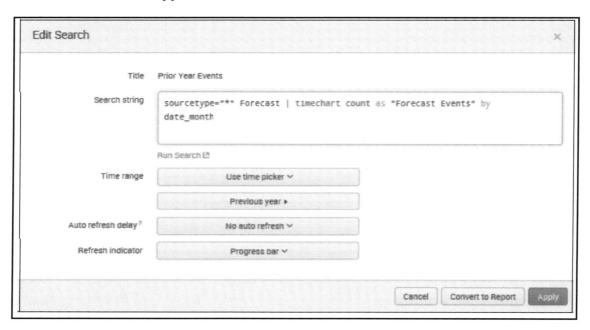

In our dashboard example, our panels use **INLINE SEARCH** as the base query. An inline search string lets us build a query directly within our dashboard. This is often convenient as many searches will have no purpose but for a particular dashboard, so there is no reason for these searches to appear in the Splunk menus. This also reduces external dependencies, making it easier to move the dashboard to another app.

In the preceding **Edit Search** screen, the edit options include: the search string, the time range, auto-refresh settings, and the refresh indicator. In addition, you can click on **Convert to Report** to convert your panel to a Splunk report. Using these options, you can modify your dashboard panel any way you like.

In version 7.0, to remove (delete) a panel from the dashboard and start again, you use the small cross (x) icon in the upper right of the panel.

Converting the panel to a report

You may want to convert your dashboard panel (that is powered by an inline search) to a Splunk report, so that it can have some of the advantages that report-based panels have over inline-search-powered panels, such as faster loading times due to report acceleration.

In the following screenshot, I have clicked on **Convert to Report** and added a **Report Title** and **Description** on the **Convert to Report** dialog:

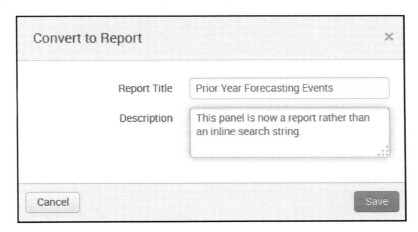

Now our dashboard panel is based on a Splunk report:

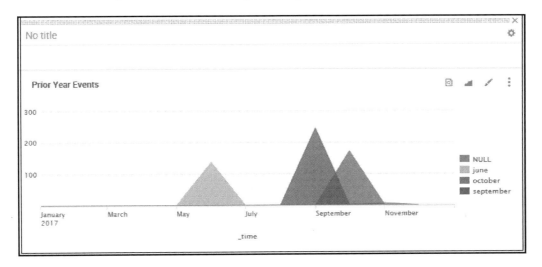

Did you notice how our magnifying icon has changed? It is no longer the **Search Report** icon. Let's click on it:

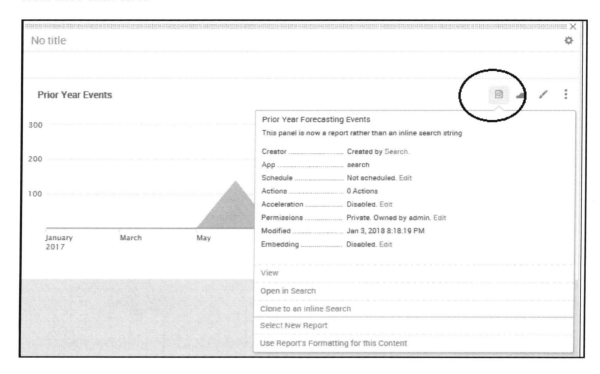

We see **Prior Year Forecasting Events** (which is what we named the report) and get a confirmation:

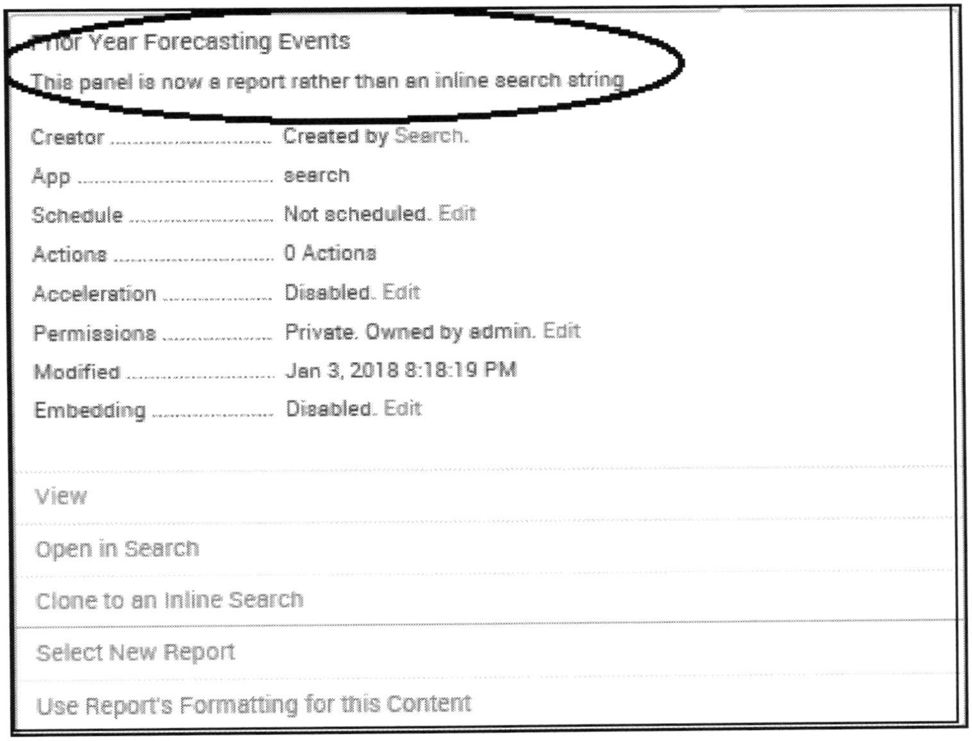

Prior Year Forecasting Events

This panel is now a report rather than an inline search string

Creator	Created by Search.
App	search
Schedule	Not scheduled. Edit
Actions	0 Actions
Acceleration	Disabled. Edit
Permissions	Private. Owned by admin. Edit
Modified	Jan 3, 2018 8:18:19 PM
Embedding	Disabled. Edit

View

Open in Search

Clone to an Inline Search

Select New Report

Use Report's Formatting for this Content

Of course, as you can see, Splunk allows us more options for our dashboard panel, such as:
View, Open in Search, Clone (back) **to an Inline Search, Select a New Report,** and **Use
Report's Formatting for this Content**. Perhaps a favorite is **View**, which opens the panel as
a full-featured Splunk report:

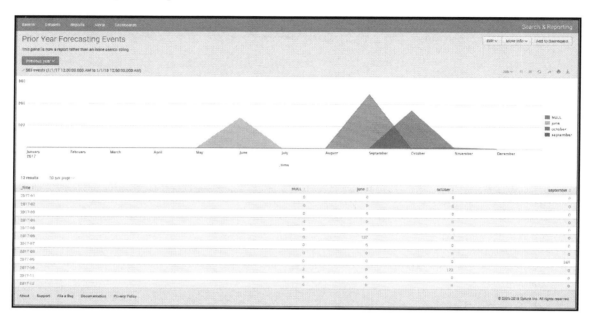

Moving on, we've already touched on the middle icon (when we switched the formatting of
our panel from pie to area). So, we'll briefly mention here that in addition to reformatting
your panel, you have the ability to click on **View Events**, which will list the raw events in
your panel similar to what you see if you run your original search string:

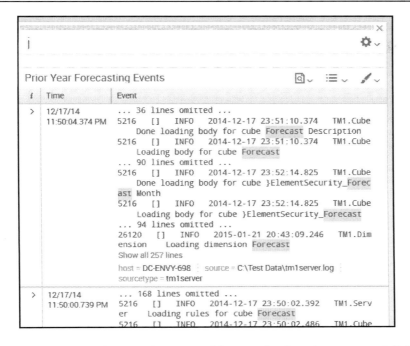

Moving on to the *third* icon, the one that resembles a paint brush, we see additional options for our panel (formatting options that will be based upon the selected panel's format). For example, our left dashboard panel is formatted as a statistical table, so the following options are selectable:

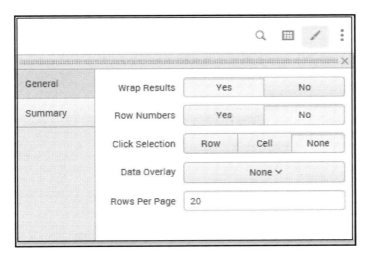

You can experiment with the various selections (they are applied dynamically) until you arrive at what you are happy with, then click on the icon again.

More options

Also on your panel, in the upper-right corner, you will find an icon resembling a gear (see the next screenshot). Clicking on this icon allows you to convert it to a prebuilt panel, or back to an **INLINE PANEL**:

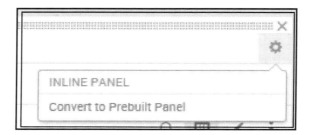

Maybe this is not so obvious; what does **Convert to Prebuilt Panel** mean? Well, so far, our panel has been an inline panel—one that you can edit with the Splunk dashboard editor and Panel Editor (you can also edit the child elements of a panel element by editing the simple XML source code; more on this later in this chapter). A prebuilt panel is a panel that is a simple XML code that can be shared between various dashboards. You cannot edit the title, search, or visualizations of a prebuilt panel from the dashboard reference.

Back to the dashboard

Our dashboard menu (changed slightly in version 7.0) includes selections in the upper-left corner, as shown in the following screenshot. We have already explored the first (**Add Panel**) in this chapter. Let's now move on to **Add Input** (we'll go over **UI** and **Source** a bit later on):

Add input

Adding an input to your dashboard will convert it to a form. All dashboards are actually made up of XML code (we touched a bit on this earlier when we introduced prebuilt panels). In the next section (**Edit Source**), we will dive deeper into this topic but, for now, understand that the dashboard that we have created is made up of or defined by the XML which Splunk is using, and adding any type of input will modify the underlying XML (in fact, after adding any input, the XML tag `<dashboard>` is changed to `<form>`).

Once you click on **Add Input,** you can select an input type from the list shown in the following screenshot:

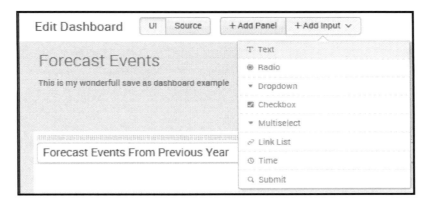

For example, you can select **Text** to add a text field for user input. You can have more than just input on your dashboard, and you can drag inputs to rearrange them on your form (dashboard). You can even drag an input onto a panel within your dashboard and make that input apply only to the panel. Once you are happy with your inputs, you can click on **Done** to indicate that you have finished editing. We will go into this in more detail later in this chapter, in the section on building forms.

Editing source

Finally, let's go on to our third option, **Source**. As I have already mentioned, all Splunk dashboards are defined by XML. If you don't have experience with XML, you can create, edit, and maintain dashboards using the dashboard editor (similar to what we've been doing with our examples). However, by using XML, Splunk gives us the ability to create dashboards as complex and robust as we need them to be.

Edit UI

Lastly, clicking back on the UI puts you back in the mode to edit the user interface (rather than the source code as described in the previous section).

Editing XML directly

Before proceeding, let me take a moment to tip my hat to Splunk for its dashboard editor. There are only a couple of reasons why you would still need to edit simplified XML dashboards: to edit forms and post-processing data. I predict that these reasons will go away in the future, as more features are added to the dashboard editor.

The documentation for simplified XML panels can be found by searching `http://www.splunk.com/` for panel reference for simple XML. The following link is a good place to start:

`http://docs.splunk.com/Documentation/Splunk/latest/Viz/PanelreferenceforSimplif iedXML`

UI examples app

Before digging into the XML behind dashboards, it may be a good idea to install the app Splunk UI examples app for 4.1+, available at Splunkbase . The examples provided in this app give a good overview of the features available in both simplified XML and advanced XML dashboards.

The simplest way to find this app is from the default Splunk home screen by clicking on **Splunk Apps**.

Building forms

Forms allow you to make a template that needs one or more pieces of information supplied to run. You can build these directly using raw XML, but I find it simpler to build a simple dashboard and then modify the XML accordingly. The other option is to copy an existing dashboard and modify it to meet your needs. We will touch on a simple use case in the following section.

Creating a form from a dashboard

First, let's think of a use case that we might be able to use with our previous example. How about a form that tells us about the forecast events for a particular year? Let's start with our previous search example:

```
sourcetype="*" Forecast | timechart count as "Forecast Events" by
  date_month
```

Since we have already created a dashboard from this query earlier in this chapter, let's look at the XML for our dashboard. As we did earlier, click on **Source** (on the dashboard editor). The XML for our dashboard looks like the following code. Notice the occurrence of two `<panel>` tags within our XML, indicating that there are two panels in our dashboard:

```
<dashboard>
 <label>Forecast Events</label>
 <description>This is my wonderful save as dashboard example.</description>
 <row>
  <panel>
   <table>
    <title>Forecast Events From Previous Year</title>
    <search>
     <query>sourcetype="*" Forecast | timechart count as "Forecast Events"
by date_month</query>
     <earliest>-1y@y</earliest>
     <latest>@y</latest>
    </search>
   </table>
  </panel>
  <panel>
   <chart>
    <title>Prior Year Forecasting Events</title>
    <search ref="Prior Year Forecasting Events"></search>
    <option name="list.drilldown">full</option>
    <option name="list.wrap">1</option>
    <option name="maxLines">5</option>
    <option name="raw.drilldown">full</option>
    <option name="rowNumbers">0</option>
    <option name="table.drilldown">all</option>
    <option name="table.wrap">1</option>
    <option name="type">list</option>
    <fields>["host","source","sourcetype"]</fields>
    <option
name="charting.axisLabelsX.majorLabelStyle.overflowMode">ellipsisNone</opti
on>
    <option name="charting.axisLabelsX.majorLabelStyle.rotation">0</option>
    <option name="charting.axisTitleX.visibility">visible</option>
```

```
        <option name="charting.axisTitleY.visibility">visible</option>
        <option name="charting.axisTitleY2.visibility">visible</option>
        <option name="charting.axisX.scale">linear</option>
        <option name="charting.axisY.scale">linear</option>
        <option name="charting.axisY2.enabled">false</option>
        <option name="charting.axisY2.scale">inherit</option>
        <option name="charting.chart">line</option>
        <option name="charting.chart.bubbleMaximumSize">50</option>
        <option name="charting.chart.bubbleMinimumSize">10</option>
        <option name="charting.chart.bubbleSizeBy">area</option>
        <option name="charting.chart.nullValueMode">gaps</option>
        <option name="charting.chart.sliceCollapsingThreshold">0.01</option>
        <option name="charting.chart.stackMode">default</option>
        <option name="charting.chart.style">shiny</option>
        <option name="charting.drilldown">all</option>
        <option name="charting.layout.splitSeries">0</option>
        <option
name="charting.legend.labelStyle.overflowMode">ellipsisMiddle</option>
        <option name="charting.legend.placement">right</option>
      </chart>
    </panel>
  </row>
</dashboard>
```

That's pretty simple. To convert our dashboard into a form, we have to do the following things.

First, we change `<dashboard>` to `<form>` within our XML. Don't forget the closing tag `</dashboard>` to `</form>`. Next, we create a `<fieldset>` tag with any form elements.

It can be something like this:

```
<form>
<label>Chapter 5 Build a Form 1</label>
<fieldset>
<input type="text" token="myyear">
<label>MyYear</label>
</input>
</fieldset>
```

Now we add the appropriate variable in `<query>` to reflect the form values:

```
<query>sourcetype="*" Forecast date_year=$myyear$ | timechart
 count as "Forecast Events" by date_month</query>
```

When we're through, our XML looks like this:

```
<form>
 <label>Forecast Events</label>
 <description>This is my wonderful save as dashboard example.</description>
 <label>Chapter 5 Build a Form 1</label>
<fieldset>
<input type="text" token="myyear">
<label>MyYear</label>
</input>
</fieldset>
 <row>
  <panel>
   <table>
    <title>Forecast Events From Previous Yeaar</title>
    <search>
     <query>sourcetype="*" Forecast date_year=$myyear$ | timechart count as
"Forecast Events" by date_month</query>
     <earliest>-1y@y</earliest>
     <latest>@y</latest>
    </search>
   </table>
  </panel>
  <panel>
   <chart>
    <title>Prior Year Forecasting Events</title>
    <search ref="Prior Year Forecasting Events"></search>
    <option name="list.drilldown">full</option>
    <option name="list.wrap">1</option>
    <option name="maxLines">5</option>
    <option name="raw.drilldown">full</option>
    <option name="rowNumbers">0</option>
    <option name="table.drilldown">all</option>
    <option name="table.wrap">1</option>
    <option name="type">list</option>
    <fields>["host","source","sourcetype"]</fields>
    <option
name="charting.axisLabelsX.majorLabelStyle.overflowMode">ellipsisNone</opti
on>
    <option name="charting.axisLabelsX.majorLabelStyle.rotation">0</option>
    <option name="charting.axisTitleX.visibility">visible</option>
    <option name="charting.axisTitleY.visibility">visible</option>
    <option name="charting.axisTitleY2.visibility">visible</option>
    <option name="charting.axisX.scale">linear</option>
    <option name="charting.axisY.scale">linear</option>
    <option name="charting.axisY2.enabled">false</option>
    <option name="charting.axisY2.scale">inherit</option>
    <option name="charting.chart">line</option>
```

```
    <option name="charting.chart.bubbleMaximumSize">50</option>
    <option name="charting.chart.bubbleMinimumSize">10</option>
    <option name="charting.chart.bubbleSizeBy">area</option>
    <option name="charting.chart.nullValueMode">gaps</option>
    <option name="charting.chart.sliceCollapsingThreshold">0.01</option>
    <option name="charting.chart.stackMode">default</option>
    <option name="charting.chart.style">shiny</option>
    <option name="charting.drilldown">all</option>
    <option name="charting.layout.splitSeries">0</option>
    <option
 name="charting.legend.labelStyle.overflowMode">ellipsisMiddle</option>
    <option name="charting.legend.placement">right</option>
   </chart>
  </panel>
 </row>
</form>
```

Let's click on **Save** and then search for **Forecast Events** that occurred in a particular year. Now, looking at our example dashboard, we notice our input field **MyYear** and a **Submit** button at the top of the panel along with a **Search is waiting for input...** message:

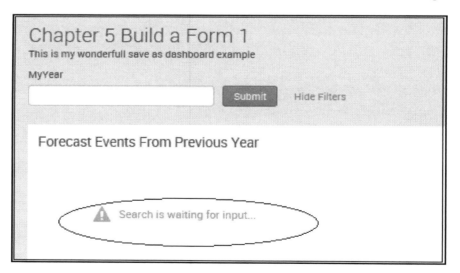

We now have a useful form for displaying the forecast events for a particular year.

Driving multiple panels from one form

A single form can also be used to drive multiple panels at once. Earlier, we had our dashboard with two panels, one of which we converted into a report. Let's revisit the dashboard in that state for a moment. If we want to (and this would probably make the most sense), we can again edit the XML source for the dashboard and this time convert all the searches, as we did in the previous example, to use our form field:

```
<form>
 <label>Forecast Events</label>
 <description>This is my wonderful save as dashboard example.</description>
 <fieldset>
  <input type="text" token="myyear">
   <label>MyYear</label>
  </input>
 </fieldset>
 <row>
  <panel>
   <table>
    <title>Forecast Events From Previous Yeaar</title>
    <search>
     <query>sourcetype="*" Forecast date_year=$myyear$ | timechart count as
"Forecast Events" by date_month</query>
     <earliest>-1y@y</earliest>
     <latest>@y</latest>
    </search>
   </table>
  </panel>
 </row>
 <row>
  <panel>
   <chart>
    <title>Forecast Events From Previous Yeaar</title>
    <search>
     <query>sourcetype="*" Forecast date_year=$myyear$ | timechart count as
"Forecast Events" by date_month</query>
     <earliest>-1y@y</earliest>
     <latest>@y</latest>
```

```
      </search>
      <option name="wrap">true</option>
      <option name="rowNumbers">true</option>
      <option name="dataOverlayMode">none</option>
      <option name="count">10</option>
      <option
name="charting.axisLabelsX.majorLabelStyle.overflowMode">ellipsisNone</opti
on>
      <option name="charting.axisLabelsX.majorLabelStyle.rotation">0</option>
      <option name="charting.axisTitleX.visibility">visible</option>
      <option name="charting.axisTitleY.visibility">visible</option>
      <option name="charting.axisTitleY2.visibility">visible</option>
      <option name="charting.axisX.scale">linear</option>
      <option name="charting.axisY.scale">linear</option>
      <option name="charting.axisY2.enabled">false</option>
      <option name="charting.axisY2.scale">inherit</option>
      <option name="charting.chart">area</option>
      <option name="charting.chart.bubbleMaximumSize">50</option>
      <option name="charting.chart.bubbleMinimumSize">10</option>
      <option name="charting.chart.bubbleSizeBy">area</option>
      <option name="charting.chart.nullValueMode">gaps</option>
      <option name="charting.chart.sliceCollapsingThreshold">0.01</option>
      <option name="charting.chart.stackMode">default</option>
      <option name="charting.chart.style">shiny</option>
      <option name="charting.drilldown">all</option>
      <option name="charting.layout.splitSeries">0</option>
      <option
name="charting.legend.labelStyle.overflowMode">ellipsisMiddle</option>
      <option name="charting.legend.placement">right</option>
    </chart>
   </panel>
  </row>
</form>
```

After clicking on **Save**, we should be back at the dashboard; it is now a form with our field, which drives both the dashboard panels.

 In the following screenshot, I've repositioned the panels horizontally for a better view.

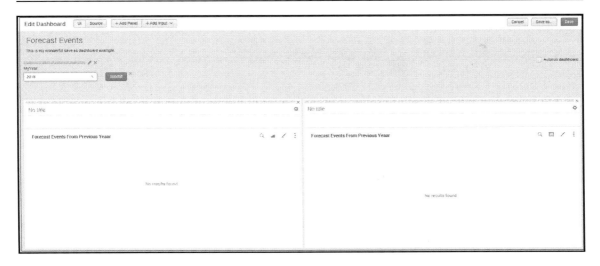

There are several other form elements available, with many options to customize their behavior. To find the official documentation, search on `http://www.splunk.com/` for build and edit forms with simple XML. There are also many useful examples in the documentation and in the UI examples app (see the *UI examples app* section earlier in this chapter).

Post-processing search results

You may have noticed that, in our previous example, both of our queries started with the same actual query:

```
sourcetype="*" Forecast date_year=$myyear$ | timechart count as
  "Forecast Events" by date_month
```

It is, of course, wasteful to run the same query four times. In prior versions of Splunk, using `<searchPostProcess>`, we can run the query once and then run commands on the results for each panel. The first step would be to move the initial query out of the panel to the top level of the XML.

The results from `<searchTemplate>` would be used by a panel if it has no query of its own, or it will be used as the source for `<searchPostProcess>`. One additional piece of information is needed: the fields that are needed by the panels. We can get this by using table, like so:

```
<?xml version='1.0' encoding='utf-8'?>
<form>
<searchTemplate>
sourcetype="*" Forecast date_year=$myyear$ | timechart count as "Forecast
Events" by date_month
</searchTemplate>
```

This technique will work exactly like our previous example but will only run the query once, drawing more quickly and saving resources for everyone. However, more work is required, as we'll see in the next section.

Another approach for limiting the number of times a query would run is to use a `<search>` tag with an `id` in the attribute, then just reference the `id` elsewhere using the base attribute.

Post-processing limitations

When using `<searchPostProcess>`, there is one big limitation and there are several smaller limitations that often require a little extra work:

- Only the first 10,000 results are passed from a raw query. To deal with this, it is necessary to run events through `stats`, `timechart`, or `table`. Transforming commands such as `stats` will reduce the number of rows produced by the initial query, increasing the performance.
- Only specifically referenced fields are passed from the original events. This can be dealt with by using table (as we did in the previous example), or by aggregating results into fewer rows with stats.

The first limitation is the most common item to affect users. The usual solution is to pre-aggregate the events into a superset of what is needed by the panels. To accomplish this, our first task would be to look at the queries and figure out which fields need to be handed along for all queries to work, and so on.

Features replaced

Moving along, in Splunk, the simple XML `<searchString>`, `<searchTemplate>`, `<searchName>`, and `<searchPostProcess>` elements were replaced by the new `<search>` element.

The following is a two-panel dashboard using the `<search>` tag and the `stats` command in version 6.2 to deal with post-processing limitations. First, the query (the search) is defined at the dashboard level (not within any panel). This is our base search (notice the search ID):

```
<dashboard>
 <label>Dashboard with post-process search</label>
 <!-- Base search cannot pass more than 10,000 events to post-process
searches-->
 <!-- This dashboard uses the stats transforming command -->
 <!-- This limits events passed to post-process search -->
 <search id="baseSearch">
  <query>sourcetype=tm1* dimension | stats count by date_month,
date_wday</query>
 </search>
</dashboard>
```

Now, within our dashboard panels, the search base is defined along with our additional search strings:

```
 <panel>
  <chart>
   <title>Dimension Events count by Month</title>
   <search base="baseSearch">
    <query>stats sum(count) AS count by date_month</query>
   </search>
   <!-- post-process search -->
   <option
name="charting.axisLabelsX.majorLabelStyle.overflowMode">ellipsisNone</opti
on>
   <option name="charting.axisLabelsX.majorLabelStyle.rotation">0</option>
   <option name="charting.axisTitleX.visibility">visible</option>
   <option name="charting.axisTitleY.visibility">visible</option>
   <option name="charting.axisTitleY2.visibility">visible</option>
   <option name="charting.axisX.scale">linear</option>
   <option name="charting.axisY.scale">linear</option>
   <option name="charting.axisY2.enabled">false</option>
   <option name="charting.axisY2.scale">inherit</option>
   <option name="charting.chart">column</option>
   <option name="charting.chart.bubbleMaximumSize">50</option>
```

```
      <option name="charting.chart.bubbleMinimumSize">10</option>
      <option name="charting.chart.bubbleSizeBy">area</option>
      <option name="charting.chart.nullValueMode">gaps</option>
      <option name="charting.chart.sliceCollapsingThreshold">0.01</option>
      <option name="charting.chart.stackMode">default</option>
      <option name="charting.chart.style">shiny</option>
      <option name="charting.drilldown">all</option>
      <option name="charting.layout.splitSeries">0</option>
      <option
name="charting.legend.labelStyle.overflowMode">ellipsisMiddle</option>
      <option name="charting.legend.placement">right</option>
    </chart>
   </panel>
   <panel>
    <chart>
     <title>Dimension Events count by Day</title>
     <search base="baseSearch">
      <query>stats sum(count) AS count by date_wday</query>
     </search>
     <!-- post-process search -->
     <option name="charting.chart">pie</option>
     <option
name="charting.axisLabelsX.majorLabelStyle.overflowMode">ellipsisNone</opti
on>
     <option name="charting.axisLabelsX.majorLabelStyle.rotation">0</option>
     <option name="charting.axisTitleX.visibility">visible</option>
     <option name="charting.axisTitleY.visibility">visible</option>
     <option name="charting.axisTitleY2.visibility">visible</option>
     <option name="charting.axisX.scale">linear</option>
     <option name="charting.axisY.scale">linear</option>
     <option name="charting.axisY2.enabled">false</option>
     <option name="charting.axisY2.scale">inherit</option>
     <option name="charting.chart.bubbleMaximumSize">50</option>
     <option name="charting.chart.bubbleMinimumSize">10</option>
     <option name="charting.chart.bubbleSizeBy">area</option>
     <option name="charting.chart.nullValueMode">gaps</option>
     <option name="charting.chart.sliceCollapsingThreshold">0.01</option>
     <option name="charting.chart.stackMode">default</option>
     <option name="charting.chart.style">shiny</option>
     <option name="charting.drilldown">all</option>
     <option name="charting.layout.splitSeries">0</option>
     <option
name="charting.legend.labelStyle.overflowMode">ellipsisMiddle</option>
     <option name="charting.legend.placement">right</option>
     <option name="wrap">true</option>
     <option name="rowNumbers">false</option>
     <option name="dataOverlayMode">none</option>
     <option name="count">10</option>
```

```
        <option name="mapping.data.maxClusters">100</option>
        <option name="mapping.map.center">(0,0)</option>
        <option name="mapping.map.zoom">2</option>
        <option name="mapping.markerLayer.markerMaxSize">50</option>
        <option name="mapping.markerLayer.markerMinSize">10</option>
        <option name="mapping.markerLayer.markerOpacity">0.8</option>
        <option name="mapping.tileLayer.maxZoom">7</option>
        <option name="mapping.tileLayer.minZoom">0</option>
      </chart>
    </panel>
  </row>
</dashboard>
```

The following is the dashboard generated by the preceding XML source:

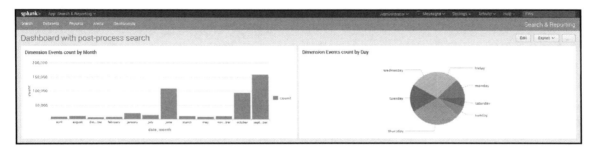

Autorun dashboard

One more important option for your dashboards is the Autorun setting. Prior versions of Splunk included a checkbox on the edit dashboard page, as is seen in the following screenshot:

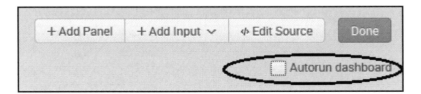

In version 7.0 and newer, Autorun is set within the dashboard source. When you add fields to submit values (for the search string in a panel, as we did in our example), the Autorun setting indicates whether the search in the panels of your dashboard should be run upon loading the page. The default is *false*. This means that the dashboard will load and wait for the user to enter or select a value and click on **Submit**. Suppose, you'd rather load your dashboard and show data right away using some default or standard value. To do that, we can modify our XML like this:

```
<fieldset autoRun="true">
  <input type="text" token="myyear"><default>2014</default>
    <label>MyYear</label>
  </input>
</fieldset>
```

In the preceding code, I've added the Autorun setting to the `<fieldset>` tag and provided the `<default>`. When I save my changes, the dashboard will execute (run) the search using the default value (`2014`) and my dashboard panels will display the results. Of course, the user still has the ability to change the search value and resubmit the query.

Depending upon a variety of factors, this convenience may or may not be a viable option as it would be foolish to rerun a search every time a dashboard loads if the underlying data is slow to change. In that case, a better option would be to set Autorun to *false* and perhaps use scheduled searches, which we will discuss in the next section.

Scheduling the generation of dashboards

As we stepped through the wizard interface to create panels, we accepted the default value of running the search each time the dashboard loads. As we mentioned earlier, this means that the user is penalized each and every time the dashboard is loaded in their web browser. It is silly (and a waste of resources) to rerun what may be multiple searches that are within a dashboard panel if the data that the search is based upon does not change very often. For example, if the indexed data is updated every evening, then rerunning a search on that data multiple times within the same day will not yield different results and would be a waste of resources.

A more prudent approach would be to convert the dashboard panels to not use inline, executed-at-load-time searches but reference reports instead (earlier in this chapter, we covered *Convert to Report*), or make it use scheduled queries.

If we use reports or scheduled queries in our dashboard, when the dashboard is loaded, the results from the last scheduled run will be used.

The dashboard will draw as quickly as the browser can draw the panels. This is particularly useful when multiple users use a dashboard, perhaps in an operations group. If there are no saved results available, the query will simply be run normally.

Be sure to ask yourself just how fresh the data on a dashboard needs to be. If you are looking at a week's worth of data, is up to 1 hour old data acceptable? What about 4 hours old? 24 hours old? The less often the search is run, the fewer the resources you will use, and the more responsive the system will be for everyone else. As your data volume increases, the searches will take more time to complete. If you notice your installation becoming less responsive, check the performance of your scheduled searches in the **Jobs** or the **Status** dashboards in the **Search** app.

For a dashboard that will be constantly monitored, real-time queries are probably more efficient, particularly if multiple people will be using the dashboard. Real-time queries are first backfilled. For instance, a real-time query watching 24 hours will first run a query against the previous 24 hours and then add new events to the results as they appear. This feature makes real-time queries over fairly long periods practical and useful.

6
Extending Search

In this chapter, we will look at some of the features that Splunk provides beyond its already powerful search language. We will cover the following with the help of examples:

- Tags and event types that help you categorize events, for both search and reporting
- Lookups that allow you to add external fields to events as though they were part of the original data
- Macros that let you reuse snippets of search in powerful ways
- Workflow actions that let you build searches and links based on the field values in an event
- External commands that allow you to use Python code to work with search results

In this chapter, we will investigate a few of the many commands included in Splunk.

Using tags to simplify search

Tags allow you to attach a marker to the fields and event types in Splunk. You can then search and report on these tags later. Let's attach a tag to a couple of users who are administrators. Start with the following search:

```
sourcetype="impl_splunk_gen"
| top user
```

This search gives us a list of our users such as **ronnie**, **tuck**, **jarde**, **shelby**, and so on:

	user ⇕	count ⇕	percent ⇕
1	ronnie	100046	10.004600
2	tuck	100044	10.004400
3	jarde	100036	10.003600
4	shelby	100031	10.003100
5	natile	99980	9.998000
6	nanette	99976	9.997600
7	steve	99975	9.997500
8	mary	99972	9.997200
9	paige	99971	9.997100
10	lou	99969	9.996900

Let's say that in our group, **shelby** and **steve** are administrators. Using a standard search, we can simply search for these two users like this:

```
sourcetype="impl_splunk_gen" (user=shelby OR user=steve)
```

Searching for these two users while going forward will still work. However, if we search for the tag value, we can avoid being forced to update multiple saved queries in the future.

To create a tag, we first need to locate the field:

```
> 2015-02-27 12:59:59 req_time=4203 msgid=420340 INFO Hello World user=shelby network=green ip=54.202.139.178
  Show as raw text
```

If the **user** field isn't already visible, click on it in the field picker, and then click on **Select and show in results**:

From our listed events, you can select an event and click on the arrow in the column **i**:

Next, we can click the **Actions** arrow for the field to create a tag for, and select **Edit Tags**:

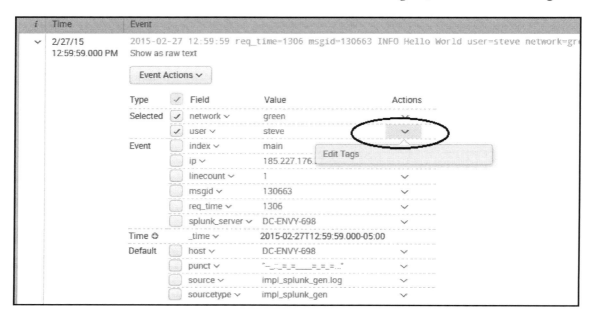

This opens the **Create Tags** dialog as shown in the following screenshot:

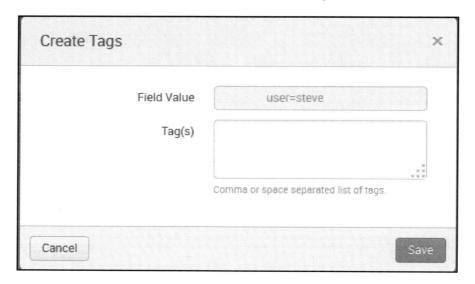

Let's tag **user=steve** with `admin`:

We now see our tag next to the field **user**:

Once this is done, follow the same steps for `user=shelby`. With these two users tagged, we can search for the tag value instead of the actual usernames:

```
sourcetype="impl_splunk_gen" tag::user="admin"
```

Under the covers, this query is unrolled into exactly the same query that we started with. The advantage is that if this tag is added to new values or removed from existing ones, no queries have to be updated.

Some other interesting features of tags are as follows:

- Tags can be searched globally simply by using `tag=tag_name`; in this case, `tag=admin`. Using this capability, you can apply any tag to any field or event type, and simply search for the tag. This is commonly used in security applications to tag hosts, users, and event types that need special monitoring.
- Any field or event type can have any number of tags. Simply choose the tag editor and enter multiple tag values separated by spaces.
- To remove a tag, simply edit the tags again and remove the value(s) you want to remove.
- Tags can also be edited in **Settings** at **Settings** | **Tags**.

Using event types to categorize results

An event type is essentially a simple search definition, with no pipes or commands.

To define an event type, first make a search. Let's search for the following:

```
sourcetype="impl_splunk_gen_SomeMoreLogs" logger=AuthClass
```

Let's say these events are login events. To make an event type, choose **Settings** and then **Event types**, as shown in the following screenshot:

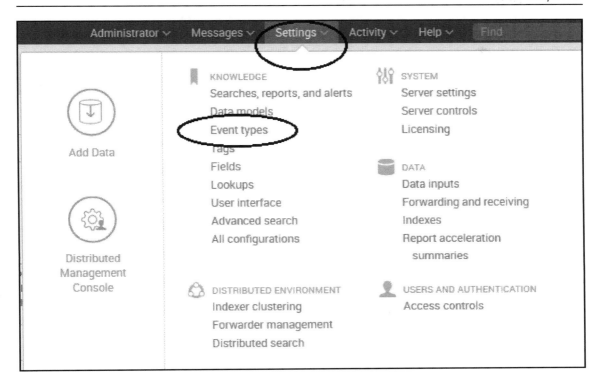

This presents us with the **Event types** page, where we view existing event types and, as we want to do here, create a new event:

First, click the button labeled **New**. Splunk will display the **Add New** page:

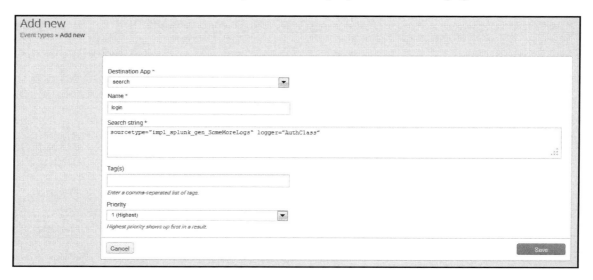

Let's name our event type `login`.

We can now search for the same events using the event type:

```
eventtype=login
```

Event types can be used as part of another search, as follows:

```
eventtype=login loglevel=error
```

Event type definitions can also refer to other event types. For example, let's assume that all login events that have a `loglevel` value of `error` are in fact failed logins. We can now save this into another event type using the same steps mentioned previously. Let's call it `failed_login`. We can now search for these events using the following:

```
eventtype="failed_login"
```

Now, let's combine this event type with the users that we tagged as `admin` in the previous section:

```
eventtype="failed_login" tag::user="admin"
```

This will find all failed logins for administrators. Let's now save this as yet another event type, `failed_admin_login`. We can now search for these events, as follows:

```
eventtype="failed_admin_login"
```

As a final step, let's tag this event type. First, make sure that the field `eventtype` is visible. Your events should look like this:

Note the three values of `eventtype` in this case. We are searching only for `eventtype=failed_admin_login`, but this event also matches the definitions of `eventtype=failed_login` and `eventtype=login`. Also note our tagged user.

We are not searching for the **admin** tag, but **steve** matches `tag::user=admin`, so the value is tagged accordingly.

Following the steps in the previous section, tag `eventtype=failed_admin_login` with the value `actionable`:

We can now search for these events with the following query:

```
tag::eventtype="actionable"
```

This technique is very useful for building up definitions of events that should appear in alerts and reports. For example, consider the following query:

```
sourcetype="impl_splunk_gen_SomeMoreLogs"
 tag::eventtype="actionable" | table _time eventtype user
```

This will now give us a very useful report, as follows:

	_time ⇕	eventtype ⇕	user ⇕
1	2015-02-28 12:59:59	login Login failed_admin_login failed_login	steve
2	2015-02-28 12:59:59	login Login failed_admin_login failed_login	shelby
3	2015-02-28 12:59:59	login Login failed_admin_login failed_login	steve
4	2015-02-28 12:59:59	login Login failed_admin_login failed_login	shelby
5	2015-02-28 12:59:59	login Login failed_admin_login failed_login	shelby
6	2015-02-28 12:59:59	login Login failed_admin_login failed_login	shelby
7	2015-02-28 12:59:59	login	steve

Think about the ways that these event types are being used in this seemingly simple query:

- **Search**: An event type definition is defined as a search, so it seems only natural that you can search for events that match an event type definition.
- **Categorization**: As events are retrieved, if the events match the definition of any event type, those events will have the name of that event type added to the eventtype field.

- **Tagging**: Since event types can also be tagged, tag values assigned to certain event types can be used for both search and categorization. This is extremely powerful for assigning common tags to varied sets of results; for instance, events that belong in a report or should cause an alert.

For clarity, let's unroll this query to see what Splunk is essentially doing under the covers.

The query is expanded from the tag and event type definitions, as follows:

```
tag::eventtype="actionable"
eventtype="failed_admin_login"
eventtype="failed_login" tag::user="admin"
(eventtype=login loglevel=error) tag::user="admin"
((sourcetype="impl_splunk_gen" logger="AuthClass")
loglevel=error) tag::user="admin"
((sourcetype="impl_splunk_gen" logger="AuthClass")
loglevel=error) (user=steve OR user=shelby)
```

Let's explain what happens at each step:

1. The initial search.
2. All event types that are tagged `actionable` are substituted. In this case, we only have one, but if there were multiple, they would be combined with OR.
3. The definition of the event type `failed_admin_login` is expanded.
4. The definition of `failed_login` is expanded.
5. The definition of `login` is expanded.
6. All values of user with the tag `admin` are substituted, separated by OR.

Any changes to tagged values or event type definitions will be reflected the next time they are used in any search or report.

Using lookups to enrich data

Sometimes, information that would be useful for reporting and searching is not located in the logs themselves, but is available elsewhere. Lookups allow us to enrich data, and even search against the fields in the lookup as if they were part of the original events.

The source of data for a lookup can be either a **comma-separated values (CSV)** file or a script. We will cover the most common use of a CSV lookup in the next section.

There are three steps for fully defining a lookup: creating the file; defining the lookup definition; and, optionally, wiring the lookup to run automatically.

Defining a lookup table file

A lookup table file is simply a CSV file. The first line is treated as a list of field names for all the other lines.

Lookup table files are managed at **Settings** | **Lookups** | **Lookup table files**. Simply upload a new file and give it a filename, preferably ending in .csv. An example lookup file (users.csv) is shown as follows:

```
user,city,department,state
steve,Dallas,HR,TX
shelby,Dallas,IT,TX
mary,Houston,HR,TX
nanette,Houston,IT,TX
tuck,Chicago,HR,IL
```

With this file uploaded, we can immediately use it with the lookup command. In the simplest case, the format of the lookup command is as follows:

```
lookup [lookup definition or file name] [matching field]
```

An example of its usage is as follows:

```
sourcetype=" impl_splunk_gen_SomeMoreLogs"
| lookup users.csv user
```

We can now see all the fields from the lookup file as if they were in the events:

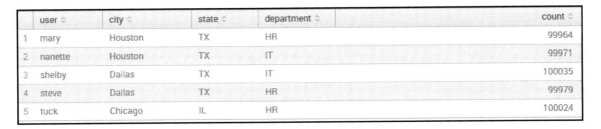

We can use these fields in reports:

```
sourcetype=" impl_splunk_gen_SomeMoreLogs"
| lookup users.csv user
| stats count by user city state department
```

This will produce results as shown in the following screenshot:

	user	city	state	department	count
1	mary	Houston	TX	HR	99964
2	nanette	Houston	TX	IT	99971
3	shelby	Dallas	TX	IT	100035
4	steve	Dallas	TX	HR	99979
5	tuck	Chicago	IL	HR	100024

This is all that is required to use a CSV lookup to enrich data, but if we do a little more configuration work, we can make the lookup even more useful.

Defining a lookup definition

Though you can access a lookup immediately by the filename, defining the lookup allows you to set other options, reuse the same file, and later make the lookup run automatically. Creating a definition also eliminates a warning message that appears when simply using the filename.

Navigate to **Settings** | **Lookups** | **Lookup definitions** and click on the **New** button:

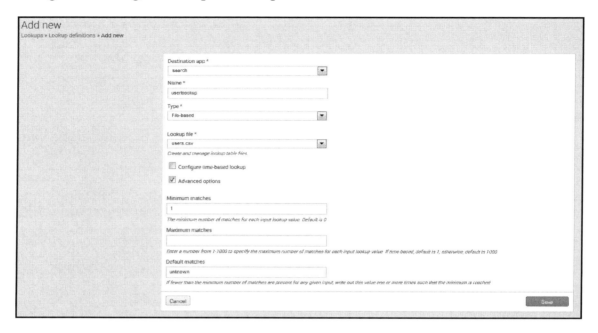

Stepping through these fields, we have the following:

- **Destination app**: This is where the lookup definition will be stored. This matters because you may want to limit the scope of a lookup to a particular application for performance reasons.
- **Name**: This is the name that you will use in search strings.
- **Type**: The options here are **File-based** or **External**.
- **Lookup file**: We have chosen `users.csv` in this case.
- **Configure time-based lookup**: Using a time-based lookup, you can have a value that changes at certain points in time while going forward. For instance, if you built a lookup for the versions of software deployed to the various hosts at different times, you could generate a report on errors or response times by the software version.
- **Advanced options**: This simply exposes the remaining fields.

- **Minimum matches**: This defines the number of items in the lookup that must be matched. With a value of 1, the value of **Default matches** will be used if no match is found.
- **Maximum matches**: This defines the maximum number of matches before stopping. For instance, if there were multiple entries for each user in our lookup file, this value would limit the number of rows that would be applied to each event.
- **Default matches**: This value will be used to populate all fields from the lookup when no match is found and **Minimum matches** is greater than 0. After clicking on **Save**, we can use our new lookup in the following manner:

```
sourcetype="impl_splunk_gen_SomeMoreLogs"
| lookup userslookup user
| stats count by user city state department
```

This will produce results as shown in the following screenshot:

	user ⇕	city ⇕	state ⇕	department ⇕	count ⇕
1	jarde	unknown	unknown	unknown	54564
2	lou	unknown	unknown	unknown	54696
3	mary	Houston	TX	HR	55235
4	nanette	Houston	TX	IT	54872
5	natile	unknown	unknown	unknown	55355
6	paige	unknown	unknown	unknown	54870
7	ronnie	unknown	unknown	unknown	54575
8	shelby	Dallas	TX	IT	55053
9	steve	Dallas	TX	HR	55176
10	tuck	Chicago	IL	HR	54932

Lookup tables have other features, including wildcard lookups, CIDR lookups, and temporal lookups. We will use those features in later chapters.

Defining an automatic lookup

Automatic lookups are, in the author's opinion, one of the coolest features in Splunk. Not only are the contents of the lookup added to events as if they were always there, but you can also search against the fields in the lookup file as if they were part of the original event.

To define the automatic lookup, navigate to **Settings** I **Lookups** I **Automatic lookups** and click on the **New** button:

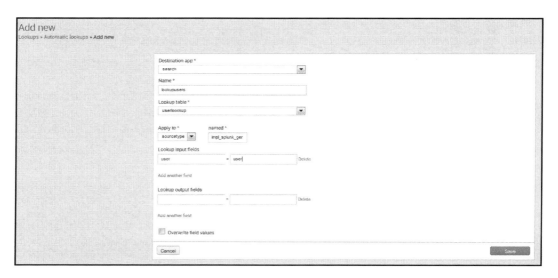

Let's step through the fields in this definition:

- **Destination app**: This is the application where the definition will live. We'll discuss the implications of this choice in Chapter 7, *Working with Apps*.
- **Name**: This name is used in the configuration. It should not contain spaces or special characters. We will discuss its significance in Chapter 10, *Configuring Splunk*.
- **Lookup table**: This is the name of the lookup definition.
- **Apply to**: This lets us choose which events are acted upon. The usual case is **sourcetype**, which must match a **sourcetype** name exactly. Alternatively, you can specify **source** or **host**, with or without wildcards.
- **Lookup input fields**: This defines the fields that will be queried in the lookup file. One field must be specified, but multiple fields can also be specified. Think of this as a join in a database. The left-hand side is the name of the field in the lookup file. The right-hand side is the name of the existing field in our events.
- **Lookup output fields**: This section lets you decide what columns to include from the lookup file and optionally override the names of those fields. The left-hand side is the name of the field in the lookup file. The right-hand side is the field to be created in the events. If left blank, the default behavior is to include all fields from the lookup, using the names defined in the lookup file.

- **Overwrite field values**: If this option is selected, any existing field values in an event will be overwritten by a value with the same name from the lookup file.

After clicking on **Save**, we see the listing of **Automatic lookups**. Initially, the **Sharing** option is **Private**, which will cause problems if you want to share searches with others. To share the lookup, first click on **Permissions**:

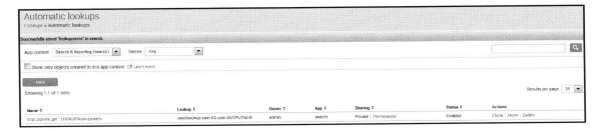

This presents us with the **Permissions** page. Change the value of `Object` should appear in to **All apps**. We will discuss these permissions in greater detail in `Chapter 10`, *Configuring Splunk*:

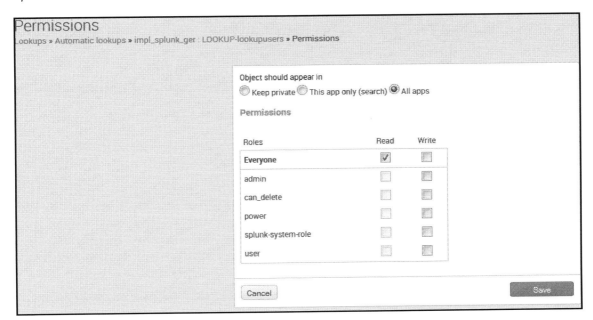

We now have a fully automatic lookup, enriching our sourcetype based on the value of user in each event. To show the power of this lookup, let's search for a field in the lookup file as if it were part of the events:

```
sourcetype="impl_splunk_gen_SomeMoreLogs" department="HR" | top user
```

Even though `department` isn't in our events at all, Splunk will reverse `lookup`, find the values of user that are in `department`, and run the search for those users.

This returns the following result:

10 Per Page ∨	Format ∨	Preview ∨		
user ⌃		**count** ⌃		**percent** ⌃
1 steve		20690		33.462720
2 tuck		20570		33.268640
3 mary		20570		33.268640

Let's combine this search with an event type that we defined earlier. To find the most recent failed login for each member of HR, we can run the following code:

```
sourcetype="impl_splunk_gen_SomeMoreLogs" department="HR"
eventtype="failed_login"
| dedup user
| table _time user department city state
```

This returns the following:

10 Per Page ∨	Format ∨	Preview ∨		
_time ⌃	user ⌃	department ⌃	city ⌃	state
1 2015-02-28 12:59:59	steve	HR	Dallas	TX
2 2015-02-28 12:59:59	tuck	HR	Chicago	IL
3 2015-02-28 12:59:59	mary	HR	Houston	TX

The purpose of the `dedup` command is simply to keep only one event for each value of user. As events are returned in the *most recent first* order, this query will return the most recent `login` for each user. We will configure more advanced lookups in later chapters.

Troubleshooting lookups

If you are having problems with a lookup, very often the cause lies within permissions. Check permissions at all three of these paths:

- **Settings | Lookups | Lookup table files**
- **Settings | Lookups | Lookup definitions**
- **Settings | Lookups | Automatic lookups**

Once permissions are squared away, be sure to keep the following points in mind:

- Check your spelling of the fields.
- By default, lookup values are case-sensitive.
- If your installation is using multiple indexers, it may take some time for the lookup files and definitions to be distributed to your indexers, particularly if the lookup files are large or you have installed many apps that have assets to be distributed.
- A rule of thumb is that a lookup file should not have more than two million rows. If a lookup is too large, an external lookup script may be required.

Using macros to reuse logic

A macro serves the purpose of replacing bits of search language with expanded phrases (additionally, macros have other uses, such as assisting in workflow creation).

Using macros can help you reuse logic and greatly reduce the length of queries.

Let's use the following as our example case:

```
sourcetype="impl_splunk_gen_SomeMoreLogs" user=mary
| transaction maxpause=5m user
| stats avg(duration) avg(eventcount)
```

Creating a simple macro

Let's take the last two lines of our query and convert them to a macro. First, navigate to **Settings** | **Advanced search** | **Search macros** and click on **New**:

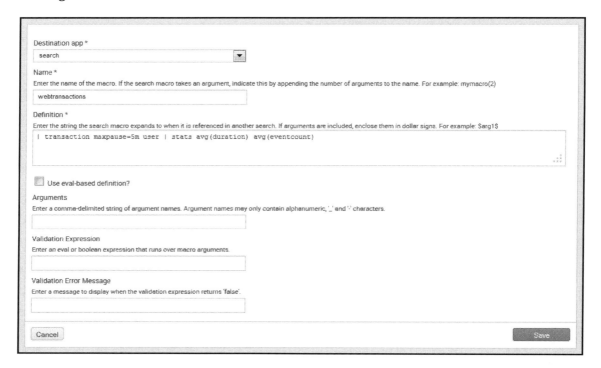

Walking through our fields, we have the following:

- **Destination app**: This is where the macro will live.
- **Name**: This is the name we will use in our searches.
- **Definition**: This is the text that will be placed in our search.
- **Use eval-based definition?**: If checked, the **Definition** string is treated as an `eval` statement instead of the raw text. We'll use this option later.

The remaining fields are used if arguments are specified. We will use these in our next example.

After clicking on **Save**, our macro is now available for use. We can use it like this:

```
sourcetype="impl_splunk_gen_SomeMoreLogs" user=mary
  `webtransactions`
```

The phrase `webtransactions` is enclosed by backticks. This is similar to the usage of backticks on a Unix command line, where a program can be executed to generate an argument. In this case, `webtransactions` is simply replaced with the raw text defined in the macro, recreating the query that we started with.

Creating a macro with arguments

Let's collapse the entire search into a macro that takes two arguments; the `user` and a value for `maxpause`:

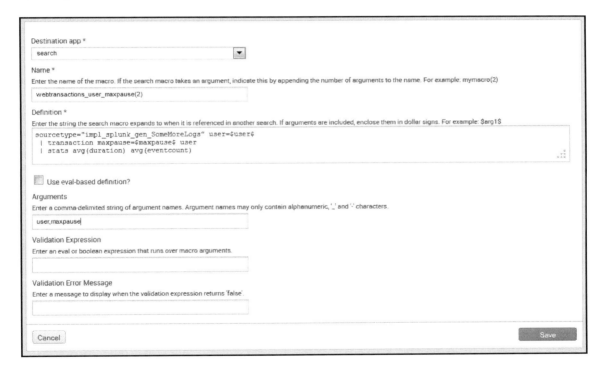

Be sure to remove newlines from your search definition. Macros do not appear to work with embedded newlines.

Walking through our fields, we have the following:

- **Name**: This is the name we will use in our searches. The parentheses and integer, (2), specify how many arguments this macro expects.
- **Definition**: We have defined the entire query in this case. The variables are defined as `$user$` and `$maxpause$`. We can use these names because we have defined the variables under `Arguments`.
- **Arguments**: This list assigns variable names to the values handed in to the macro.

After clicking on **Save**, our macro is now available for use. We can use it like this:

```
webtransactions_user_maxpause(mary,5m)
```

or:

```
`webtransactions_user_maxpause("mary","5m")`
```

 We will use this feature in conjunction with a workflow action later in this chapter. See the *Building a workflow action to show field context* section later in this chapter.

Creating workflow actions

Workflow actions allow us to create custom actions based on the values in search results. The two supported actions either run a search or link to a URL.

Running a new search using values from an event

To build a workflow action, navigate to **Settings** | **Fields** | **Workflow actions** and click on **New**. You are presented with a form as seen in the following screenshot:

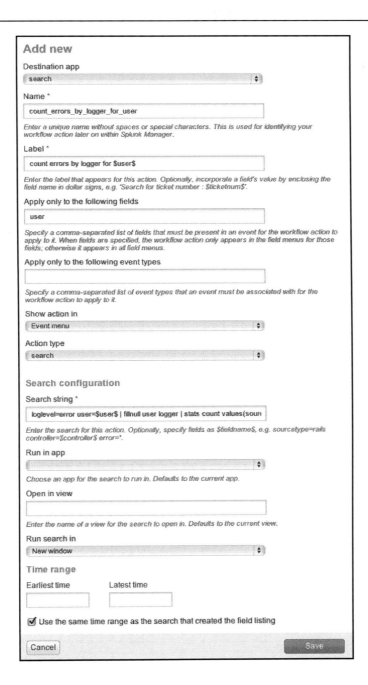

Let's walk through the following fields:

- **Destination app**: This is the app where the workflow action definition will live.
- **Name**: This is the name used in configuration files. This name cannot contain spaces, but underscores are fine.
- **Label**: This is what will appear in the menu. It can contain variables. In this case, we have included $user$, which will be populated with the value of the user field from the event.
- **Apply only to the following fields**: This workflow action will only appear on an event if all the fields specified in this list have a value. **Show action in** will determine which menus can contain the workflow action.
- **Apply only to the following event types**: Only shows this workflow action for events that match a particular event type. For instance, if you defined an event type called **login**, you might want a custom workflow action to search for all logins for this particular user over the last week.
- **Show action in**: The three options are **Event menu**, **Fields menus**, and **Both**.
  - The **Event menu** option is to the left of the event. If **Apply only to the following fields** is not empty, the workflow action will only be present if all the fields specified are present in the event.
  - The **Fields menus** option falls to the right of each field under the events. If **Apply only to the following fields** is not empty, only the fields listed will contain the workflow action. Both will show the workflow action at both places, following the same rules.
  - **Action type**: The choices here are **search** or **link**. We have chosen search.

We will try link in the next section.

- **Search string**: This is the search template to run. You will probably use field values here, but it is not required.
- **Run in app**: If left blank, the current app will be used, otherwise the search will be run in the app that is specified. You would usually want to leave this blank.
- **Open in view**: If left blank, the current view will be used. If you expect to use an events listing panel on dashboards, you probably want to set this to **flashtimeline**.
- **Run search in**: The choices here are **New window** or **Current window**.

- **Time range**: You can specify a specific time range here, either in epoch time or relative time. Leaving **Latest time** empty will allow you to search the latest data available.
- **Use the same time range as the search that created the field listing**: In most cases, you will either check this checkbox or provide a value in at least **Earliest time**. If you do not, the query will run over all time, which is not usually what you want. It is also possible to specify the time frame in our query.

After we click on **Save**, we now see our action in the event workflow action menu like this:

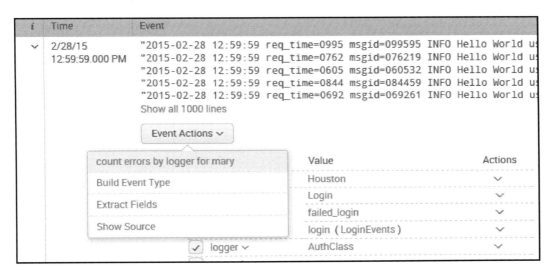

After we choose the option, a new window appears with our results, like this:

user ⬍	logger ⬍	count ⬍
1	mary	0	131
2	mary	AuthClass	64
3	mary	BarClass	251
4	mary	FooClass	46
5	mary	LogoutClass	55

Linking to an external site

A workflow action can also link to an external site, using information from an event.

Let's imagine that your organization has some other web-based tool. If that tool can accept arguments via GET or POST requests, then we can link directly to it from the Splunk results.

Create a new workflow action as we did in the previous example, but change **Action type** to link. The options change to those shown in the following screenshot:

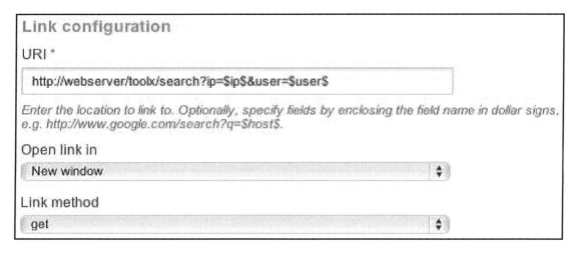

Splunk will encode any variables in the URL so that special characters survive. If you need a variable to not be encoded—for instance, if the value is actually part of the URL—add an exclamation point before the variable name, like this:

```
$!user$
```

If **Link method** is set to POST, then more input fields appear, allowing you to specify post arguments like this:

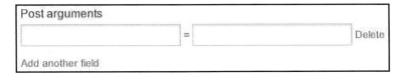

Choosing this workflow action will open a new window with the URL that we specified, either in the current window or in a new window, according to the value of **Open link in**.

The fields used by a workflow action can also come from automatic lookups. This is useful in cases where the external tool needs some piece of information that is not in your events, but can be derived from your events.

Building a workflow action to show field context

Show Source is available as a workflow action on all events. When chosen, it runs a query that finds events around the current event for the same source and host. While this is very useful, sometimes it would be nice to see events that have something else in common besides the source, and to see those events in the regular search interface, complete with the timeline and field picker.

To accomplish this, we will make a workflow action and macro that work in tandem to build the appropriate query. This example is fairly advanced, so don't be alarmed if it doesn't make a lot of sense.

Building the context workflow action

First, let's build our workflow action. As before, make a workflow action with **Action type** set to **search** as seen in the following screenshot:

Name *

    context_1m_5m

Enter a unique name without spaces or special characters. This is used for identifying your workflow action later on within Splunk Manager.

Label *

    Context for $@field_name$=$@field_value$, -1m thru 5m

Enter the label that appears for this action. Optionally, incorporate a field's value by enclosing the field name in dollar signs, e.g. 'Search for ticket number : $ticketnum$'.

Apply only to the following fields

    *

Specify a comma-separated list of fields that must be present in an event for the workflow action to apply to it. When fields are specified, the workflow action only appears in the field menus for those fields; otherwise it appears in all field menus.

Apply only to the following event types

Specify a comma-separated list of event types that an event must be associated with for the workflow action to apply to it.

Show action in

    Fields menus   ♦

Action type

    search   ♦

Search configuration

Search string *

    `context("$@field_name$", "$@field_value$", "$_time$", "-1m", "+5m")`

Enter the search for this action. Optionally. specify fields as $fieldname$, e.g. sourcetype=rails controller=$controller$ error=.*

Run in app

                                                          ♦

Choose an app for the search to run in. Defaults to the current app.

Open in view

    flashtimeline

Enter the name of a view for the search to open in. Defaults to the current view.

Run search in

    New window   ♦

Time range

Earliest time   **Latest time**

☐ Use the same time range as the search that created the field listing

Let's step through our values, which are as follows:

- **Name**: This can be anything. Let's name it after our time frame.
- **Label**: This is what will appear in the menu. You may notice two special fields, `@field_name` and `@field_value`. These two fields only make sense when **Show action in** is set to **Fields menus**.
  There are a number of `@variables` available to workflow actions. Search `http://docs.splunk.com/` for *Create workflow actions in Splunk* to find the complete documentation.

- **Apply only to the following fields**: This can be blank, or `*` to indicate all fields.
- **Show action in**: We have chosen **Fields menus** in this case.
- **Action type**: We are running a search. It's a fairly strange search, as we are using a macro, but it is still technically a search.
- **Search string**: The fact that this query is a macro doesn't matter to the workflow action, `` `context("$@field_name$", "$@field_value$", "$_ time$", "-1m", "+5m")` ``. We will create the context macro next.
- **Run in app**: With nothing chosen, this macro will execute the search in the current app.
- **Open in view**: We want to make sure that our query executes in **flashtimeline**, so we set it explicitly.
- **Run search in**: We choose **New window**.
- **Time**: Contrary to the previous advice, we have left the time frame unspecified. We will be overriding the search times in the search itself. Anything specified here will be replaced.

After clicking on **Save**, the workflow action is available on all the field menus:

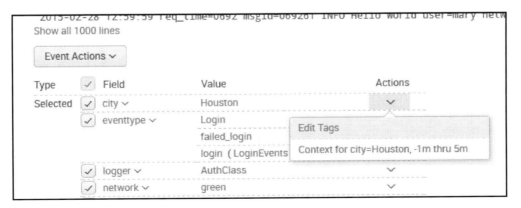

Choosing the preceding menu item generates this search:

```
'context("ip", "1.22.3.3", "2012-05-16T20:23:59-0500", "-1m", "+5m")'
```

Let's consider our query definition:

```
'context("$@field_name$", "$@field_value$", "$_time$", "-1m", "+5m")'
```

We can see that the variables were simply replaced, and the rest of the query was left unchanged. The variable `_time` is not in the format I would expect (I would have expected the epoch value), but we can work with it.

Building the context macro

When searching, you can specify the time ranges in the query itself. There are several fields that allow us to specify the time. They are as follows:

- **earliest**: This is the earliest time, inclusive. It can be specified as either a relative time or an epoch time in seconds.
- **latest**: This is the latest time, exclusive. Only events with a date before this time will be returned. This value can be specified as either a relative time or an epoch time in seconds.
- **now**: Using this field, you can redefine the relative values in **Earliest** and **Latest** that are calculated against. It must be defined as epoch time in seconds.

Now, given our inputs, let's define our variable names:

- `field_name = ip`
- `field_value = 1.22.3.3`
- `event_time = 2012-05-16T20:23:59-0500`
- `earliest_relative = -1m`
- `latest_relative = +5m`

The query we want to run looks like this:

```
earliest=-1m latest=+5m now=[epoch event time] ip=1.22.3.3
```

The only value we don't have is `now`. To calculate this, there is a function available to `eval` called `strptime`. To test this function, let's use `| stats` to create an event, build an `event_time` field, and parse the value. Consider the following code:

```
|stats count
| eval event_time="2012-05-16T20:23:59-0500"
| eval now=strptime(event_time, "%Y-%m-%dT%H:%M:%S%z")
```

This gives us the following table:

count ⇕	event_time ⇕	now ⇕
1 0	2012-05-16T20:23:59-0500	1337217839.000000

Good references for strptime formats can be found on modern Linux systems by running man strptime or man date, or by searching http://www.google.com. Splunk has several special extensions to strptime that can be found by searching for enhanced strptime() support at http://docs.splunk.com/.

Now that we have our epoch value for now, we can build and test our query like this:

```
earliest=-1m latest=+5m now=1337217839 ip=1.22.3.3
```

This gives us a normal event listing, from one minute before our event to five minutes after our selected event, only showing events that have the field in common.

Now that we have our search, and our eval statement for converting the value of now, we can actually build our macro in **Settings** | **Advanced search** | **Search macros** | **Add new**:

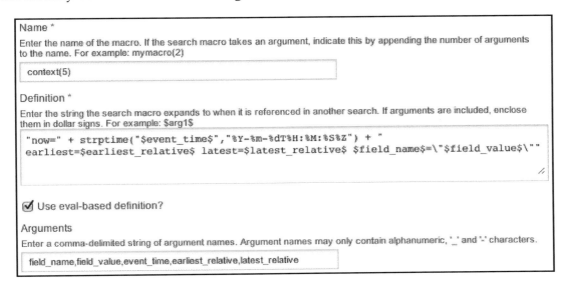

This macro is using a few interesting features, as follows:

- Macros can take arguments. The number of arguments is specified in the name of the macro by appending (`[argument count]`) to the name of the macro. In this case, we are expecting five arguments.
- The definition of a macro can actually be an `eval` statement. This means we can use `eval` functions to build our query based on some value handed to the macro. In this case, we are using `strptime`. Things to note about this feature are as follows:
    - The `eval` statement is expected to return a string. If your statement fails to return a string, for some reason, the user will see an error.
    - The variable names specified are replaced before the `eval` statement is executed. This means that there may be issues with escaping the values in the variables, so some care is required to make sure whether your value contains quotes or not is as expected.
- **Use eval-based definition?** is checked to indicate that this macro is expected to be parsed as an `eval` statement.
- In the **Arguments** field, we specify the names for the arguments handed in.

These are the names we refer to in the **Definition** field. After clicking on **Save**, we have a working macro. You might make adjustments to this workflow action to better suit your needs. Let's change the definition to sort events by ascending time, and prevent searching across indexes. Change the workflow action definition **Search string** to:

```
'context("$@field_name$", "$@field_value$", "$_time$", "-1m",
 "+5m")'
index=$index$ | reverse
```

Let's expand this just for clarity, like this:

```
'context("$@field_name$", "$@field_value$", "$_time$", "-1m", "+5m")'
index=$index$ | reverse
'context("ip", "1.22.3.3", "2012-05-16T20:23:59-0500", "-1m", "+5m")'
index=implsplunk | reverse
earliest=-1m latest=+5m now=1337217839 ip=1.22.3.3
index=implsplunk | reverse
```

You can create multiple workflow actions that specify different time frames, or include other fields; for instance, `host`.

Using external commands

The Splunk search language is extremely powerful, but at times, it may be either difficult or impossible to accomplish some piece of logic by using nothing but the search language. To deal with this, Splunk allows external commands to be written in Python. A number of commands ship with the product, and a number of commands are available in apps at `http://splunk-base.splunk.com/`.

Let's try out a few of the included commands. The documentation for the commands is included with other search commands at `http://docs.splunk.com/`. You can find a list of all included commands, both internal and external, by searching for all search commands.

Extracting values from XML

Fairly often, machine data is written in XML format. Splunk will index this data without any issue, but it has no native support for XML. Though XML is not an ideal logging format, it can usually be parsed simply enough. Two commands are included in the search app that can help us pull fields out of XML.

xmlkv

`xmlkv` uses regular expressions to create fields from tag names. For instance, given the following XML:

```
<doc><a>foo</a><b>bar</b></doc>
```

`xmlkv` will produce the fields `a=foo` and `b=bar`. To test, try this:

```
|stats count
| eval _raw="<doc><a>foo</a><b>bar</b></doc>"
| xmlkv
```

This produces a table, as shown in the following screenshot:

As this command is using regular expressions, its advantage is that malformed or incomplete XML statements will still produce results.

Using an external command is significantly slower than using the native search language, particularly if you are dealing with large sets of data. If it is possible to build the required fields using `rex` or `eval`, it will execute faster and it will introduce a smaller load on your Splunk servers. For instance, in the previous example, the fields could be extracted using:

```
| rex "<a.*?>(?<a>.*?)<" | rex "<b.*?>(?<b>.*?)<"
```

XPath

XPath is a powerful language for selecting values from an XML document. Unlike xmlkv, which uses regular expressions, XPath uses an XML parser. This means that the event must actually contain a valid XML document.

For example, consider the following XML document:

```
<d>
<a x="1">foo</a>
<a x="2">foo2</a>
<b>bar</b>
</d>
```

If we wanted the value for a tag whose x attribute equals 2, the XPath code would look like this:

```
//d/a[@x='2']
```

To test this, let's use our `|stats` trick to generate a single event and execute the `xpath` statement:

```
|stats count
| eval _raw="<d><a x='1'>foo</a><a x='2'>foo2</a><b>bar</b></d>"
| xpath outfield=a "//d/a[@x='2']"
```

This generates an output as shown in the following screenshot:

The xpath command will also retrieve multivalue fields. For instance, this xpath statement simply instructs to find any field:

```
|stats count
| eval _raw="<d><a x='1'>foo</a><a x='2'>foo2</a><b>bar</b></d>"
| xpath outfield=a "//a"
```

The result of this query is as shown:

There are many XPath references available online. My favorite quick reference is at the *Mulberry Technologies* website: http://www.mulberrytech.com/quickref/xpath2.pdf.

Using Google to generate results

External commands can also act as data generators, similar to the stats command that we used to create test events. There are a number of these commands, but let's try a fun example, Google (some organizations may not have an internet connection for use in your Splunk apps, but we'll assume you do have access for these examples). This command takes one argument, a search string, and returns the results as a set of events. Let's execute a search for Splunk:

```
|google "splunk"
```

This produces a table, as shown in the following screenshot:

	_time ⌄	_raw ⌄	title ⌄	url ⌄	description
1	2015-03-01 19:11:12	Splunk: Operational Intelligence, Log Management, Application ..... Splunk Inc. provides the leading platform for Operational Intelligence. Customers use Splunk to search, monitor, analyze and visualize machine data	Splunk: Operational Intelligence, Log Management, Application	http://www.splunk.com/	Splunk Inc. the Splunk
2	2015-03-01 19:11:12	Splunk Products	Splunk.. Splunk® Products. We make machine data accessible, usable and valuable to ...	Splunk Products	Splunk	http://www.splunk.com/en_us/products.html	Splunk® P
3	2015-03-01 19:11:12	Splunk	A Different Kind of Software Company . About Splunk. Splunk® was founded to ... We're here to help. Contact Us	Splunk	A Different Kind of Software Company	https://www.splunk.com/en_us/about-us.html	About Splun
4	2015-03-01 19:11:12	Splunk - Wikipedia, the free encyclopedia . Splunk is an American multinational corporation headquartered in San Francisco, California, which produces software for searching, monitoring, and analyzing ...	Splunk - Wikipedia, the free encyclopedia	http://en.wikipedia.org/wiki/Splunk	Splunk is an , California,
5	2015-03-01 19:11:12	Download Splunk Enterprise for free . Free Download logo splunk cloud. All the features of Splunk Enterprise All the	Download Splunk Enterprise for free	https://www.splunk.com-en_us/download.html	Free Downlo
6	2015-03-01 19:11:12	Splunk (@splunk)	Twitter. The latest Tweets from Splunk (@splunk). #Splunk was founded to pursue a disruptive new vision: make #MachineData accessible, usable & valuable to ...	Splunk (@splunk)	Twitter	https://twitter.com/splunk	The latest T disruptive n
7	2015-03-01 19:11:12	Splunk feels the heat from stronger, cheaper open source rivals ..... Feb 25, 2014 .. Splunk started strong and has only grown stronger as it's branched out to become a wide-ranging analytics platform. But the free version of ...	Splunk feels the heat from stronger, cheaper open source rivals	http://www.infoworld.com/article/2610524/log-analysis/splunk-feels-the-heat-from-stronger--cheaper-open-source-rivals.html	Feb 25, 201 branched ou of
8	2015-03-01 19:11:12	Splunk - San Francisco, CA - Computer Services	Facebook... Splunk, San Francisco, CA. 6886 likes · 93 talking about this · 1163 were here. Listen to your data. www.splunk.com.	Splunk - San Francisco, CA - Computer Services	Facebook	https://www.facebook.com/splunk	Splunk, San Listen to yo
9	2015-03-01 19:11:12	SPLK: Summary for Splunk Inc - Yahoo! Finance .. View the basic SPLK stock chart on Yahoo! Finance. Change the date range, chart type and compare Splunk Inc. against other companies	SPLK: Summary for Splunk Inc - Yahoo! Finance	http://finance.yahoo.com/q?s=SPLK	View the ba chart type a
10	2015-03-01 19:11:12	Splunk Storm.	Splunk Storm	https://www.splunkstorm.com/	

This example may not be terribly useful, but you can probably think of external sources that you would like to query as a starting point, or even to populate a subsearch for another Splunk query.

Working with Apps 7

Splunk apps are what the industry calls knowledge, or, sometimes, apps are a collection of knowledge objects. A knowledge object is a prearrangement of configurations within Splunk, based on some logic and agreed upon due to some consideration or need. With Splunk, you have the ability to create these apps to extend or customize users' Splunk experience. In this chapter, we will explore what makes up a Splunk app, as well as exploring the latest *self-service* app management (originally introduced in version 6.6) updated in version 7.0.

We will:

- Inspect included apps
- Install apps from Splunkbase
- Build our own app
- Customize app navigation
- Customize the look and feel of apps
- Self-service app management

Defining an app

In the strictest sense, an app is a directory of configurations, and sometimes code. The directories and files inside have a particular naming convention and structure.

All configurations are in plain text and can be edited using your choice of text editor. Apps generally serve one or more of the following purposes:

- **Acting as a container for searches, dashboards, and related configurations**: This is what most users will do with apps. This is useful not only for logical grouping but also for limiting what configurations are applied and at what time. This kind of app usually does not affect other apps.
- **Providing extra functionality**: Many objects can be provided in an app for use by other apps. These include field extractions, lookups, external commands, saved searches, workflow actions, and even dashboards. These apps often have no user interface at all; instead, they add functionality to other apps.
- **Configuring a Splunk installation for a specific purpose**: In a distributed deployment, there are several different purposes that are served by the multiple installations of Splunk. The behavior of each installation is controlled by its configuration, and it is convenient to wrap those configurations into one or more apps. These apps completely change the behavior of a particular installation.

Included apps

Without apps, Splunk has no user interface, rendering it essentially useless. Luckily, Splunk comes with a few apps to get us started. We'll now take a look at a few of these apps.

The Splunk Web Framework is not really an app, but a framework for developers who want to create experiences using Splunk and its analytical capabilities. The Splunk Web Framework lets you quickly create custom apps by using prebuilt components, styles, templates, and reusable samples and adding your own custom logic, interactions, reusable components, and UI:

- **Introspection_generator_addon**: Refers to the data that Splunk Enterprise logs and uses to populate the _introspection index, generating data about your Splunk instance and environment. It writes that data to log files to aid in reporting on system resource utilization and troubleshooting problems.
- **splunk_monitoring_console (or previously referred to as distributed management console)**: Provides the ability to view detailed performance information about your Splunk Enterprise deployment.
- **gettingstarted**: This app provides help screens; you can access them from the launcher. There are no searches, only a single dashboard that simply includes an HTML page.

- **Search and Reporting**: This is the app where users spend most of their time. It contains the main search dashboard that can be used from any app, external search commands that can be used from any app, admin dashboards, custom navigation, custom CSS, a custom app icon, a custom app logo, and many other useful elements.
- **SplunkForwarder and SplunkLightForwarder**: These apps, which are disabled by default, simply disable portions of a Splunk installation so that the installation is lighter in weight. If you never create or install another app, and instead simply create saved searches and dashboards in the app search, you can still be quite successful with Splunk. Installing and creating more apps, however, allows you to take advantage of others' work, organize your own work, and ultimately share your work with others.

Installing apps

Apps can either be installed from Splunkbase or uploaded through the admin interface. To get started, from the Splunk Home page, you can click on **Splunk Apps** (shown in the following screenshot):

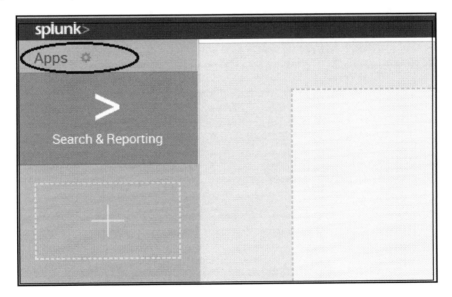

From there, the **Apps** page is displayed:

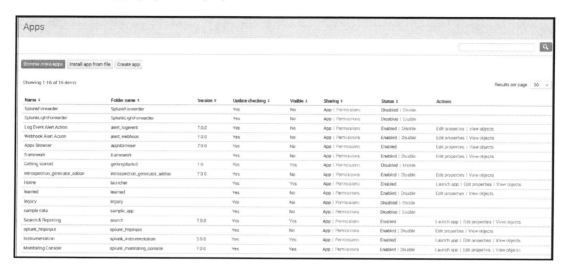

Installing apps from Splunkbase

If your Splunk server has direct access to the internet, you can install apps from Splunkbase with just a few clicks. From the **Apps** page, you can click on **Browse More Apps**, where some of the most popular apps will be available:

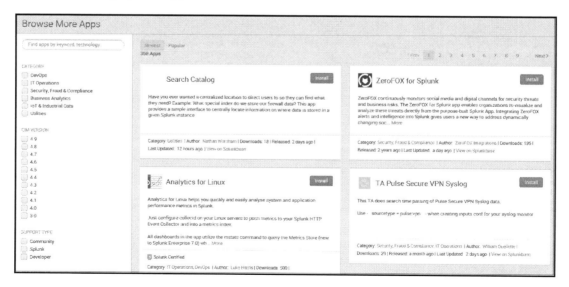

In an earlier edition of this book, we chose to use a MAXMIND app, which was popular first in Splunk version 5.0, has been updated to work with the latest version of Splunk (the app is now version 10.6), and is still worth installing and reviewing. Let's get started!

To install the **Geo Location Lookup Script** (powered by MAXMIND) app, you may have to scroll through the list of apps to find it. Or, you can also locate the app using your web browser by going to `https://apps.splunk.com`, searching for the app by name, downloading it as a file, and then uploading it into Splunk:

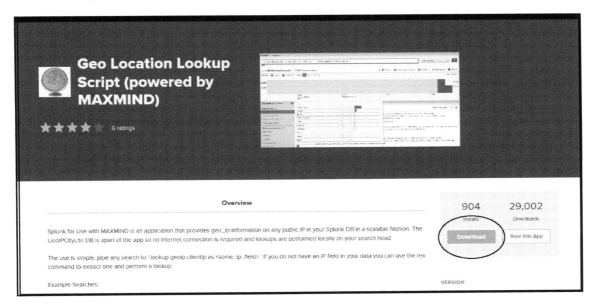

 Note: You will be prompted for your `https://www.splunk.com` login. This is the same login that you created when you downloaded Splunk. If you don't have an account, you will need to create one.

Next (as in earlier editions), we'll install the **Google Maps** app. This app was built by a Splunk customer who contributed back to the Splunk community. It (may) prompt you to restart Splunk.

Once you have restarted and logged back in, check out the menu:

Google Maps is now visible, but where is the Geo Location Lookup Script? Remember that not all apps have dashboards, nor do they necessarily have any visible components at all.

Using Geo Location Lookup Script

The Geo Location Lookup Script is a lookup script used to provide geolocation information for IP addresses. Looking at the documentation, we see this example:

```
eventtype=firewall_event | lookup geoip clientip as src_ip
```

You can find the documentation for any Splunkbase app by searching for it at https://splunkbase.com, or by clicking on **View details** on Splunk apps (next to any installed app), clicking on **Apps**, and viewing the **Apps** page.

Let's go through the arguments of the lookup command:

- geoip: This is the name of the lookup provided by Geo Location Lookup Script. You can see the available lookups by going to **Settings | Lookups | Lookup definitions**.

- `clientip`: This is the name of the field in the lookup that we are matching against.
- `as src_ip`: This says to use the value of `src_ip` to populate the field before it, in this case, `clientip`. I personally find this wording confusing. In my mind, I read this as *using* instead of *as*.

Included in the *ImplementingSplunkDataGenerator* app (available at `http://packtpub.com/support`) is a `sourcetype` instance named `impl_splunk_ips`, which looks like this:

```
2012-05-26T18:23:44 ip=64.134.155.137
```

The IP addresses in this fictitious log are from one of my websites. Let's see some information about these addresses:

```
sourcetype="impl_splunk_ips" | lookup geoip clientip AS ip | top
   client_country
```

This gives us a table similar to the one shown in the following screenshot (note that after running the command, new fields are added, such as **client_country**):

	client_country ⬍	count ⬍	percent ⬍
1	United States	447	71.634615
2	China	90	14.423077
3	Russian Federation	39	6.250000
4	Slovenia	15	2.403846
5	United Kingdom	14	2.243590
6	Ukraine	9	1.442308
7	South Africa	3	0.480769
8	Germany	2	0.320513
9	United Arab Emirates	1	0.160256
10	Turkey	1	0.160256

That's interesting. I wonder who is visiting my site from **Slovenia**.

Using Google Maps

Now, let's do a similar search in the **Google Maps** app. Choose **Google Maps** from the **App** menu. The interface looks like the standard search interface, but with a map instead of an event listing. Let's try this remarkably similar (but not identical) query using a lookup provided in the **Google Maps** app:

```
sourcetype="impl_splunk_ips"
| lookup geo ip
```

The map generated looks like this:

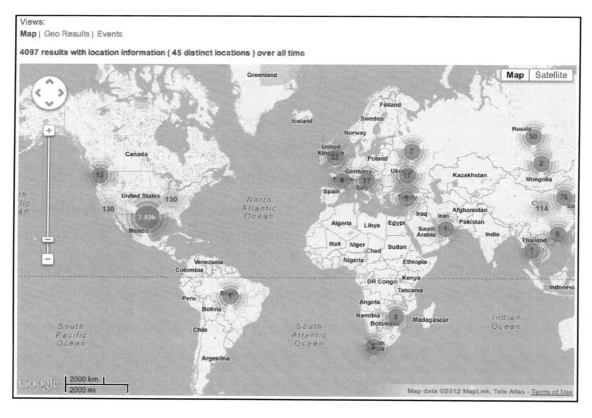

Unsurprisingly, most of the traffic to this little site came from the author's house in Austin, Texas. We'll use the Google Maps app for something more interesting in `Chapter 8`, *Building Advanced Dashboards*.

Installing apps from a file

It is not uncommon for Splunk servers to not have access to the internet, particularly in a data center. In this case, follow these steps:

1. Download the app from `https://splunkbase.com`. The file will have a `.spl` or `.tgz` extension.
2. Navigate to Splunk Apps, then to the **Apps** page.
3. Click on **Install app** from the file.
4. Upload the downloaded file using the form provided.
5. Restart if the app requires it.
6. Configure the app if required.

That's it. Some apps have a configuration form. If this is the case, you will see a **Setup** link next to the app when you go to **Manager | Apps**. If something goes wrong, contact the author of the app.

If you have a distributed environment, in most cases the app only needs to be installed on your search head. The components that your indexers need will be distributed automatically by the search head. Check the documentation for the app.

Building your first app

For our first app, we will use one of the templates provided with Splunk. To get started, navigate to the Splunk **Apps** page (as we described earlier in this chapter) and then click on **Create app**.

The following page will open:

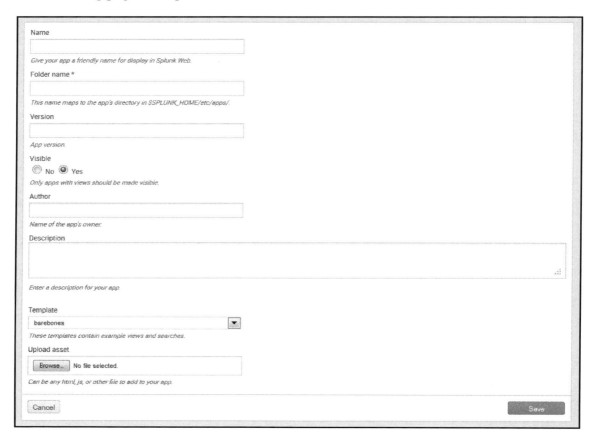

Set the fields as follows:

- Set **Name** to Implementing Splunk App One. This name will be visible on the home screen, in the **App** menu, and in the app banner on the upper-left side of the window.
- Set **Folder name** to is_app_one. This value will be the name of the app directory on the filesystem, so you should limit your name to letters, numbers, and underscores.
- Set **Version** to 1.0 (it's our first version of the app!).
- Set **Visible** to **Yes**. If your app simply provides resources for other apps to use, there may be no reason for it to be visible.
- Fill in the **Author** (your name!) and **Description** (describe your app).

- Set **Template** to **barebones**. The **barebones** template contains sample navigation and the minimal configuration required by an app. The `sample_app` template contains many example dashboards and configurations.
- **Upload asset** you can leave alone for now (we'll touch on this later).

After clicking on **Save**, we can visit our app by going back to the Splunk **Apps** page or returning to our home page. Look at the following screenshot and you will notice that we can see the apps we've installed thus far (**Goggle Maps**, **MAXMIND**, and **Implementing Splunk App One**):

Now that we have our app, we can create searches and dashboards, and maintain them in our app. The simplest way to ensure that your objects end up in your app is to verify that the app banner is correct before creating objects or before entering the Splunk manager. Our app banner looks like this:

Create a dashboard called **Errors** using the following searches (refer to `Chapter 5`, *Simple XML Dashboards*, for detailed instructions):

```
error sourcetype="impl_splunk_gen" | timechart count by user
error sourcetype="impl_splunk_gen" | top user
error sourcetype="impl_splunk_gen" | top logger
```

This produces the following result:

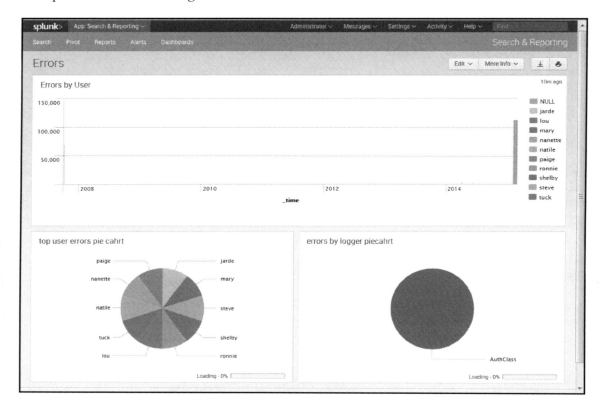

Our new dashboard appears in the navigation menu under **Dashboards**:

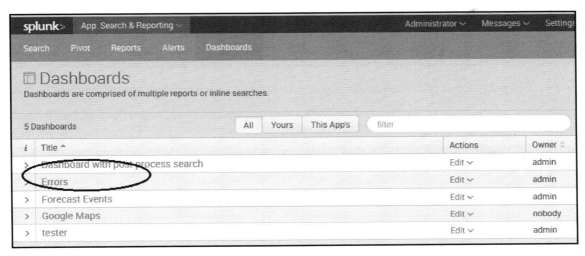

Editing navigation

Navigation is controlled by an XML file that can be accessed by going to **Settings** | **User interface** | **Navigation menus**:

Nav name ⬍	Owner ⬍	App ⬍	Sharing ⬍	Status ⬍
default	No owner	is_app_one	App | Permissions	Enabled

There can only be one active navigation file per app, and it is always called **default**.

After clicking on the name, we see the XML provided by the `barebones` template:

```
<nav search_view="search" color="#65A637">
 <view name="search" default='true' />
 <view name="data_models" />
 <view name="reports" />
 <view name="alerts" />
 <view name="dashboards" />
</nav>
```

Note that if you check the navigation for another app (*search*), you will notice the same XML.

The structure of the XML is essentially the following:

```
nav
view
saved
collection
view
a href
saved
divider
collection
```

The logic of navigation is probably best absorbed by simply editing it and seeing what happens. You should keep a backup as this XML is somewhat fragile and Splunk does not provide any kind of version control. Here are some general details about `nav`:

- Children of `nav` appear in the navigation bar.
- `collection`: Children of `collection` tags appear in a menu or submenu. If the child tags do not produce any results, the menu will not appear. The `divider` tag always produces a result, so it can be used to ensure that a menu appears.
- `view`: This tag represents a dashboard, with the following attributes:
    - `name` is the name of the dashboard `filename`, without the `.xml` extension.
    - The first view element with the attribute `default='true'` will load automatically when the app is selected.
    - The label of each `view` is based on the contents of the label tag in the dashboard XML, not the name of the dashboard `filename`.
    - `match="dashboard"` selects all dashboards whose `filename` contains dashboard. If you want to group dashboards, you may want to follow a naming convention to make grouping more predictable.
    - `source="unclassified"` essentially means *all views that have not been previously associated to a menu*. In other words, this will match dashboards that were not explicitly referenced by name or matched using the `match` attribute or a different view tag.
- `a href`: You can include standard HTML links of the form `<a href="http://a.b/c">`.

The link is untouched and passed along as written.

- `saved`: This tag represents a saved search, with the following attributes:
  - `name` is equal to the name of a saved search.
  - `match="report"` selects all the saved searches that have report in their names.
  - `source="unclassified"` essentially means *all searches that have not yet been previously associated to a menu*. In other words, this will match searches that were not explicitly referenced by name or matched using the `match` attribute or a different saved tag.

Let's customize our navigation. We'll make a few changes like these:

- Create an entry specifically for our errors dashboard
- Add `default='true'` so that this dashboard loads by default
- Simplify the `Views` and `Searches` collections

These changes are reflected in the following code:

```
<nav>
<view name="errors" default='true' />
<view name="flashtimeline" />
<collection label="Views">
<view source="unclassified" />
</collection>
<collection label="Searches">
<saved source="unclassified" />
</collection>
</nav>
```

Our navigation now looks like this screenshot:

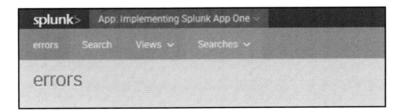

With this navigation in place, all new dashboards will appear under **Views**, and all new saved searches will appear under **Searches**. Notice that **Advanced Charting** and **Google Maps** appear under **Views**. Neither of these dashboards are part of our app, but are visible because of the permissions in their respective apps. We will discuss permissions in more detail in the *Object permissions* section.

Customizing the appearance of your app

It is helpful to further customize the appearance of your application, if for no other reason than to make it more obvious which app is currently active.

Customizing the launcher icon

The launcher icon is seen both in the `Home` app and in Splunkbase if you decide to share your app. The icon is a 36 x 36 PNG file named `appIcon.png`. I have created a simple icon for our sample app (please don't judge my art skills):

To use the icon, follow these steps:

1. Navigate to **Apps | Manage Apps**
2. Click on **Edit properties** next to our app, `Implementing Splunk App One`
3. Click on **Upload asset** and select the file
4. Click on **Save**

Our icon will now appear on the launcher screen, like the following screenshot:

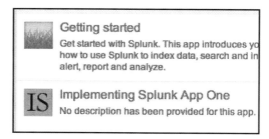

Using custom CSS

In earlier versions of Splunk, you could utilize CSS stylesheets to override the default look of a Splunk application. One common element to change was the application icon in the application bar. You could follow these steps to do just that:

1. First, create a file named `application.css`. This file will be loaded on every dashboard of the application containing it. The CSS is listed later in this section. As of Splunk Version 4.3.2, the first time `application.css` is added to an app of Version 4.3.2, a restart is required before the file is served to the users. Subsequent updates do not require a restart.
2. Next, create a file named `appLogo.png`. This file can be called anything, as we will reference it explicitly in our CSS file.
3. For each file, follow the same steps as for uploading the launcher icon:
   1. Navigate to **Apps** | **Manage Apps**
   2. Click on **Edit properties** next to our app, `Implementing Splunk App One`
   3. Click on **Upload asset** and select the file
   4. Click on **Save**

As of Splunk version 6.2, this feature was not supported. You should check back at `https://www.splunk.com` for updates on this feature.

Using custom HTML

In some apps, you will see static HTML blocks. This can be accomplished using both simple and complex dashboards.

Custom HTML in a simple dashboard

In a simple dashboard, you can simply insert an `<html>` element inside a `<row>` element (inside a `dashboard` tag, of course) and include static HTML inline. For example, after uploading an image named `graph.png`, the following block can be added to any dashboard:

```
<dashboard>
<row>
<html>
<table>
<tr>
```

```
<td><img src="/static/app/is_app_one/graph.png" /></td>
<td>
<p>Lorem ipsum ...</p>
<p>Nulla ut congue ...</p>
<p>Etiam pharetra ...</p>
</td>
</tr>
</table>
</html>
</row>
<dashboard>
```

The XML would render this panel:

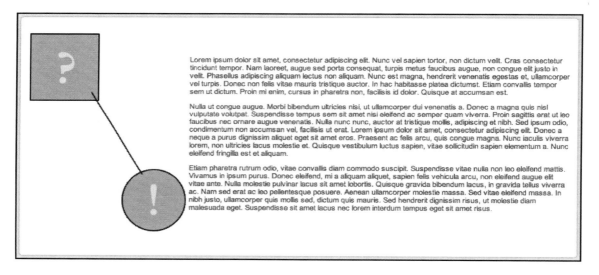

This approach has the advantage that no other files are needed. The disadvantage, however, is that you cannot build the HTML document in an external program and upload it untouched.

You can also reference custom CSS using this method by adding classes to `application.css` and then referencing those classes in your HTML block.

Using server-side include in a complex dashboard

You can also develop static pages as HTML documents, referencing other files in the same directory. Let's build a slightly more complicated page using graph.png, and also a style from application.css, as follows:

1. Place graph.png and application.css into a directory.
2. Create a new HTML file. Let's name it intro.html.
3. Add any styles for your page to application.css.
4. Upload the new HTML file and the modified CSS file.
5. Create the dashboard referencing the HTML file.

Starting with the HTML from our previous example, let's make it a complete document. Move the image to a CSS style and add a class to our text, like this:

```html
<html>
<head>
<link rel="stylesheet" type="text/css"
href="application.css" />
</head>
<body>
<table>
<tr>
<td class="graph_image"></td>
<td>
<p class="lorem">Lorem ipsum ...</p>
<p class="lorem">Nulla ut congue ...</p>
<p class="lorem">Etiam pharetra ...</p>
</td>
</tr>
</table>
</body>
</html>
```

Maintaining the classes for the navigation bar, add our page classes to the application CSS, like this:

```css
.appHeaderWrapper h1 {
display: none;
}
.appLogo {
height: 43px;
width: 155px;
padding-right: 5px;
float: left;
background: url(appLogo.png) no-repeat 0 0;
```

```
}
.appHeaderWrapper {
background: #612f00;
}
.lorem {
font-style:italic;
background: #CCCCCC;
padding: 5px;
}
.graph_image {
height: 306px;
width: 235px;
background: url(graph.png) no-repeat 0 0;
}
```

We can now open this file in a browser. Clipped for brevity, the page looks like this:

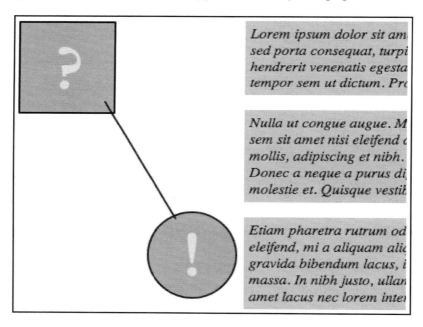

To include this external HTML document, we have to use advanced XML. We will cover advanced XML more thoroughly in Chapter 8, *Building Advanced Dashboards*.

First, build a minimal dashboard like this:

```
<view template="dashboard.html">
<label>Included</label>
<!-- chrome here -->
<module
name="ServerSideInclude"
layoutPanel="panel_row1_col1">
<param name="src">intro.html</param>
</module>
</view>
```

All simple XML dashboards are converted to advanced XML behind the scenes. We will take advantage of this later.

Now, we upload our files as we did earlier under the *Customizing the launcher icon* section. The page should render nearly identically to how the file did in the browser, with the addition of the border around the panel:

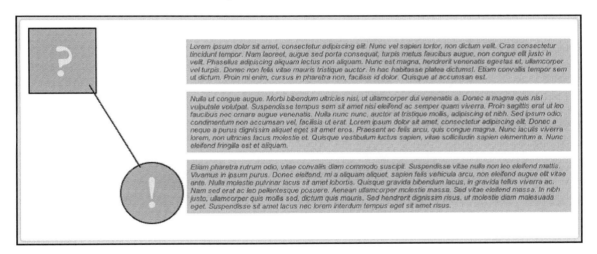

A few things to note from this overly simplified example are as follows:

1. Your CSS classes may end up merging with styles included by Splunk in unexpected ways. Using the developer tools in any modern browser will help greatly.
2. The navigation and dashboard title were excluded for brevity. They would normally go where we see `<!-- chrome here -->`. This is interesting because there are cases where you would want to exclude the navigation, something that cannot be done with simple XML.

3. The static files, such as `application.css`, can be edited directly on the filesystem and the changes will be seen immediately. This is not true for the dashboard XML file. We will cover these locations later in the *App directory structure* section.

Object permissions

Almost all objects in Splunk have permissions associated with them. These permissions essentially have the following three options:

- **Private**: Only the user that created the search can see or use the object, and only in the app where it was created
- **App**: All users that have permission to read an object may use that object in the context of the app that contains the object
- **Global**: All users that have permission to read an object may use that object in any app

How permissions affect navigation

To see a visible instance of permissions in action, let's look at our navigation.

In our application, `Implementing Splunk App One`, our navigation looks like this:

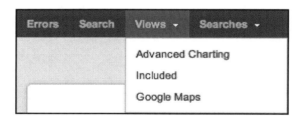

If you recall the navigation XML we built earlier, this menu is controlled by the following XML:

```
<collection label="Views">
<view source="unclassified" />
</collection>
```

There is no mention of any of these dashboards. This is where they are coming from:

- **Advanced Charting** is inherited from the **Search** app. Its permissions are set to Global.
- **Included** is from this app. Its permissions are set to **App**.
- Google Maps is inherited from the **Google Maps** app. Its permissions are set to **Global**.

If the permissions of a dashboard or search are set to **Private**, a green dot appears next to the name in the navigation.

Dashboards or searches shared from other apps can also be referenced by name.

For example, most apps, including ours, will include a link to flashtimeline, which appears as **Search**, the label in that dashboard's XML:

```
<view name="flashtimeline" />
```

This allows us to use this dashboard in the context of our app so that all the other objects that are scoped solely to our app will be available.

How permissions affect other objects

Almost everything you create in Splunk has permissions. To see all objects, navigate to **Settings** | **All configurations**:

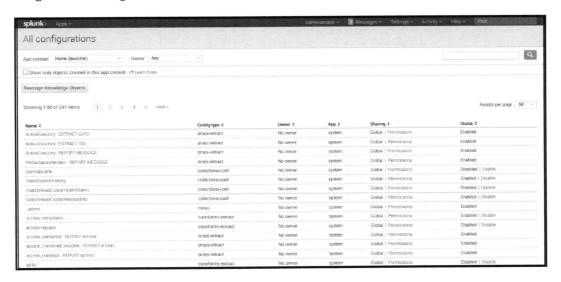

Everything with the value system in the **App** column ships with Splunk. These items live in the $SPLUNK_HOME/etc/system directory. We will cover these different configuration types in Chapter 10, *Configuring Splunk*, but the important takeaway is that the **Sharing** settings affect nearly everything.

When you create new objects and configurations, it is important to share all related objects. For instance, in Chapter 6, *Extending Search*, we created lookups.

It is important that all three parts of the lookup definition are shared appropriately, or users will be presented with error messages.

Correcting permission problems

If you see errors about permissions, it is more than likely that some object still has **Sharing** set to **Private**, or is shared at the **App** level but needs to be **Global**.

A common point of confusion is when an app is created within the Splunk search app, but with the expectation that they will be visible within another app.

Follow these steps to find the object:

1. Navigate to **Settings** | **All configurations**.
2. Change **App** context to **All**.
3. Sort by using the **Sharing** status. Click twice so that **Private** objects come to the top.
4. If there are too many items to look through, filter the list by adding terms to the search field in the upper-right corner, or changing the **App context** value.
5. Fix the permissions appropriately. In most cases, the permissions you want will look like this:

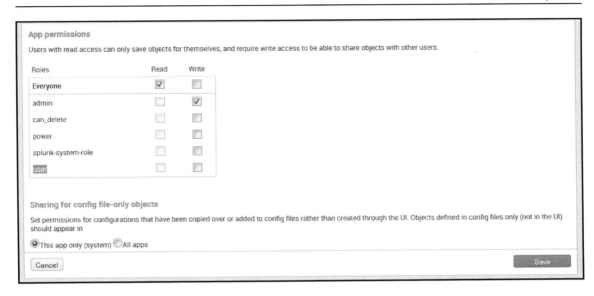

You should choose **All apps** with care. For instance, when building a lookup, it is common to share the lookup table file and lookup definition across all apps. This allows the lookup to be used in searches by other apps. It is less common to share the *automatic lookup*, as this can affect the performance in other apps in unforeseen ways.

App directory structure

If you do much beyond building searches and dashboards, sooner or later you will need to edit files in the filesystem directly. All apps live in $SPLUNK_HOME/etc/apps/. On UNIX systems, the default installation directory is /opt/splunk. On Windows, the default installation directory is C:\Program Files\Splunk.

This is the value that $SPLUNK_HOME will inherit on startup.

Stepping through the most common directories, we have:

- **appserver**: This directory contains files that are served by the Splunk web app. The files that we uploaded in earlier sections of this chapter are stored in appserver/static.

- **bin**: This is where command scripts belong. These scripts are then referenced in `commands.conf`. This is also a common location for scripted inputs to live, though they can live anywhere, although best practice it to keep all scripts contained in the `bin` folder.
- **default and local**: These two directories contain the vast majority of the configurations that make up an app.

We will discuss these configurations and how they merge in `Chapter 10`, *Configuring Splunk*.

Here is a brief look:

- Newly created, unshared objects live in:

  `$SPLUNK_HOME/etc/users/USERNAME/APPNAME/local`

- Once an object is shared at the **App** or **Global** level, the object is moved to the following path:

  `$SPLUNK_HOME/etc/APPNAME/local`

- Files in the local directory take precedence over their equivalent value in `default`
- Dashboards live in (`default|local`)/data/ui/views
- Navigations live in (`default|local`)/data/ui/nav

When editing files by hand, my general rule of thumb is to place configurations in the local directory unless the app will be redistributed. We'll discuss this in more detail in the *Adding your app to Splunkbase* section.

- **lookups**: Lookup files belong in this directory. They are then referenced in (`default|local`)/transforms.conf.
- **metadata**: The files `default.meta` and `local.meta` in this directory tell Splunk how configurations in this app should be shared. It is generally much easier to edit these settings through the **Settings** interface.

```
appserver/static/appIcon.png
appserver/static/application.css
appserver/static/appLogo.png
appserver/static/graph.png
appserver/static/intro.html
bin/README
default/app.conf
default/data/ui/nav/default.xml
default/data/ui/views/README
local/app.conf
local/data/ui/nav/default.xml
local/data/ui/views/errors.xml
local/data/ui/views/included.xml
local/savedsearches.conf
local/viewstates.conf
metadata/default.meta
metadata/local.meta
```

The `metadata/default.meta` file and all files in `default/` were provided in the template app. We created all the other files. With the exception of the PNG files, all files are plain text.

Adding your app to Splunkbase

Splunkbase (`https://splunkbase.splunk.com/`) is a wonderful community-supported site that Splunk put together for users and Splunk employees alike to share Splunk apps. The apps on Splunkbase are a mix of fully realized apps, add-ons of various sorts, and just example code.

Preparing your app

Before we upload our app, we need to make sure that all our objects are shared properly, move our files to default, and configure `app.conf`.

Confirming sharing settings

To see sharing settings for all our objects, navigate to **Settings | All configurations** and set the **App context** option:

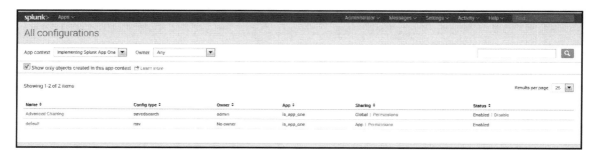

In the case of a self-contained app like ours, all objects should probably be set to **App** under **Sharing**. If you are building an app to share lookups or commands, the value should be **Global**.

Cleaning up our directories

When you upload an app, you should move everything out of `local` and into `default`. This is important because all changes that a user makes will be stored in `local`.

When your app is upgraded, all files in the app (except local files) will be replaced, and the user's changes will be lost. The following Unix commands illustrate what needs to be done:

1. First, let's copy our app to another location, perhaps `/tmp`:

   ```
   cp -r $SPLUNK_HOME/etc/apps/is_app_one /tmp/
   ```

2. Next, let's move everything from `local` to `default`. In the case of `.xml` files, we can simply move the files; but `.conf` files are a little more complicated, and we need to merge them manually. The following command does this:

   ```
   cd /tmp/is_app_one
   mv local/data/ui/nav/*.xml default/data/ui/nav/
   mv local/data/ui/views/*.xml default/data/ui/views/
   #move conf files, but don't replace conf files in default
   mv -n local/*conf default/
   ```

3. Now, we need to merge any `.conf` files that remain in `local`. The only configuration we have left is `app.conf`:

```
local/app.conf default/app.conf
[ui]
[launcher]
[package]
check_for_updates = 1
[install]
is_configured = 0
[ui]
is_visible = 1
label = Implementing Splunk
App One
[launcher]
author =
description =
version = 1.0
```

Configuration merging is additive, with any values from `local` added to the values in `default`. In this case, the merged configuration would be as follows:

```
[install]
is_configured = 0
[ui]
Working with Apps
[ 198 ]
is_visible = 1
label = Implementing Splunk App One
[launcher]
author =
description =
version = 1.0
[package]
check_for_updates = 1
```

4. Place this merged configuration in `default/app.conf` and delete `local/app.conf`.

We will cover configuration merging extensively in `Chapter 10`, *Configuring Splunk*.

Packaging your app

To package an app, we need to be sure that there are a few values in default/app.conf, and only then will we build the archive.

First, edit default/app.conf like this:

```
[install]
is_configured = 0
build = 1
[ui]
is_visible = 1
label = Implementing Splunk App One
[launcher]
author = My name
description = My great app!
version = 1.0
[package]
check_for_updates = 1
id = is_app_one
```

The identifier build is used in all URLs, so it should be incremented to defeat browser caching and the identifier ID should be a unique value in Splunkbase—you will be alerted if the value is not unique.

Next, we need to build a .tar file compressed with gzip. With a modern version of tar, the command is simply the following:

```
cd /tmp
tar -czvf is_app_one.tgz is_app_one
#optionally rename as spl
mv is_app_one.tgz is_app_one.spl
```

The Splunk documentation (https://dev.splunk.com/view/webframework-developapps/SP-CAAAEMY) covers this extensively, including hints and best practices.

Uploading your app

Now that we have our archive, all we have to do is send it up to Splunkbase. In version 7.0, submitting apps is done by pointing your browser to https://splunkbase.splunk.com/new/ and following the directions there:

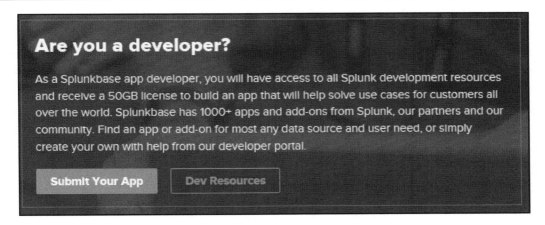

Are you a developer?

As a Splunkbase app developer, you will have access to all Splunk development resources and receive a 50GB license to build an app that will help solve use cases for customers all over the world. Splunkbase has 1000+ apps and add-ons from Splunk, our partners and our community. Find an app or add-on for most any data source and user need, or simply create your own with help from our developer portal.

Submit Your App   **Dev Resources**

If your app meets the rigid criteria, and once the Splunk personnel approve your app, it will appear in Splunkbase, ready for others to download.

> To help get your app approved, you might want to consider AppInspect, which appraises your Splunk app against a set of Splunk-defined criteria so that you can be assured of its quality and robustness.

Self-service app management

As we've seen within this chapter, Splunk apps are composed of dashboards, reports, alerts, and workflows, all optimized for a particular purpose. Splunk add-ons are a type of app that provide specific capabilities to other apps, such as getting data in, mapping data, or providing saved searches and macros.

When it comes to the Splunk Cloud environment, only pre-approved apps and add-ons can be installed. *Approved* apps are those apps that have been examined by Splunk to ensure they comply with the security requirements of Splunk Cloud.

Once deployed to the Cloud environment, management of an app starts with opening a support ticket. Sometimes timing is not optimal and in some cases, a fee is involved. To address this, there is the concept of self-service app management and the Splunk Packaging Toolkit.

The **Splunk Packaging Toolkit** is *the* tool for authoring, packaging, and validating your Splunk app in a way that eases up app management, including installation, configuration, and updating.

A note from the Splunk documentation:

> *"The Packaging Toolkit provides support for all phases of Splunk app lifecycle management. For Splunk app developers, that means they can focus on building apps without concerning themselves with different deployment topologies or the details of the deployment process"*

Like an on-premise installation, app management in the cloud now allows you to update your app directly, without relying on support services or even creating a support ticket.

Additionally, in version 7.0, there are a larger number of Splunk-approved apps in the cloud, as well as support for multiple search head configurations.

Building Advanced Dashboards

8

In Chapter 5, *Simple XML Dashboards*, we covered building dashboards using simple XML. We first used the wizards provided in Splunk and then edited the resultant XML code. When you reach the limits of what can be accomplished with simple XML, one option is to dive into Splunk's advanced XML.

In this chapter, we will explore advanced XML practices while also discussing the following topics:

- The pipe symbol
- Using top to show common field values
- Using stats to aggregate values
- Using chart to turn data
- Using timechart to show values over time
- Working with fields

Reasons for working with advanced XML

Here are a few reasons to use advanced XML:

- **More control over layout**: With advanced XML, you have better control over where form elements and chrome appear and somewhat improved control over the placement of the output.

- **Custom drilldowns**: It is only possible to create custom drilldowns from tables and charts using advanced XML.
- **Access to more parameters**: The modules in simple XML actually use advanced XML modules, but many parameters are not exposed. Sometimes, the desire is actually to disable features, and this is only possible using advanced XML.
- **Access to more modules**: There are many modules that are not available when we are using simple XML, for example, the search bar itself. All extra modules provided by the apps at Splunkbase, for example, Google Maps, are for use in advanced XML.

Reasons for not working with advanced XML

There are also a number of reasons not to work with advanced XML:

- **Steep learning curve**: Depending on what technologies you are comfortable working with, and possibly on how well the rest of this chapter is written, the learning curve for advanced XML can be steep.
- **No direct control over HTML**: If there is a particular HTML that you want to produce from search results, this may not be as simple as you had hoped. Short of writing your own module, you must work within the bounds of the options provided to the existing modules, modify the CSS with the application, or modify the HTML code using JavaScript.
- **No direct control over logic**: If you need specific things to happen when you click on specific table cells, particularly based on other values in the same row, this can only be accomplished by modifying the document using JavaScript. This is possible, but it is not well documented. Examples can be found at `https://splunkbase.splunk.com`, both in answer posts and in sample applications. Check out *customBehaviors* in the third-party app called **Sideview Utils** (**LGPL**) for an alternative.

If you have specific layout or logic requirements, you may be better served by using one of the Splunk APIs available at `https://dev.splunk.com` and writing applications in your favorite language.

Development process

When building dashboards, my approach is generally as follows:

1. Create the required queries.
2. Add the queries to a simple XML dashboard. Use the GUI tools to tweak the dashboard as much as possible. If possible, finish all graphical changes at this stage.
3. If form elements are needed, convert the simple XML dashboard to a form. If possible, make all logic work with simple XML.
4. Convert the simple XML dashboard to an advanced XML dashboard. There is no reverse conversion possible, so this should be done as late as possible and only if needed.
5. Edit the advanced XML dashboard accordingly.

The idea is to take advantage of the Splunk GUI tools as much as possible, letting the simple XML conversion process add all of the advanced XML that you would otherwise have to find yourself. We covered steps 1-3 in the previous chapters. Step 4 is covered in the *Converting simple XML to advanced XML* section.

Advanced XML structure

Before we dig into the modules provided, let's look at the structure of XML itself and cover a couple of concepts.

The tag structure of an advanced XML document is essentially as follows:

```
view
module
param
...
module
...
```

The main concept of Splunk's XML structure is that the effects of the upper modules flow downstream to the child modules.

This is a vital concept to understand. The XML structure has almost nothing to do with layout and everything to do with the flow of data.

Let's look at the following simple example:

```
<view
template="dashboard.html">
<label>Chapter 9, Example 1</label>
<module
name="HiddenSearch"
layoutPanel="panel_row1_col1"
autoRun="True">
<param name="earliest">-99d</param>
<param name="search">error | top user</param>
<module name="SimpleResultsTable"></module>
</module>
</view>
```

This document produces the following sparse dashboard with one panel:

	user ⇕	count ⇕	percent ⇕
1	ronnie	114372	10.007525
2	tuck	114352	10.005775
3	shelby	114324	10.003325
4	jarde	114310	10.002100
5	lou	114294	10.000700
6	paige	114266	9.998250
7	steve	114256	9.997375
8	mary	114242	9.996150
9	natile	114238	9.995800
10	nanette	114206	9.993000

Let's step through this example line by line:

- `<view`: This opens the outer tag. This tag begins all advanced XML dashboards.
- `template="dashboard.html">`: This sets the base HTML template. Dashboard layout templates are stored in the following path:

  $SPLUNK_HOME/share/splunk/search_mrsparkle/templates/view/

- Among other things, the templates define the panels available for use in `layoutPanel`.

- `<label>Chapter 9, Example 1</label>`: This sets the label used for navigation.
- `<module`: This begins our first module declaration.
- `name="HiddenSearch"`: This is the name of the module to use. `HiddenSearch` runs a search but displays nothing, relying instead on child modules to render the output.
- `layoutPanel="panel_row1_col1"`: This states where in the dashboard to display our panel. It seems strange to give this attribute to a module that displays nothing, but `layoutPanel` must be specified on every immediate child of `view`. See the *Understanding layoutPanel* section for more details.
- `autoRun="True">`: Without this attribute, the search does not run when the dashboard loads, and instead waits for user interaction from form elements. Since we have no form elements, we need this attribute in order to see the results.
- `<param name="earliest">-99d</param>`: It is very important to specify a value at the earliest as the query will, by default, run over all time. `param` values affect only the module tag they are nested directly inside.
- `<param name="search">error | top user</param>`: This is the actual query to run.
- `<module name="SimpleResultsTable"></module>`: This module simply displays a table of the events produced by a parent module. Since there are no `param` tags specified, the defaults for this module are used.
- `</module>`: Close the `HiddenSearch` module. This is required for valid XML, but it also implies that the scope of influence of this module is closed. To reiterate, only the downstream modules of the `HiddenSearch` module receive the events it produces.
- `</view>`: This closes the document.

This is a very simple dashboard. It lacks navigation, form elements, job status, and drilldowns. Adding all of these things is initially somewhat complicated to understand. Luckily, you can build a dashboard in simple XML, convert it to advanced XML, and then modify the provided XML as needed.

Converting simple XML to advanced XML

Let's go back to one of the dashboards we created in `Chapter 5`, *Simple XML Dashboards*—`errors_user_form`.

We built this before our app, so it still lives in the **Search** app.

Just to refresh your memory, the simple XML code behind this dashboard looks like this:

```
<?xml version='1.0' encoding='utf-8'?>
<form>
<fieldset>
<input type="text" token="user">
<label>User</label>
</input>
<input type="time" />
</fieldset>
<label>Errors User Form</label>
<row>
<chart>
<searchString>
sourcetype="impl_splunk_gen" loglevel=error user="$user$" | timechart count
as "Error count" by network
</searchString>
<title>
Dashboard - Errors - errors by network timechart
</title>
<option name="charting.chart">line</option>
</chart>
</row>
<row>
<chart>
<searchString>
sourcetype="impl_splunk_gen" loglevel=error user="$user$" | bucket bins=10
req_time | stats count by req_time
</searchString>
<title>
Error count by req_times
</title>
<option name="charting.chart">pie</option>
</chart>
<chart>
<searchString>
sourcetype="impl_splunk_gen" loglevel=error user="$user$" | stats count by
logger
</searchString>
<title>Errors by logger</title>
<option name="charting.chart">pie</option>
</chart>
</row>
<row>
<event>
<searchString>
```

```
sourcetype="impl_splunk_gen" loglevel=error user="$user$"
</searchString>
<title>Error events</title>
<option name="count">10</option>
<option name="displayRowNumbers">true</option>
<option name="maxLines">10</option>
<option name="segmentation">outer</option>
<option name="softWrap">true</option>
</event>
</row>
</form>
```

In simple XML, the layout and logic flow are tied together. Before simple XML is rendered to the user, Splunk first dynamically converts it to advanced XML in memory. We can access advanced XML by appending `?showsource=advanced` to any URL, as follows:

```
http://localhost:8000/en-US/app/is_app_one/errors?showsource=advanced
```

This produces a page (somewhat different from the earlier version of Splunk, when you used `showsource=1`) similar to this:

This is followed by a textbox containing raw XML, as shown here:

XML source

```
<view autoCancelInterval="90" isVisible="true" objectMode="SimpleDashboard" onunloadCancelJobs="true"
refresh="-1" template="dashboard.html">
  <label/>
  <module name="AccountBar" layoutPanel="appHeader"/>
  <module name="AppBar" layoutPanel="navigationHeader"/>
  <module name="Message" layoutPanel="messaging">
    <param name="filter">*</param>
    <param name="clearOnJobDispatch">False</param>
    <param name="maxSize">1</param>
  </module>
  <module name="DashboardTitleBar" layoutPanel="viewHeader"/>
  <module name="Message" layoutPanel="navigationHeader">
    <param name="level">warn</param>
    <param name="filter">splunk.search.job</param>
    <param name="clearOnJobDispatch">True</param>
    <param name="maxSize">1</param>
  </module>
</view>
```

An abbreviated version of the advanced XML version of `errors_user_form` follows:

```
<view
... template="dashboard.html">
<label>Errors User Form</label>
<module name="AccountBar" layoutPanel="appHeader"/>
<module name="AppBar" layoutPanel="navigationHeader"/>
<module name="Message" layoutPanel="messaging">
...<module name="Message" layoutPanel="messaging">
...<module name="TitleBar" layoutPanel="viewHeader">
...<module name="ExtendedFieldSearch" layoutPanel="viewHeader">
<param name="replacementMap">
<param name="arg">
<param name="user"/>
</param>
</param>
<param name="field">User</param>
<param name="intention">
... <module name="TimeRangePicker">
<param name="searchWhenChanged">False</param>
<module name="SubmitButton">
<param name="allowSoftSubmit">True</param>
<param name="label">Search</param>
```

```
<module
name="HiddenSearch"
layoutPanel="panel_row1_col1"
group="Dashboard - Errors - errors by network timechart"
autoRun="False">
<param name="search">
sourcetype="impl_splunk_gen"
loglevel=error user="$user$"
| timechart count as "Error count" by network
</param>
<param name="groupLabel">
Dashboard - Errors - errors by network timechart
</param>
<module name="ViewstateAdapter">
<param name="suppressionList">
<item>charting.chart</item>
</param>
<module name="HiddenFieldPicker">
<param name="strictMode">True</param>
<module name="JobProgressIndicator">
<module name="EnablePreview">
<param name="enable">True</param>
<param name="display">False</param>
<module name="HiddenChartFormatter">
<param name="charting.chart">line</param>
<module name="JSChart">
<param name="width">100%</param>
<module name="Gimp"/>
<module name="ConvertToDrilldownSearch">
<module name="ViewRedirector">
... </module>
<module name="ViewRedirectorLink">
... </module>
<module
name="HiddenSearch"
layoutPanel="panel_row2_col1"
group="Error count by req_times"
autoRun="False">
<param name="search">
sourcetype="impl_splunk_gen" loglevel=error
user="$user$"
| bucket bins=10 req_time | stats count by req_time
</param>
<param name="groupLabel">Error count by req_times</param>
... </module>
<module
name="HiddenSearch"
layoutPanel="panel_row2_col2"
```

```
group="Errors by logger"
autoRun="False">
<param name="search">
sourcetype="impl_splunk_gen"
loglevel=error user="$user$"
| stats count by logger
</param>
<param name="groupLabel">Errors by logger</param>
... </module>
<module
name="HiddenSearch"
layoutPanel="panel_row3_col1"
group="Error events"
autoRun="False">
<param name="search">
sourcetype="impl_splunk_gen"
loglevel=error
user="$user$"
</param>
<param name="groupLabel">Error events</param>
<module name="ViewstateAdapter">
... <module name="HiddenFieldPicker">
... <module name="JobProgressIndicator"/>
<module name="Paginator">
<param name="count">10</param>
... <module name="EventsViewer">
... <module name="Gimp"/>
... </module>
...
</view>
```

This XML code is more verbose than we actually need, but luckily, it is easier to delete code than to create it.

Module logic flow

The main concept of nested modules is that parent (upstream) modules affect child (downstream) modules. Looking at the first panel, the full module flow is as follows:

```
<module name="ExtendedFieldSearch">
<module name="TimeRangePicker">
<module name="SubmitButton">
<module name="HiddenSearch">
<module name="ViewstateAdapter">
<module name="HiddenFieldPicker">
<module name="JobProgressIndicator">
```

```
<module name="EnablePreview">
<module name="HiddenChartFormatter">
<module name="JSChart">
<module name="ConvertToDrilldownSearch">
<module name="ViewRedirector">
<module name="ViewRedirectorLink">
```

A reference to the modules installed in your instance of Splunk is available at /modules. In my case, the full URL is as follows:

```
http://localhost:8000/en-US/modules
```

Let's step through these modules in turn and discuss what each of them accomplishes:

- ExtendedFieldSearch: This provides a textbox for entry. The parameters for this module are complicated and represent arguably the most complicated aspect of advanced XML intentions. Intentions affect child modules, specifically HiddenSearch. We will cover them in the *Using intentions* section.

- TimeRangePicker: This provides the standard time picker. It affects child HiddenSearch modules that do not have times specified either using param values or in the query itself. The precedence of times used in a query is as follows:
    - Times specified in the query itself
    - Times specified via the earliest and latest param values to the search module
    - A value provided by TimeRangePicker

- SubmitButton: This draws the **Search** button and fires off any child search modules when clicked on.

- HiddenSearch: As we saw before, this runs a query and produces events for downstream modules. In this case, autoRun is set to false so that the query waits for the user.

- ViewstateAdapter: A viewstate describes what settings a user has selected in the GUI, for instance, sort order, page size, or chart type. Any time you change a chart setting or pick a time range, you create a viewstate that is saved by Splunk. This module is used to access an existing viewstate or to suppress specific viewstate settings. By suppressing specific settings, the default or specified values of child modules will be used instead. This module is rarely needed unless you are using a saved search with an associated viewstate.

- `HiddenFieldPicker`: This module limits what fields are accessible by downstream modules. This is useful when we run a query that produces many fields but only certain fields are needed. This affects the fields shown below events in an events listing or the columns displayed in a table view. This module is rarely needed.

- `JobProgressIndicator`: This module displays a progress bar until the job is completed. In this case, because of the placement of the module in XML, it appears above the results. This module does not affect downstream modules, so it can be listed on its own.

- `EnablePreview`: This module allows you to specify whether searches should refresh with incomplete results while the query is running.
  The default appears to be `true` for Splunk-provided modules, but this module allows you to control this behavior. This module does not affect downstream modules, so it can be listed on its own.
  Disabling the preview can improve the performance dramatically but it provides no information until the query is complete, which is less visually appealing, particularly during a long-running query.

- `HiddenChartFormatter`: This module is where the chart settings are specified. These settings affect any child modules that draw charts.

- `JSChart`: This draws a chart using JavaScript. Prior to Splunk 4.3, all charts were drawn using Flash. The `FlashChart` module is still included for backward compatibility.

- `ConvertToDrilldownSearch`: This module takes the values from a click on a parent module and produces a query based on the query that produced the results. This usually works, but not always, depending on the complexity of the query. We will build a custom drill-down search later.

- `ViewRedirector`: This module accepts the query from its upstream module and redirects the user to use `viewTarget` with the query specified in the URL. Usually, `flashtimeline` is specified as `viewTarget param`, but it could be any dashboard. The query affects a `HiddenSearch` or `SearchBar` module.

- `ViewRedirectorLink`: This module sends the user to a new search page with the search results for this module.

Thinking about what we have seen in this flow, we can say that modules can do the following things:

- Generate events
- Modify a query
- Modify the behavior of a downstream module
- Display an element on the dashboard
- Handle actions produced by clicks

It is also possible for a module to do the following:

- Post-process the events produced by a query
- Add custom JavaScript to the dashboard

Understanding layoutPanel

In an advanced XML dashboard, the value of the layoutPanel attribute determines which panel a module is drawn to. This separation of logic and layout can be useful—for instance, allowing you to reuse data generated by a query with multiple modules—but displays the results on different parts of the page.

A few rules for this attribute are as follows:

- The layoutPanel attribute must appear on all immediate children of <view>.
- The layoutPanel attribute can appear on descendant child module tags.
- If a module does not have a layoutPanel attribute, it will inherit the value from the closest upstream module that does.
- Modules that have visible output are added to their respective layoutPanel attributes in the order they appear in, in the XML.
- Modules flow in the panel they are placed in. Most modules take the entire width of the panel, but some do not, and flow from left to right before wrapping.

Looking through our XML, we find these elements with the layoutPanel attribute, as shown here:

```
<module name="AccountBar" layoutPanel="appHeader"/>
<module name="AppBar" layoutPanel="navigationHeader"/>
<module name="Message" layoutPanel="messaging">
<module name="TitleBar" layoutPanel="viewHeader">
<module name="ExtendedFieldSearch" layoutPanel="viewHeader">
<module name="TimeRangePicker">
```

```
<module name="SubmitButton">
<module name="HiddenSearch" layoutPanel="panel_row1_col1">...
<module name="HiddenSearch" layoutPanel="panel_row2_col1">...
<module name="HiddenSearch" layoutPanel="panel_row2_col2">...
<module name="HiddenSearch" layoutPanel="panel_row3_col1">
...
```

The first set of `layoutPanel` values are panels included in the chrome of the page. This displays the account information, navigation, and messages to the user. The second set of modules makes up the title and form elements. Note that `TimeRangePicker` and `SubmitButton` have no `layoutPanel` value but inherit from `ExtendedFieldSearch`.

The results panels all begin with a `HiddenSearch` module. All the children of each of these modules inherit this `layoutPanel` value.

Panel placement

For your dashboard panels, you will almost always use a `layoutPanel` value of the `panel_rowX_colY` form.

A simple visualization of the layout produced by our modules would look similar to the following screenshot:

In our simple XML version of this dashboard, the layout was tied directly to the order of the XML, as shown here:

```
<row>
<chart></chart>
</row>
<row>
<chart></chart>
<chart></chart>
</row>
<row>
<event></event>
</row>
```

Just to reiterate, the simple XML structure translates to the following code:

```
<row>
<chart></chart> == panel_row1_col1
</row>
<row>
<chart></chart> == panel_row2_col1
<chart></chart> == panel_row2_col2
</row>
<row>
<event></event> == panel_row3_col1
</row>
```

There is another extension available, _grp1, that allows you to create columns inside a panel. We will try that out in the *Creating a custom drill-down* section later.

Reusing a query

One example of separating layout from data would be using a single query to populate both a table and a chart.

The advanced XML for this can look like the following code:

```
<view template="dashboard.html">
<label>Chapter 9 - Reusing a query</label>
<module
name="StaticContentSample"
layoutPanel="panel_row1_col1">
<param name="text">Text above</param>
</module>
<module
name="HiddenSearch"
layoutPanel="panel_row1_col1"
autoRun="True">
<param name="search">
sourcetype="impl_splunk_gen" loglevel=error | top user
</param>
<param name="earliest">-99d</param>
<module name="HiddenChartFormatter">
<param name="charting.chart">pie</param>
<module name="JSChart"></module>
<module
name="StaticContentSample"
layoutPanel="panel_row1_col1">
<!-- this layoutPanel is unneeded, but harmless -->
<param name="text">Text below</param>
```

```
</module>
</module>
<module name="SimpleResultsTable"
layoutPanel="panel_row1_col2"></module>
</module>
</view>
```

This XML renders a dashboard similar to the following screenshot:

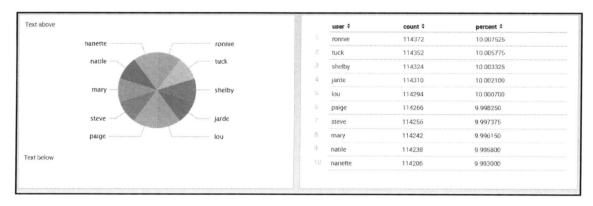

There are some things to notice in this XML:

- The data produced by `HiddenSearch` is used by both child modules.
- `JSChart` inherits `layoutPanel="panel_row1_col1"` from `HiddenSearch`.
- `SimpleResultsTable` has its own `layoutPanel` attribute set to `panel_row1_col2`, so the table draws to the right.
- Both `StaticContentSample` modules specify `layoutPanel="panel_row1_col1"` and, therefore, appear in the same panel as the chart. Even though they are at different depths in the XML, the order drawn follows the order seen in the XML.

Using intentions

Intentions allow you to affect downstream searches using values provided by other modules, for instance, form fields or the results of a click. There are a number of available intention types, but we will cover the two most common ones, `stringreplace` and `addterm`. You can see examples of other types of intentions in the UI examples app available at `http://splunkbase.com`.

stringreplace

This is the most common intention to use and maps directly to the only available action in simple XML-variable replacement. Let's look at our search field from our advanced XML example:

```
<module name="ExtendedFieldSearch" layoutPanel="viewHeader">
<param name="replacementMap">
<param name="arg">
<param name="user"/>
</param>
</param>
<param name="field">User</param>
<param name="intention">
<param name="name">stringreplace</param>
<param name="arg">
<param name="user">
<param name="fillOnEmpty">True</param>
</param>
</param>
</param>
```

Stepping through the `param` instances, we have the following terms and their descriptions:

- `field`: This is the label for the field displayed in the dashboard.
- `replacementMap`: This parameter names the variable that the `ExtendedFieldSearch` module is creating. I have been told that the nested nature means nothing, and we should simply copy and paste the entire block of XML, changing nothing but the value of the deepest `param` tag, in this case to `user`.

- `intention`: Intentions have specific structures that build blocks of queries from structured XML. In the case of `stringreplace` (which is the most common use case), we can essentially copy the entire XML and, once again, change nothing but the value of the third-level `param`, which is currently `user`. The `fillOnEmpty` value determines whether to make the substitution when the `user` variable is empty.
- All of this code simply tells us to replace `$user$` in any searches with the value of the input field. Our first `HiddenSearch` value looks like the following:

```
<module name="HiddenSearch" ...
<param name="search">
sourcetype="impl_splunk_gen"
loglevel=error user="$user$"
| timechart count as "Error count" by network
</param>
```

- The value of `$user$` will be replaced and the query will be run.

If you want to see exactly what is happening, you can insert a `SearchBar` module as a child of the form elements, and it will render the resultant query. For example, see the code of the `drilldown_chart1` dashboard in the *UI examples app* available at `http://splunkbase.com`.

addterm

This intention is useful to add search terms to a query with or without user interaction. For example, let's say you always want to ensure that a particular value of the field source is queried. You can then modify the query that will be run, appending a search term. Here is an example from the `advanced_lister_with_` dashboard.

The searchbar in the *UI examples app* is available at `http://splunkbase.com`. The following code encapsulates this discussion:

```
<module name="HiddenIntention">
<param name="intention">
<param name="name">addterm</param>
<param name="arg">
<param name="source">*metrics.log</param>
</param>
<!-- tells the addterm intention to put our term in the first search clause
no matter what. -->
<param name="flags"><list>indexed</list></param>
</param>
```

Stepping through the `param` instances, we have the following terms and their descriptions:

- `name`: This parameter sets the type of intention—in this case, `addterm`.
- `arg`: This is used to set the field to add to the query.
  The nested `param` tag sets the fieldname and value to use in the query.
  In this case, `source="*metrics.log"` is added to the query.
  Variables can be used in either the `name` attribute or body of this nested `param`
  tag. We will see an example of this under the *Creating a custom drilldown* section.
- `flags`: Every example of `addterm` that I can find includes this attribute exactly
  as written. It essentially says that the term to be added to the search should be
  added before the first pipe symbol and not at the end of the full query.

For example, consider the following query:

```
error | top logger
```

This `param` tag would amend our query like this:

```
error source="*metrics.log" | top logger
```

Creating a custom drilldown

A drilldown is a query built using values from a previous query. The
`ConvertToDrilldownSearch` module will build a query automatically from the table or
graph that it is nested inside. Unfortunately, this works well only when the query is fairly
simple and when you want to see raw events. To build a custom drilldown, we will
combine intentions and the nested nature of modules.

Building a drilldown to a custom query

Looking back at our chart in the *Reusing a query* section, let's build a custom drilldown that
shows the top instances of another field when it is clicked on.

Here is an example dashboard that draws a chart and then runs a custom query when
clicked on:

```
<view template="dashboard.html">
<label>Chapter 9 - Drilldown to custom query</label>
<!-- chrome -->
<module
```

```
name="HiddenSearch"
layoutPanel="panel_row1_col1"
autoRun="True"
group="Errors by user">
<param name="search">
sourcetype=* loglevel=error | top user
</param>
<param name="earliest">-99d</param>
<!-- draw the chart -->
<module name="HiddenChartFormatter">
<param name="charting.chart">pie</param>
<module name="JSChart">
<!-- nested modules are invoked on click -->
<!-- create a new query -->
<module name="HiddenSearch">
<param name="search">
sourcetype=* loglevel=error
| top logger
</param>
<!-- create an intention using the value from the chart.
Use addterm to add a user field to the query. -->
<module name="ConvertToIntention">
<param name="intention">
<param name="name">addterm</param>
<param name="arg">
<param name="user">$click.value$</param>
</param>
<param name="flags">
<item>indexed</item>
</param>
</param>
<!-- Send the user to flashtimeline
with the new query. -->
<module name="ViewRedirector">
<param name="viewTarget">flashtimeline</param>
</module>
</module>
</module>
</module>
</module>
</module>
</view>
```

Everything should look very similar up until the JSChart module. Inside this module, we find a HiddenSearch module. The idea is that the downstream modules of display modules are not invoked until the display module is clicked on.

`HiddenSearch` is used to build a query in this case, but instead of the query being handed to a display module, it is handed to the `ViewRedirector` module.

The magical field in all of this is `click.value`. This field contains the value that was clicked on in the chart.

Let's look at what this dashboard renders:

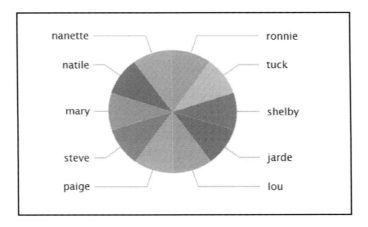

The resultant query when we click on the slice of the pie for the user `shelby` looks like the following screenshot:

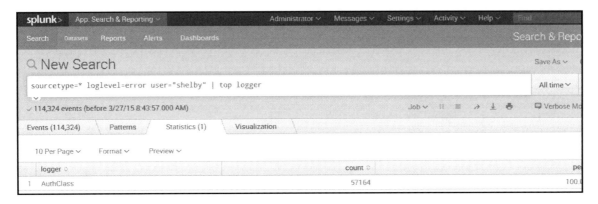

Look back to the *addterm* section for more details on how this intention works.

Building a drilldown to another panel

Another option for a drilldown is to draw a new panel on the same dashboard. This lets you create various drilldowns without redrawing the screen, which might be less jarring to the user. Here is the XML code:

```
<?xml version="1.0"?>
<view template="dashboard.html">
<label>Chapter 9 - Drilldown to new graph</label>
<!-- chrome should go here -->
<module
name="HiddenSearch"
layoutPanel="panel_row1_col1"
autoRun="True"
group="Errors by user">
<param name="search">
sourcetype=impl_splunk_gen_more error loglevel=error | top user
</param>
<param name="earliest">-99d</param>
<module name="HiddenChartFormatter">
<param name="charting.chart">pie</param>
<!-- draw the first chart -->
<module name="JSChart">
<!-- the modules inside the chart will wait for
interaction from the user -->
<module name="HiddenSearch">
<param name="earliest">-99d</param>
<param name="search">
Sourcetypeimpl_splunk_gen_more error loglevel=error
user=$user$ | timechart count by logger
</param>
<module name="ConvertToIntention">
<param name="intention">
<param name="name">stringreplace</param>
<param name="arg">
<param name="user">
<param name="value">$click.value$</param>
</param>
</param>
</param>
<!-- print a header above the new chart -->
<module name="SimpleResultsHeader">
<param name="entityName">results</param>
<param name="headerFormat">
Errors by logger for $click.value$
</param>
</module>
```

```
<!-- draw the chart. We have not specified another
layoutPanel, so it will appear below the first
chart -->
<module name="HiddenChartFormatter">
<param name="charting.chart">area</param>
<param name="chart.stackMode">stacked</param>
<module name="JSChart"/>
</module>
</module>
</module>
</module>
</module>
</module>
</view>
```

Here's what the dashboard looks like after clicking on shelby in the pie chart:

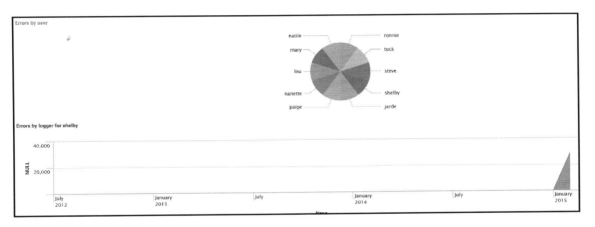

Building a drilldown to multiple panels using HiddenPostProcess

Taking the last dashboard further, let's build a number of panels from a single custom drilldown query. As we covered in Chapter 5, *Simple XML Dashboards*, search results can be post processed, allowing you to use the same query results in multiple ways. In advanced XML, this is accomplished using the HiddenPostProcess module.

We will also add the chrome for our first complete dashboard. Here is an abbreviated example. The complete dashboard is in the `Chapter9_drilldown_to_new_graph_with_postprocess.xml` file in the `Implementing Splunk App One` app:

```xml
<view template="dashboard.html">
<Label>Chapter 9 - Drilldown to new graph with postprocess</label>
<!-- The chrome at the top of the dashboard
containing navigation and the app header -->
<module name="AccountBar" layoutPanel="appHeader"/>
<module name="AppBar" layoutPanel="navigationHeader"/>
<module name="Message" layoutPanel="messaging">
<param name="filter">*</param>
<param name="clearOnJobDispatch">False</param>
<param name="maxSize">1</param>
</module>
<module name="DashboardTitleBar" layoutPanel="viewHeader"/>
<module name="Message" layoutPanel="navigationHeader">
<param name="filter">splunk.search.job</param>
<param name="clearOnJobDispatch">True</param>
<param name="maxSize">1</param>
<param name="level">warn</param>
</module>
<! -- Begin our initial search
which will populate our pie chart -->
<module
name="HiddenSearch" layoutPanel="panel_row1_col1"
autoRun="True" group="Errors by user">
<param name="search">
sourcetype="impl_splunk_gen" loglevel=error | top user
</param>
<param name="earliest">-99d</param>
<module name="HiddenChartFormatter">
<param name="charting.chart">pie</param>
<module name="JSChart">
<!-- Initially, only the pie chart will be drawn
After a click on a user wedge, this nested query will run -->
<module name="HiddenSearch">
<param name="earliest">-24h</param>
<param name="search">
sourcetype="impl_splunk_gen" loglevel=error
user="$user$" | bucket span=30m _time
| stats count by logger _time
</param>
<module name="ConvertToIntention">
<param name="intention">
<param name="name">stringreplace</param>
```

```
<param name="arg">
<param name="user">
<param name="value">$click.value$</param>
...
<!-- The remaining modules are downstream from the pie chart
and are invoked when a pie wedge is clicked -->
<module name="SimpleResultsHeader"
layoutPanel="panel_row2_col1">
<param name="entityName">results</param>
<param name="headerFormat">
Errors by logger for $click.value$
</param>
</module>
<!-- The SingleValue modules -->
<module name="HiddenPostProcess">
<param name="search">
stats sum(count) as count by logger
| sort -count | head 1
| eval f=logger + " is most common (" + count + ")" |
table f </param>
<module name="SingleValue"
layoutPanel="panel_row2_col1"></module>
</module>
...
<!-- The chart -->
<module name="HiddenPostProcess">
<param name="search">
timechart span=30m sum(count) by logger
</param>
<module name="HiddenChartFormatter">
<param name="charting.chart">area</param>
<param name="chart.stackMode">stacked</param>
<module
name="JSChart"
layoutPanel="panel_row4_col1_grp1"/>
</module>
</module>
<!-- The table -->
<module name="HiddenPostProcess">
<param name="search">
stats sum(count) as count by logger
</param>
<module name="SimpleResultsTable"
layoutPanel="panel_row4_col1_grp2"/>
</module>
...
</module>
</view>
```

This dashboard contains the chrome, which is very useful as it displays the errors in your intentions and query statements.

Let's step through the new queries. The initial query is the same and is shown here:

```
sourcetype="impl_splunk_gen" loglevel=error | top user
```

The next query may seem strange, but there's a good reason for this:

```
sourcetype="impl_splunk_gen" loglevel=error user="$user$"
| bucket span=30m _time
| stats count by logger _time
```

We used buckets and stats to slice events by `_time` and other fields. This is a convenient way to break down events for post processing, where one or more of the post-process queries use `timechart`. This query produces a row with the field count for every unique value of `logger` in each 30-minute period.

Post processing has a limit of `10,000` events. To accommodate this limit, all aggregation possible should be done in the initial query. Ideally, only what is needed by all child queries should be produced by the initial query. It is also important to note that all fields needed by post-process queries must be returned by the initial query.

The first `HiddenPostProcess` value builds a field for a module we haven't used yet, `SingleValue`, which takes the first value it sees and renders that value in a rounded rectangle. The following code shows this:

```
stats sum(count) as count by logger
| sort -count
| head 1
| eval f=logger + " is most common (" + count + ")"
| table f
The query is additive, so the full query for this module is essentially:
sourcetype="impl_splunk_gen" loglevel=error user="bob"
| bucket span=30m _time
| stats count by logger _time
| stats sum(count) as count by logger
| sort -count
| head 1
| eval f=logger + " is most common (" + count + ")"
| table f
```

The remaining `SingleValue` modules do similar work to find the count of unique loggers, the maximum errors per hour, and the average errors per hour. To step through these queries, simply copy each piece and add it to a query in the search bar.

Other things to notice in this dashboard are as follows:

- `grp` builds columns inside a single panel, for instance, in `layoutPanel="panel_row4_col1_grp2"`
- `SingleValue` modules do not stack vertically but rather flow horizontally, overflowing to the next line when the window width is reached
- `span` is used in the bucket statement and is the minimum needed by any post-process statements but as large as possible to minimize the number of events returned

Third-party add-ons

There are many excellent apps available at `http://splunkbase.com`, a number of which provide custom modules. We will cover two of the most popular, Google Maps and Sideview Utils.

Google Maps

As we saw in `Chapter 7`, *Working with Apps*, the Google Maps app provides a dashboard and lookup to draw results on a map. The underlying module is also available to use in your own dashboards.

Here is a very simple dashboard that uses the `GoogleMaps` module:

```
<?xml version="1.0"?>
<view template="search.html">
<!-- chrome -->
<label>Chapter 9 - Google Maps Search</label>
<module name="AccountBar" layoutPanel="appHeader"/>
<module name="AppBar" layoutPanel="navigationHeader"/>
<module name="Message" layoutPanel="messaging">
<param name="filter">*</param>
<param name="clearOnJobDispatch">False</param>
<param name="maxSize">1</param>
</module>
<!-- search -->
<module name="SearchBar" layoutPanel="splSearchControls-inline">
```

```
<param name="useOwnSubmitButton">False</param>
<module name="TimeRangePicker">
<param name="selected">Last 60 minutes</param>
<module name="SubmitButton">
<!-- map -->
<module
name="GoogleMaps"
layoutPanel="resultsAreaLeft"
group="Map" />
</module>
</module>
</module>
</view>
```

This code produces a search bar with a map under it, as seen here in the following screenshot:

When using the `GoogleMaps` module, you would usually convert a set of values to geographic coordinates. This is usually accomplished using the `geoip` lookup (for examples, see `Chapter 7`, *Working with Apps*) to convert IP addresses to locations or by using a custom lookup of some sort.

Just to show that the data can come from anywhere, let's make a graph by setting the `_geo` field on events from one of our example source types:

```
sourcetype="impl_splunk_gen_more" req_time
| eventstats max(req_time) as max
| eval lat=(req_time/max*360)-180
| eval lng=abs(lat)/2-15
| eval _geo=lng+","+lat
```

This query produces a *V* from our random `req_time` field, as shown in the following screenshot. See the map documentation at `http://www.splunkbase.com` for more information about the `_geo` field:

This is a very simplistic example that uses the default settings for nearly everything.

For a more complete example, see the Google Maps dashboard included with the Google Maps app. You can see the source code in the manager or using the `showsource` attribute. On my server, that URL is `http://localhost:8000/en-US/app/maps/maps?showsource=advanced`.

Sideview Utils

Sideview Utils is a third-party app for Splunk that provides an alternative set of modules for most of what you need to build an interactive Splunk dashboard. These modules remove the complexity of intentions and make it much easier to build forms, make it possible to use variables in HTML, and make it much simpler to handle values between panels and dashboards.

We will use a few of the modules to build forms and link multiple dashboards together based on URL values.

An older but still functional version of SideviewUtils is available through Splunkbase. You can download the latest version from `http://sideviewapps.com/`, which adds a number of features, including a visual editor to assemble dashboards.

The Sideview search module

Let's start with a simple search:

```
<?xml version="1.0"?>
<view template="dashboard.html">
<!-- add sideview -->
<module layoutPanel="appHeader" name="SideviewUtils"/>
<!-- chrome -->
<label>Chapter 9 - Sideview One</label>
<module name="AccountBar" layoutPanel="appHeader"/>
<module name="AppBar" layoutPanel="navigationHeader"/>
<module name="Message" layoutPanel="messaging">
<param name="filter">*</param>
<param name="clearOnJobDispatch">False</param>
<param name="maxSize">1</param>
</module>
<!-- search -->
<module
name="Search"
autoRun="True"
group="Chapter 9 - Sideview One"
layoutPanel="panel_row1_col1">
<param name="earliest">-99d</param>
<param name="search">source="impl_splunk_gen_more" | top user</param>
<!-- chart -->
<module name="HiddenChartFormatter">
<param name="charting.chart">pie</param>
<module name="JSChart"/>
</module>
</module>
</view>
```

This dashboard renders identically to the first panel, previously described in the *Building a drilldown to a custom query* section. There are two things to notice in this example:

- The `SideviewUtils` module is needed to include the code needed by all Sideview Utils apps
- We use the alternative `Search` module as a replacement for the `HiddenSearch` module to illustrate our first SideviewUtils module

In this simplistic example, `HiddenSearch` still works.

Linking views with Sideview

Starting from our simple dashboard, let's use the `Redirector` module to build a link. This link could be to anything, but we will link to another Splunk dashboard, which we will build next. Here's the XML code:

```
...
<module name="JSChart">
<module name="Redirector">
<param name="arg.user">$click.value$</param>
<param name="url">chapter_9_sideview_2</param>
</module>
</module>
...
```

After clicking on **shelby**, a new URL is built using the user value. In my case, the URL is:

```
http://localhost:8000/en-US/app/is_app_one/chapter_9_sideview_2?user=shelby
```

The dashboard referenced does not exist yet, so this URL returns an error.

Let's create the second dashboard now.

Sideview URLLoader

The `URLLoader` module provides us with the ability to set variables from the query string of a URL—a very useful feature. For our next dashboard, we will draw a table showing the error counts for the user value provided in the URL:

```
<view template="dashboard.html">
<!-- add sideview -->
<module name="SideviewUtils" layoutPanel="appHeader"/>
<!-- chrome -->
 <Label>Chapter 9 - Sideview Two</Label>
<module name="AccountBar" layoutPanel="appHeader"/>
<module name="AppBar" layoutPanel="navigationHeader"/>
<module name="Message" layoutPanel="messaging">
<param name="filter">*</param>
<param name="clearOnJobDispatch">False</param>
<param name="maxSize">1</param>
</module>
<!-- search -->
<module
```

```
name="URLLoader"
layoutPanel="panel_row1_col1"
autoRun="True">
<module name="HTML">
<param name="html"><![CDATA[
<h2>Errors by logger for $user$.</h2>
]]>
</param>
</module>
<module name="Search" group="Chapter 9 - Sideview Two">
<param name="earliest">-199d</param>
<param name="search">
sourcetype="*" user="$user$" | top user
</param>
<!-- table -->
<module name="SimpleResultsTable">
<param name="drilldown">row</param>
<module name="Redirector">
<param name="url">chapter_9_sideview_3</param>
<param name="arg.logger">
$click.fields.logger.rawValue$
</param>
<param name="arg.user">$user$</param>
<param name="arg.earliest">
$search.timeRange.earliest$
</param>
</module>
</module>
</module>
</module>
</view>
```

It is very important that `autoRun="true"` be placed in one module—most likely `URLLoader`—and that it exists only in a single module.

With the value of the user as **shelby** in our URL, this dashboard (using my data) creates the simple view (notice the logged errors for **shelby** seem to be of only one type), as shown in the following screenshot:

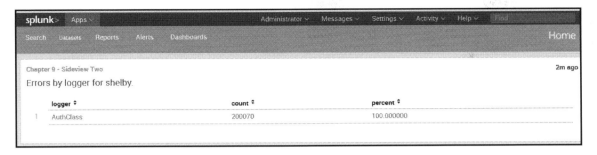

Looking at the modules in this example that are of interest, we have the following terms and their descriptions:

- `SideviewUtils`: This module is required to use any of the other Sideview modules. It is invisible to the user but is still required.
- `URLLoader`: This module takes any values specified in the URL query string and turns them into variables to be used by the descendant modules. Our URL contains `user=mary`, so `$user$` is replaced with the value `mary`.
- `HTML`: This module draws a snippet of HTML inline. Variables from `URLLoader` and from form elements are replaced.
- `Search`: This replacement for `HiddenSearch` understands variables from `URLLoader` and form elements. This completely obviates the need for intentions. In our case, `$user$` is replaced.
- `Redirector`: In this example, we are going to hand along two values to the next dashboard—user from `URLLoader` and `logger` from the table itself.

Notice the following code terms and their descriptions:

- `logger` is populated with `$click.fields.logger.rawValue$`.
- When a table is clicked on, the variable called `click.fields` contains all fields from the row of the table clicked on.
- `rawValue` makes sure that an unescaped value is returned. As the Sideview documents say:

  "Rule of Thumb for displaying in headers and sending via redirects, use $foo.rawValue$. For searches, use foo."

- This rule applies to values in `Redirector` and not in display.

- `search.timeRange` contains information about the times used by this search as to whether it comes from the URL, a `TimeRangePicker`, or `params` to the `Search` module. `arg.earliest` adds the value to the URL.

With a click on the table row for `LogoutClass`, we are taken to the following URL:

```
http://localhost:8000/en-US/app/is_app_one/chapter_9_sideview_3?
user=mar&ylogger=LogoutClass&earliest=1344188377
```

We will create the dashboard at this URL in the next section.

Sideview forms

For our final dashboard using Sideview modules, we will build a dashboard with a form that can be prefilled from a URL and allows the changing of the time range. The advantage of this dashboard is that it can be used as a destination of a click without being linked to from elsewhere. If the user accesses this dashboard directly, the default values specified in the dashboard will be used instead. Let's look at the code:

```xml
<?xml version="1.0"?>
<view template="dashboard.html">
<!-- add sideview -->
<module name="SideviewUtils" layoutPanel="appHeader"/>
<!-- chrome -->
<label>Chapter 9 - Sideview Three</label>
<module name="AccountBar" layoutPanel="appHeader"/>
<module name="AppBar" layoutPanel="navigationHeader"/>
<module name="Message" layoutPanel="messaging">
<param name="filter">*</param>
<param name="clearOnJobDispatch">False</param>
<param name="maxSize">1</param>
</module>
<!-- URLLoader -->
<module
name="URLLoader"
layoutPanel="panel_row1_col1"
autoRun="True">
<!-- form -->
<!-- user dropdown -->
<module name="Search" layoutPanel="panel_row1_col1">
<param name="search">
source="impl_splunk_gen" user user="*"
| top user
</param>
<param name="earliest">-24h</param>
<param name="latest">now</param>
```

```
<module name="Pulldown">
<param name="name">user</param>
<!-- use valueField in SideView 2.0 -->
<param name="searchFieldsToDisplay">
<list>
<param name="value">user</param>
<param name="label">user</param>
</list>
</param>
<param name="label">User</param>
<param name="float">left</param>
<!-- logger textfield -->
<module name="TextField">
<param name="name">logger</param>
<param name="default">*</param>
<param name="label">Logger:</param>
<param name="float">left</param>
<module name="TimeRangePicker">
<param name="searchWhenChanged">True</param>
<param name="default">Last 24 hours</param>
<!-- submit button -->
<module name="SubmitButton">
<param name="allowSoftSubmit">True</param>
<!-- html -->
<module name="HTML">
<param name="html"><![CDATA[
<h2>Info for user $user$, logger $logger$.</h2>
]]></param>
</module>
<!-- search 1 -->
<module
name="Search"
group="Chapter 9 - Sideview Three">
<param name="search">
source="impl_splunk_gen" user="$user$"
logger="$logger$"
| fillnull value="unknown" network
| timechart count by network
</param>
<!-- JobProgressIndicator -->
<module name="JobProgressIndicator"/>
<!-- chart -->
<module name="HiddenChartFormatter">
<param name="charting.chart">area</param>
<param name="charting.chart.stackMode">
stacked
</param>
<module name="JSChart"/>
```

```
</module>
</module>
<!-- search 2 -->
<module
name="Search"
group="Chapter 9 - Sideview Three">
<param name="search">
source="impl_splunk_gen" user="$user$"
logger="$logger$"
| fillnull value="unknown" network
| top network
</param>
<!-- table -->
<module name="SimpleResultsTable"/>
</module>
</module>
</module>
</module>
</module>
</module>
</module>
</view>
```

This draws a dashboard that is similar to the following screenshot:

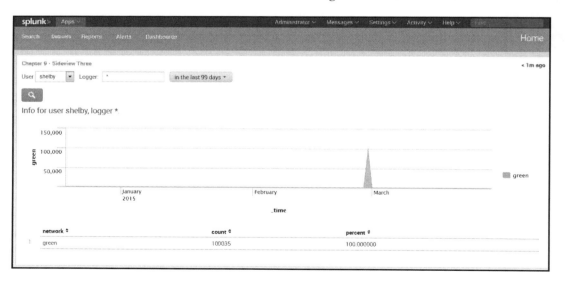

There are quite a few things to cover in this example, so let's step through portions of the XML.

Include SideviewUtils to enable the other `Sideview` modules. In this case, `URLLoader`, `HTML`, `Pulldown`, `Search`, and `TextField` are `Sideview` modules. This is done using the following code:

```
<module layoutPanel="appHeader" name="SideviewUtils"/>
```

Wrap everything in `URLLoader` so that we get values from the URL:

```
<module
name="URLLoader"
layoutPanel="panel_row1_col1"
autoRun="True">
```

Start a search to populate the user dropdown. This query will find all the users who have been active in the last 24 hours:

```
<module name="Search" layoutPanel="panel_row1_col1">
<param name="search">
source="impl_splunk_gen" user user="*"
| top user
</param>
<param name="earliest">-24h</param>
<param name="latest">now</param>
```

Using a query to populate a dropdown can be very expensive, particularly as your data volumes increase. You may need to precalculate these values, either storing the values in a CSV using `outputcsv` and `inputcsv` or using a summary index. For examples of summary indexing and using CSV files for transient data, see `Chapter 9`, *Summary Indexes and CSV Files*.

This module draws the user selector. The menu is filled by the `Search` module, but notice that the value selected is from our URL value:

```
<module name="Pulldown">
<!-- use valueField in SideView 2.0 -->
<param name="searchFieldsToDisplay">
<list>
<param name="value">user</param>
<param name="label">user</param>
</list>
</param>
<param name="name">user</param>
<param name="label">User</param>
<param name="float">left</param>
```

Next is a text field for our logger. This is a Sideview version of `ExtendedFieldSearch`. It will prepopulate using upstream variables:

```
<module name="TextField">
<param name="name">logger</param>
<param name="default">*</param>
<param name="label">Logger:</param>
<param name="float">left</param>
```

The `TimeRangePicker` module honors the earliest and latest values in the URL. Note that `searchWhenChanged` **must be** `True` to work properly in this case. As a rule of thumb, `searchWhenChanged` **should always be** `True`:

```
<module name="TimeRangePicker">
<param name="searchWhenChanged">True</param>
<param name="default">Last 24 hours</param>
```

The `SubmitButton` module kicks off a search when values are changed. `allowSoftSubmit` **allows outer modules to start the query either by choosing a value or by hitting return in a text field:**

```
<module name="SubmitButton">
<param name="allowSoftSubmit">True</param>
```

The following are two `Search` modules, each containing an output module:

```
<module
name="Search"
group="Chapter 9 - Sideview Three">
<param name="search">
source="impl_splunk_gen" user="$user$"
logger="$logger$"
| fillnull value="unknown" network
| timechart count by network
</param>
<!-- JobProgressIndicator -->
<module name="JobProgressIndicator"/>
<!-- chart -->
<module name="HiddenChartFormatter">
<param name="charting.chart">area</param>
<param name="charting.chart.stackMode">
stacked
</param>
<module name="JSChart"/>
</module>
</module>
<!-- search 2 -->
```

```
<module
group="Chapter 9 - Sideview Three"
name="Search">
<param name="search">
source="impl_splunk_gen" user="$user$"
logger="$logger$"
| fillnull value="unknown" network
| top network
</param>
<!-- table -->
<module name="SimpleResultsTable">
<param name="drilldown">row</param>
</module>
```

For greater efficiency, these two searches can be combined into one query and the PostProcess module can be used.

Summary Indexes and CSV Files

9

As the number of events retrieved by a query increases, the performance decreases linearly. Summary indexing allows you to calculate the statistics in advance and then run reports against these roll ups, dramatically increasing performance.

In this chapter, we will cover the following topics:

- Understanding summary indexes
- When to use a summary index
- When not to use a summary index
- Populating summary indexes with saved searches
- Using summary index events in a query
- Using `sistats`, `sitop`, and `sitimechart`
- How latency affects summary queries
- How and when to backfill summary data
- Reducing summary index size
- Calculating top for a large time frame
- Using CSV files to store transient data
- Speeding up queries and backfilling

Understanding summary indexes

A summary index is a place to store events calculated by Splunk. Usually, these events are aggregates of raw events broken up over time, for instance, the number of errors that occurred per hour. By calculating this information on an hourly basis, it is cheap and fast to run a query over a longer period of time, for instance, days, weeks, or months.

A summary index is usually populated from a saved search with summary indexing enabled as an action. This is not the only way, but it is certainly the most common one.

On disk, a summary index is identical to any other Splunk index. The difference is solely the source of data. We create the index through configuration or through the GUI like any other index, and we manage the index size in the same way.

Think of an index like a table, or possibly a tablespace, in a typical SQL database. Indexes are capped by size and/or time, much like a tablespace, but all the data is stored together, much like a table.

Creating a summary index

To create an index, navigate to **Settings** | **Indexes** | **New Index**:

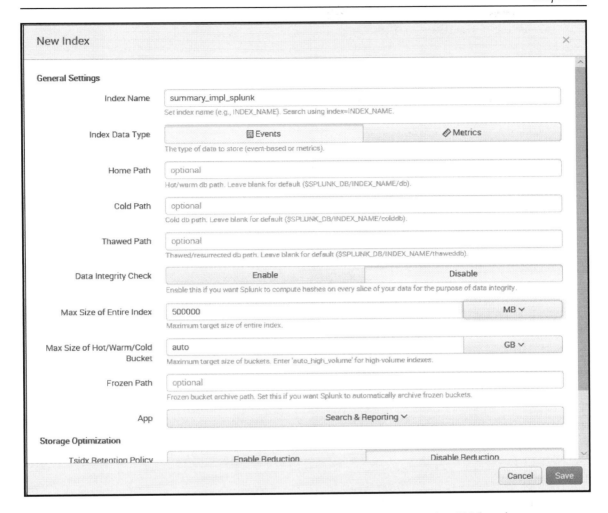

New Index ✕

General Settings

Index Name	summary_impl_splunk

Set index name (e.g., INDEX_NAME). Search using index=INDEX_NAME.

Index Data Type   ☰ Events   ⬦ Metrics

The type of data to store (event-based or metrics).

Home Path	optional

Hot/warm db path. Leave blank for default ($SPLUNK_DB/INDEX_NAME/db).

Cold Path	optional

Cold db path. Leave blank for default ($SPLUNK_DB/INDEX_NAME/colddb).

Thawed Path	optional

Thawed/resurrected db path. Leave blank for default ($SPLUNK_DB/INDEX_NAME/thaweddb).

Data Integrity Check   Enable   Disable

Enable this if you want Splunk to compute hashes on every slice of your data for the purpose of data integrity.

Max Size of Entire Index	500000	MB ⌄

Maximum target size of entire index.

Max Size of Hot/Warm/Cold Bucket	auto	GB ⌄

Maximum target size of buckets. Enter 'auto_high_volume' for high-volume indexes.

Frozen Path	optional

Frozen bucket archive path. Set this if you want Splunk to automatically archive frozen buckets.

App   Search & Reporting ⌄

Storage Optimization

Tsidx Retention Policy   Enable Reduction   Disable Reduction

Cancel   Save

Note: The **New Index** page has changed a bit in version 7.0 but for now, let's simply give our new index a name and accept the default values.

We will discuss these settings under the `indexes.conf` section in `Chapter 10`, *Configuring Splunk*. I like to put the word summary at the beginning of any summary index, but the name does not matter. I would suggest you follow some naming convention that makes sense to you.

Now that we have an index to store events in, let's do something with it.

When to use a summary index

When the question you want to answer requires looking at all or most events for a given source type, the number of events can become huge very quickly. This is what is generally referred to as a *dense search*.

For example, if you want to know how many page views happened on your website, the query to answer this question must inspect every event. Since each query uses a processor, we are essentially timing how fast our disk can retrieve the raw data and how fast a single processor can decompress that data. Doing a little math, we get the following:

1,000,000 hits per day /

10,000 events processed per second =

100 seconds

If we use multiple indexers, or possibly buy much faster disks, we can cut this time, but only linearly. For instance, if the data is evenly split across four indexers, without changing disks, this query will take roughly 25 seconds.

If we use summary indexing, we should be able to improve our time dramatically.

Let's assume we have calculated the hit counts per five minutes. Now, doing the math:

24 hours * 60 minutes per hour / 5-minute slices =

288 summary events

If we then use those summary events in a query, the math looks like the following:

288 summary events /

10,000 events processed per second =

.0288 seconds

This is a significant increase in performance. In reality, we would probably store more than 288 events. For instance, let's say we want to count the events by their HTTP response code. Assuming that there are 10 different status codes we see on a regular basis, we have:

*24 hours * 60 minutes per hour / 5-minute slices * 10 codes = 2880 events*

The math then looks as follows:

2,880 summary events /

10,000 events processed per second =

.288 seconds

That's still a significant improvement over 100 seconds.

When to not use a summary index

There are several cases where summary indexes are either inappropriate or inefficient. Consider the following:

- **When you need to see the original events**: In most cases, summary indexes are used to store aggregate values. A summary index could be used to store a separate copy of events, but this is not usually the case. The more events you have in your summary index, the less advantage it has over the original index.
- **When the possible number of categories of data is huge**: For example, if you want to know the top IP addresses seen per day, it may be tempting to simply capture a count of every IP address seen. This can still be a huge amount of data, and may not save you a lot of search time, if any. Likewise, simply storing the top 10 addresses per slice of time may not give an accurate picture over a long period of time. We will discuss this scenario under the *Calculating top for a large time frame* section.
- **When it is impractical to slice the data across sufficient dimensions**: If your data has a large number of dimensions or attributes, and it is useful to slice the data across a large number of these dimensions, then the resulting summary index may not be sufficiently smaller than your original index to bother with.

- **When it is difficult to know the acceptable time slice**: As we set up a few summary indexes, we have to pick the slice of time to which we aggregate. If you think that 1 hour is an acceptable time slice and find out later that you actually need 10 minutes of resolution, it is not the easiest task to recalculate the old data into these 10-minute slices. It is, however, very simple to later change your 10-minute search to 1 hour, as the 10-minute slices should still work for your hourly reports.

Populating summary indexes with saved searches

A search to populate a summary index is much like any other saved search (see `Chapter 3`, *Understanding Search*, for more details on creating saved searches).

The differences are that this search will run periodically, and the results will be stored in the summary index.

So, let's build a simple summary search by following these steps:

1. Start with a search that produces some statistic:

   ```
   source="impl_splunk_gen" | stats count by user
   ```

2. Save this search as **summary - count by user**.
3. Edit the search in **Settings** by navigating to **Settings** | **Searches, reports and alerts** | **summary - count by user**.
4. Set the appropriate times. This is a somewhat complicated discussion. See the *How latency affects summary queries* section discussed later:

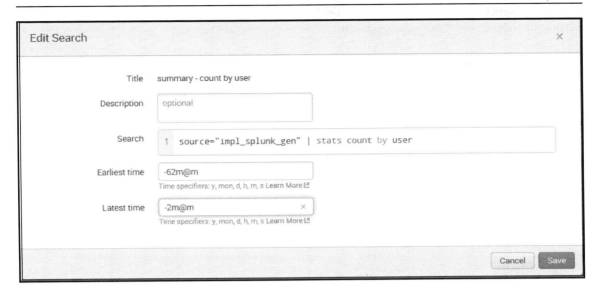

Let's look at the following fields:

- **Search**: `source="impl_splunk_gen" | stats count by user`. This is our query. Later we will use `sistats`, a special summary index version of stats.

You can stipulate *absolute* or *relative* time ranges using time modifiers:

- **Earliest time**: `-62m@m`. It may seem strange that we didn't simply say `-60m@m`, but we need to take latency into account. See the *How latency affects summary queries* section discussed later for more details.
- **Latest time**: `-2m@m`.

Using summary index events in a query

After the query to populate the summary index has run for some time, we can use the results in other queries.

If you're in a hurry or need to report against slices of time before the query was created, you will need to backfill your summary index. See the *How and when to backfill summary data section* for details about calculating the summary values for past events.

First, let's look at what actually goes into the summary index:

```
08/15/2012 10:00:00, search_name="summary - count by user",
search_now=1345046520.000, info_min_time=1345042800.000, info_max_
time=1345046400.000, info_search_time=1345050512.340, count=17,
user=mary
```

Breaking this event down, we have the following:

- `08/15/2012 10:00:00`: This is the time at the beginning of this block of data. This is consistent with how `timechart` and `bucket` work.
- `search_name="summary - count by user"`: This is the name of the search. This is usually the easiest way to find the results you are interested in.
- `search_now ... info_search_time`: These are informational fields about the summary entry, and are generally not useful to users.
- `count=17, user=mary`: The rest of the entry will be whatever fields were produced by the populating query.

There will be one summary event per row produced by the populating query.

Now, let's build a query against this data. To start the query, we need to specify the name of the index and the name of the search:

```
index="summary_impl_splunk" search_name="summary - count by user"
```

On my machine (different data will of course yield different results), this query loads 48 events, as compared to the 22,477 original events.

Using `stats`, we can quickly find the statistics by `user`:

```
index="summary_impl_splunk" | stats sum(count) count by user
```

This produces a very simple table, similar to the following screenshot:

user ⬍	sum(count) ⬍	count ⬍
Bobby	12113	16
bob	11845	16
extrauser	3612	16
jacky	12158	16
linda	12057	16
mary	24092	16

We are calculating the **sum(count)** and **count** in this query, which you might expect to produce the same number, but they are doing very different things:

- **sum(count)**: If we look back at our raw event, **count** contains the number of times that a user appeared in that slice of time. We are storing the raw value in this count field. See the *Using sistats, sitop, and sitimechart* section for a completely different approach.
- **count**: This actually represents the number of events in the summary index.

The generator that is producing these events is not very random, so all users produce at least one event per hour. Producing a `timechart` is no more complicated:

```
index="summary_impl_splunk" | timechart span=1h sum(count) by user
```

This produces our graph, as shown in the following screenshot:

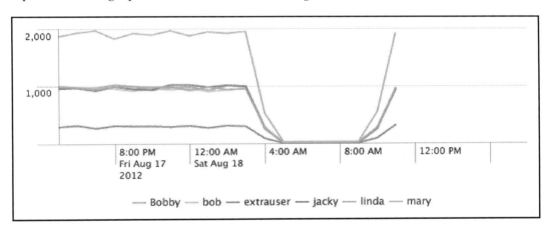

The main thing to remember here is that we cannot make a graph more detailed than the schedule of our populating query. In this case, the populating query uses a span of 1 hour. An hour is granular enough for most daily reports, and certainly fine for weekly or monthly reports, but it may not be granular enough for an operations dashboard.

The following are a few other interesting queries you can make with this simple set of data:

```
index="summary_impl_splunk" search_name="summary - count by user"
| stats avg(count) as "Average events per hour"
```

The previous code snippet tells us the average number of events per slice of time, which we know is an hour. Adding `bucket` and another `stats` command, we can calculate for a custom period of time, as follows:

```
index="summary_impl_splunk" search_name="summary - count by user"
| bucket span=4h _time
| stats sum(count) as count by _time
| stats avg(count) as "Average events per 4 hours"
```

This query would give us the user with the maximum number of events in a given hour, and the hour that it occurred in:

```
index="summary_impl_splunk" search_name="summary - count by user"
| stats first(_time) as _time max(count) as max by user
| sort -max
| head 1
| rename max as "Maximum events per hour"
```

Using sistats, sitop, and sitimechart

First, let's define some new functions:

- `sistats`: `sistats` is the summary indexing version of the `stats` command, which calculates the aggregate statistics over the dataset
- `sitop`: This is the summary indexing version of the `top` command, which returns the most frequent value of a field or a combination of fields
- `sitimechart`: `sitimechart` is the summary indexing version of the `timechart` command, which creates a time series chart visualization with the corresponding table of statistics

So far, we have used the `stats` command to populate our summary index. While this works very well, the `si*` variants have a couple of advantages:

- The remaining portion of the query does not have to be rewritten. For instance, `stats count` still works as if you were counting the raw events.
- The `stats` functions that require more data than what happened in that slice of time, will still work. For example, if your time slices each represent an hour, it is not possible to calculate the average value for a day using nothing but the average of each hour. The `sistats` function keeps enough information to make this work.

There are also a few fairly serious disadvantages to be aware of:

- The query using the summary index must use a subset of the functions, and split fields that were in the original populating query. If the subsequent query strays from what is in the original `sistats` data, the results may be unexpected and difficult to debug. For example, see the following code:

```
source="impl_splunk_gen"
| sitimechart span=1h avg(req_time) by user
| stats avg(req_time)
```

- The following code returns unpredictable and wildly incorrect values:

```
source="impl_splunk_gen"
| sitimechart span=1h avg(req_time) by user
| stats max(req_time)
```

Notice that `avg` went into `sistats`, but we tried to calculate `max` from the results.

- Using **distinct count (dc)** with `sistats` can produce huge events. This happens because to accurately determine unique values over slices of time, all original values must be kept. One common use case is to find the top IP addresses that hit a public-facing server. See the *Calculating top for a large time frame* section for alternate approaches to this problem.
- The contents of the summary index are quite difficult to read as they are not meant to be used by humans.

To see how all this works, let's build a few queries. We start with a simple stats query as follows:

```
sourcetype=impl_splunk_gen
| stats count max(req_time) avg(req_time) min(req_time) by user
```

This produces results like you would expect:

user	count	max(req_time)	avg(req_time)	min(req_time)
jarde	100036	9999	9499.569375	9000
lou	99969	6999	6499.373436	6000
mary	99972	999	499.552025	0
nanette	99976	3999	3499.401536	3000
natile	99980	8999	8499.562032	8000
paige	99971	5999	5499.620750	5000
ronnie	100046	2999	2499.403714	2000
shelby	100031	4999	4499.556048	4000
steve	99975	1999	1499.321360	1000
tuck	100044	7999	7499.468754	7000

Now, we can save this and send it straight to the summary index, but the results are not terribly nice to use, and the average of the average would not be accurate.

On the other hand, we can use the `sistats` variant as follows:

```
sourcetype=impl_splunk_gen
| sistats count max(req_time) avg(req_time) min(req_time) by user
```

The results have a lot of extra information which may be difficult to understand, as shown in the following screenshot:

	psrsvd_ct_req_time ⇕	psrsvd_gc ⇕	psrsvd_nc_req_time ⇕	psrsvd_nn_req_time ⇕	psrsvd_nx_req_time ⇕	psrsvd
1	8609	11459	8609	1	12239	52832
2	8531	11294	8531	2	12237	52104
3	3464	3464	3464	6	12239	21229
4	8674	11473	8674	1	12236	53281
5	8505	11375	8505	2	12237	51941
6	17282	23098	17282	1	12239	10597

Splunk knows how to deal with these results, and can use them in combination with the stats functions as if they were the original results. You can see how `sistats` and `stats` work together by chaining them together, as follows:

```
sourcetype=impl_splunk_gen
| sistats
count max(req_time) avg(req_time) min(req_time)
by user
| stats count max(req_time) avg(req_time) min(req_time) by user
```

Even though the `stats` function is not receiving the original events, it knows how to work with these `sistats` summary events. We are presented with exactly the same results as the original query, as shown in the following screenshot:

jarde	100036	9999	9499.569375	9000
lou	99969	6999	6499.373436	6000
mary	99972	999	499.552025	0
nanette	99976	3999	3499.401536	3000
natile	99980	8999	8499.562032	8000
paige	99971	5999	5499.620750	5000
ronnie	100046	2999	2499.403714	2000
shelby	100031	4999	4499.556048	4000
steve	99975	1999	1499.321360	1000
tuck	100044	7999	7499.468754	7000

`sitop` and `sitimechart` work in the same fashion.

Let's step through the procedure to *set up summary searches* as follows:

1. Save the query using `sistats`:

   ```
   sourcetype=impl_splunk_gen
   | sistats count max(req_time) avg(req_time) min(req_time) by
   user
   ```

2. Set the times accordingly, as we saw previously in the *Populating summary indexes with saved searches* section. See the *How latency affects summary queries* section for more information.

3. Build a query that queries the summary index, as we saw previously in the *Using summary index events in a query* section. Assuming that we saved this query as a testing `sistats`, the query would be:

```
index="summary_impl_splunk"
search_name="testing sistats".
```

4. Use the original `stats` function against the results, as follows:

```
index="summary_impl_splunk" search_name="testing sistats"
| stats count max(req_time) avg(req_time) min(req_time) by
user
```

This should produce exactly the same results as the original query.

The `si*` variants still seem somewhat magical to me, but they work so well that it is in your own best interest to dive in and trust the magic. Be very sure that your functions and fields are a subset of the original.

How latency affects summary queries

Latency is the difference between the time assigned to an event (usually parsed from the text) and the time it was written to the index. These times are captured in `_time` and `_indextime`, respectively.

This query will show us what our latency is:

```
sourcetype=impl_splunk_gen
| eval latency = _indextime - _time
| stats min(latency) avg(latency) max(latency)
```

In my case, these statistics look as shown in the following screenshot:

min(latency) ↕	avg(latency) ↕	max(latency) ↕
-0.465	31.603530	72.390

The latency in this case is exaggerated, because the script behind `impl_splunk_gen` is creating events in chunks. In most production Splunk instances, the latency is just a few seconds. If there is any slowdown, perhaps because of network issues, the latency may increase dramatically, and so it should be accounted for.

This query will produce a table showing the time for every event:

```
sourcetype=impl_splunk_gen
| eval latency = _indextime - _time
| eval time=strftime(_time,"%Y-%m-%d %H:%M:%S.%3N")
| eval indextime=strftime(_indextime,"%Y-%m-%d %H:%M:%S.%3N")
| table time indextime latency
```

The previous query produces the following table:

	time ⇕	indextime ⇕	latency ⇕
51	2012-08-22 21:38:11.107	2012-08-22 21:38:33.000	21.893
52	2012-08-22 21:38:11.011	2012-08-22 21:38:33.000	21.989
53	2012-08-22 21:38:10.546	2012-08-22 21:38:33.000	22.454
54	2012-08-22 21:38:10.433	2012-08-22 21:38:33.000	22.567
55	2012-08-22 21:38:10.419	2012-08-22 21:38:33.000	22.581
56	2012-08-22 21:38:09.588	2012-08-22 21:38:33.000	23.412
57	2012-08-22 21:38:08.955	2012-08-22 21:38:33.000	24.045
58	2012-08-22 21:38:08.502	2012-08-22 21:38:33.000	24.498
59	2012-08-22 21:38:07.867	2012-08-22 21:38:33.000	25.133

To deal with this latency, you should add enough delay in your query that populates the summary index. The following are a few examples:

```
Confidence Time slice Earliest Latest cron
2 minutes 1 hour -62m@m -2m@m 2 * * * *
15 minutes 1 hour -1h@h -0h@h 15 * * * *
5 minutes 5 minutes -10m@m -5m@m */5 * * * *
1 hour 15 minutes -75m@m -60m@m */15 * * * *
1 hour 24 hours -1d@d -0d@d 0 1 * * *
```

Sometimes you have no idea when your logs will be indexed as they are delivered in batches on unreliable networks.

This is what I call *unpredictable latency*. For one possible solution, take a look at the app `indextime search` available at `http://splunkbase.com`.

How and when to backfill summary data

If you are building reports against summary data, you need enough time represented in your summary index. If your report represents only a day or two, then you can probably just wait for the summary to have enough information. If you need the report to work sooner rather than later, or if the time frame is longer, then you can backfill your summary index.

Using fill_summary_index.py to backfill

The `fill_summary_index.py` script allows you to backfill the summary index for any time period that you like. It does this by running the saved searches which you have defined to populate your summary indexes, but only for the time periods you specify.

To use the script, follow the given procedure:

1. Create your scheduled search, as detailed previously in the *Populating summary indexes with saved searches* section.
2. Log in to the shell on your Splunk instance. If you are running a distributed environment, log in to the search head.
3. Change directories to the Splunk `bin` directory:

   cd $SPLUNK_HOME/bin

   `$SPLUNK_HOME` is the root of your Splunk installation. The default installation directory is `/opt/splunk` on Unix operating systems and `c:ProgramFilesSplunk` on Windows.

4. Run the `fill_summary_index` command. An example from inside the script is as follows:

   ```
   ./splunk cmd python fill_summary_index.py -app is_app_one -name
   "summary - count by user" -et -30d -lt now -j 8 -dedup true -auth
   admin:changeme
   ```

Let's break down these arguments in the following manner:

- `./splunk cmd`: This essentially sets the environment variables so that whatever runs next has the appropriate settings to find the Splunk libraries and included Python modules.

- `python fill_summary_index.py`: This runs the script itself using the Python executable and the modules included with the Splunk distribution.
- `-app is_app_one`: This is the name of the app that contains the summary populating queries in question.
- `-name "summary - count by user"`: This is the name of the query to run. `*` will run all summary queries contained in the app specified.
- `-et -30d`: This is the earliest time to consider. The appropriate times are determined and used to populate the summary index.
- `-lt now`: This is the latest time to consider.
- `-j 8`: This determines how many queries to run simultaneously.
- `-dedup true`: This is used to determine whether there are no results already for each slice of time. Without this flag, you could end up with duplicate entries in your summary index. For some statistics, this won't matter, but for most it would.

  If you are concerned that you have summary data that is incomplete—perhaps because summary events were produced while an indexer was unavailable—you should investigate the `delete` command to remove these events first. The `delete` command is not efficient and should be used sparingly, if at all.

- `-auth admin:changeme`: The `auth` to run the query (the admin default or if they were changed, the new credentials).

- When you run this script, it will run the query with the appropriate times as if the query had been run at those times in the past. This can be a very slow process, particularly if the number of slices is large. For instance, slices every 5 minutes for a month would be *30 * 24 * (60/5) = 8,640 queries*.

Using collect to produce custom summary indexes

If the number of events destined for your summary index could be represented in a single report, we can use the `collect` function to create our own summary index entries directly. This has the advantage that we can build our index in one shot. That could be much faster than running the `backfill` script, which must run one search per slice of time. For instance, if you want to calculate 15-minute slices over a month, the script will fire off 2,880 queries.

If you dig into the code that actually produces summary indexes, you will find that it uses the `collect` command to store events into the specified index. The `collect` command is available to us, and with a little knowledge, we can use it directly.

First, we need to build a query that slices our data by buckets of time as follows:

```
source="impl_splunk_gen"
| bucket span=1h _time
| stats count by _time user
```

This gives us a simple table, as shown in the following screenshot:

	_time ⬍	user ⬍	count ⬍
1	8/22/12 8:00:00.000 PM	Bobby	549
2	8/22/12 8:00:00.000 PM	bob	565
3	8/22/12 8:00:00.000 PM	extrauser	168
4	8/22/12 8:00:00.000 PM	jacky	551
5	8/22/12 8:00:00.000 PM	linda	588
6	8/22/12 8:00:00.000 PM	mary	1115
7	8/22/12 9:00:00.000 PM	Bobby	960
8	8/22/12 9:00:00.000 PM	bob	979
9	8/22/12 9:00:00.000 PM	extrauser	294
10	8/22/12 9:00:00.000 PM	jacky	942

Notice that there is a row per slice of time, and for each user that produced events during that slice of time.

Let's add a few more fields to make it more interesting:

```
source="impl_splunk_gen"
| bucket span=1h _time
| eval error=if(loglevel="ERROR",1,0)
| stats count avg(req_time) dc(ip) sum(error) by _time user
```

This gives us the table shown in the following screenshot:

_time ⇕	user ⇕	count ⇕	avg(req_time) ⇕	dc(ip) ⇕	sum(error) ⇕
1	8/22/12 8:00:00.000 PM	Bobby	549	5918.018913	6	144
2	8/22/12 8:00:00.000 PM	bob	565	6002.448357	6	117
3	8/22/12 8:00:00.000 PM	extrauser	168	6125.517857	6	40
4	8/22/12 8:00:00.000 PM	jacky	551	6005.267123	6	143
5	8/22/12 8:00:00.000 PM	linda	588	6215.339326	6	130
6	8/22/12 8:00:00.000 PM	mary	1115	6039.061078	6	292
7	8/22/12 9:00:00.000 PM	Bobby	960	6144.366255	6	227
8	8/22/12 9:00:00.000 PM	bob	979	6413.421622	6	229
9	8/22/12 9:00:00.000 PM	extrauser	294	6129.421769	6	88
10	8/22/12 9:00:00.000 PM	jacky	942	6115.462518	6	227

Now, to get ready for our summary index, we switch to `sistats` and add a `search_name` field as the saved search would. Use `testmode` to make sure that everything is working as expected, in the following manner:

```
source="impl_splunk_gen"
| bucket span=1h _time
| eval error=if(loglevel="ERROR",1,0)
| sistats count avg(req_time) dc(ip) sum(error) by _time user
| eval search_name="summary - user stats"
| collect index=summary_impl_splunk testmode=true
```

The results of this query show us what will actually be written to the summary index, but as this is not designed for humans, let's simply test the round trip by adding the original stats statement at the end, as follows:

```
source="impl_splunk_gen"
| bucket span=1h _time
| eval error=if(loglevel="ERROR",1,0)
| sistats count avg(req_time) dc(ip) sum(error) by _time user
| eval search_name="summary - hourly user stats - collect test"
| collect index=summary_impl_splunk testmode=true
| stats count avg(req_time) dc(ip) sum(error) by _time user
```

If we have done everything correctly, the results should be identical to the original table:

	_time ⬍	user ⬍	count ⬍	avg(req_time) ⬍	dc(ip) ⬍	sum(error) ⬍
1	8/22/12 8:00:00.000 PM	Bobby	549	5918.018913	6	144
2	8/22/12 8:00:00.000 PM	bob	565	6002.448357	6	117
3	8/22/12 8:00:00.000 PM	extrauser	168	6125.517857	6	40
4	8/22/12 8:00:00.000 PM	jacky	551	6005.267123	6	143
5	8/22/12 8:00:00.000 PM	linda	588	6215.339326	6	130
6	8/22/12 8:00:00.000 PM	mary	1115	6039.061078	6	292
7	8/22/12 9:00:00.000 PM	Bobby	960	6144.366255	6	227
8	8/22/12 9:00:00.000 PM	bob	979	6413.421622	6	229
9	8/22/12 9:00:00.000 PM	extrauser	294	6129.421769	6	88
10	8/22/12 9:00:00.000 PM	jacky	942	6115.462518	6	227

To actually run this query, we simply remove `testmode` from `collect`, as follows:

```
source="impl_splunk_gen"
| bucket span=1h _time
| eval error=if(loglevel="ERROR",1,0)
| sistats count avg(req_time) dc(ip) sum(error) by _time user
| eval search_name="summary - user stats"
| collect index=summary_impl_splunk
```

Beware that you will end up with duplicate values if you use the `collect` command over a time frame that already has results in the summary index. Either use a custom time frame to ensure that you do not produce duplicates, or investigate the `delete` command, which as mentioned earlier, is not efficient and should be avoided if possible.

No results will be available until the query is complete and the file created behind the scenes is indexed. On my installation, on querying 1 month of data, the query inspected 2.2 million events in 173 seconds, producing 2,619 summary events.

Let's use the summary data now:

```
index=summary_impl_splunk
search_name="summary - hourly user stats - collect test"
| timechart sum(error) by user
```

This will give us a neat graph, as shown in the following screenshot:

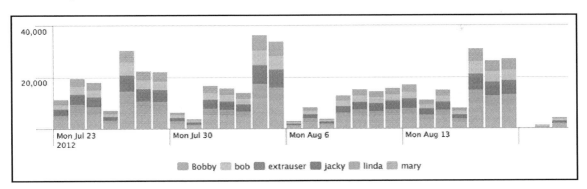

Because this is created from the summary, instead of three minutes, this query completes in around 1.5 seconds.

In this specific case, using `collect` was four times faster than using the `fill_summary_index.py` script. That said, it is much easier to make a mistake, so be very careful. Rehearse with collect `testmode=true` and a trailing `stats` or `timechart` command.

Reducing summary index size

If the saved search populating a summary index produces too many results, the summary index is less effective at speeding up searches. This usually occurs because one or more of the fields used for grouping has more unique values than expected.

One common example of a field that can have many unique values is the URL in a web access log. The number of URL values might increase in instances where:

- The URL contains a session ID
- The URL contains search terms
- Hackers are throwing URLs at your site trying to break in
- Your security team runs tools looking for vulnerabilities

On top of this, multiple URLs can represent exactly the same resource, as follows:

- `/home/index.html`
- `/home/`
- `/home/index.html?a=b`
- `/home/?a=b`

We will cover a few approaches to flatten these values. These are just examples and ideas, and your particular case may require a different approach.

Using eval and rex to define grouping fields

One way to tackle this problem is to make up a new field from the URL using `rex`.

Perhaps you only really care about the hits by directories. We can accomplish this with `rex`, or if needed, multiple `rex` statements.

Looking at the fictional source type `impl_splunk_web`, we see results that look like the following:

```
2012-08-25T20:18:01 user=bobby GET /products/x/?q=10471480 uid=Mzg2NDc0OA
2012-08-25T20:18:03 user=user3 GET /bar?q=923891 uid=MjY1NDI5MA
2012-08-25T20:18:05 user=user3 GET /products/index.html?q=9029891
uid=MjY1NDI5MA
2012-08-25T20:18:08 user=user2 GET /about/?q=9376559 uid=MzA4MTc5OA
```

URLs are tricky, as they might or might not contain certain parts of the URL. For instance, the URL may or may not have a query string, a page, or a trailing slash. To deal with this, instead of trying to make an all-encompassing regular expression, we will take advantage of the behavior of `rex`, which is used to make no changes to the event if the pattern does not match.

Consider the following query:

```
sourcetype="impl_splunk_web"
| rex "s[A-Z]+s(?P<url>.*?)s"
| rex field=url "(?P<url>.*)?"
| rex field=url "(?P<url>.*/)"
| stats count by url
```

In our case, this will produce the following report:

url ⬍	count ⬍
1	/	5741
2	/about/	2822
3	/contact/	2847
4	/products/	5653
5	/products/x/	5637
6	/products/y/	2786

Stepping through these `rex` statements, we have:

- `rex "s[A-Z]+s(?P<url>.*?)s"`: This pattern matches a space followed by uppercase letters, followed by a space, and then captures all characters until a space into the field `url`. The field `attribute` is not defined, so the `rex` statement matches against the `_raw` field. The values extracted look like the following:
    - `/products/x/?q=10471480`
    - `/bar?q=923891`
    - `/products/index.html?q=9029891`
    - `/about/?q=9376559`

- `rex field=url "(?P<url>.*)?"`: Searching the field `url`, this pattern matches all characters until a question mark. If the pattern matches, the result replaces the contents of the `url` field. If the pattern doesn't match, `url` stays the same. The values of `url` will now be as follows:
    - `/products/x/`
    - `/bar`
    - `/products/index.html`
    - `/about/`

- `rex field=url "(?P<url>.*/)"`: Once again, while searching the field `url`, this pattern matches all characters until, and including, the last slash. The values of `url` are then as follows:
    - `/products/x/`
    - `/`
    - `/products/`
    - `/about/`

This should effectively reduce the number of possible URLs and hopefully make our summary index more useful and efficient. It may be that you only want to capture up to three levels of depth. You can accomplish that with the following rex statement:

```
rex field=url "(?P<url>/(?:[^/]/){,3})"
```

The possibilities are endless. Be sure to test as much data as you can when building your summary indexes.

Using a lookup with wildcards

Splunk lookups also support wildcards, which we can use in this case.

One advantage is that we can define arbitrary fields for grouping, independent of the values of url.

For a lookup wildcard to work, first we need to set up our url field and the lookup:

1. Extract the url field. The rex pattern we used before should work:

    s[AZ]+s(?P<url>.*?)s. See Chapter 3, *Tables, Charts, and Fields*, for detailed instructions on setting up a field extraction. Don't forget to set permissions on the extraction.

2. Create our lookup file. Let's call the lookup file flatten_summary_lookup.csv. Use the following contents for our example log:

    ```
    url,section
    /about/*,about
    /contact/*,contact
    /*/*,unknown_non_root
    /*,root
    *,nomatch
    ```

    If you create your lookup file in Excel on a Mac, be sure to save the file using the Windows comma-separated values (.csv) format.

3. Upload the lookup table file and create our lookup definition and automatic lookup. See the *Using lookups to enrich the data section* in Chapter 6, *Extending Search*, for detailed instructions. The automatic lookup definition should look like the following screenshot (the value of *Name* doesn't matter):

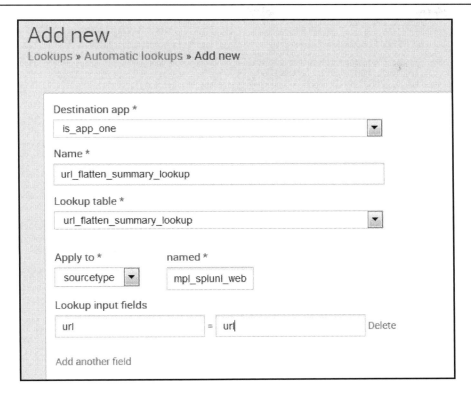

4. Set the permissions on all the objects. I usually opt for **All Apps** for **Lookup table** files and **Lookup definitions**, and **This app** only for **Automatic lookups**. See Chapter 6, *Extending Search*, for details.

5. Edit `transforms.conf`. In this version (actually as of Splunk 4.3), not all the features of lookups can be defined through the admin interface. To access these features, the configuration files that actually drive Splunk must be edited manually.

We will cover configuration files in greater detail in Chapter 10, *Configuring Splunk*, but for now, let's add two lines to one file and move on:

1. Edit `$SPLUNK_HOME/etc/apps/is_app_one/local/transforms.conf`. The name of the directory `is_app_one` may be different depending on what app was active when you created your lookup definition. If you can't find this file, check your permissions and the app column in the admin interface.

2. You should see these two lines, or something similar, depending on what you
    named your **Lookup table** file and **Lookup definition** instances:

    ```
    [flatten_summary_lookup]
    filename = flatten_summary_lookup.csv
    ```

    If you do not see these lines in this file, check your permissions.

3. Add two more lines below `filename`:

    ```
    match_type = WILDCARD(url)
    max_matches = 1
    ```

    These two lines effectively say the following:

*   `match_type = WILDCARD(url)`: When evaluating the field URL, honor
    wildcard characters. Without this setting, matches are always exact.
*   `max_matches = 1`: Stop searching after the first match. By default, up to 10
    matches are allowed. We want to match only the first line that matches,
    effectively using the lookup like a case statement.

If everything is wired up properly, we should now be able to run the search:

```
sourcetype=impl_splunk_web | stats count by section
```

This should give us the following simple report:

section ⇕	count ⇕
about	2822
contact	2847
root	5741
unknown_non_root	14076

To see in greater detail what is really going on, let's try the following search:

```
sourcetype=impl_splunk_web
| rex field=url "(?P<url>.*)?"
| stats count by section url
```

The `rex` statement is included to remove the query string from the value of `url` created by our extracted field. This gives us the following report:

section ⬍	url ⬍	count ⬍
about	/about/	2822
contact	/contact/	2847
root	/bar	2847
root	/foo	2894
unknown_non_root	/products/	5653
unknown_non_root	/products/x/	5637
unknown_non_root	/products/y/	2786

Looking back at our lookup file, our matches appear to be as follows:

```
url pattern section
/about/ /about/* about
/contact/ /contact/* contact
/bar /* root
/foo /* root
/products/ /*/* unknown_non_root
/products/x/ /*/* unknown_non_root
/products/y/ /*/* unknown_non_root
```

If you read the lookup file from top to bottom, the first pattern that matches wins.

Using event types to group results

Another approach for grouping results to reduce the summary index size would be to use event types in creative ways. For a refresher on event types, see `Chapter 6`, *Extending Search*.

This approach has the following advantages:

- All definitions are defined through the web interface
- It is possible to create arbitrarily complex definitions
- You can easily search for only those events that have defined section names
- You can place events in multiple groups if desired

The disadvantages to this approach are as follows:

- This is a non-obvious approach.
- It is inconvenient to not place events in multiple groups if more than one event type matches. For instance, if you want a page to match /product/x/* but not /product/*, it is not convenient to do so.

The following is the procedure to create these event types:

1. For each section, create an event type, as follows:

2. Set the permissions to either **This app only** or **Global**, depending on the scope.

3. Repeat this for each section that you want to summarize. The clone link in the manager makes this process much faster.

With our event types in place, we can now build queries. The `Tag` value that we included means we can search easily for only those events that match a section, like the following:

```
tag::eventtype="summary_url" | top eventtype
```

The previous code returns a table, as shown in the following screenshot:

	eventtype ‡	count ‡	percent ‡
1	bogus	19745	100.000000
2	url_products	14076	71.288934
3	url_contact	2847	14.418840
4	url_about	2822	14.292226

Our results contain the new event types that we created, along with an unwanted event type, **bogus**. Remember that all event type definitions that match an event are attached. This is very powerful, but sometimes is not what you expect. The **bogus** event type definition is `*`, which means it matches everything. The **bogus** event type was added purely to illustrate the point and has no practical use.

Let's create a new field from our summary event type name and then aggregate based on the new field:

```
tag::eventtype="summary_url"
| rex field=eventtype "url_(?P<section>.*)"
| stats count by section
```

The previous code gives us the results that we are looking for, as shown in the following screenshot:

	section ‡	count ‡
1	about	2822
2	contact	2847
3	products	14076

This search finds only the events that have defined event types, which may be what you want. To group all other results into an other group, we instead need to search for all events in the following manner:

```
sourcetype=impl_splunk_web
| rex field=eventtype "url_(?P<section>.*)"
| fillnull value="other" section
| stats count by section
```

The previous code then produces the following report:

section ‡	count ‡
1 about	2822
2 contact	2847
3 other	5741
4 products	14076

Hopefully, these examples will be food for thought when it comes to collapsing your results into more efficient summary results.

Calculating top for a large time frame

One common problem is to find the top contributors out of a huge set of unique values. For instance, if you want to know what IP addresses are using the most bandwidth in a given day or week, you may have to keep a track of the total of request sizes across millions of unique hosts to definitively answer this question. When using summary indexes, this means storing millions of events in the summary index, quickly defeating the purpose of summary indexes.

Just to illustrate, let's look at a simple set of data:

```
Time 1.1.1.1 2.2.2.2 3.3.3.3 4.4.4.4 5.5.5.5 6.6.6.6
12:00 99 100 100 100
13:00 99 100 100 100
14:00 99 100 101 100
15:00 99 99 100 100
16:00 99 100 100 100
total 495 300 299 401 400 100
```

If we only stored the top three IPs per hour, our dataset would look like the following:

```
Time 1.1.1.1 2.2.2.2 3.3.3.3 4.4.4.4 5.5.5.5 6.6.6.6
12:00 100 100 100
13:00 100 100 100
14:00 100 101 100
15:00 99 100 100
16:00 100 100 100
total 300 299 401 400 100
```

According to this dataset, our top three IP addresses are 4.4.4.4, 5.5.5.5, and 2.2.2.2. The actual largest value was for 1.1.1.1, but it was missed because it was never in the top three.

To tackle this problem, we need to keep track of more data points for each slice of time. But how many?

Using our generator data, let's count a random number and see what kind of results we see. In my dataset, it is the following query:

```
source="impl_splunk_gen" | top req_time
```

When run over a week, this query gives me the following results:

	req_time ‡	count ‡	percent ‡
1	10	402	0.072102
2	34	383	0.068694
3	15	377	0.067618
4	118	374	0.067080
5	26	373	0.066901
6	21	370	0.066362
7	18	366	0.065645
8	46	365	0.065466
9	140	365	0.065466
10	291	363	0.065107

How many unique values were there? The following query will tell us that:

```
source="impl_splunk_gen" | stats dc(req_time)
```

This tells us there are (based on my data) 12,239 unique values of `req_time`. How many different values are there per hour? The following query will calculate the average unique values per hour:

```
source="impl_splunk_gen"
| bucket span=1h _time
| stats dc(req_time) as dc by _time
| stats avg(dc)
```

This tells us that each hour there are an average of (again, given my data) 3,367 unique values of `req_time`.

So, if we stored every count of every `req_time` for a week, we will store *3,367 * 24 * 7 = 565,656 values*. How many values would we have to store per hour to get the same answer that we received before?

The following is a query that attempts to answer this question:

```
source="impl_splunk_gen"
| bucket span=1h _time
| stats count by _time req_time
| sort 0 _time -count
| streamstats count as place by _time
| where place<50
| stats sum(count) as count by req_time
| sort 0 -count
| head 10
```

Breaking this query down, we have:

- `source="impl_splunk_gen"`: This finds the events.
- `| bucket span=1h _time`: This floors our `_time` field to the beginning of the hour. We will use this to simulate hourly summary queries.
- `| stats count by _time req_time`: This generates a `count` per `req_time` per hour.
- `| sort 0 _time -count`: This sorts and keeps all events (that's what 0 means), first ascending by `_time` and then descending by `count`.
- `| streamstats count as place by _time`: This loops over the events, incrementing `place`, and starting the count over when `_time` changes. Remember that we flattened `_time` to the beginning of each hour.
- `| where place<50`: This keeps the first 50 events per hour. These will be the largest 50 values of `count` per hour, since we sorted descending by `count`.

- | `stats sum(count) as count by req_time`: This adds up what we have left across all hours.
- | `sort 0 -count`: This sorts the events in descending order by `count`.
- | `head 10`: This shows the first 10 results.

How did we do? Keeping the top 50 results per hour, my results look as shown in the following screenshot:

	req_time ⬍	count ▾
1	10	139
2	257	125
3	101	109
4	103	109
5	140	107
6	46	107
7	15	98
8	21	98
9	24	97
10	211	96

That really isn't close. Let's try this again. We'll try where `place<1000`. This gives us the following results:

	req_time ⬍	count ▾
1	10	401
2	34	367
3	15	361
4	26	356
5	101	354
6	118	351
7	18	350
8	21	349
9	46	345
10	291	344

That is much closer, but we're still not quite there. After experimenting a little more, `place<2000` was enough to get the expected top 10. This is better than storing 3,367 rows per hour. This may not seem like a big enough difference to bother about, but increase the number of events by 10 or 100, and it can make a huge difference.

To use these results in a summary index, you would simply eliminate the results going into your dataset. One way to accomplish this might be as follows:

```
source="impl_splunk_gen"
| sitop req_time
| streamstats count as place
| where place<2001
```

The first row produced by `sitop` contains the total value.

Another approach, using a combination of `eventstats` and `sistats`, is as follows:

```
source="impl_splunk_gen"
| eventstats count by req_time
| sort 0 -req_time
| streamstats count as place
| where place<2001
| sistats count by req_time
```

Luckily, this is not a terribly common problem, so most of this complexity can be avoided. For another option, see the *Storing a running calculation* section.

Summary index searches

You can use established summary indexes for just about any saved search or report. Using Splunk Web, summary indexing is an alert option for scheduled reports. To leverage a summary index for a saved report:

1. Navigate to **Settings > Searches, Reports, and Alerts**
2. Select the name of your report
3. Under **Schedule and alert**, select **Schedule**
4. Schedule the report (`Splunk.com` states that "*searches that populate summary indexes should run on a fairly frequent basis in order to create statistically accurate final reports*")
5. Under **Alert**, set **Condition** to **Always**

6. Set **Alert mode** to **Once per search**
7. Under summary indexing, select **Enable**
8. Select the name of the summary index that the report populates from the **Select the summary index** list

That's it! Your search or report will now use your summary index.

Using CSV files to store transient data

Sometimes it is useful to store small amounts of data outside a Splunk index. Using the inputcsv and outputcsv commands, we can store tabular data in CSV files on the filesystem.

Pre-populating a dropdown

If a dashboard contains a dynamic dropdown, you must use a search to populate the dropdown. As the amount of data increases, the query to populate the dropdown will run more and more slowly, even from a summary index. We can use a CSV file to store just the information needed, simply adding new values when they occur.

First, we build a query to generate the CSV file. This query should be run over as much data as possible:

```
source="impl_splunk_gen"
| stats count by user
| outputcsv user_list.csv
```

Next, we need a query to run periodically and append any new entries to the file. Schedule this query to run periodically as a saved search:

```
source="impl_splunk_gen"
| stats count by user
| append [inputcsv user_list.csv]
| stats sum(count) as count by user
| outputcsv user_list.csv
```

To then use this in our dashboard, our populating query will simply be:

```
|inputcsv user_list.csv
```

A simple dashboard XML using this query would look like the following:

```
<input type="dropdown" token="sourcetype">
<label>User</label>
<populatingSearch fieldForValue="user" fieldForLabel="user">
|inputcsv user_list.csv
</populatingSearch>
</input>
```

Creating a running calculation for a day

If the number of events per day is in millions or tens of millions, querying all events for that day can be extremely expensive. For that reason, it makes sense to do part of the work in smaller periods of time.

Using a summary index to store these interim values can sometimes be an overkill if those values are not needed for long. In the *Calculating top for a large time frame* section, we ended up storing thousands of values every few minutes. If we simply want to know the top 10 per day, this might be seen as a waste. To cut down on the noise in our summary index, we can use a CSV as cheap interim storage.

The steps are essentially to:

1. Periodically query recent data and update the CSV
2. Capture top values in summary at the end of the day
3. Empty the CSV file

Our periodic query looks like the following:

```
source="impl_splunk_gen"
| stats count by req_time
| append [inputcsv top_req_time.csv]
| stats sum(count) as count by req_time
| sort 10000 -count
| outputcsv top_req_time.csv
```

Let's break down the query line by line:

- `source="impl_splunk_gen"`: This is the query to find the events for this slice of time.
- `| stats count by req_time`: This helps calculate the count by `req_time`.
- `| append [inputcsv top_req_time.csv]`: This loads the results generated so far from the CSV file, and adds the events to the end of our current results.
- `| stats sum(count) as count by req_time`: This uses `stats` to combine the results from our current time slice and the previous results.
- `| sort 10000 -count`: This sorts the results descending by `count`. The second term, `10000`, specifies that we want to keep the first 10,000 results.
- `| outputcsv top_req_time.csv`: This overwrites the CSV file.

Schedule the query to run periodically, perhaps every 15 minutes. Follow the same rules about latency as discussed in the *How latency affects summary queries* section.

When the rollup is expected, perhaps each night at midnight, schedule two more queries a few minutes apart, as follows:

- `| inputcsv top_req_time.csv | head 100`: Save this as a query adding to a summary index, as in the *Populating summary indexes with saved searches* section
- `| stats count |outputcsv top_req_time.csv`: This query will simply overwrite the CSV file with a single line

10
Configuring Splunk

Everything that controls Splunk lives in its configuration files, sitting in the filesystem of each instance of Splunk. These files are unencrypted, easily readable, and easily editable. Almost all of the work that we have done so far has been accomplished through the web interface, but everything actually ends up in these configuration files.

While the web interface does a lot, there are many options that are not represented in the admin interface. There are also some things that are simply easier to accomplish by editing the files directly.

In this chapter, we will cover the following topics:

- Locating configuration files
- Merging configurations
- Debugging configurations
- Common configurations and their parameters

Locating Splunk configuration files

Splunk's configuration files live in `$SPLUNK_HOME/etc`. This is reminiscent of Unix's `/etc` directory but is instead contained within Splunk's directory structure.

This has the advantage that the files don't have to be owned by root. In fact, the entire Splunk installation can run as an unprivileged user (assuming you don't need to open a port below `1024` or read files only readable by another user).

The directories that contain configurations are as follows:

- `$SPLUNK_HOME/etc/system/default`: These are the default configuration files that ship with Splunk. Never edit these files as they will be overwritten each time you upgrade.
- `$SPLUNK_HOME/etc/system/local`: This is the location of the global configuration overrides specific to this host. There are very few configurations that need to live here—most configurations that do live here are created by Splunk itself. In almost all cases, you should make your configuration files inside an app.
- `$SPLUNK_HOME/etc/apps/$app_name/default`: This is the proper location for configurations in an app that will be shared either through Splunkbase or otherwise.
- `$SPLUNK_HOME/etc/apps/$app_name/local`: This is where most configurations should live and where all non-private configurations created through the web interface will be placed.
- `$SPLUNK_HOME/etc/users/$user_name/$app_name/local`: When a search configuration is created through the web interface, it will have a permission setting of *Private* and will be created in a user- or app-specific configuration file. Once permissions are changed, the configuration will move to the corresponding directory named `$app_name/local`.

There are a few more directories that contain files that are not `.conf` files. We'll talk about those later in this chapter, in the *User interface resources* section.

The structure of a Splunk configuration file

The `.conf` files used by Splunk look very similar to `.ini` files. A simple configuration looks like this:

```
#settings for foo
[foo]
bar=1
la = 2
```

Let's look at the following couple of definitions:

- **stanza**: A stanza is used to group attributes. Our stanza in this example is `[foo]`. A common synonym for this is **section**. Keep in mind the following key points:
    - A stanza name must be unique in a single file
    - The order does not matter
- **attribute**: An attribute is a name-value pair. Our attributes in this example are `bar` and `la`. A common synonym is `parameter`. Keep in mind the following key points:
    - The attribute name must not contain whitespace or the equals sign.
    - Each attribute belongs to the stanza defined previously; if the attribute appears before all stanzas, the attribute belongs to the stanza `[default]`.
    - The attribute name must be unique in a single stanza but not in a configuration.
    - Each attribute must have its own line and can only use one line. Spaces around the equals sign do not matter.

These are a few rules that may not apply in other implementations:

- Stanza and property names are case-sensitive
- The comment character is #
- Bare attributes at the top of a file are added to the `[default]` stanza
- Any attributes in the `[default]` stanza are added to all stanzas that do not have an attribute with that name already

The configuration merging logic

Configurations in different locations merge behind the scenes into one super-configuration. Luckily, the merging happens in a predictable way and is fairly easy to learn; there is also a tool to help us preview this merging.

The merging order

The merging order is slightly different depending on whether the configuration is being used by the search engine or another part of Splunk. The difference is whether there is an active user and app.

The merging order outside of search

Configurations being used outside of search are merged in a fairly simple order. These configurations include the files to read, the indexed fields to create, the indexes that exist, deployment server and client configurations, and other settings. These configurations merge in this order:

1. `$SPLUNK_HOME/etc/system/default`: This directory contains the base configurations that ship with Splunk.
   Never make changes in `$SPLUNK_HOME/etc/system/default` as your changes will be lost when you upgrade Splunk.

2. `$SPLUNK_HOME/etc/apps/*/default`: Configurations are overlaid in the reverse ASCII order by app directory name, that is, *a beats z*.

3. `$SPLUNK_HOME/etc/apps/*/local`.

4. `$SPLUNK_HOME/etc/system/local`:
   - The configurations in this directory are applied last.
   - Outside of search, these configurations cannot be overridden by an app configuration. Apps are a very convenient way to compartmentalize control and distribute configurations. This is particularly relevant if you use the deployment server.

Don't edit configurations in `$SPLUNK_HOME/etc/system/local` even if you have a very specific reason. An app is almost always the correct place for configuration.

A little pseudocode to describe this process might look like this:

```
$conf = new Configuration('$SPLUNK_HOME/etc/')
$conf.merge( 'system/default/$conf_name' )
for $this_app in reverse(sort(@all_apps)):
$conf.merge( 'apps/$this_app/default/$conf_name' )
for $this_app in reverse(sort(@all_apps)):
$conf.merge( 'apps/$this_app/local/$conf_name' )
$conf.merge( 'system/local/$conf_name' )
```

The merging order when searching

When you are searching, configuration merging is slightly more complicated. When you are running a search, there is always an active user and app, and they come into play. The logical order looks like this:

1. `$SPLUNK_HOME/etc/system/default`.

2. `$SPLUNK_HOME/etc/system/local`.

3. `$SPLUNK_HOME/etc/apps/not app`.

    - Each app, other than the current app, is looped through in the ASCII order of the directory name (not the visible app name). Unlike merging outside of search, here *z beats a*.

    - All configuration attributes that are shared globally are applied, first from `default` and then from `local`.

4. `$SPLUNK_HOME/etc/apps/app`:

    All configurations from `default` and then `local` are merged.

5. `$SPLUNK_HOME/etc/users/user/app/local`:

    Maybe a little pseudocode would make this clearer:

    ```
    $conf = new Configuration('$SPLUNK_HOME/etc/')
    $conf.merge( 'system/default/$conf_name' )
    $conf.merge( 'system/local/$conf_name' )
    for $this_app in sort(@all_apps):
    if $this_app != $current_app:
    $conf.merge_shared( 'apps/$this_app/default/$conf_name' )
    $conf.merge_shared( 'apps/$this_app/local/$conf_name' )
    $conf.merge( 'apps/$current_app/default/$conf_name' )
    $conf.merge( 'apps/$current_app/local/$conf_name' )
    $conf.merge( 'users/$current_user/$current_app/local/$conf_name' )
    ```

The configuration merging logic

Now that we know what configurations will merge in what order, let's cover the logic for how they actually merge. The logic is fairly simple:

- The configuration name, stanza name, and attribute name must match exactly
- The last configuration added wins

The best way to understand configuration merging is through examples.

Configuration merging – example 1

Say we have the base configuration, `default/sample1.conf`:

```
[foo]
bar=10
la=20
```

And, say we merge a second configuration, `local/sample1.conf`:

```
[foo]
bar=15
```

The resultant configuration would be as follows:

```
[foo]
bar=15
la=20
```

The things to note here are as follows:

- The second configuration does not simply replace the prior configuration
- The value of `bar` is taken from the second configuration
- The lack of a `la` property in the second configuration does not remove the value from the final configuration

Configuration merging – example 2

Suppose we have the `default/sample2.conf` base configuration:

```
[foo]
bar = 10
la=20
[pets]
cat = red
Dog=rex
```

And we merge a second configuration, `local/sample2.conf`:

```
[pets]
cat=blue
dog=fido
fish = bubbles
```

```
[foo]
bar= 15
[cars]
ferrari =0
```

The resultant configuration would be:

```
[foo]
bar=15
la=20
[pets]
cat=blue
dog=rex
Dog=fido
fish=bubbles
[cars]
ferrari=0
```

The things to note in this example are as follows:

- The order of the stanzas does not matter
- The spaces around the equals sign do not matter
- `Dog` does not override `dog` as all stanza names and property names are case-sensitive
- The `cars` stanza is added fully

Configuration merging – example 3

Let's do a little exercise, merging four configurations from different locations. In this case, we are not in search, so we will use the rules from the *Merging order outside of search* section.

Let's walk through a few sample configurations.

For `$SPLUNK_HOME/etc/apps/d/default/props.conf`, we have the following code:

```
[web_access]
MAX_TIMESTAMP_LOOKAHEAD = 25
TIME_PREFIX = ^[
[source::*.log]
BREAK_ONLY_BEFORE_DATE = true
```

For `$SPLUNK_HOME/etc/system/local/props.conf`, we have this code:

```
BREAK_ONLY_BEFORE_DATE = false
[web_access]
TZ = CST
```

For `$SPLUNK_HOME/etc/apps/d/local/props.conf`, we have the following code:

```
[web_access]
TZ = UTC
[security_log]
EXTRACT-<name> = [(?P<user>.*?)]
```

For `$SPLUNK_HOME/etc/apps/b/default/props.conf`, we have this:

```
[web_access]
MAX_TIMESTAMP_LOOKAHEAD = 20
TIME_FORMAT = %Y-%m-%d $H:%M:%S
[source::*/access.log]
BREAK_ONLY_BEFORE_DATE = false
```

I've thrown a bit of a curveball here by placing the files out of merging order.

These configurations actually merge in this order:

```
$SPLUNK_HOME/etc/apps/d/default/props.conf
$SPLUNK_HOME/etc/apps/b/default/props.conf
$SPLUNK_HOME/etc/apps/d/local/props.conf
$SPLUNK_HOME/etc/system/local/props.conf
```

Walking through each merge, the configuration would look like this:

1. We will start with `$SPLUNK_HOME/etc/apps/d/default/props.conf`:

   ```
   [web_access]
   MAX_TIMESTAMP_LOOKAHEAD = 25
   TIME_PREFIX = ^[
   [source::*.log]
   BREAK_ONLY_BEFORE_DATE = true
   ```

2. We will then merge `$SPLUNK_HOME/etc/apps/b/default/props.conf`:

   ```
   [web_access]
   MAX_TIMESTAMP_LOOKAHEAD = 30
   TIME_PREFIX = ^[
   TIME_FORMAT = %Y-%m-%d $H:%M:%S
    [source::*.log]
   BREAK_ONLY_BEFORE_DATE = true
   ```

```
[source::*/access.log]
BREAK_ONLY_BEFORE_DATE = false
```

Even though [source::*.log] and [source::*/access.log] both match a file called access.log, they will not merge in the configuration because the stanza names do not match exactly. This logic is covered later, in the *Stanza types* section under the *props.conf* heading.

3. Then, we will merge $SPLUNK_HOME/etc/apps/d/local/props.conf:

```
[web_access]
MAX_TIMESTAMP_LOOKAHEAD = 30
TIME_PREFIX = ^[
TIME_FORMAT = %Y-%m-%d $H:%M:%S
TZ = UTC
[source::*.log]
BREAK_ONLY_BEFORE_DATE = true
[source::*/access.log]
BREAK_ONLY_BEFORE_DATE = false
[security_log]
EXTRACT-<name> = [(?P<user>.*?)]
```

4. We will finally merge the globally-overriding $SPLUNK_HOME/etc/system/ configuration:

```
local/props.conf file:
[default]
BREAK_ONLY_BEFORE_DATE = false
[web_access]
MAX_TIMESTAMP_LOOKAHEAD = 25
TIME_PREFIX = ^[
TIME_FORMAT = %Y-%m-%d $H:%M:%S
TZ = CST
BREAK_ONLY_BEFORE_DATE = false
[source::*.log]
BREAK_ONLY_BEFORE_DATE = true
[source::*/access.log]
Configuring Splunk
[ 288 ]
BREAK_ONLY_BEFORE_DATE = false
[security_log]
EXTRACT-<name> = [(?P<user>.*?)]
BREAK_ONLY_BEFORE_DATE = false
```

The setting with the biggest impact here is the BREAK_ONLY_BEFORE_DATE = false bare attribute. It is first added to the [default] stanza and then added to all stanzas that do not already have any value.

> As a general rule, avoid using the [default] stanza and bare word attributes. The final impact may not be what you expect.

Configuration merging – example 4, search

In this case, we are in search, so we will use the more complicated merging order.

Assuming that we are currently working in the d app, let's merge the same configurations again. For simplicity, we are assuming that all attributes are shared globally. We will merge the same configurations listed previously in *Configuration merging – example 3*.

With d as our current app, we will now merge in this order:

```
$SPLUNK_HOME/etc/system/local/props.conf
$SPLUNK_HOME/etc/apps/b/default/props.conf
$SPLUNK_HOME/etc/apps/d/default/props.conf
$SPLUNK_HOME/etc/apps/d/local/props.conf
```

Walking through each merge, the configuration will look like this:

1. We will start with `$SPLUNK_HOME/etc/system/local/props.conf`:

   ```
   BREAK_ONLY_BEFORE_DATE = false
   [web_access]
   TZ = CST
   ```

2. Now, we will merge the default for apps other than our current app (which, in this case, is only one configuration):

   `$SPLUNK_HOME/etc/apps/b/default/props.conf`:

   ```
   BREAK_ONLY_BEFORE_DATE = false
   [web_access]
   MAX_TIMESTAMP_LOOKAHEAD = 20
   TIME_FORMAT = %Y-%m-%d $H:%M:%S
   TZ = CST
     [source::*/access.log]
   BREAK_ONLY_BEFORE_DATE = false
   ```

3. Next, we will merge the default of our current app:

   `$SPLUNK_HOME/etc/apps/d/default/props.conf`:

   ```
   BREAK_ONLY_BEFORE_DATE = false
   [web_access]
   MAX_TIMESTAMP_LOOKAHEAD = 25
   TIME_PREFIX = ^[
   TIME_FORMAT = %Y-%m-%d $H:%M:%S
   TZ = CST
   [source::*/access.log]
   BREAK_ONLY_BEFORE_DATE = false
   [source::*.log]
   BREAK_ONLY_BEFORE_DATE = true
   ```

4. Now, we will merge our current app local

   `$SPLUNK_HOME/etc/apps/d/local/props.conf`:

   ```
   BREAK_ONLY_BEFORE_DATE = false
   [web_access]
   MAX_TIMESTAMP_LOOKAHEAD = 25
   TIME_PREFIX = ^[
   TIME_FORMAT = %Y-%m-%d $H:%M:%S
   TZ = UTC
   [source::*/access.log]
   BREAK_ONLY_BEFORE_DATE = false
   [source::*.log]
   BREAK_ONLY_BEFORE_DATE = true
   [security_log]
   EXTRACT-<name> = [(?P<user>.*?)]
   ```

5. And finally, we will apply our default stanza to stanzas that don't already have
   the attribute:

   ```
   BREAK_ONLY_BEFORE_DATE = false
     [web_access]
   MAX_TIMESTAMP_LOOKAHEAD = 25
   TIME_PREFIX = ^[
   TIME_FORMAT = %Y-%m-%d $H:%M:%S
   TZ = UTC
   BREAK_ONLY_BEFORE_DATE = false
   [source::*/access.log]
   BREAK_ONLY_BEFORE_DATE = false
   [source::*.log]
   BREAK_ONLY_BEFORE_DATE = true
   [security_log]
   EXTRACT-<name> = [(?P<user>.*?)]
   BREAK_ONLY_BEFORE_DATE = false
   ```

I know this is fairly confusing, but with practice, it will make sense. Luckily, btool, which we will cover in the next section, makes it easier to see this.

Using btool

To help preview merged configurations, we call on btool, a command-line tool that prints the merged version of configurations. The Splunk site has one of my favorite documentation notes of all time, as follows:

> *"btool is not tested by Splunk and is not officially supported or guaranteed. That said, it's what our Support team uses when trying to troubleshoot your issues."*

With that warning in mind, btool has never steered me wrong. The tool has a number of functions, but the only one I have ever used is list, as follows:

```
$SPLUNK_HOME/bin/splunk cmd btool props list
```

This produces 5,277 lines of output, which I won't list here. Let's list the impl_splunk_gen stanza by adding it to the end of the command line, as shown here:

```
/opt/splunk/bin/splunk cmd btool props list impl_splunk_gen
```

This will produce an output such as this:

```
[impl_splunk_gen]
ANNOTATE_PUNCT = True
BREAK_ONLY_BEFORE =
BREAK_ONLY_BEFORE_DATE = True
... truncated ...
LINE_BREAKER_LOOKBEHIND = 100
LOOKUP-lookupusers = userslookup user AS user OUTPUTNEW
MAX_DAYS_AGO = 2000
... truncated ...
TRUNCATE = 10000
TZ = UTC
maxDist = 100
```

Our configuration file at $SPLUNK_HOME/etc/apps/ImplementingSplunkDataGenerator/local/props.conf contains only the following lines:

```
[impl_splunk_web]
LOOKUP-web_section = flatten_summary_lookup url AS url OUTPUTNEW
EXTRACT-url = s[A-Z]+s(?P<url_from_app_local>.*?)s
EXTRACT-foo = s[A-Z]+s(?P<url_from_app>.*?)s
```

So, where did the rest of this configuration come from? With the use of the -debug flag, we can get more details:

```
/opt/splunk/bin/splunk cmd btool props list impl_splunk_gen -debug
```

This produces the following query:

```
Implementi [impl_splunk_gen]
system ANNOTATE_PUNCT = True
system BREAK_ONLY_BEFORE =
system BREAK_ONLY_BEFORE_DATE = True
... truncated ...
system LINE_BREAKER_LOOKBEHIND = 100
Implementi LOOKUP-lookupusers = userslookup user AS user OUTPUTNEW
system MAX_DAYS_AGO = 2000
... truncated ...
system TRUNCATE = 10000
Implementi TZ = UTC
system maxDist = 100
```

The first column, truncated though it is, tells us what we need to know. The vast majority of these lines are defined in the system, most likely in system/default/props.conf.

The remaining items from our file are labeled Implementi, which is the beginning of our app directory, ImplementingSplunkDataGenerator. If you ever have a question about where some setting is coming from, btool will save you a lot of time. Also, check out the *Splunk on Splunk* app at Splunkbase for access to btool from the Splunk web interface.

An overview of Splunk.conf files

If you have spent any length of time in the filesystem investigating Splunk, you must have seen many different files ending in .conf. In this section, we will give you a quick overview of the most common .conf files. The official documentation is the best place to look for a complete reference to files and attributes.

The quickest way to find the official documentation is with your favorite search engine, by searching for Splunk filename.conf. For example, a search for Splunk props.conf pulled up (and will pull up) the Splunk documentation for props.conf first in every search engine I tested.

props.conf

The stanzas in `props.conf` define which events to match based on host, source, and sourcetype. These stanzas are merged into the master configuration based on the uniqueness of stanza and attribute names, as with any other configuration, but there are specific rules governing when each stanza is applied to an event and in what order. Stated as simply as possible, attributes are sorted by type, then by priority, and then by the ASCII value.

We'll cover those rules in the *Stanza types* section. First, let's look at common attributes.

Common attributes

The full set of attributes allowed in `props.conf` is vast. Let's look at the most common attributes and try to break them down by the time when they are applied.

Search-time attributes

The most common attributes that users will make in `props.conf` are field extractions. When a user defines an extraction through the web interface, it ends up in `props.conf`, as shown here:

```
[my_source_type]
EXTRACT-foo = s(?<bar>d+)ms
EXTRACT-cat = s(?<dog>d+)s
```

This configuration defines the fields `bar` and `dog` for the `my_source_type` source type. Extracts are the most common search-time configurations. Any of the stanza types listed in the *Stanza types* section can be used, but the source type is definitely the most common one.

Other common search-time attributes include:

- `REPORT-foo = bar`: This attribute is a way to reference stanzas in `transforms.conf`, but apply them at search time instead of index time. This approach predates `EXTRACT` and is still useful in a few special cases.

  We will cover this case later, in the *transforms.conf* section.

- KV_MODE = auto: This attribute allows you to specify whether Splunk should automatically extract fields, in the form of key=value, from events. The default value is auto. The most common change is to disable automatic field extraction for performance reasons by setting the value to none. Other possibilities are multi, JSON, and XML.
- LOOKUP-foo = mylookup barfield: This attribute lets you wire up a lookup to automatically run for a set of events. The lookup itself is defined in transforms.conf.

Index-time attributes

As discussed in Chapter 3, *Tables, Charts, and Fields* under *Indexed Fields Versus Extracted Fields* section, it is possible to add fields to the metadata of events. This is accomplished by specifying a transform in transforms.conf, and an attribute in props.conf, to tie the transformation to specific events.

The attribute in props.conf looks like this: TRANSFORMS-foo = bar1,bar2.

This attribute references stanzas in transforms.conf by name, in this case, bar1 and bar2. These transform stanzas are then applied to the events matched by the stanza in props.conf.

Parse-time attributes

Most of the attributes in props.conf actually have to do with parsing events. To successfully parse events, a few questions need to be answered, such as these:

- When does a new event begin? Are events multiline? Splunk will make fairly intelligent guesses, but it is best to specify an exact setting. Attributes that help with this include:
  - SHOULD_LINEMERGE = false: If you know that your events will never contain the newline character, setting this to false will eliminate a lot of processing.
  - BREAK_ONLY_BEFORE = ^dddd-dd-dd: If you know that new events always start with a particular pattern, you can specify it using this attribute.

- `TRUNCATE = 1024`: If you are certain you only care about the first *n* characters of an event, you can instruct Splunk to truncate each line. What is considered a line can be changed with the next attribute.
- `LINE_BREAKER = ([rn]+)(?=d{4}-dd-dd)`: The most efficient approach to multiline events is to redefine what Splunk considers a line. This example says that a line is broken on any number of newlines followed by a date of the form `1111-11-11`. The big disadvantage to this approach is that, if your log changes, you will end up with garbage in your index until you update your configuration. Try the props helper app available at Splunkbase for help in making this kind of configuration.

- Where is the date? If there is no date, see `DATETIME_CONFIG` further down this bullet list. The relevant attributes are as follows:
  - `TIME_PREFIX = ^[`: By default, dates are assumed to fall at the beginning of the line. If this is not true, give Splunk some help and move the cursor past the characters preceding the date. This pattern is applied to each line, so if you have redefined `LINE_BREAKER` correctly, you can be sure only the beginnings of actual multiline events are being tested.
  - `MAX_TIMESTAMP_LOOKAHEAD = 30`: Even if you change no other setting, you should change this one. This setting says how far after `TIME_PREFIX` to test for dates. With no help, Splunk will take the first 150 characters of each line and then test regular expressions to find anything that looks like a date. The default regular expressions are pretty lax, so what it finds may look more like a date than the actual date. If you know that your date is never more than *n* characters long, set this value to n or n+2. Remember that the characters retrieved come after `TIME_PREFIX`.

- What does the date look like? These attributes will be of assistance here:
  - `TIME_FORMAT = %Y-%m-%d %H:%M:%S.%3N %:z`: If this attribute is specified, Splunk will apply `strptime` to the characters immediately following `TIME_PREFIX`. If this matches, then you're done. This is, by far, the most efficient and least error-prone approach. Without this attribute, Splunk actually applies a series of regular expressions until it finds something that looks like a date.

- DATETIME_CONFIG = /etc/apps/a/custom_datetime.xml: As mentioned, Splunk uses a set of regular expressions to determine the date. If TIME_FORMAT is not specified, or won't work for some strange reason, you can specify a different set of regular expressions or disable time extraction completely by setting this attribute to CURRENT (the indexer clock time) or NONE (file modification time, or if there is no file, clock time). I personally have never had to resort to a custom datetime.xml file, though I have heard of it being done.

- The data preview function available when you are adding data through the manager interface builds a good, usable configuration. The configuration generated does not use LINE_BREAKER, which is definitely safer but less efficient.

Here is a sample stanza that uses LINE_BREAKER for efficiency:

```
[mysourcetype]
TIME_FORMAT = %Y-%m-%d %H:%M:%S.%3N %:z
MAX_TIMESTAMP_LOOKAHEAD = 32
TIME_PREFIX = ^[
SHOULD_LINEMERGE = False
LINE_BREAKER = ([rn]+)(?=[d{4}-d{1,2}-d{1,2}s+
d{1,2}:d{1,2}:d{1,2})
TRUNCATE = 1024000
This configuration would apply to log messages that looked like
this:
[2011-10-13 13:55:36.132 -07:00] ERROR Interesting message.
More information.
And another line.
[2011-10-13 13:55:36.138 -07:00] INFO All better.
[2011-10-13 13:55:37.010 -07:00] INFO More data
and another line.
```

Let's walk through how these settings affect the first line of this sample configuration:

- LINE_BREAKER states that a new event starts when one or more newline characters are followed by a bracket and series of numbers and dashes in the [1111-11-11 11:11:11] pattern.
- SHOULD_LINEMERGE=False tells Splunk not to bother trying to recombine multiple lines.
- TIME_PREFIX moves the cursor to the character after the [character.
- TIME_FORMAT is tested against the characters at the current cursor location. If it succeeds, we are done.

- If TIME_FORMAT fails, MAX_TIMESTAMP_LOOKAHEAD characters are read from the cursor position (after TIME_PREFIX) and the regular expressions from DATE_CONFIG are tested.
- If the regular expressions fail against the characters returned, the time last parsed from an event is used. If there is no last time parsed, the modification date from the file will be used if known; otherwise, the current time will be used.

This is the most efficient and precise way to parse events in Splunk, but also the most brittle. If your date format changes, you will almost certainly have junk data in your index. Use this approach only if you are confident that the format of your logs will not change without your knowledge.

Input-time attributes

There are only a few attributes in props.conf that matter at the input stage, but they are generally not needed:

- CHARSET = UTF-16LE: When reading data, Splunk has to know the character set used in the log.
- 8859-1 or UTF-8 is handled by the default settings just fine. Some Windows applications write logs in 2-byte little endian, which is indexed as garbage.
- Setting CHARSET = UTF-16LE takes care of the problem. Check out the official documentation for a list of supported encodings.
- NO_BINARY_CHECK = true: If Splunk believes that a file is binary, it will not index the file at all. If you find that you have to change this setting to convince Splunk to read your files, it is likely that the file is in an unexpected character set. You might try other CHARSET settings before enabling this setting.

Stanza types

Now that we have looked at common attributes, let's talk about the different types of stanzas in props.conf. Stanza definitions can take the following three forms:

- [foo]
    - This is the exact name of a source type and is the most common type of stanza to be used; the source type of an event is usually defined in inputs.conf
    - Wildcards are not allowed

- `[source::/logs/.../*.log]`
    - This matches the source attribute, which is usually the path to the log where the event came from
    - `*` matches a file or directory name
    - `...` matches any part of a path
- `[host::*nyc*]`
    - This matches the host attribute, which is usually the value of the hostname on a machine running Splunk Forwarder
    - `*` is allowed

Types follow this order in taking precedence:

1. Source
2. Host
3. Source type

For instance, say an event has the following fields:

```
sourcetype=foo_type
source=/logs/abc/def/gh.log
host=dns4.nyc.mycompany.com
```

Given this configuration snippet and our preceding event, we have the following code:

```
[foo_type]
TZ = UTC
[source::/logs/.../*.log]
TZ = MST
[host::*nyc*]
TZ = EDT
```

`TZ = MST` will be used during parsing because the source stanza takes precedence.

To extend this example, say we have this snippet:

```
[foo_type]
TZ = UTC
TRANSFORMS-a = from_sourcetype
[source::/logs/.../*.log]
TZ = MST
BREAK_ONLY_BEFORE_DATE = True
TRANSFORMS-b = from_source
[host::*nyc*]
```

```
TZ = EDT
BREAK_ONLY_BEFORE_DATE = False
TRANSFORMS-c = from_host
```

The attributes applied to our event would, therefore, be as shown here:

```
TZ = MST
BREAK_ONLY_BEFORE_DATE = True
TRANSFORMS-a = from_sourcetype
TRANSFORMS-b = from_source
TRANSFORMS-c = from_host
```

Priorities inside a type

If there are multiple source or host stanzas that match a given event, the order in which settings are applied also comes into play. A stanza with a pattern has a priority of 0, while an exact stanza has a priority of 100. Higher priorities win. For instance, say we have the following stanza:

```
[source::/logs/abc/def/gh.log]
TZ = UTC
[source::/logs/.../*.log]
TZ = CDT
```

Our TZ value will be UTC since the exact match of source::/logs/abc/def/gh.log has a higher priority.

When priorities are identical, stanzas are applied by the ASCII order. For instance, say we have this configuration snippet:

```
[source::/logs/abc/.../*.log]
TZ = MST
[source::/logs/.../*.log]
TZ = CDT
```

The attribute TZ=CDT will win because /logs/.../*.log is first in the ASCII order.

This may seem counterintuitive since /logs/abc/.../*.log is arguably a better match. The logic for determining what makes a better match, however, can quickly become fantastically complex, so the ASCII order is a reasonable approach.

You can also set your own value of priority, but luckily, it is rarely needed.

Attributes with class

As you dig into configurations, you will see attribute names of the FOO-bar form.

The word after the dash is generally referred to as the class. These attributes are special in a few ways:

- Attributes merge across files like any other attribute.
- Only one instance of each class will be applied according to the rules described previously.
- The final set of attributes is applied in the ASCII order by the value of the class. Once again, say we are presented with an event with the following fields:

```
sourcetype=foo_type
source=/logs/abc/def/gh.log
host=dns4.nyc.mycompany.com
```

And, say this is the configuration snippet:

```
[foo_type]
TRANSFORMS-a = from_sourcetype1, from_sourcetype2
[source::/logs/.../*.log]
TRANSFORMS-c = from_source_b
[source::/logs/abc/.../*.log]
TRANSFORMS-b = from_source_c
[host::*nyc*]
TRANSFORMS-c = from_host
The surviving transforms would then be:
TRANSFORMS-c = from_source_b
TRANSFORMS-b = from_source_c
TRANSFORMS-a = from_sourcetype1, from_sourcetype2
```

To determine the order in which the transforms are applied to our event, we will sort the stanzas according to the values of their classes, in this case, c, b, and a. This gives us:

```
TRANSFORMS-a = from_sourcetype1, from_sourcetype2
TRANSFORMS-b = from_source_c
TRANSFORMS-c = from_source_b
```

The transforms are then combined into a single list and executed in this order:

```
from_sourcetype1, from_sourcetype2, from_source_c, from_source_b
```

The order of transforms usually doesn't matter, but it is important to understand it if you want to chain transforms and create one field from another. We'll try this later, in the *transforms.conf* section.

inputs.conf

This configuration, as you might guess, controls how data makes it into Splunk.

By the time this data leaves the input stage, it still isn't an event but has some basic metadata associated with it: `host`, `source`, `sourcetype`, and optionally `index`. This basic metadata is then used by the parsing stage to break the data into events according to the rules defined in `props.conf`.

Input types can be broken down into files, network ports, and scripts. First, we will look at the attributes that are common to all inputs.

Common input attributes

These common bits of metadata are used in the parsing stage to pick the appropriate stanzas in `props.conf`:

- `host`: By default, `host` will be set to the hostname of the machine producing the event. This is usually the correct value, but it can be overridden when appropriate.
- `source`: This field is usually set to the path, file, or network port that an event came from, but this value can be hardcoded.
- `sourcetype`: This field is almost always set in `inputs.conf` and is the primary field to determine which set of parsing rules in `props.conf` to apply to these events.

> It is very important to set `sourcetype`. In the absence of a value, Splunk will create automatic values based on the source, which can easily result in an explosion of `sourcetype` values.

- `index`: This field says what index to write events to. If it is omitted, the default `index` will be used.

All of these values can be modified using transforms, the only caveat being that these transforms are applied after the parsing step. The practical consequence of this is that you cannot apply different parsing rules to different events in the same file, for instance, different time formats on different lines.

Files as inputs

The vast majority of events in Splunk come from files. Usually, these events are read from the machine where they are produced and as the logs are written. Very often, the entire input's stanza will look like this:

```
[monitor:///logs/interesting.log*]
sourcetype=interesting
```

This is often all that is needed. This stanza says:

- Read all logs that match the /logs/interesting.log* pattern, and going forward, watch them for new data
- Name the source type interesting
- Set the source to the name of the file in which the log entry was found
- Default the host to the machine where the logs originated
- Write the events to the default index

These are usually perfectly acceptable defaults. If sourcetype is omitted, Splunk will pick a default source type based on the filename, which you don't want—your source type list will get very messy very fast.

Using patterns to select rolled logs

You may notice that the previous stanza ended in *. This is important because it gives Splunk a chance to find events that were written to a log that has recently rolled. If we simply watch /logs/interesting.log, it is likely that events will be missed at the end of the log when it rolls, particularly on a busy server.

There are specific cases where Splunk can get confused, but in the vast majority of cases, the default mechanisms do exactly what you would hope for. See the *When to use crcSalt* section further on for a discussion about special cases.

Using blacklist and whitelist

It is also possible to use a blacklist and whitelist pattern for more complicated patterns. The most common use case is to blacklist files that should not be indexed, for instance, gz and zip files. This can be done as follows:

```
[monitor:///opt/B/logs/access.log*]
sourcetype=access
blacklist=.*.gz
```

This stanza will still match `access.log.2012-08-30`, but if we had a script that compressed older logs, Splunk will not try to read `access.log.2012-07-30.gz`.

Conversely, you can use a whitelist to apply very specific patterns, as shown here:

```
[monitor:///opt/applicationserver/logs]
sourcetype=application_logs
whitelist=(app|application|legacy|foo).log(.d{4})?
blacklist=.*.gz
```

This whitelist will match `app.log`, `application.log`, `legacy.log.2012-08-13`, and `foo.log`, among others. The blacklist will negate any `gz` files.

Since a log is a directory, the default behavior will be to recursively scan that directory.

Selecting files recursively

The layout of your logs or your application may dictate a recursive approach.

For instance, say we have these stanzas:

```
[monitor:///opt/*/logs/access.log*]
sourcetype=access
[monitor:///opt/.../important.log*]
sourcetype=important
```

The character `*` will match a single file or directory, while `...` will match any depth. This will match the files you want, with the caveat that all of `/opt` will continually be scanned.

Splunk will continually scan all directories from the first wildcard in a monitor path.

If `/opt` contains many files and directories, which it almost certainly does, Splunk will use an unfortunate amount of resources scanning all directories for matching files, constantly using memory and CPU. I have seen a single Splunk process watching a large directory structure use 2 gigabytes of memory. A little creativity can take care of this, but it is something to be aware of.

The takeaway is that if you know the possible values for `*`, you are better off writing multiple stanzas. For instance, assuming our directories in `/opt` are A and B, the following stanzas will be far more efficient:

```
[monitor:///opt/A/logs/access.log*]
sourcetype=access
[monitor:///opt/B/logs/access.log*]
sourcetype=access
```

It is also perfectly acceptable to have stanzas matching files and directories that simply don't exist. This causes no errors, but be careful not to include patterns that are so broad that they match unintended files.

Following symbolic links

When scanning directories recursively, the default behavior is to follow symbolic links. Often this is very useful, but it can cause problems if a symbolic link points to a large or slow filesystem. To control this behavior, simply do this:

```
followSymlink = false
```

It's probably a good idea to put this on all of your monitor stanzas until you know you need to follow a symbolic link.

Setting the value of the host from the source

The default behavior of using the hostname from the machine forwarding the logs is almost always what you want. If, however, you are reading logs for a number of hosts, you can extract the hostname from the source using host_regex or host_segment. For instance, say we have the path:

```
/nfs/logs/webserver1/access.log
```

To set host to webserver1, you could use:

```
[monitor:///nfs/logs/*/access.log*]
sourcetype=access
host_segment=3
```

You could also use:

```
[monitor:///nfs/logs/*/access.log*]
sourcetype=access
host_regex=/(.*?)/access.log
```

The host_regex variable could also be used to extract the value of the host from the filename. It is also possible to reset the host using a transform, with the caveat that this will occur after parsing, which means any settings in props.conf that rely on matching the host will already have been applied.

Ignoring old data at installation

It is often the case that, when Splunk is installed, months or years of logs are sitting in a directory where logs are currently being written. Logs that are appended to infrequently may also have months or years of events that are no longer interesting and would be wasteful to index.

The best solution is to set up archive scripts to compress any logs older than a few days, but in a large environment, this may be difficult to do. Splunk has two settings that help ignore older data, but be forewarned: once these files have been ignored, there is no simple way to change your mind later. If, instead, you compress older logs and blacklist the compressed files as explained in the *Using blacklist and whitelist* section, you can simply decompress, at a later stage, any files you would like to index. Let's look at a sample stanza:

```
[monitor:///opt/B/logs/access.log*]
sourcetype = access
ignoreOlderThan = 14d
```

In this case, `ignoreOlderThan` says to ignore, forever, all events in any files, the modification date of which is older than `14` days. If the file is updated in the future, any new events will be indexed.

The `followTail` attribute lets us ignore all events written until now, instead starting at the end of each file. Let's look at an example:

```
[monitor:///opt/B/logs/access.log*]
sourcetype = access
followTail = 1
```

Splunk will note the length of files matching the pattern, but `TailfollowTail` instructs Splunk to ignore everything currently in these files. Any new events written to the files will be indexed. Remember that there is no easy way to alter this if you change your mind later.

It is not currently possible to say *ignore all events older than x*, but since most logs roll on a daily basis, this is not commonly a problem.

When to use crcSalt

To keep track of what files have been seen before, Splunk stores a checksum of the first 256 bytes of each file it sees. This is usually plenty as most files start with a log message, which is almost guaranteed to be unique. This breaks down when the first 256 bytes are not unique on the same server.

I have seen two cases where this happens, as follows:

1. The first case is when logs start with a common header containing information about the product version, for instance:

   ```
   ================================================================
   == Great product version 1.2 brought to you by Great company ==
   == Server kernel version 3.2.1 ==
   ```

2. The second case is when a server writes many thousands of files with low time resolution, for instance:

   ```
   12:13:12 Session created
   12:13:12 Starting session
   ```

To deal with these cases, we can add the path to the log to the checksum, or salt our crc. This is accomplished as shown here:

```
[monitor:///opt/B/logs/application.log*]
sourcetype = access
crcSalt = <SOURCE>
```

It says to include the full path to this log in the checksum.

This method will only work if your logs have a unique name. The easiest way to accomplish this is to include the current date in the name of the log when it is created. You may need to change the pattern for your log names so that the date is always included and the log is not renamed.

Do not use **crcSalt** if your logs change names!

If you enable crcSalt in an input where it was not already enabled, you will re-index all the data! You need to ensure that the old logs are moved aside or uncompressed and blacklisted before enabling this setting in an existing configuration.

Destructively indexing files

If you receive logfiles in batches, you can use the batch input to consume `logs` and then delete them. This should only be used against a copy of the logs.

See the following example:

```
[batch:///var/batch/logs/*/access.log*]
sourcetype=access
host_segment=4
move_policy = sinkhole
```

This stanza would index the files in the given directory and then delete the files. Make sure this is what you want to do!

Network inputs

In addition to reading files, Splunk can listen to network ports. The stanzas take the following form:

```
[protocol://<remote host>:<local port>]
```

The remote host portion is rarely used, but the idea is that you can specify different input configurations for specific hosts. The usual stanzas look like this:

- [tcp://1234]: Specify that we will listen to port 1234 for TCP connections. Anything can connect to this port and send data in.
- [tcp-ssl://importanthost:1234]: Listen on TCP using SSL, and apply this stanza to the importanthost host. Splunk will generate self-signed certificates the first time it is launched.
- [udp://514]: This is generally used to receive syslog events. While this does work, it is generally considered a best practice to use a dedicated syslog receiver, such as rsyslog or syslog-ng.
- [splunktcp://9997] or [splunktcp-ssl://9997]: In a distributed environment, your indexers will receive events on the specified port. It is a custom protocol used between Splunk instances. This stanza is created for you when you go to **Settings** | **Forwarding and receiving** | **Receive data** and configure your Splunk instance to receive data forwarded from other Splunk instances.

For TCP and UDP inputs, the following attributes apply:

- source: If it is not specified, the source will default to protocol:port, for instance, udp:514.

- `sourcetype`: If it is not specified, `sourcetype` will also default to `protocol:port`, but this is generally not what you want. It is best to specify a source type and create a corresponding stanza in `props.conf`.
- `connection_host`: With network inputs, what value to capture for `host` is somewhat tricky. Your options essentially are:
  - `connection_host = dns` uses reverse DNS to determine the hostname from the incoming connection. When reverse DNS is configured properly, this is usually your best bet. This is the default setting.
  - `connection_host = ip` sets the host field to the IP address of the remote machine. This is your best choice when reverse DNS is unreliable.
  - `connection_host = none` uses the hostname of the Splunk instance receiving the data. This option can make sense when all traffic is going to an interim host.
  - `host = foo` sets the hostname statically.
  - It is also common to reset the value of the host using a transform, for instance, with syslog events. This happens after parsing, though, so it is too late to change things such as time zone based on the host.
- `queueSize`: This value specifies how much memory Splunk is allowed to set aside for an input queue. A common use for a queue is to capture spiky data until the indexers can catch up.
- `persistentQueueSize`: This value specifies a persistent queue that can be used to capture data to the disk if the in-memory queue fills up. If you find yourself building a particularly complicated setup around network ports, I would encourage you to talk to Splunk support as there may be a better way to accomplish your goals.

Native Windows inputs

One nice thing about Windows is that system logs and many application logs go to the same place.

Unfortunately, that place is not a file, so native hooks are required to access these events. Splunk makes those inputs available using stanzas of the `[WinEventLog:LogName]` form. For example, to index the `Security` log, the stanza simply looks like this:

```
[WinEventLog:Security]
```

There are a number of supported attributes, but the defaults are reasonable. The only attribute I have personally used is `current_only`, which is the equivalent of `followTail` for monitor stanzas. For instance, this stanza says to monitor the `Application` log, but also to start reading from now:

```
[WinEventLog:Application]
current_only = 1
```

This is useful when there are many historical events on the server.

The other input available is **Windows Management Instrumentation (WMI)**. With WMI, you can accomplish the following:

- Monitor native performance metrics as you would find in Windows Performance Monitor
- Monitor the Windows Event Log API
- Run custom queries against the database behind WMI
- Query remote machines

Even though it is theoretically possible to monitor many Windows servers using WMI and a few Splunk forwarders, this is not advised. The configuration is complicated, does not scale well, introduces complicated security implications, and is not thoroughly tested. Also, reading Windows Event Logs via WMI produces different output than the native input, and most apps that expect Windows events will not function as expected.

The simplest way to generate the `inputs.conf` and `wmi.conf` configurations needed for Windows Event Logs and WMI is to install Splunk for Windows on a Windows host and then configure the desired inputs through the web interface. See the official Splunk documentation for more examples.

Scripts as inputs

Splunk will periodically execute processes and capture the output. For example, here is input from the `ImplementingSplunkDataGenerator` app:

```
[script://./bin/implSplunkGen.py 2]
interval=60
sourcetype=impl_splunk_gen_sourcetype2
source=impl_splunk_gen_src2
host=host2
index=implSplunk
```

Things to note in this example are as follows:

- The present working directory is the root of the app that contains `inputs.conf`.
- Files that end with `.py` will be executed using the Python interpreter included with Splunk. This means the Splunk Python modules are available. To use a different Python module, specify the path to Python in the stanza.
- Any arguments specified in the stanza will be handed to the script as if it was executed at the command line.
- The interval specifies how often, in seconds, this script should be run:
    - If the script is still running, it will not be launched again.
    - Long-running scripts are fine. Since only one copy of a script will run at a time, the interval will instead indicate how often to check whether the script is still running.
    - This value can also be specified in the `cron` format.

Any programming language can be used as long as it can be executed at the command line. Splunk simply captures the standard output from whatever is executed.

Included with Splunk for Windows are scripts to query WMI. One sample stanza looks like this:

```
[script://$SPLUNK_HOMEbinscriptssplunk-wmi.path]
```

The things to note are as follows:

- Windows paths require backslashes instead of slashes
- `$SPLUNK_HOME` will expand properly

transforms.conf

The `transforms.conf` configuration is where we specify transformations and lookups that can then be applied to any event. These transforms and lookups are referenced by name in `props.conf`.

For our examples in the later subsections, we will use this event:

```
2012-09-24T00:21:35.925+0000 DEBUG [MBX] Password reset called.
[old=1234, new=secret, req_time=5346]
```

We will use it with these metadata values:

```
sourcetype=myapp
source=/logs/myapp.session_foo-jA5MDkyMjEwMTIK.log
host=vlbmba.local
```

Creating indexed fields

One common task accomplished with `transforms.conf` is the creation of new indexed fields. Indexed fields are different from extracted fields in that they must be created at index time and can be searched for whether the value is in the raw text of the event or not. It is usually preferable to create extracted fields instead of indexed fields. See `Chapter 3`, *Tables, Charts, and Fields* under *Indexed Fields Versus Extracted Fields* section, for a deeper discussion about when indexed fields are beneficial.

Indexed fields are only applied to events that are indexed after the definition is created. There is no way to backfill a field without re-indexing.

Creating a loglevel field

The format of a typical stanza in `transforms.conf` looks like this:

```
[myapp_loglevel]
REGEX = s([A-Z]+)s
FORMAT = loglevel::$1
WRITE_META = True
```

This will add to our events the field `loglevel=DEBUG`. This is a good idea if the values of `loglevel` are common words outside of this location, for instance `ERROR`.

Walking through this stanza, we have the following:

- `[myapp_loglevel]`: The stanza can be any unique value, but it is in your best interest to make the name meaningful. This is the name referenced in `props.conf`.
- `REGEX = s([A-Z]+)s`: This is the pattern to test against each event that is handed to us. If this pattern does not match, this transform will not be applied.
- `FORMAT = loglevel::$1`: Create the `loglevel`. Under the hood, all indexed fields are stored using a `::` delimiter, so we have to follow that form.
- `WRITE_META = True`: Without this attribute, the transform won't actually create an indexed field and store it with the event.

Creating a session field from the source

Using our event, let's create another field, `session`, which appears only to be in the value of the source:

```
[myapp_session]
SOURCE_KEY = MetaData:Source
REGEX = session_(.*?).log
FORMAT = session::$1
WRITE_META = True
```

Note the `SOURCE_KEY` attribute. The value of this field can be any existing metadata field or another indexed field that has already been created. See the *Attributes with class* subsection within the *props.conf* section for a discussion about the transform execution order. We will discuss these fields in the `Modifying metadata fields` subsection.

Creating a tag field

It is also possible to create fields simply to tag events that would be difficult to search for otherwise. For example, if we wanted to find all events that were slow, we could search for:

```
sourcetype=myapp req_time>999
```

Without an indexed field, this query would require parsing every event that matches `sourcetype=myapp` over the time that we are interested in. The query will then discard all events whose `req_time` value was 999 or less.

If we know ahead of time that a value of `req_time>999` is bad, and we can come up with a regular expression to specify what *bad* is, we can tag these events for quicker retrieval. Say we have this `transforms.conf` stanza:

```
[myapp_slow]
REGEX = req_time=d{4,}
FORMAT = slow_request::1
WRITE_META = True
```

This `REGEX` will match any event containing `req_time=` followed by four or more digits.

After adding `slow_request` to `fields.conf` (see the *fields.conf* section), we can search for `slow_request=1` and find all slow events very efficiently. This will not apply to events that were indexed before this transform existed. If the events that are slow are uncommon, this query will be much faster.

Creating host categorization fields

It is common to have parts of a hostname mean something in particular. If this pattern is well known and predictable, it may be worthwhile to pull the value out into fields. Working from our fictitious host value `vlbmba.local` (which happens to be my laptop), we might want to create fields for the owner and the host type. Our stanza might look like this:

```
[host_parts]
SOURCE_KEY = MetaData:Host
REGEX = (...)(...).
FORMAT = host_owner::$1 host_type::$2
WRITE_META = True
```

With our new fields, we can now easily categorize errors by whatever information is encoded into the hostname. Another approach would be to use a lookup, which has the advantage of being retroactive. This approach has the advantage of faster searches for the specific fields.

Modifying metadata fields

It is sometimes convenient to override the main metadata fields. We will look at one possible reason for overriding each base metadata value.

Remember that transforms are applied after parsing, so changing metadata fields via transforms cannot be used to affect which `props.conf` stanzas are applied for date parsing or line breaking.

For instance, with `syslog` events that contain the hostname, you cannot change the time zone, because the date has already been parsed before the transforms are applied. The keys provided by Splunk include:

- `_raw` (this is the default value for SOURCE_KEY)
- `MetaData:Source`
- `MetaData:Sourcetype`
- `MetaData:Host`
- `_MetaData:Index`

Overriding the host

If your hostnames are appearing differently from different sources, for instance, `syslog` versus Splunk forwarders, you can use a transform to normalize these values. Given our hostname, `vlbmba.local`, we may want to only keep the portion to the left of the first period. The stanza would look like this:

```
[normalize_host]
SOURCE_KEY = MetaData:Host
DEST_KEY = MetaData:Host
REGEX = (.*?).
FORMAT = host::$1
```

This will replace our hostname with `vlbmba`. Note these two things:

- `WRITE_META` is not included, because we are not adding to the metadata of this event; we are instead overwriting the value of a core metadata field
- `host::` must be included at the beginning of the format

Overriding the source

Some applications will write a log for each session, conversation, or transaction. One problem this introduces is an explosion of source values. The values of the source will end up in `$SPLUNK_HOME/var/lib/splunk/*/db/Sources.data`—one line per unique value of the source. This file will eventually grow to a huge size, and Splunk will waste a lot of time updating it, causing unexplained pauses. A new setting in `indexes.conf`, called `disableGlobalMetadata`, can also eliminate this problem.

To flatten this value, we could use a stanza like this:

```
[myapp_flatten_source]
SOURCE_KEY = MetaData:Source
DEST_KEY = MetaData:Source
REGEX = (.*session_).*.log
FORMAT = source::$1x.log
```

This would set the value of source to /logs/myapp.session_x.log, which would eliminate our growing source problem. If the value of session is useful, the transform in the *Creating a session field from source* section could be run before this transform to capture the value. Likewise, a transform could capture the entire value of the source and place it into a different metadata field.

A huge number of logfiles on a filesystem introduces a few problems, including running out of inodes and the memory used by the Splunk process tracking all of the files. As a general rule, a cleanup process should be designed to archive older logs.

Overriding sourcetype

It is not uncommon to change the sourcetype field of an event based on the contents of the event, particularly from syslog. In our fictitious example, we want a different source type for events that contain [MBX] after the log level so that we can apply different extracts to these events. The following examples will do this work:

```
[mbx_sourcetype]
DEST_KEY = MetaData:Sourcetype
REGEX = d+s[A-Z]+s([MBX])
FORMAT = sourcetype::mbx
```

Use this functionality carefully as it easy to go conceptually wrong, and this is difficult to fix later.

Routing events to a different index

At times, you may want to send events to a different index, either because they need to live longer than other events or because they contain sensitive information that should not be seen by all users. This can be applied to any type of event from any source, be it a file, network, or script.

All that we have to do is match the event and reset the index.

```
[contains_password_1]
DEST_KEY = _MetaData:Index
```

```
REGEX = Password reset called
FORMAT = sensitive
```

The things to note are as follows:

- In this scenario, you will probably make multiple transforms, so make sure to make the name unique
- DEST_KEY starts with an underscore
- FORMAT does not start with index::
- The index sensitive must exist on the machine indexing the data, or else the event will be lost

Lookup definitions

A simple lookup simply needs to specify a filename in transforms.conf, as shown here:

```
[testlookup]
filename = test.csv
```

Assuming that test.csv contains the user and group columns and our events contain the user field, we can reference this lookup using the lookup command in search, as follows:

```
* | lookup testlookup user
```

Otherwise, we can wire this lookup to run automatically in props.conf, as follows:

```
[mysourcetype]
LOOKUP-testlookup = testlookup user
```

That's all you need to get started, and this probably covers most cases. See the *Using lookups to enrich data* section in Chapter 6, *Extending Search*, for instructions on creating lookups.

Wildcard lookups

In Chapter 9, *Summary Indexes and CSV Files*, we edited transforms.conf but did not explain what was happening. Let's take another look. Our transform stanza looks like this:

```
[flatten_summary_lookup]
filename = flatten_summary_lookup.csv
match_type = WILDCARD(url)
max_matches = 1
```

Walking through what we added, we have the following terms and their descriptions:

- `match_type = WILDCARD(url)`: This says that the value of the `url` field in the lookup file may contain wildcards. In our example, the URL might look like `/contact/*` in our CSV file.
- `max_matches = 1`: By default, up to 10 entries that match in the lookup file will be added to an event, with the values in each field being added to a multivalue field. In this case, we only want the first match to be applied.

CIDR wildcard lookups

CIDR wildcards look very similar to text-based wildcards but use **Classless Inter-Domain Routing (CIDR)** rules to match lookup rows against an IP address.

Let's try an example. Say we have this lookup file:

```
ip_range,network,datacenter
10.1.0.0/16,qa,east
10.2.0.0/16,prod,east
10.128.0.0/16,qa,west
10.129.0.0/16,prod,west
```

It has this corresponding definition in `transforms.conf`:

```
[ip_address_lookup]
filename = ip_address_lookup.csv
match_type = CIDR(ip_range)
max_matches = 1
```

And, there are a few events such as these:

```
src_ip=10.2.1.3 user=mary
src_ip=10.128.88.33 user=bob
src_ip=10.1.35.248 user=bob
```

We could use `lookup` to enrich these events as follows:

```
src_ip="*"
| lookup ip_address_lookup ip_range as src_ip
| table src_ip user datacenter network
```

This would match the appropriate IP address and give us a table like this one:

	src_ip ⬍	user ⬍	datacenter ⬍	network ⬍
1	10.2.1.3	mary	east	prod
2	10.128.88.33	bob	west	qa
3	10.1.35.248	bob	east	qa

The query also shows that you could use the same lookup for different fields using the as keyword in the lookup call.

Using time in lookups

A temporal lookup is used to enrich events based on when the event happened. To accomplish this, we specify the beginning of a time range in the lookup source and then specify a format for this time in our lookup configuration. Using this mechanism, lookup values can change over time, even retroactively.

Here is a very simple example to attach a version field based on time. Say we have the following CSV file:

```
sourcetype,version,time
impl_splunk_gen,1.0,2012-09-19 02:56:30 UTC
impl_splunk_gen,1.1,2012-09-22 12:01:45 UTC
impl_splunk_gen,1.2,2012-09-23 18:12:12 UTC
```

We then use the lookup configuration in transforms.conf to specify which field in our lookup will be tested against the time in each event and what the format of the time field will be:

```
[versions]
filename = versions.csv
time_field = time
time_format = %Y-%m-%d %H:%M:%S %Z
```

With this in place, we can now use our lookup in search, as shown here:

```
sourcetype=impl_splunk_gen error
| lookup versions sourcetype
| timechart count by version
```

This would give us a chart of errors (by version) over time, as shown here:

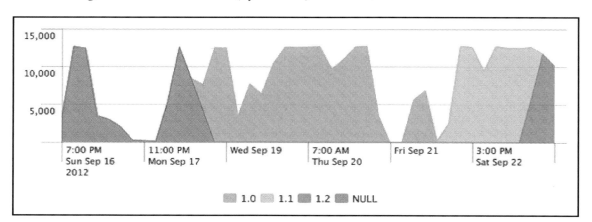

Other use cases include tracking deployments across environments and tracking activity from disabled accounts.

Using REPORT

Attributes of the format REPORT-foo in props.conf call stanzas in transforms.conf at search time, which means that they cannot affect metadata fields. EXTRACT definitions are more convenient to write, as they live entirely in a single attribute in props.conf, but there are a couple of things that can only be done using a REPORT attribute paired with a transform defined in transforms.conf.

Creating multivalue fields

Assuming some value might occur multiple times in a given event, an EXTRACT definition can only match the first occurrence. For example, say we have the event:

```
2012-08-25T20:18:09 action=send a@b.com c@d.com e@f.com
```

We could pull the first email address using the following extraction:

```
EXTRACT-email = (?i)(?P<email>[a-zA-Z0-9._]+@[a-zA-Z0-9._]+)
```

This would set the field `email` to `a@b.com`. Using a `REPORT` attribute and the transform stanza, we can capture all of the email addresses using the `MV_ADD` attribute. The props stanza would look like this:

```
REPORT-mvemail = mvemail
```

The `transforms.conf` stanza would then look like this:

```
[mvemail]
REGEX = (?i)([a-zA-Z0-9._]+@[a-zA-Z0-9._]+)
FORMAT = email::$1
MV_ADD = true
```

The `MV_ADD` attribute also has the effect that, if some other configuration has already created the email field, all values that match will be added to the event.

Creating dynamic fields

Sometimes, it can be useful to dynamically create fields from an event. For instance, say we have an event, such as:

```
2012-08-25T20:18:09 action=send from_335353("a@b.com") to_223523("c@d.com")
cc_39393("e@f.com") cc_39394("g@h.com")
```

It would be nice to pull `from`, `to`, and `cc` as fields, but we may not know all of the possible field names. This stanza in `transforms.conf` would create the fields we want, dynamically:

```
[dynamic_address_fields]
REGEX=s(S+)_S+("(.*?)")
FORMAT = $1::$2
MV_ADD=true
```

While we're at it, let's put the numeric value after the field name into a value:

```
[dynamic_address_ids]
REGEX=s(S+)_(S+)("
FORMAT = $1::$2
MV_ADD=true
```

This gives us multivalue fields such as the ones in the following screenshot:

action ⇕	cc ⇕	from ⇕	to ⇕
send	e@f.com g@h.com 39393 39394	a@b.com 335353	c@d.com 223523

One thing that we cannot do is add extra text to the FORMAT attribute. For instance, in the second case, it would be nice to use a FORMAT attribute such as this one:

```
FORMAT = $1_id::$2
```

Unfortunately, this will not function as we hope and will instead create the field id.

Chaining transforms

As covered before in the *Attributes with class* section, transforms are executed in a particular order. In most cases, this order does not matter, but there are occasions when you might want to chain transforms together, with one transform relying on a field created by a previous transform.

A good example is the source flattening that we used previously, in the *Overriding source* section. If this transform happened before our transform in the *Creating a session field from source* section, our session field will always have the value x.

Let's reuse two transforms from previous sections and then create one more transform. We will chain them to pull the first part of session into yet another field. Say we have these transforms:

```
[myapp_session]
SOURCE_KEY = MetaData:Source
REGEX = session_(.*?).log
FORMAT = session::$1
WRITE_META = True
[myapp_flatten_source]
SOURCE_KEY = MetaData:Source
DEST_KEY = MetaData:Source
REGEX = (.*session_).*.log
FORMAT = source::$1x.log
[session_type]
SOURCE_KEY = session
```

```
REGEX = (.*?)-
FORMAT = session_type::$1
WRITE_META = True
```

To ensure that these transforms run in order, the simplest thing would be to place them in a single TRANSFORMS attribute in props.conf, as shown here:

```
[source:*session_*.log]
TRANSFORMS-s = myapp_session,myapp_flatten_source,session_type
```

We can use the source from our sample event specified inside tranforms.conf as follows:

```
source=/logs/myapp.session_foo-jA5MDkyMjEwMTIK.log
```

Walking though the transforms, we have the following terms and their descriptions:

- myapp_session: Reading from the metadata field, source, creates the indexed field session with the foo-jA5MDkyMjEwMTIK value
- myapp_flatten_source: This resets the metadata field, source, to /logs/myapp.session_x.log
- session_type: Reading from our newly-indexed field, session, creates the session_type field with the value foo

This same ordering logic can be applied at search time using the EXTRACT and REPORT stanzas. This particular case needs to be calculated as indexed fields if we want to search for these values, since the values are part of a metadata field.

Dropping events

Some events are simply not worth indexing. The hard part is figuring out which ones these are and making very sure you're not wrong. Dropping too many events can make you blind to real problems at critical times, and can introduce more problems than tuning Splunk to deal with the greater volume of data in the first place.

With that warning stated, if you know what events you do not need, the procedure for dropping events is pretty simple. Say we have an event such as this one:

```
2012-02-02 12:24:23 UTC TRACE Database call 1 of 1,000. [...]
```

I know absolutely that, in this case and for this particular source type, I do not want to index TRACE-level events.

In `props.conf`, I will create a stanza for my source type, as shown here:

```
[mysourcetype]
TRANSFORMS-droptrace=droptrace
```

Then, I will create the following transform in `transforms.conf`:

```
[droptrace]
REGEX=^d{4}-d{2}-d{2}s+d{1,2}:d{2}:d{1,2}s+[A-Z]+sTRACE
DEST_KEY=queue
FORMAT=nullQueue
```

Splunk compares `nullQueue` to `nulldevice`, which (according to the product documentation) tells Splunk not to forward or index the filtered data.

This `REGEX` attribute is purposely as strict as I can make it. It is vital that I do not accidentally drop other events, and it is better for this brittle pattern to start failing and to let through `TRACE` events rather than for it to do the opposite.

fields.conf

We need to add to `fields.conf` any indexed fields we create, or else they will not be searched efficiently, or may even not function at all. For our examples in the *transforms.conf* section, `fields.conf` would look like this:

```
[session_type]
INDEXED = true
[session]
INDEXED = true
[host_owner]
INDEXED = true
[host_type]
INDEXED = true
[slow_request]
INDEXED = true
[loglevel]
INDEXED = true
```

These stanzas instruct Splunk not to look in the body of the events for the value being queried. Take, for instance, the following search:

```
host_owner=vlb
```

Without this entry, the actual query would essentially be:

```
vlb | search host_owner=vlb
```

With the expectation that the value `vlb` is in the body of the event, this query simply won't work. Adding the entry to `fields.conf` fixes this. In the case of loglevel, since the value is in the body, the query will work, but it will not take advantage of the indexed field, instead only using it to filter events after finding all events that contain the bare word.

outputs.conf

This configuration controls how Splunk will forward events. In the vast majority of cases, this configuration exists on Splunk forwarders, which send their events to Splunk indexers. An example would look like this:

```
[tcpout]
defaultGroup = nyc
[tcpout:nyc]
autoLB = true
server = 1.2.3.4:9997,1.2.3.6:9997
```

It is possible to use transforms to route events to different server groups, but it is not commonly used as it introduces a lot of complexity that is generally not needed.

indexes.conf

Put simply, `indexes.conf` determines where data is stored on the disk, how much is kept, and for how long. An index is simply a named directory with a specific structure. Inside this directory structure, there are a few metadata files and subdirectories; the subdirectories are called buckets and actually contain the indexed data.

A simple stanza looks like this:

```
[implSplunk]
homePath = $SPLUNK_DB/implSplunk/db
coldPath = $SPLUNK_DB/implSplunk/colddb
thawedPath = $SPLUNK_DB/implSplunk/thaweddb
```

Let's walk through these attributes:

- `homePath`: This is the location for recent data.
- `coldPath`: This is the location for older data.

- `thawedPath`: This is a directory where buckets can be restored. It is an unmanaged location. This attribute must be defined, but I, for one, have never actually used it.

An aside about the terminology of buckets is probably in order. It is as follows:

- `hot`: This is a bucket that is currently open for writing. It lives in `homePath`.
- `warm`: This is a bucket that was created recently but is no longer open for writing. It also lives in `homePath`.
- `cold`: This is an older bucket that has been moved to `coldPath`. It is moved when `maxWarmDBCount` has been exceeded.
- `frozen`: For most installations, this simply means deleted. For customers who want to archive buckets, `coldToFrozenScript` or `coldToFrozenDir` can be specified to save buckets.
- `thawed`: A thawed bucket is a frozen bucket that has been brought back. It is special in that it is not managed, and it is not included in all time queries. When using `coldToFrozenDir`, only the raw data is typically kept, so Splunk rebuild will need to be used to make the bucket searchable again.

How long data stays in an index is controlled by these attributes:

- `frozenTimePeriodInSecs`: This setting dictates the oldest data to keep in an index. A bucket will be removed when its newest event is older than this value. The default value is approximately 6 years.
- `maxTotalDataSizeMB`: This setting dictates how large an index can be. The total space used across all hot, warm, and cold buckets will not exceed this value. The oldest bucket is always frozen first. The default value is 500 gigabytes. It is generally a good idea to set both of these attributes. `frozenTimePeriodInSecs` should match what users expect. `maxTotalDataSizeMB` should protect your system from running out of disk space.

Less commonly used attributes include:

- `coldToFrozenDir`: If specified, buckets will be moved to this directory instead of being deleted. This directory is not managed by Splunk, so it is up to the administrator to make sure that the disk does not fill up.
- `maxHotBuckets`: A bucket represents a slice of time and will ideally span as small a slice of time as is practical. I would never set this value to less than 3, but ideally, it should be set to 10.

- `maxDataSize`: This is the maximum size for an individual bucket. The default value is set by the processor type and is generally acceptable. The larger a bucket, the fewer the buckets to be opened to complete a search, but the more the disk space needed before a bucket can be frozen. The default is auto, which will never top 750 MB. The setting `auto_high_volume`, which equals 1 GB on 32-bit systems and 10 GB on 64-bit systems, should be used for indexes that receive more than 10 GB a day.

authorize.conf

This configuration stores definitions of capabilities and roles. These settings affect search and the web interface. They are generally managed through the interface at **Settings** | **Access controls**, but a quick look at the configuration itself may be useful.

A role stanza looks like this:

```
[role_power]
importRoles = user
schedule_search = enabled
rtsearch = enabled
srchIndexesAllowed = *
srchIndexesDefault = main
srchDiskQuota = 500
srchJobsQuota = 10
rtSrchJobsQuota = 20
```

Let's walk through these settings:

- `importRoles`: This is a list of roles to import capabilities from. The set of capabilities will be the merging of capabilities from imported roles and added capabilities.
- `schedule_search` and `rtsearch`: These are two capabilities enabled for the role power that were not necessarily enabled for the imported roles.
- `srchIndexesAllowed`: This determines what indexes this role is allowed to search. In this case, all are allowed.

- `srchIndexesDefault`: This determines the indexes to search by default. This setting also affects the data shown in **Search** | **Summary**. If you have installed the `ImplementingSplunkDataGenerator` app, you will see the `impl_splunk_*` source types on this page even though this data is actually stored in the `implsplunk` index.
- `srchDiskQuota`: Whenever a search is run, the results are stored on the disk until they expire. The expiration can be set explicitly when creating a saved search, but the expiration is automatically set for interactive searches. Users can delete old results from the **Jobs** view.
- `srchJobsQuota`: Each user is limited to a certain number of concurrently running searches. The default is three. Users with the power role are allowed 10, while those with the admin role are allowed 50.
- `rtSrchJobsQuota`: Similarly, this is the maximum number of concurrently running real-time searches. The default is six.

savedsearches.conf

This configuration contains saved searches and is rarely modified by hand.

times.conf

This holds definitions for time ranges that appear in the time picker.

commands.conf

This configuration specifies commands provided by an app.

web.conf

The main settings changed in this file are the port for the web server, the SSL certificates, and whether to start the web server at all.

User interface resources

Most Splunk apps consist mainly of resources for the web application. The app layout for these resources is completely different from all other configurations.

Views and navigation

Like `.conf` files, view and navigation documents take precedence in the following order:

- `$SPLUNK_HOME/etc/users/$username/$appname/local`: When a new dashboard is created, it lands here. It will remain here until the permissions are changed to **App** or **Global**.
- `$SPLUNK_HOME/etc/apps/$appname/local`: Once a document is shared, it will be moved to this directory.
- `$SPLUNK_HOME/etc/apps/$appname/default`: Documents can only be placed here manually. You should do this if you are going to share an app. Unlike `.conf` files, these documents do not merge.

Within each of these directories, views and navigation end up under the directories `data/ui/views` and `data/ui/nav`, respectively. So, given a view `foo`, for the user `bob`, in the app `app1`, the initial location for the document will be as follows:

```
$SPLUNK_HOME/etc/users/bob/app1/local/data/ui/views/foo.xml
```

Once the document is shared, it will be moved to the following location:

```
$SPLUNK_HOME/etc/apps/app1/local/data/ui/views/foo.xml
```

Navigation follows the same structure, but the only navigation document that is ever used is called `default.xml`, for instance:

```
$SPLUNK_HOME/etc/apps/app1/local/data/ui/nav/default.xml
```

You can edit these files directly on the disk instead of through the web interface, but Splunk will probably not realize the changes without a restart—unless you use a little trick. To reload changes to views or navigation made directly on the disk, load the URL `http://mysplunkserver:8000/debug/refresh`, replacing `mysplunkserver` appropriately. If all else fails, restart Splunk.

Appserver resources

Outside of views and navigation, there are a number of resources that the web application will use. For instance, applications and dashboards can reference CSS and images, as we did in Chapter 7, *Working with Apps*. These resources are stored under `$SPLUNK_HOME/etc/apps/$appname/appserver/`. There are a few directories that appear under this directory, as follows:

- `static`: Any static files that you would like to use in your application are stored here. There are a few magic documents that Splunk itself will use, for instance, `appIcon.png`, `screenshot.png`, `application.css`, and `application.js`. Other files can be referenced using includes or templates. See the *Using ServerSideInclude in a complex dashboard* section in Chapter 7, *Working with Apps*, for an example of referencing includes and static images.
- `event_renderers`: Event renderers allow you to run special display code for specific event types.
- `templates`: It is possible to create special templates using the *mako* template language. It is not commonly done.
- `modules`: This is where new modules that are provided by apps are stored. Examples of this include the Google Maps and Sideview Utils modules. See `https://dev.splunk.com` for more information about building your own modules, or use existing modules as an example.

Metadata

Object permissions are stored in files located at `$SPLUNK_HOME/etc/apps/$appname/metadata/`. The two possible files are `default.meta` and `local.meta`.

These files have certain properties:

- They are only relevant to the resources in the app where they are contained
- They do merge, with entries in `local.meta` taking precedence
- They are generally controlled by the admin interface
- They can contain rules that affect all configurations of a particular type, but this entry must be made manually

In the absence of these files (not all apps will have this folder), resources are limited to the current app.

Let's look at `default.meta` for `is_app_one`, as created by Splunk:

```
# Application-level permissions
[]
access = read : [ * ], write : [ admin, power ]
### EVENT TYPES
[eventtypes]
export = system
### PROPS
[props]
export = system
### TRANSFORMS
[transforms]
export = system
### LOOKUPS
[lookups]
Chapter 10
[ 329 ]
export = system
### VIEWSTATES: even normal users should be able to create shared
viewstates
[viewstates]
access = read : [ * ], write : [ * ]
export = system
```

Walking through this snippet, we have the following terms and their descriptions:

- The `[]` stanza states that all users should be able to read everything in this app but that only users with the admin or power roles should be able to write to this app.
- The `[eventtypes]`, `[props]`, `[transforms]`, and `[lookups]` states say that all configurations of each type in this app should be shared by all users in all apps, by default. `export=system` is equivalent to `Global` in the user interface.
- The `[viewstates]` stanza gives all users the right to share `viewstates` globally. A viewstate contains information about dashboard settings made through the web application, for instance, chart settings. Without this, chart settings applied to a dashboard or saved search would not be available.

Looking at local.meta, we see settings produced by the web application for the configurations we created through the web application:

```
[indexes/summary_impl_splunk]
access = read : [ * ], write : [ admin, power ]
[views/errors]
access = read : [ * ], write : [ admin, power ]
export = system
owner = admin
version = 4.3
modtime = 1339296668.151105000
[savedsearches/top%20user%20errors%20pie%20chart]
export = none
owner = admin
version = 4.3
modtime = 1338420710.720786000
[viewstates/flashtimeline%3Ah2v14xkb]
owner = nobody
version = 4.3
modtime = 1338420715.753642000
[props/impl_splunk_web/LOOKUP-web_section]
access = read : [ * ]
export = none
owner = admin
version = 4.3
modtime = 1346013505.279379000
```

Hopefully, you get the idea. The web application will make very specific entries for each object created. When distributing an application, it is generally easier to make blanket permissions in metadata/default.meta as appropriate for the resources in your application.

For an application that simply provides dashboards, no metadata at all will be needed as the default for all resources (apps) will be acceptable. If your application provides resources to be used by other applications, for instance, lookups or extracts, your `default.meta` file might look like this:

```
### PROPS
[props]
export = system
### TRANSFORMS
[transforms]
export = system
### LOOKUPS
[lookups]
export = system
```

This states that everything in your `props.conf` and `transforms.conf` files, and all lookup definitions, are merged into the logical configuration of every search.

11
Play Time – Getting Data In

In this chapter, we will cover the basic ways to get data into **Splunk**, in addition to some other recipes that will help prepare you for later chapters. You will learn about the following recipes:

- Indexing files and directories
- Getting data through network ports
- Using scripted inputs
- Using modular inputs
- Using the Universal Forwarder to gather data
- Receiving data using the HTTP Event Collector
- Getting data from databases using DB Connect
- Loading the sample data for this book
- Data onboarding: Defining field extractions
- Data onboarding: Defining event types and tags
- Installing the Machine Learning Toolkit

Introduction

The machine data that facilitates operational intelligence comes in many different forms and from many different sources. Splunk can collect and index data from several sources, including log files written by web servers or business applications, syslog data streaming in from network devices, or the output of custom developed scripts. Even data that looks complex at first can be easily collected, indexed, transformed, and presented back to you in real time.

This chapter will walk you through the basic recipes that will act as the building blocks to get the data you want into Splunk. The chapter will further serve as an introduction to the sample data sets that we will use to build our own operational intelligence Splunk app. The datasets will be coming from a hypothetical three-tier e-commerce web application and will contain web server logs, application logs, and database logs.

Splunk Enterprise can index any type of data; however, it works best with time-series data (data with timestamps). When Splunk Enterprise indexes data, it breaks it into events, based on timestamps and/or event size, and puts them into indexes. Indexes are data stores that Splunk has engineered to be very fast, searchable, and scalable across a distributed server environment.

All data indexed into Splunk is assigned a source type. The source type helps identify the data format type of the event and where it has come from. Splunk has several preconfigured source types, but you can also specify your own. The example source types include `access_combined`, `cisco_syslog`, and `linux_secure`. The source type is added to the data when the indexer indexes it into Splunk. It is a key field that is used when performing field extractions and when conducting many searches to filter the data being searched.

The Splunk community plays a big part in making it easy to get data into Splunk. The ability to extend Splunk has provided the opportunity for the development of inputs, commands, and applications that can be easily shared. If there is a particular system or application you are looking to index data from, there is most likely someone who has developed and published relevant configurations and tools that can be easily leveraged by your own Splunk Enterprise deployment.

Splunk Enterprise is designed to make the collection of data very easy, and it will not take long before you are being asked or you yourself try to get as much data into Splunk as possible—at least as much as your license will allow for!

Indexing files and directories

File- and directory-based inputs are the most commonly used ways of getting data into Splunk. The primary need for these types of input will be to index logfiles. Almost every application or system produces a logfile, and it is generally full of data that you want to be able to search and report on.

Splunk can continuously monitor for new data being written to existing files or new files being added to a directory, and it is able to index this data in real time. Depending on the type of application that creates the logfiles, you would set up Splunk to either monitor an individual file based on its location, or scan an entire directory and monitor all the files that exist within it. The latter configuration is more commonly used when the logfiles being produced have unique filenames, such as filenames containing a timestamp.

This recipe will show you how to configure Splunk to continuously monitor and index the contents of a rolling logfile located on the Splunk server. The recipe specifically shows how to monitor and index a Red Hat Linux system's messages logfile (/var/log/messages). However, the same principle can be applied to a logfile on a Windows system, and a sample file is provided. Do not attempt to index the Windows event logs this way, as Splunk has specific Windows event inputs for this.

Getting ready

To step through this recipe, you will need a running Splunk Enterprise server and access to read the /var/log/messages file on Linux. No other prerequisites are required. If you are not using Linux and/or do not have access to the /var/log/messages location on your Splunk server, use the cp01_messages.log file that is provided and upload it to an accessible directory on your Splunk server.

You can download the example code files for all Packt books you have purchased from your account at http://www.packtpub.com. If you purchased this book elsewhere, you can visit http://www.packtpub.com/support and register to have the files emailed directly to you.

How to do it...

Follow these steps to monitor and index the contents of a file:

1. Log in to your Splunk server.
2. From the menu in the top right-hand corner, click on the **Settings** menu and then click on the **Add Data** link:

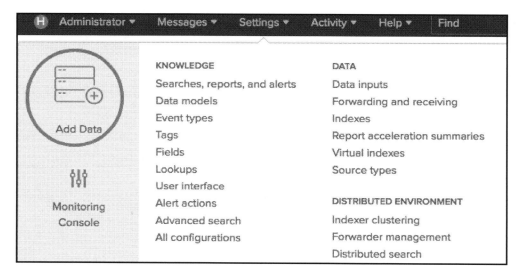

3. If you are prompted to take a quick tour, click on **Skip**.
4. In the **How do you want to add data** section, click on **monitor**:

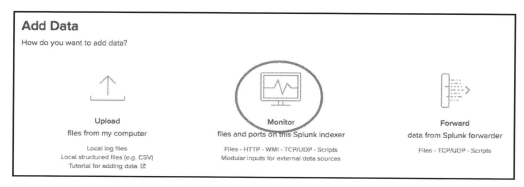

5. Click on the **Files & Directories** section:

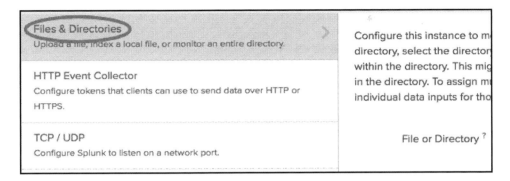

6. In the **File or Directory** section, enter the path to the logfile (`/var/log/messages` or the location of the `cp01_messages.log` file), ensure **Continuously Monitor** is selected, and click on **Next**:

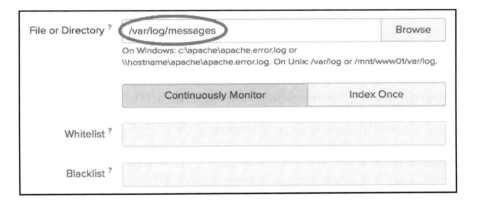

If you are just looking to do a one-time upload of a file, you can select **Index Once** instead. This can be useful to index a set of data that you would like to put into Splunk, either to backfill some missing or incomplete data or just to take advantage of its searching and reporting tools.

7. If you are using the provided file or the native `/var/log/messages` file, the data preview will show the correct line breaking of events and timestamp recognition. Click on the **Next** button.

8. A **Save Source Type** box will pop up. Enter `linux_messages` as the **Name** and then click on **Save**:

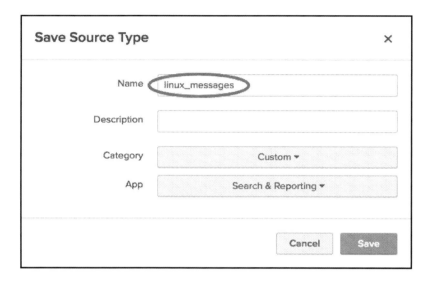

9. On the **Input Settings** page, leave all the default settings and click **Review**.
10. Review the settings and if everything is correct, click **Submit**.
11. If everything was successful, you should see a **File input has been created successfully** message:

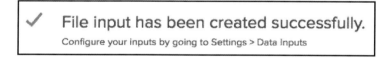

12. Click on the **Start** searching button. The **Search & Reporting** app will open with the search already populated based on the settings supplied earlier in the recipe.

 In this recipe, we could have simply used the common syslog source type or let Splunk choose a source type name for us; however, starting a new source type is often a better choice. The syslog format can look completely different depending on the data source. As knowledge objects, such as field extractions, are built on top of source types, using a single syslog source type for everything can make it challenging to search for the data you need.

How it works...

When you add a new file or directory data input, you are basically adding a new configuration stanza into an `inputs.conf` file behind the scenes. The Splunk server can contain one or more `inputs.conf` files, and these files are either located in `$SPLUNK_HOME/etc/system/local` or in the local directory of a Splunk app.

Splunk uses the monitor input type and is set to point to either a file or a directory. If you set the monitor to a directory, all the files within that directory will be monitored. When Splunk monitors files, it initially starts by indexing all the data that it can read from the beginning. Once complete, Splunk maintains a record of where it last read the data from, and if any new data comes into the file, it reads this data and advances the record. The process is nearly identical to using the tail command in Unix-based operating systems. If you are monitoring a directory, Splunk also provides many additional configuration options, such as blacklisting files you don't want Splunk to index.

For more information on Splunk's configuration files, visit `https://docs.splunk.com/Documentation/Splunk/latest/Admin/Aboutc` `onfigurationfiles`.

There's more...

While adding inputs to monitor files and directories can be done through the web interface of Splunk, as outlined in this recipe, there are other approaches to add multiple inputs quickly. These allow for customization of the many configuration options that Splunk provides.

Adding a file or directory data input using the CLI

Instead of using the GUI, you can add a file or directory input through the Splunk **command-line interface (CLI)**. Navigate to your `$SPLUNK_HOME/bin` directory and execute the following command (replacing the file or directory to be monitored with your own):

For Unix, we will be using the following code to add a file or directory input:

```
./splunk add monitor /var/log/messages -sourcetype linux_messages
```

For Windows, we will be using the following code to add a file or directory input:

```
splunk add monitor c:/filelocation/cp01_messages.log –sourcetype
linux_messages
```

There are a number of different parameters that can be passed along with the file location to monitor.

See the Splunk documentation for more on data inputs using the CLI (`https://docs.splunk.com/Documentation/Splunk/latest/Data/Monito rfilesanddirectoriesusingtheCLI`).

Adding a file or directory input using inputs.conf

Another common method of adding the file and directory inputs is to manually add them to the `inputs.conf` configuration file directly. This approach is often used for large environments or when configuring Splunk forwarders to monitor for files or directories on endpoints.

Edit `$SPLUNK_HOME/etc/system/local/inputs.conf` and add your input. After your inputs are added, Splunk will need to be restarted to recognize these changes.

For Unix, we will use the following code:

```
[monitor:///var/log/messages]
sourcetype = linux_messages
```

For Windows, we will use the following code:

```
[monitor://c:/filelocation/cp01_messages.log]
sourcetype = linux_messages
```

Editing `inputs.conf` directly is often a much faster way of adding new files or directories to monitor when several inputs are needed. When editing `inputs.conf`, ensure that the correct syntax is used and remember that Splunk will need a restart for modifications to take effect. Additionally, specifying the source type in the `inputs.conf` file is the best methods for assigning source types.

One-time indexing of data files using the Splunk CLI

Although you can select **Upload and Index a file** from the Splunk GUI to upload and index a file, there are a couple of CLI functions that can be used to perform one-time bulk loads of data.

Use the `oneshot` command to tell Splunk where the file is located and which parameters to use, such as the source type:

```
./splunk add oneshot XXXXXXX
```

Another way is to place the file you wish to index into the Splunk `spool` directory, `$SPLUNK_HOME/var/spool/splunk`, and then add the file using the `spool` command, as shown in the following code:

```
./splunk spool XXXXXXX
```

If using Windows, omit the dot and slash (`./`) that is in front of the Splunk commands mentioned earlier.

Indexing the Windows event logs

Splunk comes with special `inputs.conf` configurations for some source types, including monitoring Windows event logs. Typically, the Splunk **Universal Forwarder** (**UF**) would be installed on a Windows server and configured to forward the Windows events to the Splunk indexer(s). The configurations for `inputs.conf` to monitor the Windows security, application, and event logs in real time are as follows:

```
[WinEventLog://Application]
disabled = 0
[WinEventLog://Security]
disabled = 0
[WinEventLog://System]
disabled = 0
```

By default, the event data will go into the main index, unless another index is specified.

See also

- The *Getting data through network ports* recipe
- The *Using scripted inputs* recipe
- The *Using modular inputs* recipe

Getting data through network ports

Not every machine has the luxury of being able to write logfiles. Sending data over network ports and protocols is still very common. For instance, sending logs through syslog is still the primary method to capture network device data such as firewalls, routers, and switches.

Sending data to Splunk over network ports doesn't need to be limited to network devices. Applications and scripts can use socket communication to the network ports that Splunk is listening on. This can be a very useful tool in your back pocket, as there can be scenarios where you need to get data into Splunk but don't necessarily have the ability to write to a file.

This recipe will show you how to configure Splunk to receive syslog data on a UDP network port, but it is also applicable to the TCP port configuration.

Getting ready

To step through this recipe, you will need a running Splunk Enterprise server. No other prerequisites are required.

How to do it...

Follow these steps to configure Splunk to receive network UDP data:

1. Log in to your Splunk server.
2. From the menu in the top right-hand corner, click on the **Settings** menu and then click on the **Add Data** link.
3. If you are prompted to take a quick tour, click on **Skip**.
4. In the **How do you want to add data** section, click on **Monitor**.

5. Click on the **TCP / UDP** section:

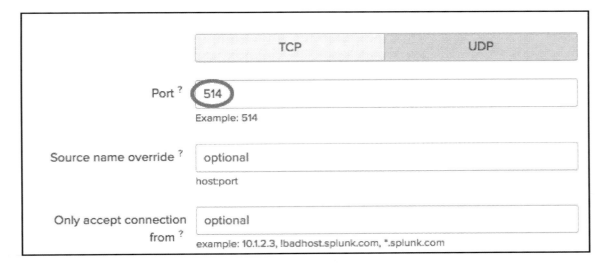

6. Ensure the **UDP** option is selected and in the **Port** section, enter 514. On Unix/Linux, Splunk must be running as root to access privileged ports such as 514. An alternative would be to specify a higher port, such as port 1514, or route data from 514 to another port using routing rules in iptables. Then, click on **Next**:

7. In the **Source type** section, select **Select** and then select **syslog** from the **Select Source Type** drop-down list and click **Review**:

Source type

The source type is one of the default fields that Splunk assigns to all incoming data. It tells Splunk what kind of data you've got, so that Splunk can format the data intelligently during indexing. And it's a way to categorize your data, so that you can search it easily.

Select   New

syslog ▾

8. Review the settings and if everything is correct, click **Submit**.
9. If everything was successful, you should see a **UDP input has been created successfully** message:

 UDP input has been created successfully.

Configure your inputs by going to Settings > Data Inputs

10. Click on the **Start Searching** button. The **Search & Reporting** app will open with the search already populated based on the settings supplied earlier in the recipe. Splunk is now configured to listen on UDP port 514. Any data sent to this port now will be assigned the syslog source type. To search for the syslog source type, you can run the following search:

```
source="udp:514" sourcetype="syslog"
```

Understandably, you will not see any data unless you happen to be sending data to your Splunk server IP on UDP port 514.

How it works...

When you add a new network port input, you basically add a new configuration stanza into an `inputs.conf` file behind the scenes. The Splunk server can contain one or more `inputs.conf` files, and these files are either located in the `$SPLUNK_HOME/etc/system/local` or the local directory of a Splunk app.

To collect data on a network port, Splunk will set up a socket to listen on the specified TCP or UDP port and will index any data it receives on that port. For example, in this recipe, you configured Splunk to listen on port 514 for UDP data. If data was received on that port, then Splunk would index it and assign a syslog source type to it.

Splunk also provides many configuration options that can be used with network inputs, such as how to resolve the host value to be used on the collected data.

For more information on Splunk's configuration files, visit
`https://docs.splunk.com/Documentation/Splunk/latest/Admin/Aboutc`
`onfigurationfiles`.

There's more...

While adding inputs to receive data from network ports can be done through the web interface of Splunk, as outlined in this recipe, there are other approaches to add multiple inputs quickly; these inputs allow for customization of the many configuration options that Splunk provides.

Adding a network input using the CLI

You can also add a file or directory input via the Splunk CLI. Navigate to your `$SPLUNK_HOME/bin directory` and execute the following command (just replace the protocol, port, and source type you wish to use):

- We will use the following code for Unix:

`./splunk add udp 514 -sourcetype syslog`

- We will use the following code for Windows:

`splunk add udp 514 -sourcetype syslog`

There are a number of different parameters that can be passed along with the port. See the Splunk documentation for more on data inputs using the CLI
(`https://docs.splunk.com/Documentation/Splunk/latest/Data/Monitorfilesanddirect`
`oriesusingtheCLI`).

Adding a network input using inputs.conf

Network inputs can be manually added to the `inputs.conf` configuration files. Edit `$SPLUNK_HOME/etc/system/local/inputs.conf` and add your input. You will need to restart Splunk after modifying the file. For example, to enable UDP port 514 use the following code:

```
[udp://514]
sourcetype = syslog
```

 It is best practice to not send syslog data directly to an indexer. Instead, always place a forwarder between the network device and the indexer. The Splunk forwarder will be set up to receive the incoming syslog data (`inputs.conf`) and will load balance the data across your Splunk indexers (`outputs.conf`). The forwarder can also be configured to cache the syslog data in the event communication to the indexers is lost.

See also

- The *Indexing files and directories* recipe
- The *Using scripted inputs* recipe
- The *Using modular inputs* recipe

Using scripted inputs

Not all data that is useful for operational intelligence comes from logfiles or network ports. Splunk will happily take the output of a command or script and index it along with all your other data.

Scripted inputs are a very helpful way to get that hard-to-reach data. For example, if you have third-party-supplied command-line programs that can output data you would like to collect, Splunk can run the command periodically and index the results. Typically, scripted inputs are often used to pull data from a source, whereas network inputs await a push of data from a source.

This recipe will show you how to configure Splunk on an interval to execute your command and direct the output into Splunk.

Getting ready

To step through this recipe, you will need a running Splunk server and the provided scripted input script suited to the environment you are using. For example, if you are using Windows, use the `cp01_scripted_input.bat` file. This script should be placed in the `$SPLUNK_HOME/bin/scripts` directory. No other prerequisites are required.

How to do it...

Follow these steps to configure a scripted input:

1. Log in to your Splunk server.
2. From the menu in the top right-hand corner, click on the **Settings** menu and then click on the **Add Data** link.
3. If you are prompted to take a quick tour, click on **Skip**.
4. In the **How do you want to add data** section, click on **Monitor**.
5. Click on the **Scripts** section:

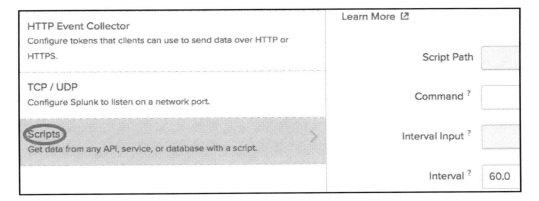

6. A form will be displayed with a number of input fields. In the **Script Path** drop-down, select the location of the script. All scripts must be located in a Splunk `bin` directory, either in `$SPLUNK_HOME/bin/scripts` or an appropriate bin directory within a Splunk app, such as `$SPLUNK_HOME/etc/apps/search/bin`.
7. In the **Script Name** dropdown, select the name of the script. In the **Commands** field, add any command-line arguments to the auto-populated script name.

8. Enter the value in the **Interval** field (in seconds) in which the script is to be run (the default value is **60.0** seconds) and then click **Next**:

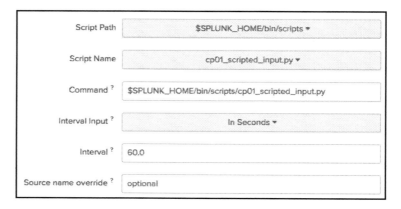

9. In the **Source Type** section, you have the option to either select a predefined source type or to select **New** and enter your desired value. For the purpose of this recipe, select **New** as the source type and enter `cp01_scripted_input` as the value for the source type. Then click **Review**:

10. By default, data will be indexed into the Splunk index of `main`. To change this destination index, select your desired index from the drop-down list in the **Index** section of the form.

11. Review the settings. If everything is correct, click **Submit**.

12. If everything was successful, you should see a **Script input has been created successfully** message:

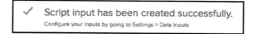

13. Click on the **Start searching** button. The **Search & Reporting** app will open with the search already populated based on the settings supplied earlier in the recipe. Splunk is now configured to execute the scripted input you provided every 60 seconds, in accordance with the specified interval. You can search for the data returned by the scripted input using the following search:

```
sourcetype=cp01_scripted_input
```

How it works...

When adding a new scripted input, you are directing Splunk to add a new configuration stanza into an `inputs.conf` file behind the scenes. The Splunk server can contain one or more `inputs.conf` files, located either in `$SPLUNK_HOME/etc/system/local` or the local directory of a Splunk app.

After creating a scripted input, Splunk sets up an internal timer and executes the command that you have specified, in accordance with the defined interval. It is important to note that Splunk will only run one instance of the script at a time, so if the script gets blocked for any reason, it will cause the script to not be executed again, until after it has been unblocked.

Since Splunk 4.2, any output of the scripted inputs that are directed to `stderr` (causing an error) are captured to the `splunkd.log` file, which can be useful when attempting to debug the execution of a script. As Splunk indexes its own data by default, you can search for that data and put an alert on it if necessary.

For security reasons, Splunk does not execute scripts located outside of the bin directories mentioned earlier. To overcome this limitation, you can use a wrapper script (such as a shell script in Linux or batch file in Windows) to call any other script located on your machine.

See also

- The *Indexing files and directories* recipe
- The *Getting data through network ports* recipe
- The *Using modular inputs* recipe

Using modular inputs

Since Splunk 5.0, the ability to extend data input functionality has existed such that custom input types can be created and shared while still allowing for user customization to meet needs.

Modular inputs build further upon the scripted input model. Originally, any additional functionality required by the user had to be contained within a script. However, this presented a challenge, as no customization of this script could occur from within Splunk itself. For example, pulling data from a source for two different usernames needed two copies of a script or meant playing around with command-line arguments within your scripted input configuration.

By leveraging the modular input capabilities, developers are now able to encapsulate their code into a reusable app that exposes parameters in Splunk and allows for configuration through processes familiar to Splunk administrators.

This recipe will walk you through how to install the **Command Modular Input**, which allows for periodic execution of commands and subsequent indexing of the command output. You will configure the input to collect the data outputted by the `vmstat` command in Linux and the `systeminfo` command in Windows.

Getting ready

To step through this recipe, you will need a running Splunk server with a connection to the internet. No other prerequisites are required.

You will also need to download the Command Modular Input Add-on app from Splunkbase. This app can be found at `https://splunkbase.splunk.com/app/1553/`.

How to do it...

Follow the steps in this recipe to configure a modular input:

1. Log in to your Splunk server.
2. From the **Apps** menu in the upper left-hand corner of the home screen, click on the gear icon:

3. The **Apps settings** page will load. Then, click on the **Install App from file** button.

4. Click the **Choose File** button and select the app file that was previously downloaded from Splunkbase, then click the **Upload** button:

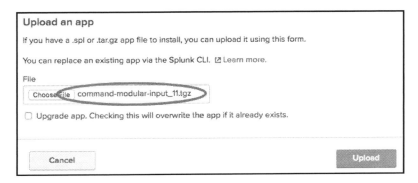

5. After the app has been installed, from the menu in the top right-hand corner, click on the **Settings** menu and then click on the **Data inputs** link.

6. Click on the **Command** section:

7. In the **Mod Input Name** field, enter a name for the input of `SystemInfo`. If you are using Linux, enter `/usr/bin/vmstat` in the **Command Name** field. If you are using Windows, enter `C:\Windows\System32\systeminfo.exe` in the **Command Name** field:

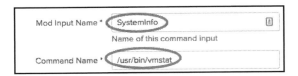

Use the full path if the command to be executed cannot be found on the system PATH.

8. In the **Command Arguments** field, enter any argument that needs to be passed to the command listed in the **Command Name** field. In the **Command Execution Interval** field, enter a value in seconds for how often the command should be executed (in this case, we will use 60 seconds). If the output is streamed, then leave this field empty and check the **Streaming Output** field:

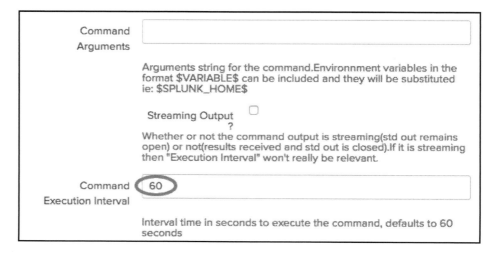

9. In the **Source type** section, you have the option to either select a predefined source type or select **Manual** and enter a value. For this recipe, select **Manual** as the source type and enter `cp01_modular_input` as the value for the source type.
10. Click **Next**.
11. If everything was successful, you should see a **Modular input has been created successfully** message:

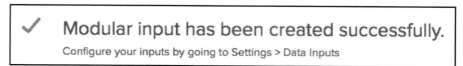

12. Click on the **Start searching** button. The **Search & Reporting** app will open with the search already populated based on the settings supplied earlier in the recipe. Splunk is now configured to execute the modular input you provided, every 60 seconds, in accordance with the specified interval. You can search for this data returned by the scripted input using the following search over an **All time** time range:

```
sourcetype=cp01_modular_input
```

How it works...

Modular inputs are bundled as Splunk apps and, once installed, contain all the necessary configuration and code to display them in the **Data inputs** section of Splunk. In this recipe, you installed a modular input application that allows for periodic execution of commands. You configured the command to execute every minute and to index the results of the command each time, giving the results a source type of cp01_modular_input.

Modular inputs can be written in several languages and need to follow only a set of interfaces that expose the configuration options and runtime behaviors. Depending on the design of the input, they will either run persistently or run at an interval and will send data to Splunk as they receive it.

 You can find several other modular inputs, including REST API, SNMP, and PowerShell, on the Splunk Apps site (https://splunkbase.splunk.com).

There's more...

To learn how to create your own modular input, refer to the *Modular Inputs* section of the *Developing Views and Apps for Splunk* web manual located at https://docs.splunk.com/Documentation/Splunk/latest/AdvancedDev/ModInputsIntro.

See also

- The *Indexing files and directories* recipe
- The *Getting data through network ports* recipe
- The *Using scripted inputs* recipe

Using the Universal Forwarder to gather data

Most IT environments today range from multiple servers in the closet of your office to hundreds of endpoint servers located in multiple geographically distributed data centers.

When the data we want to collect is not located directly on the server where Splunk is installed, the **Splunk Universal Forwarder** (**UF**) can be installed on your remote endpoint servers and used to forward data back to Splunk to be indexed.

The Universal Forwarder is like the Splunk server in that it has many of the same features, but it does not contain Splunk web and doesn't come bundled with the Python executable and libraries. Additionally, the Universal Forwarder cannot process data in advance, such as performing line breaking and timestamp extraction.

This recipe will guide you through configuring the Splunk Universal Forwarder to forward data to a Splunk indexer and will show you how to set up the indexer to receive the data.

Getting ready

To step through this recipe, you will need a server with the Splunk Universal Forwarder installed but not configured. You will also need a running Splunk Enterprise server. No other prerequisites are required.

To obtain the Universal Forwarder software, you need to go to `https://www.splunk.com/download` and register for an account if you do not already have one. Then, either download the software directly to your server or download it to your laptop or workstation and upload it to your server using a file transfer process such as SFTP.
For more information on how to install and manage the Universal Forwarder, visit `https://docs.splunk.com/Documentation/Forwarder/latest/Forwarder/Abouttheuniversalforwarder`.

How to do it...

Follow these steps to configure the Splunk Forwarder to forward data and the Splunk indexer to receive data:

1. On the server with the Universal Forwarder installed, open a command prompt if you are a Windows user or a terminal window if you are a Unix user.
2. Change to the `$SPLUNK_HOME/bin` directory, where `$SPLUNK_HOME` is the directory in which the Splunk forwarder was installed.
3. For Unix, the default installation directory will be `/opt/splunkforwarder/bin`. For Windows, it will be `C:/Program Files/SplunkUniversalForwarder/bin`.

 If using Windows, omit `./` in front of the Splunk command in the upcoming steps.

4. Start the Splunk forwarder, if not already started, using the following command:

   ```
   ./splunk start
   ```

5. Accept the license agreement.
6. Enable the Universal Forwarder to autostart, using the following command:

   ```
   ./splunk enable boot-start
   ```

7. Set the indexer that this Universal Forwarder will send its data to. Replace the host value with the value of the indexer as well as the username and password for the Universal Forwarder, using the following command:

   ```
   ./splunk add forward-server <host>:9997 -auth <username>:<password>
   ```

8. The username and password to log in to the forwarder (default is `admin:changeme`) is `<username>:<password>`.

 Additional receiving indexers can be added in the same way by repeating the command in the previous step with a different indexer host or IP. Splunk will automatically load balance the forwarded data if more than one receiving indexer is specified in this manner. Port 9997 is the default Splunk TCP port and should only be changed if it cannot be used for some reason.

9. On the receiving Splunk indexer servers, log in to your receiving Splunk indexer server. From the home launcher, in the top right-hand corner, click on the **Settings** menu item and then select the **Forwarding and receiving** link:

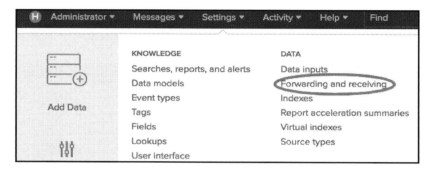

10. Click on the **Configure receiving** link:

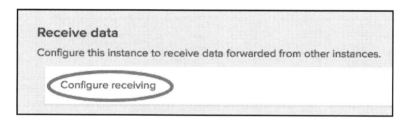

11. Click on **New**.

12. Enter 9997 in the **Listen on this port** field:

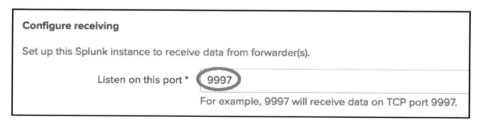

13. Click on **Save** and restart Splunk. The Universal Forwarder is installed and configured to send data to your Splunk server, and the Splunk server is configured to receive data on the default Splunk TCP port 9997.

How it works...

When you tell the forwarder which server to send data to, you basically add a new configuration stanza into an `outputs.conf` file behind the scenes. On the Splunk server, an `inputs.conf` file will contain a `[splunktcp]` stanza to enable receiving. The `outputs.conf` file on the Splunk forwarder will be located in `$SPLUNK_HOME/etc/system/local`, and the `inputs.conf` file on the Splunk server will be located in the local directory of the app you were in (the launcher app in this case) when configuring receiving.

Using forwarders to collect and forward data has many advantages. The forwarders communicate with the indexers on TCP port 9997 by default, which makes for a very simple set of firewall rules that need to be opened. Forwarders can also be configured to load balance their data across multiple indexers, increasing search speeds and availability. Additionally, forwarders can be configured to queue the data they collect if communication with the indexers is lost. This can be extremely important when collecting data that is not read from logfiles, such as performance counters or syslog streams, as the data cannot be re-read.

There's more...

While configuring the settings of the Universal Forwarder can be performed using the command-line interface of Splunk, as outlined in this recipe, there are several other methods to update the settings quickly and to allow for customization of the many configuration options that Splunk provides.

Adding the receiving indexer via outputs.conf

The receiving indexers can be directly added to the `outputs.conf` configuration file on the Universal Forwarder. Edit `$SPLUNK_HOME/etc/system/local/outputs.conf`, add your input, and then restart the UF. The following example configuration is provided, where two receiving indexers are specified. The `[tcpout-server]` stanza can be leveraged to add output configurations specific to an individual receiving indexer:

```
[tcpout]
defaultGroup = default-autolb-group

[tcpout:default-autolb-group]
disabled = false
server = mysplunkindexer1:9997,mysplunkindexer2:9997
```

```
[tcpout-server://mysplunkindexer1:9997]
[tcpout-server://mysplunkindexer2:9997]
```

If nothing has been configured in `inputs.conf` on the UF, but `outputs.conf` is configured with at least one valid receiving indexer, the Splunk forwarder will only send internal forwarder health-related data to the indexer. It is therefore possible to configure a forwarder correctly and the forwarder be detected by the Splunk indexers, but not actually send any real data.

Receiving data using the HTTP Event Collector

The **HTTP Event Collector (HEC)** is another highly scalable way of getting data into Splunk. The HEC listens for HTTP requests containing JSON objects and sends the data that has been collected to be indexed.

In this recipe, you will learn how to configure the Splunk HTTP Event Collector to receive data coming from an example Inventory Scanner. This example inventory scan HEC configuration will be used in Chapter 15, *Above and Beyond – Customization, Web Framework, REST API, HTTP Event Collector, and SDKs*.

Getting ready

To step through this recipe, you will need a running Splunk Enterprise server. You should be familiar with navigating the Splunk user interface and using the Splunk search language. This recipe will use the open source command-line tool, `curl`. There are other command-line tools available, such as `wget`. The curl tool is usually installed by default on most Mac and Linux systems but can be downloaded for Windows systems as well.

For more information on curl, visit http://curl.haxx.se/.

How to do it...

Perform these steps to create a custom search command to format product names:

1. Log in to your Splunk server.
2. Select the **Search & Reporting** application.
3. Click on **Settings** and then on **Data Inputs**:

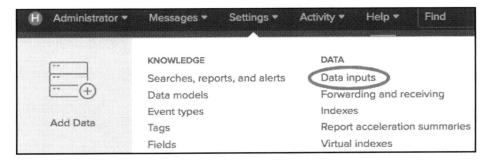

4. Click on **HTTP Event Collector**:

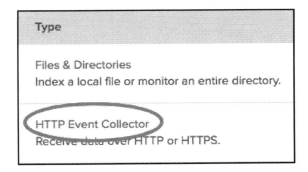

5. Click the **Global Settings** button:

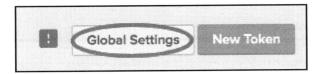

6. Set **All Tokens** to **Enabled**, and set the **DefaultIndex** to **main**. Then, click the **Save** button:

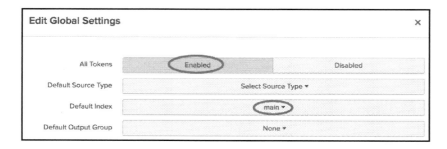

7. Click the **New Token** button:

8. Set the **Name** to Inventory Scanner and the **Source name override** to inventory:scanner, and click the **Next** button:

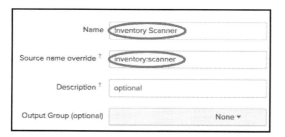

9. Select **New** for the **Source Type** and enter inventory:scanner as the value:

10. Under the Index section, click on **main** so that it gets moved to the **SelectedItem(s)** list and click the **Review** button:

11. Click **Review** and confirm your selections, then click **Submit**.
12. After the form submits, you will be presented with the token. This token will be needed for the recipe in `Chapter 15`, *Above and Beyond – Customization, Web Framework, REST API, HTTP Event Collector, and SDKs:*

How it works...

To get the HEC to work, you firstly configured a few global settings. These included the default index, default source type, and the HTTP port that Splunk will listen on. These default values, such as index and source type, will be used by the HEC, unless the data itself contains the specific values to use. The port commonly used for the HEC is port 8088. This single port can receive multiple different types of data since it is all differentiated by the token that is passed with it and by interpreting the data within the payload of the request.

After configuring the defaults, you then generated a new token, specifically for the inventory scanner data. You provided a specific source type for this data source and selected the index that the data should go to. These values will override the defaults and help to ensure that data is routed to the correct index.

The HEC is now up and running and listening on port 8088 for the inventory scan HTTP data to be sent to it.

Getting data from databases using DB Connect

Splunk DB Connect is a popular application developed by Splunk that allows you to easily get data into Splunk from many common databases. In this recipe, you will install DB Connect and configure it to connect to an external database's product inventory table.

 DB Connect has a dedicated Splunk manual that can be found at
https://docs.splunk.com/Documentation/DBX/latest/DeployDBX.

Getting ready

To step through this recipe, you will need a running Splunk Enterprise server. You should be familiar with navigating the Splunk user interface.

Additionally, it is recommended that you have one of the following supported databases installed:

- DB2
- Informix
- MemSQL
- MS SQL
- MySQL
- Oracle
- PostgreSQL
- SAP SQL
- Sybase
- Teradata

DB Connect might work with other JDBC-compatible databases and data stores, but this is **not** guaranteed. DB Connect 3 has several prerequisites detailed in the installation manual. Before attempting this recipe, please ensure that you have installed the **Java Platform, Standard Edition Development Kit (JDK) 8** from Oracle. Additionally, you will also need to download the database drivers for your specific database.

How to do it...

Assuming JDK 8 is installed and your required database drivers are downloaded, follow the steps in this recipe to generate a local Splunk lookup using data from an external database and DB Connect:

1. In your database application, create a new database called productdb, and within the database, create a new table called productInventory. Insert the contents of the provided productInventory.csv file into the new database table. The new table will resemble the following screenshot:

```
mysql> use productdb
Reading table information for completion of table and column names
You can turn off this feature to get a quicker startup with -A

Database changed
mysql> select * from productInventory;
+---------+-------------------+------------------------------------------------+---------------+
| itemId  | itemName          | itemDescription                                | itemInventory |
+---------+-------------------+------------------------------------------------+---------------+
| 4728475 | Rolux Navigator   | Stylish mens watch with metal band             |           400 |
|   38492 | Rolux Sportsman   | Mens sport watch with timer                    |           600 |
| 1000014 | Ripple BookPro 13 | 13 inch laptop - 5PB HDD/200GB RAM             |          1000 |
| 1000015 | Ripple Jukebox 500| Portable music player - 984 hour battery life  |           405 |
| 1000016 | Poku Castbox      | Video streaming device - HDMI compatible       |           605 |
| 1000017 | Ripple Jukebox 300| Music streaming device 300GB storage capacity  |           350 |
| 1000020 | Ripple MyPhone 8  | The latest phone from Ripple - 8 inch with 8TB of |        500 |
+---------+-------------------+------------------------------------------------+---------------+
7 rows in set (0.00 sec)
```

2. Once the DB table is built, you need to install the DB Connect application to connect to it. From the drop-down application menu, select **Find More Apps**:

3. Search for the `Splunk DB Connect` application and then select it to install it. You will have to enter your splunk.com account credentials after hitting the **Install** button. When prompted, select to **Restart** Splunk:

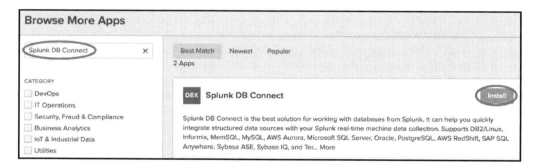

 If your environment has no internet access, you can download the DB Connect application from the Splunk app store at `https://splunkbase.splunk.com/app/2686/`. Once it is downloaded, you can upload and install the application to your Splunk environment by selecting **Manage Apps** from *Step 2*.

4. After logging back in, select the **Splunk DB Connect** from the drop-down application menu. You will see a welcome notice initially. Click on the green **Setup** button to continue.

5. The next screen will display an error warning if the DB Connect task server is not running. If it is not running, then you will need to enter the correct **JRE Installation Path**. The rest of the settings we will leave as they are for now. Click **Save** and ensure the task server is running, then click the **Drivers** tab:

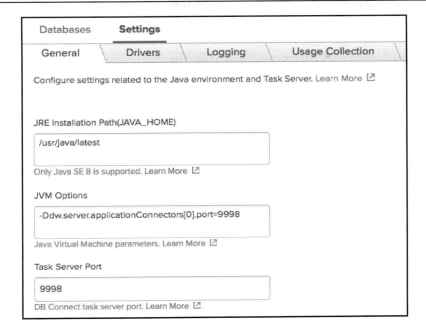

6. On the next screen, you will see a list of supported databases and whether any drivers are correctly installed. At this point, you must copy the database driver for your database over to DB Connect. Follow the instructions in the DB Connect installation manual to do this. Then, click the **Reload** button to ensure the driver is now installed. Once you see a green check mark next to the database you are looking to use, the driver has been detected properly:

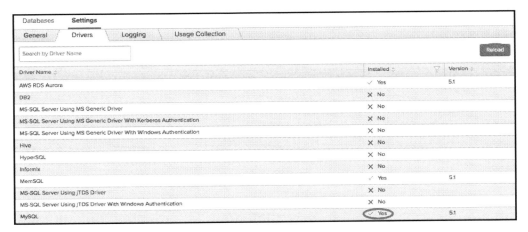

7. In the navigation bar, click on **Configuration**, then **Settings**, then select the **Identities** tab. Then, click **New Identity** to add a new database identity:

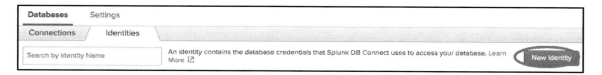

8. Add a new database identity by entering the **Identity Name**, **Username**, and **Password** for the user that will be connecting to the database. Then, click **Save** to create the identity:

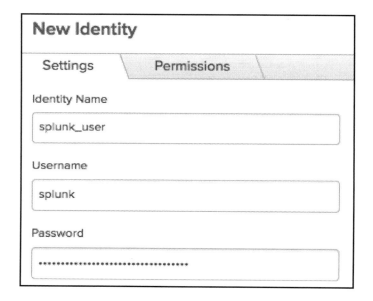

9. In the navigation bar, click on **Configuration**, then **Settings**, then select the **Connections** tab. Then, click the **New Connection** to add a new database identity. Enter in the required database connection details. You will need to enter the **Host**, the **Connection Type**, the **Default Database**, and then select the newly created identity from the **Identity** drop-down box. The **Default Database** will match the name of your database—in this case, **productdb**. When done, select **Save**. The connection will be validated when saved and will report back any errors:

10. Now, test that you are able to view the product inventory table by clicking on **Data Lab** and then **SQL Explorer**. Select your product database and then run the following SQL query:

```
select * from productInventory;
```

You should now be able to see the inventory table and your database connection is ready to go.

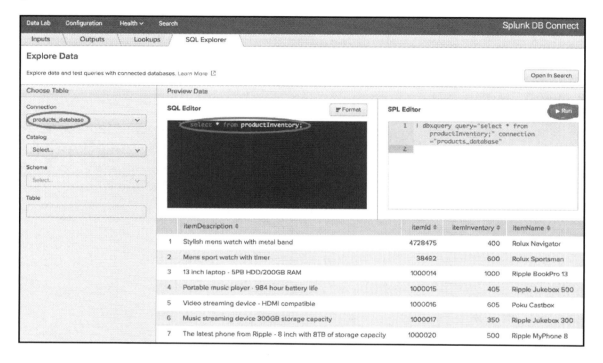

How it works...

DB Connect enables real-time integration between Splunk and traditional relational databases. In this recipe, you installed the DB Connect application and configured it to talk to a database. When installed, DB Connect sets up something called a Java Bridge Server that is essentially a **Java Virtual Machine** (**JVM**) constantly running in the background. The Java Bridge Server helps speed up connectivity to external databases by allocating memory and caching a lot of the metadata associated with the database tables.

Loading the sample data for this book

While most of the data you will index with Splunk will be collected in real time, there might be instances where you have a set of data that you would like to put into Splunk, either to backfill some missing or incomplete data, or just to take advantage of its searching and reporting tools.

This recipe will show you how to perform one-time bulk loads of data from files located on the Splunk server. We will also use this recipe to load the data samples that will be used throughout the subsequent chapters as we build our operational intelligence app in Splunk.

There are three files that make up our sample data. The first is `access_log`, which represents the data from our web layer and is modeled on an Apache web server. The second file is `app_log`, which represents the data from our application layer and is modeled on `log4j` log data from our custom middleware application. The third file is `metric_csv` data that represents sensor readings from HVAC units.

Getting ready

To step through this recipe, you will need a running Splunk server and you should have a copy of the sample data generation app (`OpsDataGen.spl`) for this book.

How to do it...

Follow these steps to load the sample data generator on your system:

1. Log in to your Splunk server using your credentials.
2. From the **Apps** menu in the upper left-hand corner of the home screen, click on the gear icon.

3. The **Apps settings** page will load. Then, click on the **Install app from file** button:

4. Select the location of the OpsDataGen.spl file on your computer and then click on the **Upload** button to install the application:

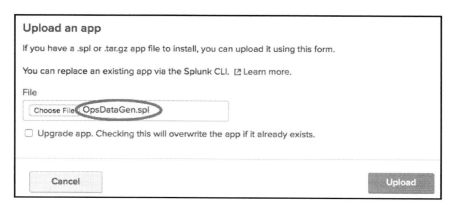

5. After installation, a message should appear in a blue bar at the top of the screen, letting you know that the app has installed successfully. You should also now see the OpsDataGen app in the list of apps:

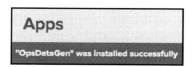

6. By default, the app installs with the data-generation scripts disabled. In order to generate data, you will need to enable either a Windows or Linux script, depending on your Splunk operating system. To enable the script, select the **Settings** menu from the top right-hand side of the screen and then select **Data inputs**:

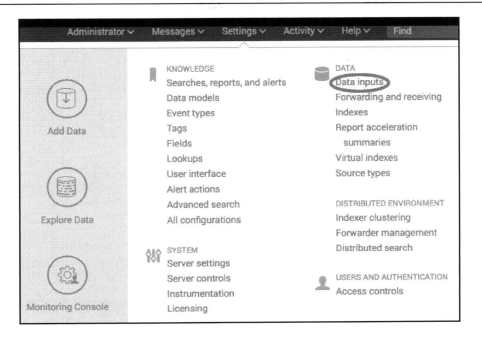

7. From the **Data inputs** screen that follows, select **Scripts**.
8. On the **Scripts** screen, locate the **OpsDataGen** script for your operating system and click on **Enable**:
    * For Linux, it will
      be `$SPLUNK_HOME/etc/apps/OpsDataGen/bin/AppGen.path`
    * For Windows, it will
      be `$SPLUNK_HOME/etc/appsOpsDataGen/bin/AppGen-win.path`

The following screenshot displays both the Windows and Linux inputs that are available after installing the **OpsDataGen** app. It also displays where to click to enable the correct one based on the operating system Splunk is installed on:

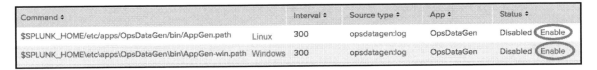

Command ⬍		Interval ⬍	Source type ⬍	App ⬍	Status ⬍
$SPLUNK_HOME/etc/apps/OpsDataGen/bin/AppGen.path	Linux	300	opsdatagen:log	OpsDataGen	Disabled Enable
$SPLUNK_HOME\etc\apps\OpsDataGen\bin\AppGen-win.path	Windows	300	opsdatagen:log	OpsDataGen	Disabled Enable

9. Select the **Settings** menu from the top right-hand side of the screen, select **Data inputs**, and then select **Files & directories**.

10. On the **Files & directories** screen, locate the three **OpsDataGen** inputs for your operating system and for each click on **Enable**:

      - For Linux, it will be `$SPLUNK_HOME/etc/apps/OpsDataGen/data/access_log`, `$SPLUNK_HOME/etc/apps/OpsDataGen/data/app_log`, and `$SPLUNK_HOME/etc/apps/OpsDataGen/data/hvac_log`

      - For Windows, it will be `$SPLUNK_HOME\etc\apps\OpsDataGendata\access_log`, `$SPLUNK_HOME\etc\apps\OpsDataGendata\app_log`, and `$SPLUNK_HOME\etc\apps\OpsDataGendata\hvac_log`

    The following screenshot displays both the Windows and Linux inputs that are available after installing the **OpsDataGen** app. It also displays where to click to enable the correct one based on the operating system Splunk is installed on:

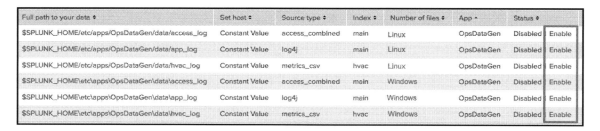

Full path to your data ◆	Set host ◆	Source type ◆	Index ◆	Number of files ◆	App ▲	Status ◆	
$SPLUNK_HOME/etc/apps/OpsDataGen/data/access_log	Constant Value	access_combined	main	Linux	OpsDataGen	Disabled	Enable
$SPLUNK_HOME/etc/apps/OpsDataGen/data/app_log	Constant Value	log4j	main	Linux	OpsDataGen	Disabled	Enable
$SPLUNK_HOME/etc/apps/OpsDataGen/data/hvac_log	Constant Value	metrics_csv	hvac	Linux	OpsDataGen	Disabled	Enable
$SPLUNK_HOME\etc\apps\OpsDataGen\data\access_log	Constant Value	access_combined	main	Windows	OpsDataGen	Disabled	Enable
$SPLUNK_HOME\etc\apps\OpsDataGen\data\app_log	Constant Value	log4j	main	Windows	OpsDataGen	Disabled	Enable
$SPLUNK_HOME\etc\apps\OpsDataGen\data\hvac_log	Constant Value	metrics_csv	hvac	Windows	OpsDataGen	Disabled	Enable

11. The data will now be generated in real time. You can test this by navigating to the Splunk search screen and running the following search over an **All time (real-time)** time range:

    ```
    index=main sourcetype=log4j OR sourcetype=access_combined
    ```

12. After a short while, you should see data from both the source types flowing into Splunk. The data generation is now working, as displayed in the following screenshot:

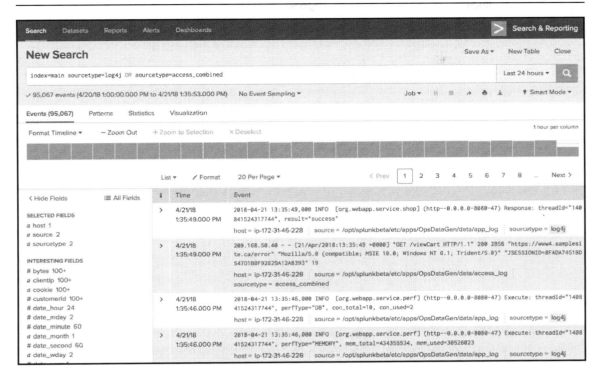

13. You can also test that the metric data is being generated by navigating to the Splunk search screen and running the following search over an **All Time** range:

```
| mcatalog values(_dims) WHERE index=hvac
```

How it works...

In this case, you installed a Splunk application that leverage a scripted input. The script we wrote generates data for three source types. The `access_combined` source type contains sample web access logs, the `metrics_csv` source type contains sensor metrics, and the `log4j` source type contains application logs. These data sources will be used throughout the recipes in the book. Applications will also be discussed in more detail later on.

See also

- The *Indexing files and directories* recipe
- The *Getting data through network ports* recipe
- The *Using scripted inputs* recipe

Data onboarding – defining field extractions

Splunk has many built-in features, including knowledge of several common source types, which lets it automatically know which fields exist within your data. Splunk, by default, also extracts any key-value pairs present within the log data and all the fields within JSON-formatted logs. However, often the fields within raw log data cannot be interpreted out of the box, and this knowledge must be provided to Splunk to make these fields easily searchable.

The sample data that we will be using in subsequent chapters contains data we wish to present as fields to Splunk. Much of the raw log data contains key-value fields that Splunk will extract automatically, but there is one field we need to tell Splunk how to extract, representing the page response time. To do this, we will be adding a custom field extraction, which will tell Splunk how to extract the field for us.

Getting ready

To step through this recipe, you will need a running Splunk server with the operational intelligence sample data loaded. No other prerequisites are required.

How to do it...

Follow these steps to add a custom field extraction for a response:

1. Log in to your Splunk server.
2. In the top right-hand corner, click on the **Settings** menu and then click on the **Fields** link.

3. Click on the **Field extractions** link:

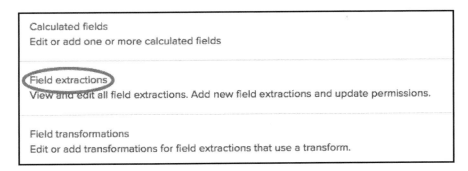

4. Click on **New**.
5. In the **Destination app** field, select the **search** app, and in the **Name** field, enter
   response. Set the **Apply to** dropdown to **sourcetype** and the **named** field to
   access_combined. Set the **Type** dropdown to **Inline**, and for the
   Extraction/Transform field, carefully enter the
   (?i)^(?:[^"]*"){8}s+(?P<response>.+) regex:

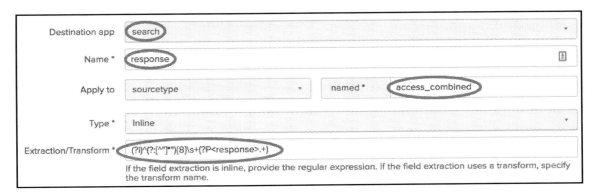

6. Click on **Save**.
7. On the **Field extractions** listing page, find the recently added extraction, and in
   the **Sharing** column, click on the **Permissions** link:

8. Update the **Object should appear in** setting to **All apps**. In the **Permissions** section, for the **Read** column, check **Everyone**, and in the **Write** column, check **admin**. Then, click on **Save**:

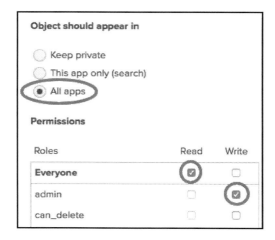

9. Navigate to the Splunk search screen and enter the following search over the **Last 60 minutes** time range:

```
index=main sourcetype=access_combined
```

10. You should now see a field called **response** extracted on the left-hand side of the search screen under the **Interesting Fields** section.

How it works...

All field extractions are maintained in the `props.conf` and `transforms.conf` configuration files. The stanzas in `props.conf` include an extraction class that leverages regular expressions to extract field names and/or values to be used at search time. The `transforms.conf` file goes further and can be leveraged for more advanced extractions, such as reusing or sharing extractions over multiple sources, source types, or hosts.

See also

- The *Loading the sample data for this book* recipe
- The *Data onboarding – defining event types and tags* recipe

Data onboarding - defining event types and tags

Event types in Splunk are a way of categorizing common types of events in your data to make them easier to search and report on. One advantage of using event types is that they can assist in applying a common classification to similar events. Event types essentially turn chunks of search criteria into field/value pairs. Tags help you search groups of event data more efficiently and can be assigned to any field/value combination, including event types.

For example, Windows log-on events could be given an event type of `windows_logon`, Unix log-on events could be given an event type of `unix_logon`, and VPN log-on events could be given an event type of `vpn_logon`. We could then tag these three event types with a tag of `logon_event`. A simple search for `tag="logon_event"` would then search across the Windows, Unix, and VPN source types and return all the log-on events. Alternatively, if we want to search only for Windows log-on events, we will search for `eventtype=windows_logon`.

This recipe will show how to define event types and tags for use with the sample data. Specifically, you will define an event type for successful web server events.

 For more information on event types and tags in Splunk, check out
`https://docs.splunk.com/Documentation/Splunk/latest/Knowledge/Abouteventtypes` and
`https://docs.splunk.com/Documentation/Splunk/latest/Knowledge/Abouttagsandaliases`.

Getting ready

To step through this recipe, you will need a running Splunk server with the operational intelligence sample data loaded. No other prerequisites are required.

How to do it...

Follow these steps to define an event type and associated tag:

1. Log in to your Splunk server.

2. From the home launcher in the top right-hand corner, click on the **Settings** menu item and then click on the **Event types** link:

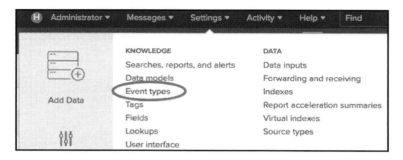

3. Click on the **New** button.

4. In the **Destination App** dropdown, select **search**. Enter HttpRequest-Success in the **Name** field. In the **Search string** text area, enter sourcetype=access_combined status=2*. In the **Tag(s)** field, enter webserver and then click on **Save**:

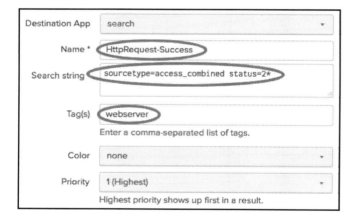

5. The event type is now created. To verify that this worked, you should now be able to search by both the event type and the tag that you created. Navigate to the Splunk search screen in the **Search and Reporting** app and enter the following search over the **Last 60 minutes** time range to verify that eventtype is working:

```
eventtype="HttpRequest-Success"
```

6. Enter the following search over the **Last 60 minutes** time range to verify that the tag is working:

```
tag="webserver"
```

How it works...

Event types are applied to events at search time and introduce an `eventtype` field with user-defined values that can be used to quickly sift through large amounts of data. An event type is essentially a Splunk search string that is applied against each event to see if there is a match. If the event type search matches the event, the `eventtype` field is added, with the value of the field being the user-defined name for that event type.

The common tag value allows for a grouping of event types. If multiple event types had the same tag, then your Splunk search could just search for that particular tag value, instead of needing to list out each individual event type value.

Event types can be added, modified, and deleted at any time without the need to change or reindex your data, as they are applied at search time.

Event types are stored in `eventtypes.conf`, which can be found in `$SPLUNK_HOME/etc/system/local/`, a custom app directory in `$SPLUNK_HOME/etc/apps/`, or a user's private directory, `$SPLUNK_HOME/etc/users/`.

There's more...

While adding event types and tags can be done through the web interface of Splunk, as outlined in this recipe, there are other approaches to add them in bulk quickly and to allow for customization of the many configuration options that Splunk provides.

Adding event types and tags using eventtypes.conf and tags.conf

Event types in Splunk can be manually added to the `eventtypes.conf` configuration files. Edit or create `$SPLUNK_HOME/etc/system/local/eventtypes.conf` and add your event type. You will need to restart Splunk after this:

```
[HttpRequest-Success]
search = status=2*
```

Tags in Splunk can be manually added to the `tags.conf` configuration file. Edit or create `$SPLUNK_HOME/etc/system/local/tags.conf` and add your tag. You will need to restart Splunk after this:

```
[eventtype=HttpRequest-Success]
webserver = enabled
```

In this recipe, you tagged an event type. However, tags do not always need to be associated with event types. You can tag any field/value combination found in an event. To create new tags independently, click on the **Settings** menu and select **Tags**.

See also

- The *Loading the sample data for this book* recipe
- The *Data onboarding – defining field extractions* recipe

Installing the Machine Learning Toolkit

The Splunk Machine Learning Toolkit extends Splunk with additional search commands, visualizations, assistants, and examples to assist in developing and working with machine learning concepts. Machine learning tools and processes can be applied to your Splunk data to assist in predictive analytics, trending, anomaly detection, and outlier detection.

This recipe will show you how to install the Machine Learning Toolkit and the necessary prerequisites, which will be used in `Chapter 13`, *Diving Deeper – Advanced Searching, Machine Learning, and Predictive Analytics*.

For more information on the Machine Learning Toolkit, check out `https://docs.splunk.com/Documentation/MLApp/latest/User/Abou t`.

Getting ready

To step through this recipe, you will need a running Splunk server with the operational intelligence sample data loaded. No other prerequisites are required.

How to do it...

Follow these steps to define an event type and associated tag:

1. Log in to your Splunk server.

2. From the **Apps** menu in the upper left-hand corner of the home screen, click on the gear icon.

3. The **Apps settings** page will load. Then, click on the **Browse More Apps** button.

4. In the search field, enter `Scientific Computing` and press enter.

5. The search results will return multiple Python for Scientific Computing apps — one for each different supported operating system (Windows and Linux 32-bit or 64-bit). In the search results, click on the **Install** button for the app that matches the correct operating system you have Splunk installed on:

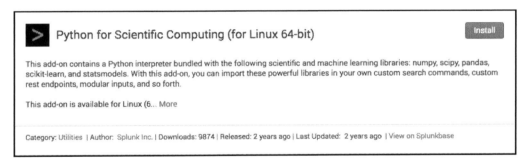

6. Enter your `splunk.com` credentials, check the checkbox to accept the terms and conditions, and click on **Login and Install**. Splunk should return with a message saying that the app was installed successfully.

7. If prompted to restart Splunk, click the **Restart later** button.

8. In the search field, enter `Machine Learning` and press enter.

9. In the search results, click on the **Install** button for **Splunk Machine Learning Toolkit**:

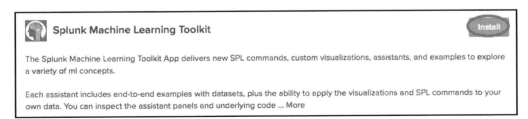

10. Enter your Splunk.com credentials, check the checkbox to accept the terms and conditions, and click on **Login and Install**. Splunk should return with a message saying that the app was installed successfully.

11. After the app has installed, click the Restart Splunk button. After Splunk restarts, log back in to Splunk. You should then, in the Apps launcher, see the **Machine Learning Toolkit** installed, as shown in the following screenshot:

How it works...

The **Machine Learning Toolkit (MLTK)** app is the main Splunk app that contains all the necessary knowledge objects and user interfaces that make working with machine learning possible. On its own, that would be enough to provide some basic functionality. However, to take advantage of more advanced machine learning concepts, Splunk needs to take advantage of additional Python libraries.

The Python for Scientific Computing add-on contains a Python interpreter bundled with the numpy, scipy, pandas, scikit-learn, and statsmodels libraries. These libraries are platform-specific, which is why the correct version must be installed.

The Machine Learning Toolkit also provides the ability to customize and extend the application with your own custom models and algorithms, which makes it a very powerful platform.

With the MLTK installed, you are now ready for Chapter 13, *Diving Deeper - Advanced Searching, Machine Learning and Predictive Analytics*.

12
Building an Operational Intelligence Application

In this chapter, we will learn how to build and modify a Splunk application. We will cover the following topics:

- Creating an Operational Intelligence application
- Adding dashboards and reports
- Organizing the dashboards more efficiently
- Dynamically drilling down on activity reports
- Creating a form to search web activity
- Linking web page activity reports to the form
- Displaying a geographical map of visitors
- Highlighting Average Product Price
- Scheduling the PDF delivery of a dashboard

Introduction

In the previous chapter, we were introduced to Splunk's awesome dashboarding and visualization capabilities. We created several basic dashboards and populated them with various operational intelligence-driven visualizations. In this chapter, we will continue to build on what we have learned in the previous chapters and further advance our Splunk dashboarding knowledge. You will learn how to create a Splunk application and populate it with several dashboards. You will also learn to use some of Splunk's more advanced dashboarding capabilities such as forms, drill downs, maps, and column highlighting.

Splunk applications (or **apps**) are best thought of as workspaces designed specifically around certain use cases. In this chapter, we will be building a new application that focuses specifically on Operational Intelligence. Splunk apps can vary in complexity from a series of saved reports and dashboards, through to complex, fully-featured standalone solutions. After logging in to Splunk for the first time, you are actually interfacing with Splunk through the **launcher** application, which displays a dashboard that lists other applications installed on the system. The **Search and Reporting** application that we have been using throughout this book so far is an example of another bundled Splunk application.

 Several vendors, developers, and customers have developed applications that can be used to get you started with your datasets. Most of these applications are available for free download from the Splunk App store at https://splunkbase.splunk.com.

In this chapter, you will also start to get to grips with the dashboard form functionality. The best way to think about forms in Splunk is that they are essentially dashboards with an interface, allowing users to easily supply values to the underlying dashboard searches. For example, a basic form in Splunk would be a dashboard with a user-selectable time range at the top. The user might then select to run the dashboard over the last 24 hours, and all the searches that power the dashboard visualizations will run over this selected time range.

Forms, by their very nature, require inputs. Luckily, for us, Splunk has several common form inputs out of the box that can be readily used using the dashboard editor or SimpleXML. The available form inputs and an explanation of their common usage are detailed in the following table:

Input	Common usage
Dropdown	Used to display lists of user selectable values from which a user may select a single value. Dropdowns can be populated dynamically using Splunk searches and even filtered based on the user selection of another dropdown.
Multiselect	Used to display lists of user selectable values from which a user may select multiple values. Dynamic value population and filtering is possible, in addition to determining how the multiple values are delimited.
Radio	Used for simple yes/no or single selection type values. You can only select one value at a time with radio buttons, unlike dropdowns.
Checkbox	Used for simple on/off type option values. The option is either selected or not. Multiple checkboxes can be arranged together to allow you to select multiple options.
Text	A simple textbox, allowing the user to type whatever value they want to search for. The textbox is great for searching for wildcard type values, such as field values of abc*.

Time	A time range picker. This is the same as the time range picker found on the main Splunk search dashboard. You can add a time range for the entire dashboard or for individual dashboard panels.

Dashboards in Splunk are coded behind the scenes in something known as Simple XML. This Simple XML code can be edited directly or by use of Splunk's interactive, **GUI**-based dashboard editor. For the most part, this chapter will focus on using the GUI-based dashboard editor, which allows for dashboards to be edited without touching a line of code - nice! However, you will be introduced to direct Simple XML editing in order to take advantage of more advanced capabilities and options.

OK, enough discussion; let's get started!

Creating an Operational Intelligence application

This recipe will show you how to create an empty Splunk app that we will use as the starting point for building our Operational Intelligence application.

Getting ready

To step through this recipe, you will need a running Splunk Enterprise server, with the sample data loaded from Chapter 11, *Play Time - Getting Data In*. You should have also completed the recipes from the earlier chapters. You should be familiar with navigating the Splunk user interface.

How to do it...

Follow these steps to create the Operational Intelligence application:

1. Log in to your Splunk server.

2. From the **Apps** menu in the upper left-hand corner of the home screen, click on the gear icon, as shown in the following screenshot:

3. Click on the **Create app** button:

4. Complete the fields in the box that follows. Name the app `Operational Intelligence` and give it a folder name of `operational_intelligence`. Add in a version number and provide an author name. Ensure that **Visible** is set to **Yes**, and the **barebones** template is selected, as shown in the following screenshot:

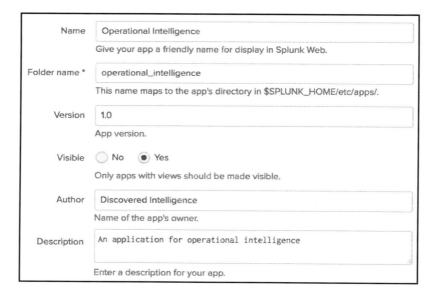

5. When the form is completed, click on **Save**. This should be followed by a blue bar with the message, **Successfully saved operational_intelligence**.

Congratulations, you just created a Splunk application!

How it works...

When an app is created through the Splunk GUI, as in this recipe, Splunk essentially creates a new folder (or directory) named `operational_intelligence` within the `$SPLUNK_HOME/etc/apps` directory. Within the `$SPLUNK_HOME/etc/apps/operational_intelligence` directory, you will find four new subdirectories that contain all the configuration files needed for our barebones Operational Intelligence app that we just created, as shown in the following screenshot:

The eagle-eyed among you would have noticed that there were two templates that could have been selected from when creating the app: `barebones` and `sample_app`. The `barebones` template creates an application with nothing much inside of it, and the `sample_app` template creates an application populated with sample dashboards, searches, views, menus, and reports. If you wish to, you can also develop your own custom template if you create lots of apps, which might enforce certain color schemes for example.

There's more...

As Splunk apps are just a collection of directories and files, there are other methods to add apps to your Splunk Enterprise deployment.

Creating an application from another application

It is relatively simple to create a new app from an existing app without going through the Splunk GUI, should you wish to do so. This approach can be very useful when we are creating multiple apps with different `inputs.conf` files for deployment to Splunk Universal Forwarders.

Taking the app we just created as an example, copy the entire directory structure of the `operational_intelligence` **app and name it** `copied_app`, as shown in the following code:

```
cp -r $SPLUNK_HOME/etc/apps/operational_intelligence
  $SPLUNK_HOME/etc/apps/copied_app
```

Within the directory structure of `copied_app`, we must now edit the `apps.conf` file in the default directory.

Open `$SPLUNK_HOME/etc/apps/copied_app/default/apps.conf` and change the label field to `My Copied App`, provide a new description, and then save the `conf` file, as shown in the following code:

```
#
# Splunk app configuration file
#
[install]
is_configured = 0

[ui]
is_visible = 1
label = My Copied App

[launcher]
author = John Smith
description = My Copied application
version = 1.0
```

Now, restart Splunk, and the new **My Copied App** application should be seen in the application menu, using the following code:

```
$SPLUNK_HOME/bin/splunk restart
```

Downloading and installing a Splunk app

Splunk has an entire application website with hundreds of applications, created by Splunk, other vendors, and even users of Splunk. These are great ways to get started with a base application, which you can then modify to meet your needs.

If the Splunk server that you are logged in to has access to the internet, from the **Apps** page you can select the **Browse More Apps** button. From here, you can search for apps and install them directly.

An alternative way to install a Splunk app is to visit `https://splunkbase.splunk.com` and search for the app. You will then need to download the application locally. From your Splunk server, on the **Apps** page, click on the **Install app from file** button and upload the app you just downloaded to install it.

Once the app has been installed, go and look at the directory structure that the installed application just created. Familiarize yourself with some of the key files and where they are located.

> When downloading applications from the Splunk apps site, it is best practice to test and verify them in a non-production environment first. The Splunk apps site is community driven and, as a result, quality checks and/or technical support for some of the apps might be limited.

See also

- The *Adding dashboards and reports* recipe
- The *Organizing the dashboards more efficiently* recipe
- The *Dynamically drilling down on activity reports* recipe

Adding dashboards and reports

As we saw in the previous chapter, dashboards are a great way to present many different pieces of information. Rather than having lots of disparate dashboards across your Splunk environment, it makes a lot of sense to group related dashboards into a common Splunk application, for example, putting operational intelligence dashboards into a common Operational Intelligence application.

In this recipe, you will learn how to move the dashboards and associated reports you created in the last couple of chapters into our new Operational Intelligence application.

Getting ready

To step through this recipe, you will need a running Splunk Enterprise server, with the sample data loaded from `Chapter 11`, *Play Time - Getting Data In*. You should have also completed the recipes from the earlier chapters. You should be familiar with navigating the Splunk user interface.

How to do it...

Follow these steps to move your dashboards into the new application:

1. Log in to your Splunk server.
2. Select the newly created **Operational Intelligence** application.
3. From the top menu, select **Settings** and then select the **User interface** menu item, as shown in the following screenshot:

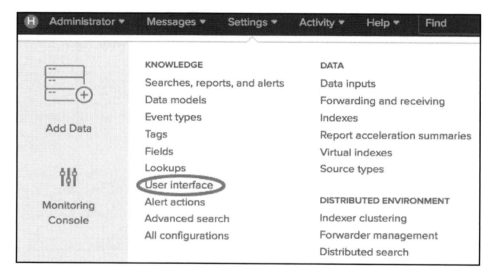

4. Click on the **Views** section:

5. In the **App Context** dropdown, select **Search & Reporting (search)** or whatever application you were in when creating the dashboards in the previous chapter, as shown in the following screenshot:

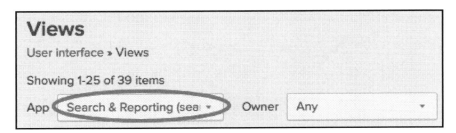

6. Locate the `website_monitoring` dashboard row in the list of views and click on the **Move** link to the right of the row.

7. In the **Move Object** popup, select the **Operational Intelligence (operational_intelligence)** application that was created earlier and then click on the **Move** button, as shown in the following screenshot:

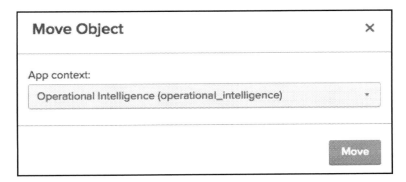

8. A message bar will then be displayed at the top of the screen to confirm that the dashboard was moved successfully.

9. Repeat from step 5 to move the `product_monitoring` dashboard as well, as shown in the following screenshot:

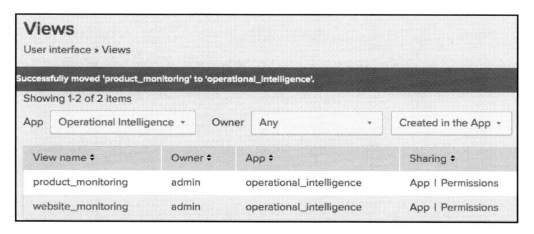

10. After the **Website Monitoring** and **Product Monitoring** dashboards have been moved, we now want to move all the reports you created in the previous recipes, as these power the dashboards and provide operational intelligence insight. From the top menu, select **Settings**, but this time, select **Searches, Reports, and Alerts**.

11. Select the **Search & Reporting (search)** app context and filter by *cp** to view the searches (reports). Click on the **Edit** link of the first *cp0** search in the list and select **Move,** as shown in the following screenshot:

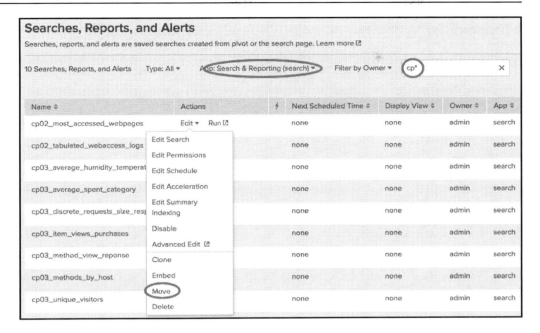

12. Select to move the object to the **Operational Intelligence (operational_intelligence)** application and click on the **Move** button:

13. Select the **Search & Reporting (search)** context and repeat from step 11 to move all the other searches over to the new Operational Intelligence application-this seems like a lot but will not take you long!

All of the dashboards and reports are now moved over to your new Operational Intelligence application.

How it works...

In the previous recipe, we revealed how Splunk apps are essentially just collections of directories and files. Dashboards are XML files found within the $SPLUNK_HOME/etc/apps directory structure. When moving a dashboard from one app to another, Splunk is essentially just moving the underlying file from a directory inside one app to a directory in the other app. In this recipe, you moved the dashboards from the **Search & Reporting** app to the **Operational Intelligence** app, as represented in the following screenshot:

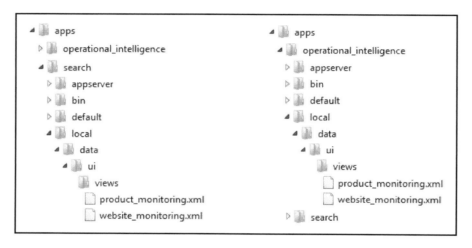

As visualizations on the dashboards leverage the underlying saved searches (or reports), you also moved these reports to the new app so that the dashboards maintain permissions to access them. Rather than moving the saved searches, you could have changed the permissions of each search to **Global** such that they could be seen from all the other apps in Splunk. However, the other reason you moved the reports was to keep everything contained within a single Operational Intelligence application, which you will continue to build out going forward.

It is best practice to avoid setting permissions to **Global** for reports and dashboards, as this makes them available to all the other applications when they most likely do not need to be. Additionally, setting global permissions can make things a little messy from a housekeeping perspective and crowd the lists of reports and views that belong to specific applications. The exception to this rule might be for knowledge objects such as tags, event types, macros, and lookups, which often have advantages to being available across all applications.

There's more...

As you went through this recipe, you likely noticed that the dashboards had application-level permissions, but the reports had private-level permissions. The reports are private as this is the default setting in Splunk when they are created. This private-level permission restricts access to only your user account and admin users. To make the reports available to other users of your application, you will need to change the permissions of the reports to **Shared in App** as we did when adjusting the permissions of reports.

Changing permissions of saved reports

Changing the sharing permission levels of your reports from the default Private to App is relatively straightforward:

1. Ensure that you are in your newly created Operational Intelligence application.
2. Select the **Reports** menu item to see the list of reports.
3. Click on **Edit** next to the report you wish to change the permissions for. Then, click on **Edit Permissions** from the drop-down list, as shown in the following screenshot:

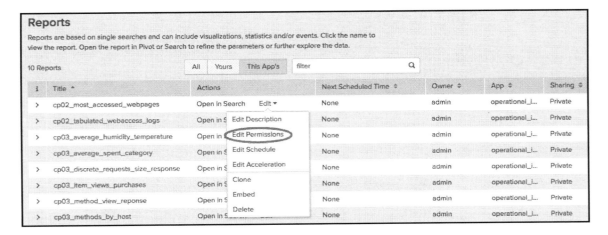

4. An **Edit Permissions** pop-up box will appear. In the **Display for** section, change from **Owner** to **App**, and then click on **Save**.
5. The box will close, and you will see that the Sharing permissions in the table will now display **App** for the specific report. This report will now be available to all the users of your application.

See also

- The *Creating an Operational Intelligence application* recipe
- The *Organizing the dashboards more efficiently* recipe
- The *Dynamically drilling down on activity reports* recipe

Organizing the dashboards more efficiently

In this recipe, you will learn how to use Splunk's dashboard editor to use more efficient visualizations and organize the dashboards more efficiently. This feature was introduced in **Splunk 6** and enhanced even further in more recent versions.

Getting ready

To step through this recipe, you will need a running Splunk Enterprise server, with the sample data loaded from *Chapter 11*, *Play Time - Getting Data In*, and should have completed the earlier recipes in this chapter. You should also be familiar with navigating the Splunk user interface.

How to do it...

Follow these steps to organize the dashboards more efficiently:

1. Log in to your Splunk server.
2. Select the **Operational Intelligence** application.
3. Click on the **Dashboards** menu item, as shown in the following screenshot:

4. You should see the **Product Monitoring** and **Website Monitoring** dashboards that we moved into the Operational Intelligence app in the previous recipe. Select the **Website Monitoring** dashboard and it will be displayed.

5. You will notice that there are several visualizations on the dashboard; in Splunk, they are known as **panels**. Click the **Edit** button, as shown in the following screenshot:

6. In the **Total Number of Errors** panel, change the **Radial Gauge** to a **Single Value** visualization by clicking on the radial gauge icon and selecting **Single Value**, as shown in the following screenshot:

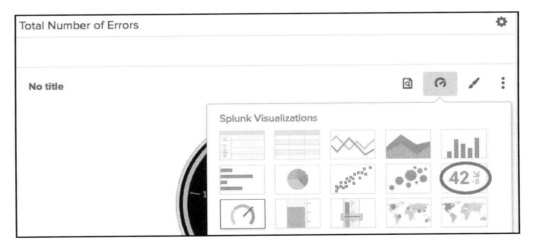

7. Move the other panels around until your dashboard resembles the layout in the following screenshot. Notice how we have our single value panels at the top, our various charts in the middle, and then our time series-based charts at the bottom:

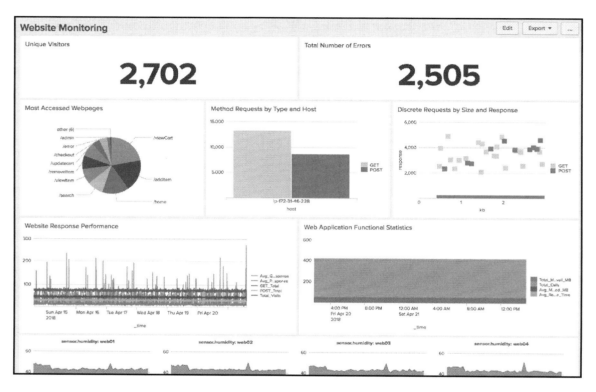

8. Click on the **Save** button when complete. I think you will agree that this dashboard looks a lot better than the earlier one! Everything fits on the screen for the most part, and it is much easier on the eye.

How it works...

In this recipe, we started to experience the power of Splunk's amazing dashboard editor. The dashboard editor provides a nice usable interface that essentially shields the user from what is happening underneath the covers. When we edit dashboard panels and visualizations in this manner, Splunk is actually writing the required Simple XML code into the respective view's XML file on your behalf. When you click on **Save**, the file is essentially saved with the newly written XML under the covers. If you are hungry for more, don't worry; we are just getting started with the editor. There is plenty more to come later in this chapter!

 Dashboards in Splunk are also called **Views**. In the management interface and in the backend, they are commonly known as Views, but in the application menu, they are called Dashboards. We may use the terms interchangeably in this book.

There's more...

Instead of using the dashboard editor, you can edit the Simple XML directly.

Modifying the Simple XML directly

Let's take a look at the Simple XML that is behind the **Website Monitoring** dashboard. Ensure that the dashboard is displayed onscreen. Then, click on the **Edit** button as you did earlier, then click the **Source** toggle. The underlying Simple XML source code will now be displayed.

Dashboards in Simple XML consist of rows, panels, and visualization elements. Dashboards can have many rows (`<row></row>`), but around three rows is advisable. Within each row, you can have multiple panels (`<panel></panel>`), and within each panel, you can have multiple visualization elements (for example, `<chart></chart>` for a chart). On the **Website Monitoring** dashboard, you should see four row elements and multiple panels with a single dashboard element on each panel.

We can edit the Simple XML directly to swap the single elements around on the top row of the dashboard. Simply select the first panel group (The Unique Visitors panel XML):

Move it below the second panel group (The Total Number of Errors panel XML), as shown in the following screenshot:

Then, once done, click on the **Save** button. This is an extremely simple example, but you should start to see how we can edit the code directly rather than use the dashboard editor.

Note that there might be some `<option>` data within the panel groups that we have removed in the screenshots to simplify things. However, ensure that you move everything within the panel group.

Familiarizing yourself with Simple XML and how to tweak it manually will provide more functionality and likely make the process of creating a dashboard a lot more efficient.

A great way to learn Simple XML can be to modify something using the Splunk dashboard editor and then select to view the source code to see what has happened in the underlying Simple XML code. Splunk also has a great Simple XML reference that allows for quick access to many of the key Simple XML elements. Visit `https://docs.splunk.com/Documentation/Splunk/latest/Viz/PanelreferenceforSimplifiedXML` for more information.

See also

- The *Adding dashboards and reports* recipe
- The *Dynamically drilling down on activity reports* recipe
- The *Creating a form for searching web activity* recipe

Dynamically drilling down on activity reports

When viewing a dashboard in Splunk, there is usually a very high probability that you will look at a chart or report and want to know more details about the information that you are looking at.

Splunk dashboards can be configured to let the user drill down into more details. By linking results or data points to an underlying dashboard or report, information about what the user clicked can provide them with the next level of detail or the next step in the process they are following.

This recipe will show you how you can configure reports to drill down into subsequent searches and other dashboards so that you can link them together into a workflow that gets the user to the data they are interested in seeing within your Operational Intelligence application.

Getting ready

To step through this recipe, you will need a running Splunk Enterprise server, with the sample data loaded from Chapter 11, *Play Time - Getting Data In*, and should have completed the earlier recipes in this chapter. You should also be familiar with navigating the Splunk user interface.

How to do it...

Follow these steps to configure a dashboard report with row drilldown capabilities:

1. Log in to your Splunk server.
2. Select the Operational Intelligence application.
3. Click on the **Dashboards** menu:

4. Click on the **Create New Dashboard** button, as shown in the following screenshot:

5. Name the dashboard Visitor Monitoring and set the **Permissions** field to **Shared in App:**

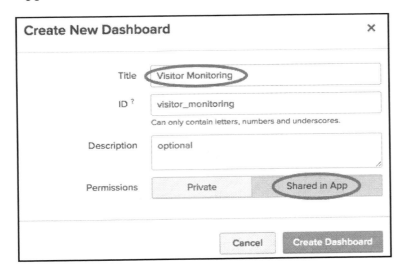

6. Click on **Create Dashboard**.

7. When the empty dashboard is displayed, click on the **Add Panel** button, as shown in the following screenshot:

8. From the flyout panel, expand the **New** section and then click on **StatisticsTable**.

9. Set the **Content Title** panel to `Session Listing`.

10. Set the **Search String** field to the one mentioned in the following code:

```
index=main sourcetype=access_combined | iplocation clientip | fillnull
value="Unknown" City, Country, Region| replace "" with "Unknown" in City,
Country, Region | stats count by JSESSIONID, clientip, City, Country,
Region | fields clientip, City, Region, Country
```

11. Set the time range to **Last 24 hours**, as shown in the following screenshot:

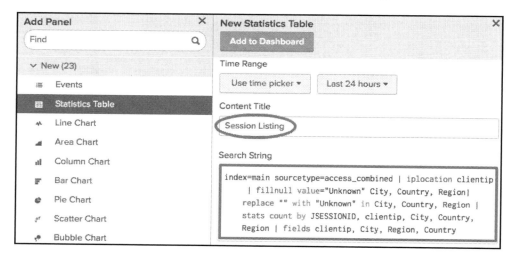

12. Click on the **Add to Dashboard** button.

13. Click anywhere on the dashboard to have the flyout panel disappear.

14. Click on the panel edit icon, select the **Row** option for the **Click Selection** setting and click anywhere on the page, as shown in the following screenshot:

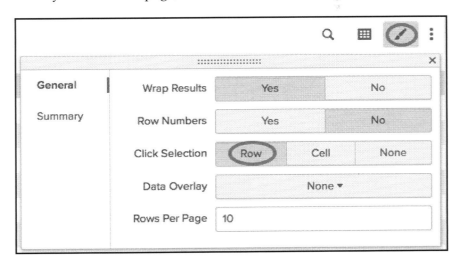

15. Click on the **Save** button to finish editing the dashboard:

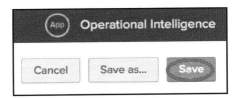

16. Click on a row in the dashboard table, and Splunk will now drill down to the search screen and execute a search that is filtered by the `clientip` value in the row you selected to drill down on.

How it works...

The drilldown feature of dashboards can be utilized to get your users to the next set of data they need. When they click on a table entry or a part of a chart, they set off a search that can drill down into more details of the item they clicked. The behavior of the drilldown is controlled by the configuration of the panel in the Simple XML but also has a few options displayed by the dashboard editor.

When displaying a table of results, there are three options that can be chosen from, as shown in the following table:

Option	Description
Row	When a row is clicked, the search that is launched by the drilldown is based on the x-axis value, which is the first column in the row.
Cell	When a particular cell is clicked, the search that is launched by the drilldown is based on both the x-axis and y-axis values represented by that cell.
None	The drilldown functionality is disabled. When a user clicks on the table, the page will not change.

When displaying a chart, there are two options for the drilldown behavior that can be chosen from, as shown in the following table:

Option	Description
On	When a row is clicked, the search that is launched by the drilldown is based on the values of the portion of that chart.
Off	The drilldown functionality is disabled. When a user clicks on the table, the page will not change.

When the drilldown search is started after the table or chart is clicked on, it is generally derived by taking the original search, backing off the final transforming commands, and then adding the values that were selected depending on the drilldown setting.

When a new panel item is added, such as a chart, table, or map, the default drilldown is always turned off by default.

There's more...

The drilldown options can be customized and provide many different options to control the behavior when dashboards are clicked on.

Disabling the drilldown feature in tables and charts

To disable the drilldown feature, you can specify the **None** option in the **Drilldown** setting of the edit panel form or add/modify the following Simple XML option to the panel source:

```
<option name="drilldown">none</option>
```

A full reference of drilldown options can be found in the Splunk documentation at `https://docs.splunk.com/Documentation/Splunk/latest/Viz/Panelref erenceforSimplifiedXML#drilldown`.

See also

- The *Organizing the dashboards more efficiently* recipe
- The *Creating a form for searching web activity* recipe
- The *Linking web page activity reports to the form* recipe

Creating a form for searching web activity

Presenting users with dashboards is a great way to visualize data, as we have seen. However, often, people like to *slice n dice* data in many different ways, and to do this, we need to make our dashboards more interactive. We can do this using the dashboard forms functionality of Splunk, which allows users to filter dashboard visualizations and data based upon the criteria that are important to them.

This recipe will build on the tabular **Visitor Monitoring** dashboard you created in the previous recipe to allow for granular filtering of the tabulated results.

Getting ready

To step through this recipe, you will need a running Splunk Enterprise server, with the sample data loaded from *Chapter 11*, *Play Time - Getting Data In*, and should have completed the earlier recipes in this chapter. You should also be familiar with navigating the Splunk user interface.

How to do it...

Follow these steps to create a form to filter data on a dashboard:

1. Log in to your Splunk server.
2. Select the **Operational Intelligence** application.
3. Click on the **Dashboards** menu item.

4. Select to view the **Visitor Monitoring** dashboard we created in the previous recipe.

5. Once loaded, click on the **Edit** button.

6. Click on **+ Add Input** and then select **Time**, as shown in the following screenshot:

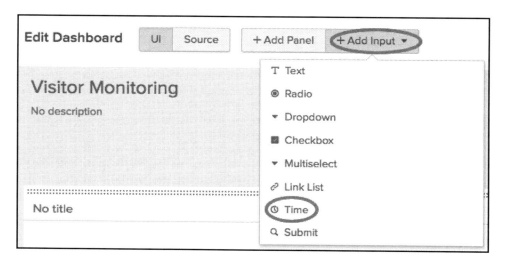

7. Click on **Add Input** again, and this time, select **Text**.

8. A new text input named **field2** will appear. Above the text input, you will see a little pencil icon. Click on the pencil icon to edit the input. A pop up will be displayed.

9. Complete the box with the values in the following table:

Label	IP
Search on Change	Checked
Token	ip
Default	*
Token Suffix	*

10. Then, click on **Apply**:

11. The box will disappear, and you will see that the input is now titled IP.
12. Repeat from step 7 to add and edit the three other textbox fields (one at a time) using the following values for each:
13. For **field3**, we will use the following values:

Label	City
Search on Change	Checked
Token	city
Default	*
Token Suffix	*

14. For **field4,** we will use the following values:

Label	Region
Search on Change	Checked
Token	region
Default	*
Token Suffix	*

15. For **field5,** we will use the following values:

Label	Country
Search on Change	Checked
Token	country
Default	*
Token Suffix	*

16. Once complete, you should have a total of five fields. Let's now do a bit of rearrangement. Move the **Time input** field on the far right-hand side so that it is the last input field at the top. Additionally, check the **Autorun dashboard** checkbox on the far right-hand side, as shown in the following screenshot:

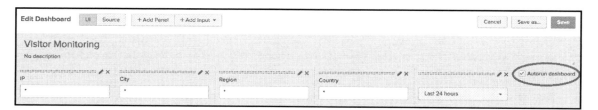

17. Click on the pencil icon above the time input and ensure the default time range from **All Time** to **Last 24 Hours** and that **Search on Change** is checked. Then, click on **Apply**, as shown in the following screenshot:

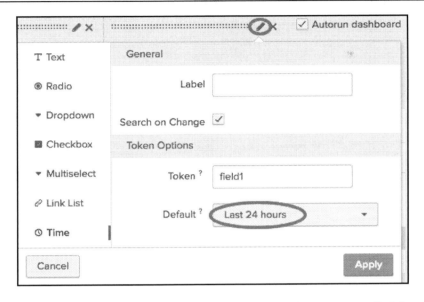

18. Next, click on **Save** in the top right-hand side of the screen to finish editing the form. You should see all your fields nicely labeled across the top with wildcard asterisks (*) in each textbox.

19. Next, we need to link the new fields we just created with the table. Click on **Edit**.

20. Select **Edit Search** icon on the panel with the table. A pop-up box will appear with the current search string, as shown in the following screenshot:

21. Replace the existing search string with the following search string. The modifications to the search have been highlighted:

```
index=main sourcetype=access_combined clientip="$ip$" | iplocation clientip
| fillnull value="Unknown" City, Country, Region| replace "" with "Unknown"
in City, Country, Region | stats count by JSESSIONID, clientip, City,
Country, Region | fields clientip, City, Region, Country | search
City="$city$" Region="$region$" Country="$country$"
```

22. Change **Time Range** to **Shared Time Picker (field1)**, as shown in the following screenshot:

23. Click on **Apply** and then on **Save**.
24. Refresh/reload the dashboard in your browser.
25. That's it! You now have a nice form-driven table. Try testing it out. For example, if you want to filter by all IP addresses that begin with 134, simply enter `134` into the IP textbox and press *Enter*.

How it works...

In this recipe, we only used the GUI editor, which means that Splunk was changing the underlying Simple XML for us. As soon as we added the first input field, Splunk changed the opening Simple XML `<dashboard>` element to a form `<form>` element behind the scenes. Each of the five inputs we added are contained within a `<fieldset>` element. For each of the inputs, Splunk creates an `<input>` element, and each input type can have a number of fields: some optional, some required. One of the key fields for each type is the **Token** field, the values of which are then used by searches on the dashboard. We assigned a token name to each input, such as `ip`, `city`, and `country`.

Other fields that we populated for the text inputs were the **Default** and **Suffix** field values of `*`. This tells Splunk to search for everything (`*`) by default if nothing is entered into the textbox and to add a wildcard (`*`) suffix to everything entered into the textbox. This means that if we were to search for a city using a value of `Tor`, Splunk will search for all the cities that begin with Tor (`Tor*`), such as Toronto. We also checked the **Search on Change** box, which forces a rerun of any searches in the dashboard should we change a value of the input. After completing the editing of the inputs, we selected to autorun the dashboard, which adds `autoRun="true"` in the `<fieldset>` element of the Simple XML and ensures that the dashboard runs as soon as it is loaded with the default values, rather than waiting for something to be submitted in the form.

Once we built the form inputs and configured them appropriately, we needed to tell the searches that power the dashboard visualizations to use the tokens from each of the form inputs. The **Token** field for each input will contain the value for that input. We edited the search for the table on the dashboard and added additional search criteria to force Splunk to search, based upon these tokens. Token names must be encapsulated by `$` signs, so our `ip` token is entered into the search as `$ip$`, and our country token is entered as `$country$`. We also told our search to use the `Shared Time Picker` input rather than its own time range. This allows us to then search using the time picker input we added to the form.

The end result is that anything entered into the form inputs is encapsulated into the respective tokens, and the values of these tokens are then passed to the search that powers the table in the dashboard. If we change the value of an input, then the value of the input's token in the search changes, the search immediately reruns, and the search results in the table change accordingly.

There's more...

In this recipe, we began to scratch the surface of form building, using only textbox inputs and the time picker. Later in this book, we will leverage the drop-down input, and you will learn how to prepopulate drop-down values as a result of a search and how to filter drop-down values as a result of other drop-down selections.

Adding a Submit button to your form

In this recipe, you probably will have noticed that there was no **Submit** button. The reason for this was primarily because no **Submit** button was needed. We selected to autorun the dashboard and selected **Search on Change** for each input. However, there are times when you might not want the form to run as soon as something is changed; perhaps, you want to modify multiple inputs and then search. Additionally, many users like the reassurance of a **Submit** button, as it is commonly used on forms across websites and applications.

Adding a **Submit** button is extremely simple. When the dashboard is in editing mode, simply click on the **Add Input** dropdown and select **Submit**. You will notice that a green **Submit** button now appears on the form. If you now edit the text inputs and uncheck the **Search on Change** checkbox for each of them, the form will only be submitted when someone clicks on the **Submit** button.

See also

- The *Dynamically drilling down on activity reports* recipe
- The *Linking web page activity reports to the form* recipe
- The *Displaying a geographical map of visitors* recipe

Linking web page activity reports to the form

Form searches in Splunk do not need to be limited to displaying events and table-driven data. Rich visualizations can also be linked to forms and be updated when the forms are submitted.

This recipe will show you how you can extend a form to include charts and other visualizations that can be driven by the form created to show visitor traffic and location data.

Getting ready

To step through this recipe, you will need a running Splunk Enterprise server, with the sample data loaded from `Chapter 11`, *Play Time - Getting Data In*, and should have completed the earlier recipes in this chapter. You should also be familiar with navigating the Splunk user interface.

How to do it...

Follow these steps to add a web page activity chart and link it to a form:

1. Log in to your Splunk server.
2. Select the default Operational Intelligence application.
3. Select the **Dashboards** menu item, as shown in the following screenshot:

4. Select the **Visitor Monitoring** dashboard.
5. Click on the **Edit** button:

6. Click on the **+ Add Panel** button:

7. From the flyout panel, expand the **New** section and then click on **Line Chart**.
8. Set the **Content Title** panel to `Session Over Time`.

9. Set the **Search String** field according to the following code:

```
index=main sourcetype=access_combined clientip="$ip$" | iplocation clientip
| fillnull value="Unknown" City, Country, Region| replace "" with "Unknown"
in City, Country, Region | search City="$city$" Region="$region$"
Country="$country$" | timechart dc(JSESSIONID)
```

10. Set the **Time Range** field to **Shared Time Picker (field1)**, as shown in the following screenshot:

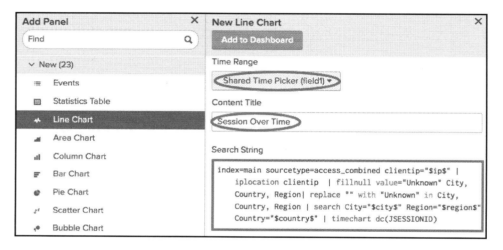

11. Click on the **Add to Dashboard**.
12. Click anywhere on the dashboard to have the flyout panel disappear.
13. Click on the edit panel icon in the panel we just added to the dashboard, as shown in the following screenshot:

14. Update the **X-Axis** label with a **Custom** Title set to `Time`.
15. Update the **Y-Axis** label with a **Custom** Title set to `UniqueSessions`.
16. Set the **Legend Position** option to **None**.
17. Click anywhere on the page and the pop-up box will disappear with the changes reflected on the panel, as shown in the following screenshot:

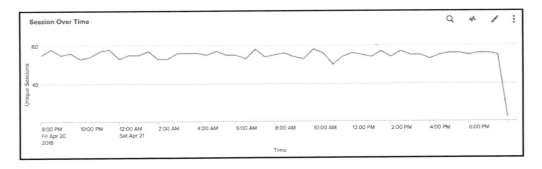

18. Next, click on **Save** to finish editing the dashboard:

19. Filter by an IP of 134 or similar again, and you should see that the chart panel also changes along with the table panel.

How it works...

Adding a chart to the dashboard works in a manner very similar to the way in which the original form was created. You can utilize the field variables defined in the form in the inline search that is used for the chart. Splunk will set them when the form is submitted. The panel can also utilize the time range that was used in the form or contain a separate time range dropdown.

By building a form and several different charts and tables, you can build a very useful form-driven dashboard. One of the great uses of a form-driven dashboard is for investigative purposes. For example, you could take any of the fields and view all sessions coming from a particular country and then see the level of activity over the time period you are interested in.

There's more...

Additional customizations can be added to the charts to give them more meaning.

Adding an overlay to the Sessions Over Time chart

You can have Splunk overlay a field value on top of your existing chart to provide trendlines and so on. Add the following line to the end of the inline search used for the Sessions Over Time search:

```
| eventstats avg(dc(JSESSIONID)) as average | eval average=round(average,0)
```

Then, add the following line to the Simple XML of the panel:

```
<option name="charting.chart.overlayFields">average</option>
```

The following screenshot illustrates this process:

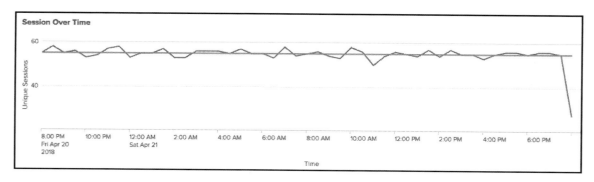

```
<chart>
  <title>Session Over Time</title>
  <search>
    <query>index=main sourcetype=access_combined clientip="$ip$" | iploca
      Region| replace "" with "Unknown" in City, Country, Region | search
      timechart dc(JSESSIONID) | eventstats avg(dc(JSESSIONID)) as avera
    <earliest>$field1.earliest$</earliest>
    <latest>$field1.latest$</latest>
  </search>
  <option name="charting.axisTitleX.text">Time</option>
  <option name="charting.axisTitleY.text">Unique Sessions</option>
  <option name="charting.chart">line</option>
  <option name="charting.drilldown">none</option>
  <option name="charting.legend.placement">none</option>
  <option name="refresh.display">progressbar</option>
  <option name="charting.chart.overlayFields">average</option>
</chart>
```

It will then add a line that charts the average of the session count over top of the actual values, as shown in the following screenshot:

The chart overlay functionality can also be added from the panel editor under the edit panel icon.

See also

- The *Creating a form for searching web activity* recipe
- The *Displaying a geographical map of visitors* recipe
- The *Scheduling the PDF delivery of a dashboard* recipe

Displaying a geographical map of visitors

Operational intelligence doesn't always need to come in the form of pie charts, bar charts, and data tables. With a wide range of operational data being collected from IT systems, there is the opportunity to display this data in ways that can be more meaningful to users or help present it in ways that can be easier to identify trends or anomalies.

One way that always provides great visibility is by representing your data using a geographical map. With geolocation data available for many different data types, it becomes very easy to plot. Using IP addresses from web server logs is a very common use case for this type of visualization. Splunk allows for the easy addition of a map to a dashboard with all the capabilities to zoom and update the portion of the map that the user is viewing.

This recipe will show you how you can configure a map panel within a dashboard and link it to a search that contains IP addresses in order to visualize from where in the world the IP traffic is originating.

Getting ready

To step through this recipe, you will need a running Splunk Enterprise server, with the sample data loaded from Chapter 1, *Play Time - Getting Data In*, and should have completed the earlier recipes in this chapter. You should also be familiar with navigating the Splunk user interface.

How to do it...

Follow these steps to add a map to your form-driven dashboard:

1. Log in to your Splunk server.
2. Select the Operational Intelligence application.
3. Click on the **Dashboards** menu item, as shown in the following screenshot:

4. Select the **Visitor Monitoring** dashboard.
5. Click on the **Edit** button.

6. Click on the **+ Add Panel** button, as shown in the following screenshot:

7. From the flyout panel, expand the **New** section and then click on **Choropleth Map**.
8. Set the **Content Title** panel to Sessions By Location.
9. Set the **Search String** field to:

```
index=main sourcetype=access_combined clientip="$ip$" | iplocation clientip
| fillnull value="Unknown" Country | search City="$city$" Region="$region$"
Country="$country$" | stats count by Country | fields Country, count | geom
geo_countries featureIdField=Country
```

10. Set the **Time range** field to **Shared Time Picker (field1)**, as shown in the following screenshot:

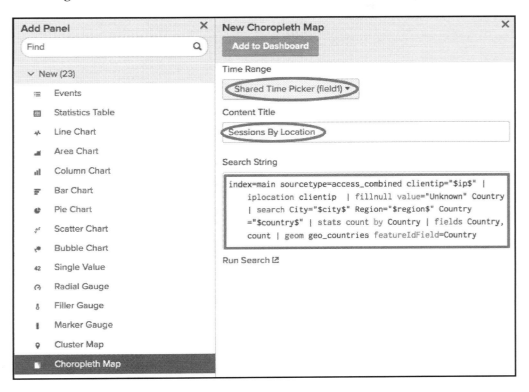

11. Click on the **Add to Dashboard** button.
12. Click anywhere on the dashboard to have the flyout panel disappear.
13. Click on **Save** to finish editing the dashboard:

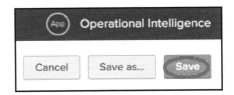

14. Filter by an IP of 134 or similar again, and you should now see that the map panel also changes along with the table and chart panels you added earlier, as shown in the following screenshot:

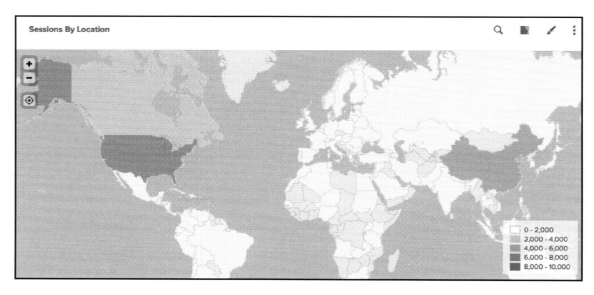

The map panel obtained after applying the filter

How it works...

The rendering of the map is done in the same way in which most browser-based maps are generated, using many small images known as tiles that are put together in a grid layout and swapped in and out depending on the zoom level and the visible area being requested. This results in the browser and services not needing to load an entire world's worth of image data into memory. Layers are then rendered on top of the tiles based on either markers or shapes (polygons).

Splunk currently has two built-in mapping types that can be used:

Type	Description
Choropleth	A choropleth map uses shading to show relative metrics, such as population or election results, for predefined geographic regions.
Cluster	Cluster maps can plot geographic coordinates as interactive markers. These markers can be configured to represent a metric, such as a pie chart with details about that location.

Splunk supports both a native tile server that can be used to serve the actual map images or can be configured to use the external OpenStreetMap service (openstreetmap.org). The native tiles do not have a very granular level of mapping detail, but will work in situations where there is no external connectivity or security reasons for not calling the external service.

In this recipe, the map panel depends on the result of the `geom` command, which looks for the necessary feature id fields in the search results and adds its own data to that the map can use to render the shapes properly. The `iplocation` command is commonly used to map network traffic-originating locations.

The built-in IP location data within Splunk is provided by Splunk as part of Splunk Enterprise but is not always the most up-to-date data available from the internet. It's often best practice to purchase a third-party service to get the most accurate and real-time data available, especially when it is used on critical security-monitoring dashboards and searches.

The map panel has many different configuration options that can be used to specify the initial latitude, longitude, and zoom level that should be applied when the map is initially loaded, as well as the minimum and maximum zoom levels. Drilling down into the maps is also supported.

For more details on mapping in Splunk, you can visit `https://docs.splunk.com/Documentation/Splunk/latest/Viz/Choroplethmaps`.
A full reference of map drilldown options can be found in the Splunk documentation at `https://docs.splunk.com/Documentation/Splunk/latest/Viz/PanelreferenceforSimplifiedXML#drilldown`.

There's more...

The map panel option can also be configured in several different ways in Splunk.

Adding a map panel using Simple XML

A map panel can be added directly to a dashboard by adding the following Simple XML when editing the dashboard source:

```
<row>
  <panel>
    <map>
      <title>Count by location</title>
      <search>
        <query>index=main sourcetype=access_combined clientip="$ip$" |
iplocation clientip  | fillnull value="Unknown" City, Country, Region|
replace "" with "Unknown" in City, Country, Region | search City="$city$"
Region="$region$" Country="$country$" | geostats count</query>
        <earliest>-24h@m</earliest>
        <latest>now</latest>
      </search>
      <option name="mapping.data.maxClusters">100</option>
      <option name="mapping.drilldown">all</option>
      <option name="mapping.map.center">(0,0)</option>
    </map>
  </panel>
</row>
```

Mapping different distributions by area

The `geostats` command takes an aggregation term as its main argument. This term is what is used to render the pie charts that are located on the map. In this recipe, we simply ran | `geostats count`, which is the most commonly used command and simply does a single count. However, you can break out the data by product, and then the pie charts will provide segmented visual information and can be moused over to see the breakdown:

```
MySearch | geostats count by product
```

See also

- The *Linking web page activity reports to the form* recipe
- The *Scheduling the PDF delivery of a dashboard* recipe

Highlighting average product price

As we have seen in previous recipes, visualizing data with charts can be a great way to gain visibility into the meaning of your data. However, certain types of data may be best represented by a table rather than a chart. In these cases, we can add some visual benefit by highlighting specific cells based on some logic that we define.

This recipe will show you how to create a new dashboard panel containing a table of purchase locations for the past week and how to highlight the cell based on the average purchase price. We will then place this new dashboard into the **Operational Intelligence** application.

Getting ready

To step through this recipe, you will need a running Splunk Enterprise server, with the sample data loaded from Chapter 1, *Play Time - Getting Data In*. You should be familiar with navigating the Splunk user interface and using the Splunk search language.

How to do it...

Follow the steps in this recipe to create a new dashboard that contains a table with average purchase price cell highlighting:

1. Log in to your Splunk server.
2. Select the **Operational Intelligence** application.
3. From the search bar, enter the following search and select to run over **Last 60 Minutes**:

```
index=main sourcetype=log4j requestType="checkout" | eval
avg_price=round(total/numberOfItems,2) | table customerId orderId
numberOfItems total avg_price
```

4. Click on the **Save As** dropdown and select **Report** from the list:

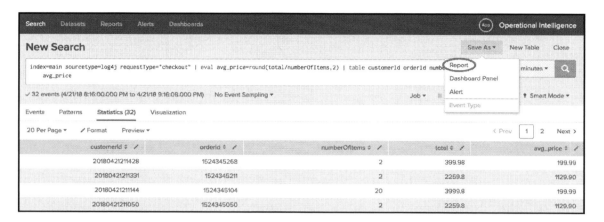

5. In the pop-up box that gets displayed, enter
   cp04_average_checkout_product_price as the title of the report and select
   No in the **Time Range Picker** field; then, click on **Save**:

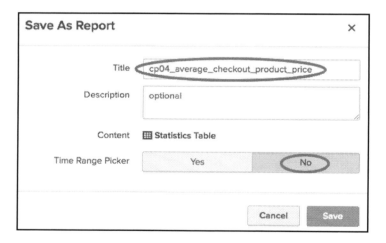

6. On the next screen, click on the **Add to Dashboard** button.

7. In the pop-up box that appears, select **Existing** and select **Product Monitoring**.
   Give the panel we are adding a title of Average Checkout Product Price.
   Ensure the panel is powered by **Report** and then click on **Save** to create the new
   dashboard with the statistics table:

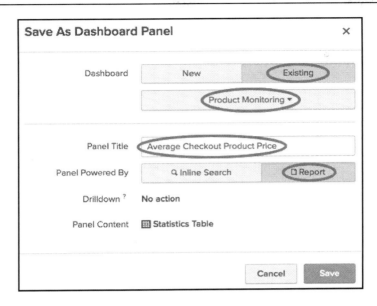

8. Click on **View Dashboard** to see the panel that's been added to your Product Monitoring dashboard.
9. Click on the **Edit** button.
10. In the **avg_price** column, click the pencil icon and then click the **Color** dropdown and select **Ranges**, as shown in the following screenshot:

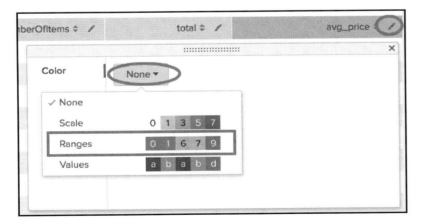

11. Remove the second and third rages and update the ranges to, **min to 1000** is **green**, **1000 to 2000** is **orange**, and **2000 to max** is **red**, as shown in the following screenshot:

12. Click anywhere on the page and you should now see the cells of the **avg_price** column highlighted based on the amount, as shown in the following screenshot:

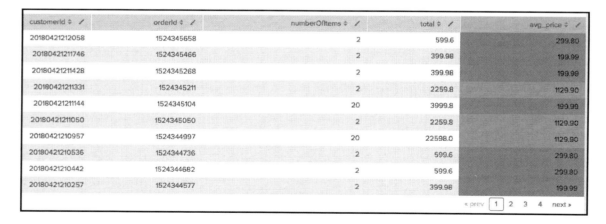

How it works...

First, we created a search. Let's break down the search piece by piece:

Search fragment	Description
`index=main    sourcetype=log4j requestType="checkout"`	You should be familiar with this search from the recipes in previous chapters. It is used to return events from the application logs. For this search, we just take the checkout requests.
`| eval avg_price=round(total/numberOfItems,2)`	Using the `eval` command, we calculate the average price per product by taking the total amount spent over the total number of items purchased. We then round the average to two significant digits.
`| table    customerId orderId numberOfItems total avg_price`	Using the `table` command, we return just the fields we want to see in our table and the order in which we want to see them.

Splunk has been improving the capabilities of the dashboard editor interface with each release. In older versions of Splunk, you had to leverage JavaScript and CSS to enable cell highlighting. Splunk now enables you to do this highlighting directly within the GUI along with multiple options for customization. You can currently have column values highlighted in either sequential or divergent scales, color ranges, or specific values.

 For more details on table visualizations in Splunk, you can go to `https://docs.splunk.com/Documentation/SplunkCloud/latest/Viz/ TableFormatsFormatting`.

See also

- The *Dynamically drilling down on activity reports* recipe
- The *Linking web page activity reports to the form* recipe
- The *Displaying a geographical map of visitors* recipe

Scheduling the PDF delivery of a dashboard

Getting Operational Intelligence to users who need it the most can be challenging. They can be users who are not IT savvy, don't have the correct access to the right systems, or are executives about to walk into a client meeting to go over the latest results data.

Sometimes, all a user needs is to have data emailed to their inbox every morning so that they can review it on their commute to the office or have an assistant prepare for a morning briefing. Splunk allows the user to schedule a dashboard so that it can be delivered as a PDF document via email to a customizable list of recipients.

This recipe will show you how to schedule the delivery of a dashboard within the Operational Intelligence application as a PDF document to an internal email distribution list.

Getting ready

To step through this recipe, you will need a running Splunk Enterprise server, with the sample data loaded from Chapter 1, *Play Time - Getting Data In*, and should have completed the earlier recipes in this chapter. You should also be familiar with navigating the Splunk user interface. You should also have configured your email server to work with Splunk so that Splunk can send emails to specified addresses.

How to do it...

Follow these steps to schedule a PDF delivery of your dashboard:

1. Log in to your Splunk server.
2. Select the Operational Intelligence application.
3. Click on the **Dashboards** menu item:

4. From the dashboard listing, select the dashboard you would like to deliver as a PDF document. Only the **Website Monitoring** and **Product Monitoring** dashboards can leverage PDF delivery, as the PDF delivery function is not (currently) compatible with dashboards driven by form inputs.

5. Once the selected dashboard loads, click on the **Edit** drop-down menu in the top right-hand side of the screen.
6. Click the **Export** button and then click on the **Schedule PDF Delivery** option, as shown in the following screenshot:

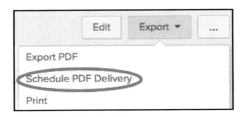

7. On the **Edit PDF Schedule** form, check the **Schedule PDF** box:

8. Modify the **Schedule** field to suit your needs. Update the dropdown and select the appropriate schedule type, as shown in the following screenshot:

9. Enter the list of email addresses you wish to send the PDF to in **the Email To** field, using commas to separate multiple email addresses.
10. Select the priority of the email.
11. Customize the **Subject** field with the content of the message subject you would like the recipients to see.

12. Customize the **Message** field with the content of the message you would like the recipients to see, as shown in the following screenshot:

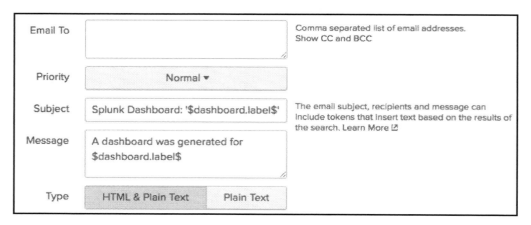

13. Update the layout options of the generated PDF by updating the **Paper Size** and **Paper Layout** options:

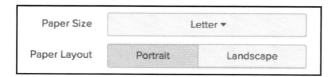

14. You can test your PDF and email formatting using the preview options. Click on the **Send Test Email** link to send to the recipients the dashboard as it looks when the link is clicked. Then, click on the **Preview PDF** link to view a version of the PDF as it looks when the link is clicked, as shown in the following screenshot:

15. Click on the **Save** button, and the PDF delivery of the dashboard is now scheduled.

How it works...

Splunk Enterprise can natively produce PDFs of dashboards and reports. This integrated PDF features allow quicker and easier access to generate PDFs either via a schedule and emailed, or directly from the web.

There are some situations where Splunk cannot produce PDFs, including form-driven dashboards, dashboards created using advanced XML, and Simple XML dashboards that contain Flash components. There are also some visualizations and features that may not render properly.

PDFs are generated when requested by native libraries built into Splunk that render what would normally be output as HTML and encode this into the PDF. This is not an easy feat, as you must take the page layout and orientation into consideration and the PDF is much more constrained than the browser window.

When delivering a scheduled PDF of a dashboard, you are using the same mechanism that scheduled reports and alerts are using. Every scheduled dashboard generates an associated scheduled report responsible for executing the scheduled dashboard on the defined schedule. The `sendemail` command is the backbone of the process and allows many different configuration options for the format of the message, including a full range of tokens that can be inserted into the subject and body of the messages that are replaced with job- and schedule-specific details.

 For more information on the configuration options to schedule reports and dashboards, check out `https://docs.splunk.com/Documentation/Splunk/latest/Report/Schedulereports`.

See also

- The *Displaying a geographical map of visitors* recipe

13
Diving Deeper – Advanced Searching, Machine Learning and Predictive Analytics

In this chapter, we will cover some of the more advanced search commands available in Splunk. We will cover the following recipes:

- Calculating the average session time on a website
- Calculating the average execution time for multi-tier web requests
- Displaying the maximum concurrent checkouts
- Analyzing the relationship of web requests
- Predicting website traffic volumes
- Finding abnormally sized web requests
- Identifying potential session spoofing
- Detecting outliers in server response times
- Forecasting weekly sales

Introduction

In the previous chapter, we learned about Splunk's new data model and Pivot functionality, and how they can be used to further intelligence reporting. In this chapter, we will return to Splunk's SPL, diving deeper and making use of some very powerful search commands to facilitate a better understanding and correlation of event data. You will learn how to create transactions, build subsearches and understand concurrency, leverage field associations, leverage the Splunk Machine Learning Toolkit, and much more.

Looking at event counts, applying statistics to calculate averages, or finding the top values over time only provide a view of the data limited to one angle. Splunk's SPL contains some very powerful search commands that provide the ability to correlate data from different sources and understand or build relationships between the events. Through the building of relationships between data sets and looking at different angles of the data, you can better understand the impact one event might have over another. Additionally, correlating related values can provide a much more contextual value to teams when reviewing or analyzing a series of data.

Identifying and grouping transactions

Single events can be easily interpreted and understood, but these single events are often part of a series of events, where the event might be influenced by preceding events or might affect other events to come. By leveraging Splunk's ability to group associated events into transactions based on field values, the data can be presented in a way that allows the reader to understand the full context of an event and what led up to this point. Building transactions can also be useful when needing to understand the time duration between the start and finish of specific events, or calculating values within a given transaction and comparing them to the values of others.

Converging data sources

Context is everything when it comes to building successful Operational Intelligence, and when you are stuck analyzing events from a single data source at a time, you might be missing out on rich contextual information that other data sources can provide. With Splunk's ability to converge multiple data sources using the `join` or `append` search commands and search across them as if they are a single source, you can easily enrich the single data source and understand events from other sources that occurred at, or around, the same time.

For example, you might notice there are more timeouts than usual on your website, but when you analyze the website access log, everything appears normal. However, when you look at the application log, you notice that there are numerous failed connections to the database. Even so, by looking at each data source individually, it is hard to understand where the actual issue lies. Using Splunk's SPL to converge the data sources will allow for both the web access and application logs to be brought together into one view, to better understand and troubleshoot the sequence of events that might lead to website timeouts.

Identifying relationships between fields

In the Operational Intelligence world, the ability to identify relationships between fields can be a powerful asset. Understanding the values of a field, and how these values might have a relationship with other field values within the same event, allows you to calculate the degree of certainty the values will provide in future events. By continually sampling events as they come in over time, you can become more accurate at predicting values in events as they occur. When used correctly, this can provide tremendous value in being able to actively predict the values of fields within events, leading to more proactive incident or issue identification.

Predicting future values

Understanding system, application, and user behavior will always prove to be extremely valuable when building out any intelligence program; however, the ability to predict future values can provide values more immense than simple modeling actions. The addition of predictive capabilities to an Operational Intelligence program enables the ability to become more proactive with issue identification, forecast system behavior, and plan and optimize thresholds more effectively.

Imagine being able to predict the number of sessions on your website, number of purchases of a specific product, response times during peak periods, or general tuning alerting thresholds to values that are substantiated rather than taking an educated guess. All of this is possible with predictive analytics; by looking back over past events, you can better understand what the future will hold.

Discovering anomalous values

With the volume of data ever increasing, looking for events that are outliers is becoming more difficult and requires different techniques for their detection. The value of identifying these values is that it can lead to the identification of a resource issue, highlight malicious activities hidden within high volumes of events, or simply detect users attempting to interact with the application in a way they were not designed to. Capitalize on these opportunities to capture the abnormalities and triage them accordingly.

Leveraging machine learning

The pace to keep up with the vast number of systems, applications, and infrastructure generating data in today's technology-first world can feel at times like an all-out sprint. Unfortunately, as fast and as smart as your analysts are trying to keep up to the pace of the data streaming may just not be possible leading to delays in analysis, missed detections, failed transactions or general poor future business planning. Enter machine learning. Machine learning has the potential to simplify prediction, better identify patterns through supervised or unsupervised training, and generally speed up issue discovery and investigations. Think of the endless possibilities of having machine learning models that are continuously "learning" from your data and adapting thresholds or generating more precise predictions on the fly as the data changes. This is the power of machine learning and why it should become the next step in your Splunk journey.

Calculating the average session time on a website

In previous chapters, we created methods to assess various values that show how consumers interact with our website. However, what these values did not outline is how long consumers spend on our website. By leveraging Splunk's more powerful search commands, we can calculate the average session time of consumers interacting with our website, which can act as supporting information when articulating data such as engagement rates, resource requirements, or consumer experience.

In this recipe, you will write a Splunk search to calculate the average time of a session on the website over a given period of time. You will then graphically display this value on a dashboard using the single-value visualization.

Getting ready

To step through this recipe, you will need a running Splunk Enterprise server, with the sample data loaded from Chapter 11, *Play Time - Getting Data In*. You should be familiar with navigating the Splunk user interface.

How to do it...

Follow the steps in this recipe to calculate the average session time on a website:

1. Log in to your Splunk server.
2. Select the **Operational Intelligence** application.
3. Ensure the time range picker is set to **Last 24 Hours**, and type the following search into the Splunk search bar. Then, click on the magnifying glass button or hit *Enter*:

```
index=main sourcetype=access_combined | transaction
JSESSIONID | stats avg(duration) AS Avg_Session_Time
```

4. Splunk will return a single value representing the average duration in seconds for a session on the website.
5. Click on the **Visualization** tab.
6. Since there are a number of visualizations within Splunk, the single-value visualization might not be displayed by default within the **Visualization** tab. Click on the dropdown listing the visualization types and select **Single Value**:

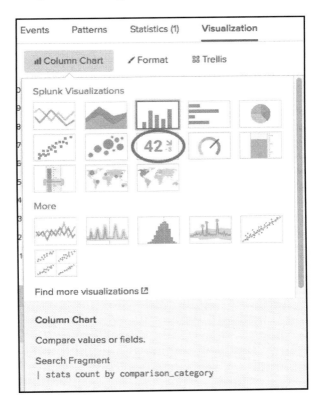

7. You should now see the value represented as the single-value visualization.

8. Let's add more context to the visualization. Click on **Format**. Enter `Avg Session Time` in the **Caption**:

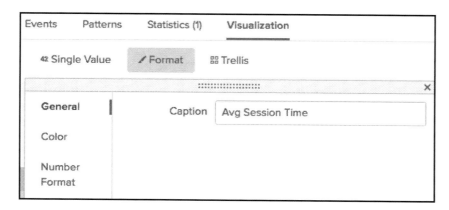

9. Click on **Number Format**. Enter `secs` in the **Unit** and then click anywhere on the page:

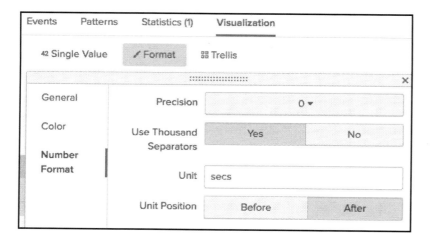

10. Your single-value visualization should now look similar to the following example:

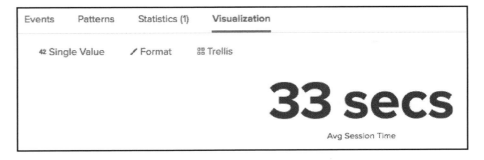

11. Let's save this search as a report. Click on **Save As** and choose **Report** from the drop-down menu:

12. In the **Save As Report** window that appears, enter cp06_average_session_time as the title and click on **Save**:

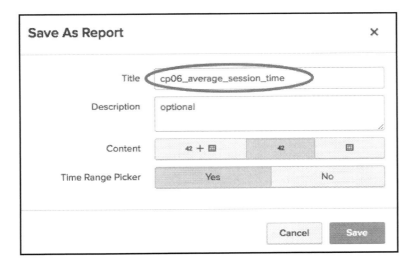

13. You will receive confirmation that your report has been created. Now, let's add this report to a dashboard. In the next window, click on **Add to Dashboard**:

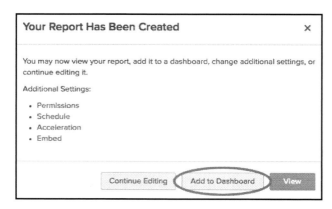

14. You will create a new dashboard for this report. On the **Save As Dashboard Panel** screen, ensure **New** is selected and enter `Session Monitoring` as the dashboard title. Select **Shared in App** for the dashboard permissions and **Report** to power the panel by a report. Finally, click on **Save** to create the dashboard:

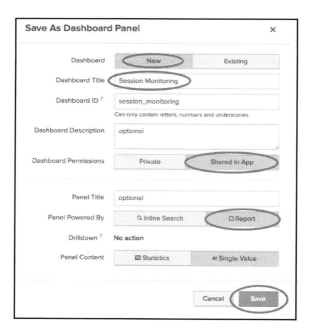

15. The report is saved and a new Session Monitoring dashboard is created. You can now choose to click on View Dashboard to see your newly created dashboard with the Average Session Time report.

How it works...

Let's break down the search piece by piece:

Search fragment	Description
`index=main sourcetype=access_combined`	You should be familiar with this search from the recipes in previous chapters. It is used to return events from the website access log.
`| transaction JSESSIONID`	Using the `transaction` command, we group events together based on their given JSESSIONID to form a single transaction. The JSESSIONID field is chosen as each visitor to the website is given a random session identifier whose value is stored in this field. One of the fields created by the `transaction` command is the `duration` field. The `duration` field represents the amount of time, in seconds, between the first and last events in the transaction.
`| stats avg(duration) AS Avg_Session_Time`	Using the `stats` command, we calculate the average value of the `duration` field. Using the AS operator, we rename the resulting field that is created with the given value to something more readable, for example, `Avg_Session_Time`.

There's more...

The `transaction` command provides many parameters to control the way in which transactions are grouped. Using the `startswith` and `endswith` parameters, you can control what marks the start and end of a transaction based on data inside the events. Using the `maxspan`, `maxpause`, or `maxevents` parameters, you can control the constraints around how long a transaction will be, the amount of time between events before splitting it into a new transaction, or the total number of events within a transaction.

Where possible, using the parameters available for the `transaction` command is highly encouraged. Using the `transaction` command without any other parameter can result in a processing intensive (and inefficient) search that takes a while to run.

Starts with a website visit, ends with a checkout

To mark where a transaction begins and ends, you can make use of two parameters available within the `transaction` command, called `startswith` and `endswith`, respectively. In the following example, we modify the search in the recipe to include the `startswith="GET /home"` and `endswith="checkout"` parameters. This constrains the `transaction` command to only group events together with a general website request when the first event begins and the last event is a request to checkout. Any other event, or transaction, that does not meet these criteria will be discarded and not included in the returned results:

```
index=main sourcetype=access_combined | transaction JSESSIONID
  startswith="GET /home" endswith="checkout" | stats avg(duration)
  AS Avg_Session_Time
```

By making use of these parameters, you can be more explicit on what gets treated as a transaction or focus on specific groupings of data.

Defining maximum pause, span, and events in a transaction

Three more very useful parameters available, apart from the `transaction` command, are `maxpause`, `maxspan`, and `maxevents`. These parameters allow you to apply more constraints around the duration and size of transactions and can be used individually or all together for even more precise constriction.

Adding the `maxpause=30s` parameter to the search in the recipe tells the `transaction` command that there must be no pause between events greater than 30 seconds, otherwise the grouping breaks. By default, there is no limit:

```
index=main sourcetype=access_combined | transaction JSESSIONID
  maxpause=30s | stats avg(duration) AS Avg_Session_Time
```

Adding the `maxspan=30m` parameter to the search in the recipe tells the `transaction` command that when building the transaction, the first and last events cannot be greater than 30 minutes, otherwise the grouping breaks. By default, there is no limit:

```
index=main sourcetype=access_combined | transaction JSESSIONID
   maxspan=30m | stats avg(duration) AS Avg_Session_Time
```

Adding the `maxevents=300` parameter to the search in the recipe tells the `transaction` command that when building the transaction, the total number of events contained within cannot be greater than 300, otherwise the grouping breaks. By default, the value is 1,000:

```
index=main sourcetype=access_combined | transaction JSESSIONID
   maxevents=300 | stats avg(duration) AS Avg_Session_Time
```

As mentioned, these parameters can be combined to create an even more constrained transaction for specific use cases. Here is an example of a transaction that starts with a home page request, ends with a checkout, is no longer than 30 minutes, has no events where there is a pause greater than 30 seconds, and the maximum number of events contained within is 300:

```
index=main sourcetype=access_combined | transaction JSESSIONID
   startswith="GET /home" endswith="checkout" maxpause=30s
   maxspan=30m maxevents=300 | stats avg(duration) AS
   Avg_Session_Time
```

> For more information on the `transaction` command, visit `https://docs.splunk.com/Documentation/Splunk/latest/SearchReference/Transaction`.

See also

- The *Calculating the average execution time for multi-tier web requests* recipe
- The *Displaying the maximum concurrent checkouts* recipe

Calculating the average execution time for multi-tier web requests

With components existing at many different layers to provide varying functionalities, web applications are no longer as straightforward as they once were. Understanding the execution time for a web request across the entire application stack, rather than at a single layer, can be extremely beneficial in correctly articulating the average time that requests take to execute in their entirety. This can lead to the identification of issues in relation to increasing website response times.

In this recipe, you will write a Splunk search to calculate the average execution time of a web request that traverses not only the website access logs, but also application logs. You will then graphically display this value on a dashboard using a single-value visualization.

Getting ready

To step through this recipe, you will need a running Splunk Enterprise server, with the sample data loaded from `Chapter 11`, *Play Time - Getting Data In*. You should also complete the recipes in previous chapters and be familiar with navigating the Splunk user interface.

How to do it...

Follow the steps in this recipe to calculate the average execution time for multi-tier web requests:

1. Log in to your Splunk server.
2. Select the **Operational Intelligence** application.
3. Ensure the time range picker is set to **Last 24 Hours**, and type the following search into the Splunk search bar. Then, click on the search button or hit *Enter*:

```
index=main sourcetype=access_combined | join JSESSIONID
usetime=true earlier=false [ search index=main
sourcetype=log4j | transaction threadId maxspan=5m | eval
JSESSIONID=sessionId ] | stats avg(duration) AS
Avg_Request_Execution_Time
```

4. After a little while, Splunk will return a single value representing the average execution time in seconds for a complete web request on the website.

5. Click on the **Visualization** tab.

6. Since there are a number of visualizations within Splunk, the single-value visualization might not be displayed by default within the **Visualization** tab. Click on the dropdown listing the visualization types and select **Single Value**:

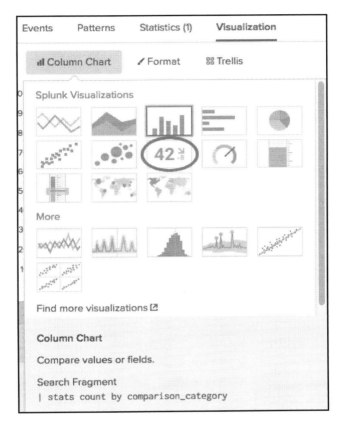

7. You should now see the value represented as the single-value visualization.

8. Let's add more context to the visualization. Click on **Format**. On the General tab, enter `Avg Request Execution` in the **Caption** field:

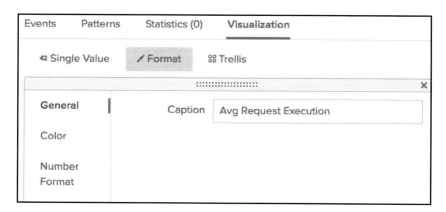

9. Click on the **NumberFormat** tab and select **0.00** for **Precision**, enter `secs` for the **Unit**, and then click anywhere on the page:

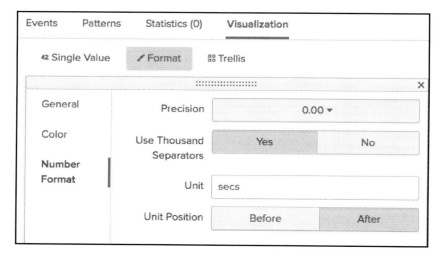

10. Your single-value visualization should now look similar to the following example:

11. Let's save this search as a report. Click on **Save As**, and choose **Report** from the drop-down menu as shown in the following snapshot:

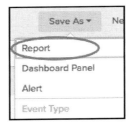

12. In the **Save As Report** window that appears, enter `cp06_average_request_execution_time` as the title and click on **Save**:

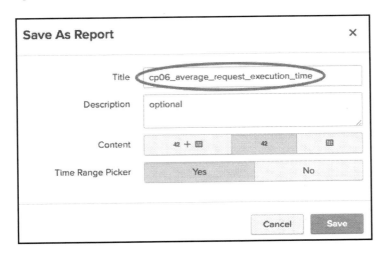

13. You will receive a confirmation that your report has been created. Now, let's add this report to a dashboard. In the next window, click on **Add to Dashboard**:

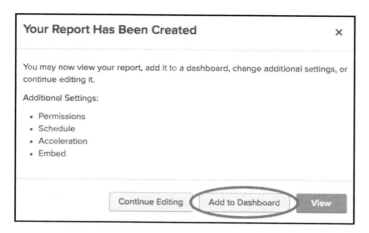

14. You will now add this to the dashboard that was created in the previous recipe named **Session Monitoring**. In the **Save As Dashboard Panel** window, click on the **Existing** button beside the **Dashboard** label. From the drop-down menu that appears, select **Session Monitoring**. For the **Panel Powered By** field, click on the **Report** button. Finally, click on **Save**:

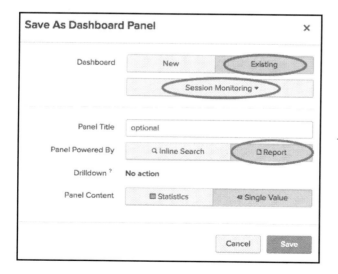

15. Click on **View Dashboard** to see the panel that's been added to your Session Monitoring dashboard.

16. Now, let's arrange the panels so they are side by side. Click on **Edit**:

17. Now, drag the newly added panel so that both single-value visualizations are on the same row, as shown in the following screenshot. When finished, click on **Save**:

How it works...

Let's break down the search piece by piece:

Search fragment	Description
index=main sourcetype=access_combined	You should be familiar with this search from the recipes in previous chapters. It is used to return events from the website access log.

`| join JSESSIONID`
`   usetime=true`
`earlier=false`
`   [ search index=main`
`   sourcetype=log4j |`
`   transaction threadId`
`   maxspan=5m | eval`
`   JSESSIONID=sessionId ]`
	Using the `join` command, we execute a subsearch to return matching events from the web application log. The `JSESSIONID` field is used as the unique value to join the events on. Within the subsearch, we leverage the `transaction` command to group all application events together based on their `threadId`, which is a unique value for each function execution. The `maxspan` parameter is used with the assumption that application events common to the transaction will all be within 5 minutes of each other. Then, we create a field named `JSESSIONID` using `eval` because it does not exist within the web application events, which has a field named `sessionId` instead. By creating this field, the join will work properly as it knows how to associate the events. The `usetime` and `earlier` parameters passed to the `join` command tell it to limit matches to only those events that come after the originating web access event. This ensures that only web application events that occurred after the website access log event will be returned, since we know the natural method of execution for our application requires a user interaction with the website before the application will trigger a function execution.

`| stats avg(duration) AS` `Avg_Request_Execution_Time`	Using the `stats` command, we calculate the average value of the duration field, since this field has been carried through by the use of the `transaction` command within the subsearch. Using the `AS` operator, we rename the resulting field that is created with the given value to something more readable, for example, `Avg_Request_Execution_Time`.

There's more...

In this recipe, you used the `join` command to join an inner subsearch with an outer main search. This is similar to a join in an SQL database. Another command that is similar to join is `append`. The `append` command allows you to string two different searches together, such that the results of the second search will be appended to the results of the first search. The maximum value is obtained from `append` if the searches you append together share common fields; use of the `eval` command or implementation of **Common Information Model (CIM)** can help with this.

 For more information on `join`, visit
https://docs.splunk.com/Documentation/Splunk/latest/SearchReference/Join.

 For more information on the `append` command, visit
https://docs.splunk.com/Documentation/Splunk/latest/SearchReference/Append.

While both the `join` and `append` commands can be useful, they are not the most efficient commands. This is because both commands execute multiple searches instead of just one. Often, the `stats` or `transaction` command can be used in creative ways to avoid using `join` or `append`, and to increase search performance as a result.

Calculating the average execution time without using a join

Often, there are many ways to write a search that results in providing the same or similar insight. While there is nothing wrong with the search used in this recipe, we can amend the search so that it does not use the `join` command. An example search might be as follows:

```
index=main sourcetype=access_combined OR sourcetype=log4j
| eval action=substr(uri_path,2) | eval
 action=lower(if(isnull(action),requestType,action))
| eval JSESSIONID=if(isnull(JSESSIONID),sessionId,JSESSIONID)
| transaction threadId, JSESSIONID, action maxspan=1m
| stats avg(duration) AS Avg_Request_Execution_Time
```

Here, we search both the web access and application logs in the same search. We evaluated a new field called `action` using similar field values found in the web access (`uri_path`) and application logs (`requestType`). For example, a checkout web request generates a checkout application request. Using the `transaction` command, we transact all events across both sourcetypes that share a session ID, thread ID, or our new action field. We also make the assumption that our requests do not take longer than a minute to execute, and subsequently we set a `maxspan` of one minute. Setting this tightened criteria will make the `transaction` command more efficient. Splunk will now group all web requests and subsequent application events related to the web requests together into transactions, with duration calculated for each. We then apply the same `stats` command to work out the average request execution time. This might actually provide a more accurate execution time as we incorporate the timestamp of the web access logs into the transaction duration.

See also

- The *Calculating the average session time on the website* recipe
- The *Displaying the maximum concurrent checkouts* recipe
- The *Analyzing the relationship of web requests* recipe

Displaying the maximum concurrent checkouts

Typically, when analyzing web requests, events often overlap with one another due to multiple users issuing requests concurrently. By identifying these overlapping requests, and further understanding the concurrency of events, you will gain a clearer picture of the true demand for both resources and consumer demands.

In this recipe, you will write a Splunk search to find the number of concurrent checkouts over a given period of time. You will then graphically display this value on a dashboard using the line chart visualization.

Getting ready

To step through this recipe, you will need a running Splunk Enterprise server, with the sample data loaded from Chapter 11, *Play Time - Getting Data In*. You should also complete the earlier recipes in this chapter and be familiar with navigating the Splunk user interface.

How to do it...

Follow the steps in this recipe to identify the number of concurrent checkouts over a given period of time:

1. Log in to your Splunk server.
2. Select the **Operational Intelligence** application.
3. Ensure the time range picker is set to **Last 24 Hours**, and type the following search into the Splunk search bar. Then, click on the search button or hit *Enter*:

```
index=main sourcetype=access_combined | transaction
 JSESSIONID startswith="GET /home" endswith="checkout"
 | concurrency duration=duration | timechart max(concurrency)
AS "Concurrent Checkouts"
```

4. Splunk will return the values associated with the maximum concurrent checkout's split in 30-minute durations.
5. Click on the **Visualization** tab.
6. Since there are a number of visualizations within Splunk, the line chart visualization might not be displayed by default within the **Visualization** tab. Click on the dropdown listing the visualization types, and select **Line**:

7. You should now see the value represented as the line chart visualization.

8. Let's add more context to the visualization and correct some values. Click on **Format**, and then click on the **Y-Axis** tab. Click on the dropdown **Title** menu and choose **Custom**. Enter Count as the title, and click anywhere on the page:

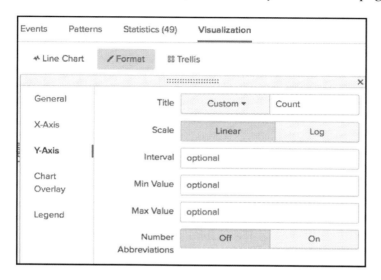

9. Your line chart visualization should now look similar to the following example:

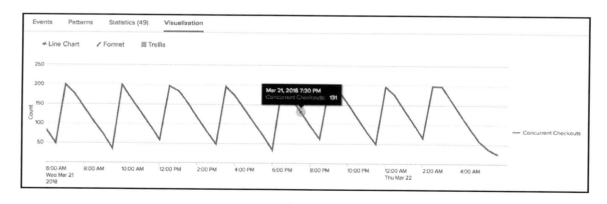

10. Let's save this search as a report. Click on **Save As** and choose **Report** from the drop-down menu:

11. In the pop-up box that appears, enter cp06_concurrent_checkouts in the **Title** field and then click on **Save**:

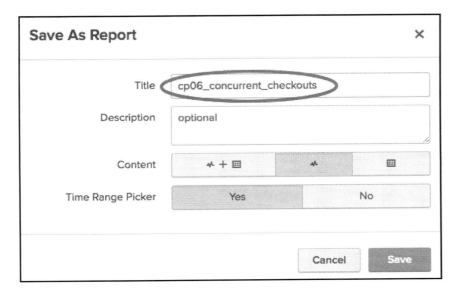

12. You will receive a confirmation that your report has been created. Now, let's add this report to a dashboard. In the next window, click on **Add to Dashboard**:

13. You add this report to the Session Monitoring dashboard that was created in an earlier recipe. In the **Save As Dashboard Panel** pop-up box, click on the **Existing** button beside the **Dashboard** label. From the drop-down menu that appears, select **Session Monitoring**. Enter `Maximum Concurrent Checkouts` in the **Panel Title** field, and ensure the panel is powered by a **Report**. Then, click on **Save**:

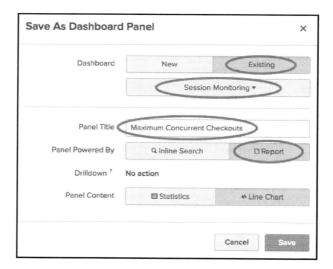

14. You can now click on **View Dashboard** to see the panel on your Session Monitoring dashboard.

How it works...

Let's break down the search piece by piece:

Search fragment	Description
`index=main` `    sourcetype=access_combined`	You should be familiar with this search from the earlier recipes in this chapter. It is used to return events from the website access log.

`| transaction JSESSIONID`
`    startswith="GET /home"`
`    endswith="checkout"`
	Using the `transaction` command, we group events together based on their given `JSESSIONID` to form a single transaction, and apply transaction parameters so that events start with a `GET` request for the main page and end with `checkout`.

`| concurrency` `    duration=duration`	The `concurrency` command is used to find the concurrent number of events, given a duration value, that occurred at the same start time. The `duration` field being used here is generated by the use of the `transaction` command. A field named `concurrency` will be created by the `concurrency` command, and this will store the value of concurrent events.

`| timechart`
`    max(concurrency) AS`
`    "Concurrent Checkouts"`
	The `timechart` command is leveraged to plot the maximum values of the `concurrency` field over the given period of time. The `AS` operator is leveraged to rename the field to a more readable value, for example, `Concurrent Checkouts`.

The `concurrency` command is a useful way of calculating concurrent events without using too much logic. In this recipe, you were able to use the command to identify the maximum number of concurrent checkouts throughout the day.

For more information on the `concurrency` command, visit
`https://docs.splunk.com/Documentation/Splunk/latest/SearchRefere`
`nce/Concurrency`.

See also

- The *Calculating the average execution time for multi-tier web requests* recipe
- The *Analyzing the relationship of web requests* recipe
- The *Predicting website traffic volumes* recipe

Analyzing the relationship of web requests

To better understand the events occurring within a web application environment, you need to start building relationships between the pieces of data within events. By leveraging these relationships, efforts can become more targeted on the events requiring attention and a more proactive stance on issue identification can be taken. Imagine being able to say with confidence that when a certain page is requested, it will have a status of 404, or when a specific product is added to a cart, the service becomes unresponsive. Having this type of relationship capability added into your Operational Intelligence application opens up a vast array of possibilities when performing event analysis.

In this recipe, you will write a Splunk search to analyze the relationship of web requests between the status of the request and the pages where the request originated from, over a given period of time. You will then add this table as a panel to a dashboard.

Getting ready

To step through this recipe, you will need a running Splunk Enterprise server, with the sample data loaded from Chapter 11, *Play Time - Getting Data In*. You should also complete the earlier recipes in this chapter and be familiar with navigating the Splunk user interface.

How to do it...

Follow the steps in this recipe to analyze the relationship of web requests over time:

1. Log in to your Splunk server.
2. Select the **Operational Intelligence** application.
3. Ensure the time range picker is set to **Last 24 Hours**, and type the following search into the Splunk search bar. Then, click on the search button or hit *Enter*:

```
index=main sourcetype=access_combined NOT status=200 |
associate uri status supcnt=50 | table Description
Reference_Key Reference_Value Target_Key
Top_Conditional_Value
```

4. Splunk will return the results in a tabular format similar to the following example:

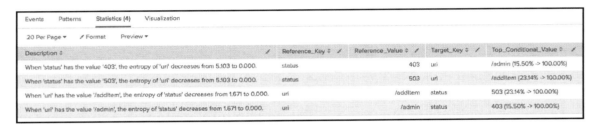

5. Let's save this search as a report. Click on **Save As** and choose **Report** from the drop-down menu:

6. In the pop-up box that appears, enter `cp06_status_uri_relationships` in the **Title** field and click on **Save**:

7. You will receive a confirmation that your report has been created. Now, let's add this report to our Session Monitoring dashboard we created earlier in this chapter. In the next window, click on **Add to Dashboard**:

8. In the **Save As Dashboard Panel** pop-up box, click on the **Existing** button beside the **Dashboard** label. From the drop-down menu that appears, select **Session Monitoring**. Enter Status and URI Relationships in the **Panel Title** field, ensure the panel is powered by a **Report**, and then click on **Save**:

9. You can now click on **View Dashboard** to see the panel that has been added to the Session Monitoring dashboard.

How it works...

In this recipe, you used the associate command to find relationships between the status and uri fields in the web access events. The associate command works by calculating a change in entropy based upon field-pair values. It is able to provide a prediction of a field value based upon another field value.

Let's break down the search piece by piece:

Search fragment	Description
`index=main sourcetype=access_combined NOT status="200"`	You should be familiar with this search from the earlier recipes in this chapter. However, we added search criteria to not return any event where the status field is equal to `200` (success).
`| associate uri status supcnt=50`	The `associate` command is used to identify correlations between the `uri` and `status` fields. The `associate` command creates multiple new fields. The `Reference_Key`, `Reference_Value`, and `Target_Key` fields are used to indicate the fields being analyzed. The `supcnt` parameter is used to specify the minimum number of times the "`reference key=reference value`" combination must appear. The `Unconditional_Entropy`, `Conditional_Entropy`, and `Entropy_Improvement` fields contain the entropy that was calculated for each pair of field values. The `Description` field provides a more easily readable summarization of the result.
`| table Description Reference_Key Reference_Value Target_Key Top_Conditional_Value`	The `table` command is used last to format the output of the results. Here, we chose to display only a few of the available fields generated by the `associate` command.

Examining the tabulated results in more detail, we selected to display the `Description`, `Reference_Key`, `Reference_Value`, `Target_Key`, and `Top_Conditional_Value` fields. The `Description` field provides a textual description in the following format:

```
"When the 'Reference_Key' has the value 'Reference_Value', the
  entropy of 'Target_Key' decreases from Unconditional_Entropy to
  Conditional_Entropy."
```

Taking a row from the results table, when the `Reference_Key` field is equal to the `Reference_Value` field, then the `Target_Key` field is most likely to be the `Top_Conditional_Value` field. For example, a `status` code of X might most likely have a `uri` value of Y.

It is highly recommended that you review the documentation for the `associate` command, as there is quite a bit to it and some of the concepts are fairly complex. The documentation is available at `https://docs.splunk.com/Documentation/Splunk/latest/Searchreference/Associate`.

There's more...

The `associate` command does not require that you explicitly pass field names to it, so when starting out with your event data, it is best to just call the command without any parameters and explore the results that are returned. At times, this can prove to be most useful, as you will likely identify relationships that you might previously not have thought of.

Analyzing relationships of DB actions to memory utilization

The `associate` command is most useful to analyze events related to system resource utilization. It can be leveraged to understand if there is any relationship between the type of DB action being executed by the web application and the current memory utilization. The following search will group events together into transactions based on their given `threadId`, and then compile relationships between the `dbAction` and `mem_user` fields using the `associate` command:

```
index=main sourcetype=log4j | transaction threadId | associate
  supcnt=50 dbAction mem_used
```

This can be most beneficial when trying to understand how function calls have an impact on resource utilization by drawing out direct relationships of the values.

See also

- The *Displaying the maximum concurrent checkouts* recipe
- The *Predicting website traffic volumes* recipe
- The *Finding abnormally sized web requests* recipe

Predicting website traffic volumes

In any environment, the capability to predict events provides immense value. In many cases, predictive analytics involves looking back over past events to predict what might occur in the future with a certain degree of confidence. When applied to the Operational Intelligence space and used correctly, predictive analytics can become a key asset that is more heavily relied on by teams rather than any other part of an Operational Intelligence program. For example, imagine having the ability to know the appropriate thresholds to set to alert key staff of impending issues, the capability to understand that a problem is beginning to occur even before it does, or simply being able to predict what consumers will purchase and ensuring the items are in stock. These examples just scratch the surface on use cases for predictive analytics.

In this recipe, you will write a Splunk search to predict website traffic volumes over a given time period. You will then graphically represent these values on a dashboard using a line chart.

Getting ready

To step through this recipe, you will need a running Splunk Enterprise server, with the sample data loaded from `Chapter 11`, *Play Time - Getting Data In*. You should be familiar with navigating the Splunk user interface.

How to do it...

Follow the steps in this recipe to predict website traffic volumes over a given period of time:

1. Log in to your Splunk server.
2. Select the **Operational Intelligence** application.
3. Ensure the time range picker is set to **Last 24 Hours**, and type the following search into the Splunk search bar. Then, click on the search button or hit *Enter*:

   ```
   index=main sourcetype=access_combined | timechart span=1h
   count | predict count
   ```

4. Splunk will return the resulting calculations in a tabular format in 1-hour intervals.

5. Click on the **Visualization** tab.
6. Since there are a number of visualizations within Splunk, the line chart visualization might not be displayed by default within the **Visualization** tab. Click on the dropdown listing the visualization types and select **Line**:

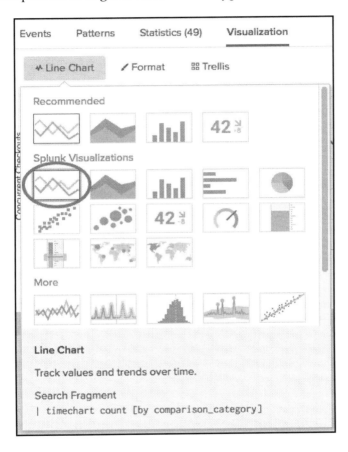

7. You should now see the value represented as line chart visualization, which is similar to the following example:

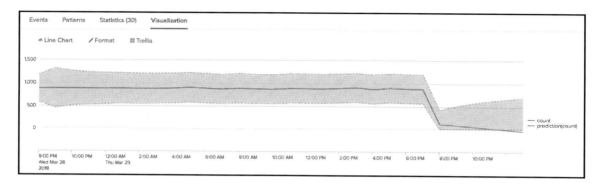

8. Let's save this search as a report. Click on **Save As** and choose **Report** from the drop-down menu:

9. A **Save As Report** pop-up box will appear. Enter
    cp06_website_traffic_prediction in the **Title** field, and then click on **Save**:

10. You will receive a confirmation that your report has been created. Now, let's add
    this report to a dashboard. In the next window, click on **Add to Dashboard**:

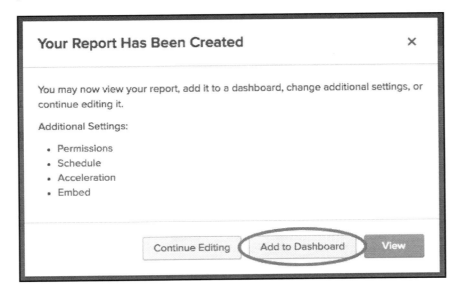

11. You will create a new dashboard for this report. On the **Save As Dashboard Panel** pop-up screen, make sure **New** is selected. Enter `Predictive Analytics` in the **Dashboard Title** field. Ensure the dashboard permissions are set to **Shared in App**. Enter `Website Traffic Volume Predictions` as the panel title and ensure the panel is powered by a **Report**. Then, click on **Save** to create the dashboard:

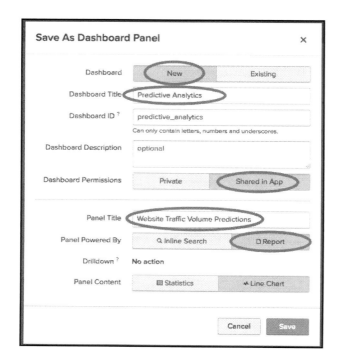

12. You can now click on **View Dashboard** to view your newly created Predictive Analytics dashboard.

How it works...

Let's break down the search piece by piece:

Search fragment	Description
`index=main sourcetype=access_combined`	You should now be familiar with this search from the earlier recipes. It is used to return events from the website access log.

`| timechart span=1h count`	The `timechart` command simply performs a count of events in 1-hour intervals. This produces the total count in a tabular form.
`| predict count`	The `predict` command is used to look back over the given data set and generate three new fields: `prediction`, which is the predicted future value for the given data point; `upper95`, which is the upper confidence interval; and `lower95`, which is the lower confidence interval. The confidence intervals specify the percentage of predictions that are expected to fail. The default value is `95%` but can be adjusted as needed.

There's more...

Predictive analytics can be applied to many different aspects of Operational Intelligence. The following are a few more short examples of other ways that prediction can be performed within Splunk using the `predict` command or the Machine Learning ToolKit to provide operational insight.

Create and apply a machine learning model of traffic over time

The Splunk Machine Learning Toolkit introduces the ability to create and train a machine learning model, which in this example will store the results of running a machine learning algorithm on a dataset of traffic counts over time to be applied later against the same dataset. First, create and train the machine learning model:

```
index=main sourcetype=access_combined | timechart span=1h count | fit
LinearRegression fit_intercept=true "count" from "_time" into
"ml_traffic_over_time"
```

Here, we calculate the number of events in 1-hour intervals. Then, we use the `fit` command to create the model named `ml_traffic_over_time`, using the LinearRegression algorithm, to predict the `count` over `_time`; this process is effectively training the machine learning model being created.

Now that the machine learning model has been created, it can be applied back against the dataset again using the `apply` command:

```
index=main sourcetype=access_combined | timechart span=1h count | apply
"ml_traffic_over_time" | table _time, "count", "predicted(count)"
```

Here, we again calculate the number of events in 1-hour intervals; however, using the `apply` command we compute predictions based on the `ml_traffic_over_time` model that was previously learned by the `fit` command. The output is then best visualized using the Downsampled Line Chart visualization.

For more information on the `fit` and `apply` commands, visit
`https://docs.splunk.com/Documentation/MLApp/latest/User/Customse`
`archcommands`.

Predicting the total number of items purchased

The `predict` command can be used to analyze the number of items being purchased from a website, therefore ensuring that the right quantity of a product is always stocked. The Splunk search will be written as shown:

```
index=main sourcetype=log4j requestType=checkout | timechart
span=1h sum(numberOfItems) as count | predict count
```

Here, we simply look for all of the checkout events within the web application log and create a time chart of the sum of items purchased in 1-hour intervals. Then, we pipe the results into the `predict` command.

Predicting the average response time of function calls

Predicting the average response time of function calls can allow you to better tune your alerting thresholds if, or when, a function call falls outside the acceptable range. This can allow teams to better prioritize and hone in on issues as they occur, or even when they begin to occur. The Splunk search will be written as shown:

```
index=main sourcetype=log4j | transaction threadId | timechart
span=1h avg(duration) as avg_duration | predict upper98=high
lower98=low avg_duration
```

Here, we must first calculate the duration of a function call by using the `transaction` command to group the events by `threadId`. Next, the `timechart` command will calculate the average duration by 1-hour intervals, and rename the field to `avg_duration`. Then, the results are piped to the `predict` command, where we have specified an upper and lower `98%` confidence interval in which predictions are expected to fail.

 For more information on the `predict` command, visit `https://docs.splunk.com/Documentation/Splunk/latest/SearchReference/Predict`.

See also

- The *Analyzing the relationship of web requests* recipe
- The *Finding abnormally sized web requests* recipe
- The *Identifying potential session spoofing* recipe

Finding abnormally-sized web requests

The identification of abnormalities within events can prove to be valuable for many reasons: it can lead to the identification of a resource issue, highlight malicious activities hidden within high volumes of events, or simply detect users attempting to interact with the application in a way they were not designed to. When building an Operational Intelligence application for your website, the ability to detect abnormal activities should be at the top of your list. Frequently, after issues are identified, remediated, and due diligence has been done, it is common to see that some abnormality in the system or application was an early identifier of the cause. Capitalize on these opportunities to capture the abnormalities and triage them accordingly.

In this recipe, you will create a Splunk search to highlight abnormal web requests based on the size of the request over a given time period. You will then present all findings in a tabular format.

Getting ready

To step through this recipe, you will need a running Splunk Enterprise server, with the sample data loaded from `Chapter 11`, *Play Time - Getting Data In*. You should also complete the earlier recipes in this chapter and be familiar with navigating the Splunk user interface.

How to do it...

Follow the steps in this recipe to identify abnormally-sized web requests:

1. Log in to your Splunk server.
2. Select the **Operational Intelligence** application.
3. Ensure the time range picker is set to **Last 24 Hours**, and type the following search into the Splunk search bar. Then, click on the search button or hit *Enter*:

```
index=main sourcetype=access_combined | eventstats
mean(bytes) AS mean_bytes, stdev(bytes) AS stdev_bytes |
eval Z_score=round(((bytes-mean_bytes)/stdev_bytes),2) |
where Z_score>1.5 OR Z_score<-1.5 | table _time, clientip,
uri, bytes, mean_bytes, Z_score
```

4. Splunk will return the results in a tabulated form, similar to the following example:

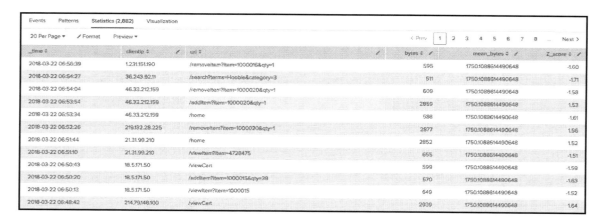

_time ≑	clientip ≑	uri ≑	bytes ≑	mean_bytes ≑	Z_score ≑
2018-03-22 06:56:39	1.231.151.190	/removeitem?item=1000016&qty=1	595	1750.1088614490648	-1.60
2018-03-22 06:54:27	36.243.92.11	/search?terms=Hooble&category=3	511	1750.1088614490648	-1.71
2018-03-22 06:54:04	46.33.212.159	/removeitem?item=1000020&qty=1	609	1750.1088614490648	-1.58
2018-03-22 06:53:54	46.33.212.159	/additem?item=1000020&qty=1	2859	1750.1088614490648	1.53
2018-03-22 06:53:34	46.33.212.159	/home	588	1750.1088614490648	1.61
2018-03-22 06:52:26	219.132.28.225	/removeitem?item=1000020&qty=1	2877	1750.1088614490648	1.56
2018-03-22 06:51:44	21.31.99.210	/home	2852	1750.1088614490648	1.52
2018-03-22 06:51:10	21.31.99.210	/viewitem?item=4728475	655	1750.1088614490648	-1.51
2018-03-22 06:50:43	18.5.171.50	/viewCart	599	1750.1088614490648	-1.59
2018-03-22 06:50:20	18.5.171.50	/additem?item=1000015&qty=39	570	1750.1088614490648	-1.63
2018-03-22 06:50:13	18.5.171.50	/viewitem?item=1000015	649	1750.1088614490648	-1.52
2018-03-22 06:48:42	214.79.148.100	/viewCart	2939	1750.1088614490648	1.64

5. Let's save this search as a report. Click on **Save As** and choose **Report** from the drop-down menu:

6. In the **Save As Report** pop-up box that appears, enter `cp06_abnormal_web_request_size` as the title and then click on **Save**:

7. You will receive a confirmation that your report has been created. Now, let's add this report to the Session Monitoring dashboard you created earlier in this chapter. In the next window, click on **Add to Dashboard**:

8. In the **Save As Dashboard Panel** pop-up box, click on the **Existing** button beside the **Dashboard** label, and then select **Session Monitoring** from the drop-down menu. Enter Abnormal Web Requests by Size in the **Panel Title** field and ensure it is powered by a **Report**. Then, click on **Save**:

9. You can now click on **View Dashboard** to see your newly added panel.

How it works...

Let's break down the search piece by piece:

Search fragment	Description
`index=main sourcetype=access_combined`	You should now be familiar with this search from the earlier recipes. It is used to return events from the website access log.
`| eventstats mean(bytes) AS mean_bytes, stdev(bytes) AS stdev_bytes`	The `eventstats` command is used to calculate the mean value and standard deviation of bytes over a given time period. The resulting values are added as new fields to each event.
`| eval Z_score=round(((bytes-mean_bytes)/stdev_bytes),2)`	Using the `eval` command, we calculate a new field called `Z-score` for each event and round it to two decimal places. The `Z-score` associated with each event will enable us to understand the amount and direction of variation from what is normal.
`| where Z_score>1.5 OR Z_score<-1.5`	Using the `where` command, we filter for only those Z-scores that are deemed to be too far away from what is normal. This numeric threshold should be tuned as you get a better understanding of your data and events. As a standard best practice, 1.5 is used here. The higher the values, the more extreme the abnormalities will become.
`| table _time, clientip, uri, bytes, mean_bytes, Z_score`	The `table` command is used here to format the output of our search to make it more easily understandable.

You can make use of the `predict` command to look at previous events and to provide a better insight into the most accurate threshold values used to filter Z-scores.

There's more...

In this recipe, we looked at the use of the `eventstats` command with some general statistics applied to isolate events that might deviate too far from what is considered normal. There are a few other prebuilt commands that Splunk has to perform similar tasks. We will cover these commands in the following sections.

The anomalies command

The `anomalies` command is used to look for events based on the values of a field and return only the values that you won't expect to find. As the `anomalies` command is running, it assigns an unexpectedness score to each event, and the event is only considered unexpected if the unexpectedness score passes the defined threshold. In the following example, we use the `anomalies` command to assess the bytes field within our website access logs, and we define a threshold of unexpectedness at `0.03`. The `table` and `sort` commands are just to make data presentation a little bit nicer:

```
index=main sourcetype=access_combined | anomalies field=bytes
    threshold=0.03 | table unexpectedness, _raw | sort -unexpectedness
```

The results that are returned will be those that the `anomalies` command deems to be unexpected events. The algorithm that scores the events is proprietary to Splunk, but a short description can be found on the Splunk documentation site for the `anomalies` command.

 For more information on the `anomalies` command, visit
https://docs.splunk.com/Documentation/Splunk/latest/SearchRefere
nce/Anomalies.

The anomalousvalue command

The `anomalousvalue` command provides yet another means to find irregular or uncommon search results. It will look at the entire event set for the given time range, take into consideration the distribution of values, and then make a decision on whether a value is anomalous. In the following example, we use the `anomalousvalue` command against the website access logs and set a probability threshold of `0.03` that must be met:

```
index=main sourcetype=access_combined | anomalousvalue
    pthresh=0.03
```

The results that are returned will be those that the `anomalousvalue` command deems to be anomalous.

 For more information on the `anomalousvalues` command, visit https://docs.splunk.com/Documentation/Splunk/latest/SearchReference/Anomalousvalue.

The anomalydetection command

The `anomalydetection` command provides yet another means to find irregular or uncommon search results. It identifies anomalous events by computing a probability for each event and then detecting unusually small probabilities. The probability is defined as the product of the frequencies of each individual field value in the event. In the following example, we use the `anomalydetection` command against the website access logs bytes field and set a probability threshold of `0.03` that must be met:

```
index=main sourcetype=access_combined | anomalydetection action=filter
pthresh=0.03 bytes
```

The results that are returned will be those that the `anomalydetection` command deems to be anomalous.

The `anomalydetection` command includes the capabilities of existing `anomalousvalue` and `outlier` SPL commands and offers a histogram-based approach for detecting anomalies.

 For more information on the `anomalydetection` command, visit https://docs.splunk.com/Documentation/Splunk/latest/SearchReference/Anomalydetection.

The cluster command

The `cluster` command provides a method to cluster similar events together, making it easier for you to identify outliers. Outliers are those events that are part of very small clusters or are on their own; all other events are a part of large-sized clusters. In the following example, we use the `cluster` command against the website access logs to identify any potential outlier. The `showercount` parameter is used to ensure the size of each cluster displayed. The `table` and `sort` commands are just to make data presentation a little bit nicer:

```
index=main sourcetype=access_combined | cluster showcount=t |
  table cluster_count _raw | sort +cluster_count
```

The results that are returned will be sorted with the smallest cluster being listed first. Additional filtering, such as `NOT status=200`, can be applied to the event search to further filter out false positives and allow for proper prioritization of event investigation.

 For more information on the `cluster` command, visit
`https://docs.splunk.com/Documentation/Splunk/latest/SearchReference/Cluster`.

See also

- The *Predicting website traffic volumes* recipe
- The *Identifying potential session spoofing* recipe

Identifying potential session spoofing

Sometimes, the most common website operational issues relate to malicious users operating on the site or attempting malicious activities. One of the simpler and more common activities is to attempt to spoof the session identifier of a legitimate one in the hope that a session can be hijacked. Typically, web applications are built for proper session handling, but mistakes can be made, and even the best web applications can fall victim to simple session spoofing or hijacking. Understanding the impact that this can have on the operation of the website, we will leverage a common command we used throughout this chapter to identify any potential malicious use and flag it for investigation.

In this recipe, you will write a Splunk search to aid in the identification of potential session spoofing over a given period of time. The results will be presented in a tabular format and added to a dashboard.

Getting ready

To step through this recipe, you will need a running Splunk Enterprise server, with the sample data loaded from `Chapter 11`, *Play Time - Getting Data In*. You should also complete the earlier recipes in this chapter and be familiar with navigating the Splunk user interface.

How to do it...

Follow the steps in this recipe to identify potential session spoofing activity:

1. Log in to your Splunk server.
2. Select the **Operational Intelligence** application.
3. Ensure the time range picker is set to **Last 24 Hours**, and type the following search into the Splunk search bar. Then, click on the search button or hit *Enter*:

```
index=main sourcetype=access_combined | transaction
JSESSIONID | eval count_of_clientips=mvcount(clientip) |
where count_of_clientips > 1 | table _time,
count_of_clientips, clientip, JSESSIONID | sort
count_of_clientips
```

4. Splunk will return the results in a tabular format.
5. Let's save this search as a report. Click on **Save As** and choose **Report** from the drop-down menu:

6. In the **Save As Report** pop-up box that appears, enter
   `cp06_potential_session_spoofing` in the **Title** field, and then click on **Save**:

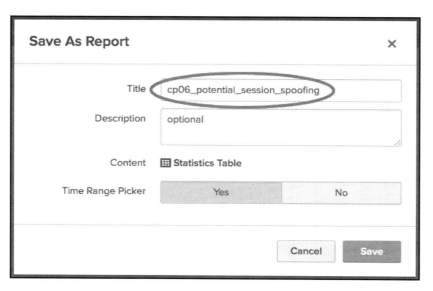

7. You will receive a confirmation that your report has been created. Now, let's add
   this report to the Session Monitoring dashboard you created earlier in this
   chapter. In the next window, click on **Add to Dashboard**:

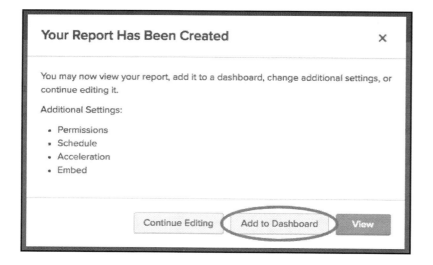

8. In the **Save As Dashboard Panel** pop-up box, click on the **Existing** button beside the **Dashboard** label and select **Session Monitoring** from the drop-down menu. Enter `Potential Session Spoofing` in the **Panel Title** field and ensure the panel is powered by a **Report**. Then, click on **Save**:

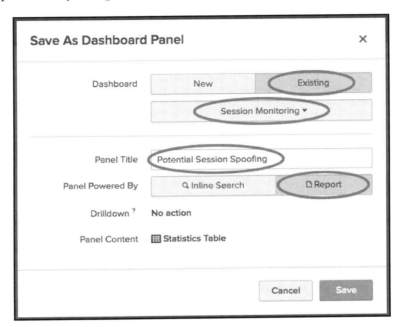

9. You can now click on **View Dashboard** to see your newly added panel.

It is best practice to save these types of searches as *alerts* so that you are automatically notified at the time a security incident occurs. It will help to lessen the impact of any potential repercussions due to malicious activity.

How it works...

In this recipe, you wrote a search to detect spoofed sessions. Essentially, the search looks for where a single session identifier (`JSESSIONID`) is associated with multiple client IP addresses over the given time range of 24 hours. Understandably, in almost all cases, a session identifier will only come from a single client IP address. So, if there are sessions that have multiple IPs, then this can very well detect spoofing of a session. Results will only be displayed where there is more than one client IP associated with a specific session.

Let's break down the search piece by piece:

Search fragment	Description
`index=main sourcetype=access_combined`	You should now be familiar with this search from the earlier recipes. It is used to return events from the website access log.
`| transaction JSESSIONID`	Using the `transaction` command, we group events together based on their given `JESSIONID` to form a single transaction.
`| eval count_of_clientips=mvcount (clientip)`	Using the `eval` command, we create a new field called `count_of_clientips`, which is populated by the output of the `mvcount` function. The `mvcount` function is responsible for providing a count of the values contained within a multivalued field.
`| where count_of_clientips > 1`	Using the `where` command, we tell Splunk to only return events where the value of the `count_of_clientips` field is greater than 1.
`| table _time, count_of_clientips, clientip, JSESSIONID`	The `table` command is used here to format the output of our search to make it more easily understandable.
`| sort count_of_clientips`	The `sort` command is used to sort the results based on the values stored within the field named `count_of_clientips`.

There's more...

Besides presenting the data sorted based on the count of client IPs that were associated with a given session identifier, logic can be applied to ensure events that meet specific criteria and are raised higher in the list when compared to others.

Creating logic for urgency

Not all session spoofing is alike, and therefore it needs to be responded to differently according to the urgency associated with the event. For example, a session might be spoofed, but this session is not in the middle of any purchasing, and therefore the potential financial loss to either the website or the consumer is extremely low. Another session is spoofed in the middle of making over $1,000 in purchases, and therefore the potential financial loss to the parties involved is substantial.

You can build some common logic into your search, based upon given values, to increase the urgency associated with an event. In the following example, we bring together the website access and web application logs to enhance the amount of information we have access to. We then set up specific conditions that increase the urgency based on the values stored within the given events:

```
index=main sourcetype=access_combined
  | join JSESSIONID usetime=true earlier=false [ search index=main
  sourcetype=log4j | transaction threadId | eval
  JSESSIONID=sessionId ]
  | transaction JSESSIONID
  | eval count_of_clientips=mvcount(clientip) | where
  count_of_clientips > 1
  | eval cost_urgency=if(itemPrice>=1000,"2","1")
  | eval frequency_urgency=case(count_of_clientips=="2","1",
  count_of_clientips=="3","2",1=1,"3")
  | eval urgency=cost_urgency + frequency_urgency
  | table _time, count_of_clientips, clientip, JSESSIONID
  | sort urgency
```

In this example, we join the field values from the web application log with the website access log, and then build a transaction of the session identifiers within the website access log. Next, we count the number of `clientip` values associated with each unique session identifier and ensure that only events with more than one `clientip` are returned. We now add further logic to say that if the `itemPrice` field value is greater than or equal to $1,000, then the `cost_urgency` field value will be raised to 2; otherwise, it will remain at 1. The next piece of logic looks at the number of `clientip` fields associated with the unique session identifier and assigns a value to `frequency_urgency` accordingly. The values of `cost_urgency` and `frequency_urgency` are then added together to form the overall urgency value. The tabulated results are then sorted based on the overall urgency, allowing teams to focus more clearly on the most important incidents.

See also

- The *Predicting website traffic volumes* recipe
- The *Finding abnormally sized web requests* recipe

Detecting outliers in server response times

A marker of success for any website is its ability to respond to user requests in an appropriate amount of time, when response times fall outside of what is normal it can lead to a negative experience for the end user or consumer. Increases in website response times could be attributed to any number of factors, or just simply a natural effect of demand during peak business hours. Being able to detect response time outliers in a series of what may seem like normal response time events can help website operators get ahead of potential issues before they become a greater problem.

In this recipe, you will write a Splunk search with the assistance of the Splunk Machine Learning Toolkit to detect outliers in server response times over a given period of time. The results will be visualized and added to a dashboard.

Getting ready

To step through this recipe, you will need a running Splunk Enterprise server, with the sample data loaded from Chapter 11, *Play Time - Getting Data In*, as well as have installed the Splunk Machine Learning Toolkit application. You should also complete the earlier recipes in this chapter and be familiar with navigating the Splunk user interface.

How to do it...

Follow the steps in this recipe to identify potential session spoofing activity:

1. Log in to your Splunk server.
2. Select the Splunk Machine Learning Toolkit application.
3. Click on the Assistants dropdown menu and select Detect Numeric Outliers:

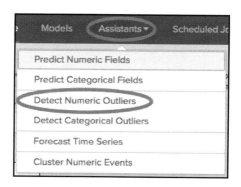

4. Ensure the time range picker is set to **Last 24 Hours**, and type the following search into the search bar. Then, click on the search button or hit *Enter*:

```
index=main sourcetype="access_combined" | table _time response
```

5. The Splunk Machine Learning Toolkit will now return a **Raw Data Preview** of the results:

6. Now, let's choose the appropriate options to perform outlier detection. From the **Field to analyze** dropdown, select `response`; from the **Threshold method** dropdown, select `Median Absolute Deviation`; in the **Threshold multiplier** input box, enter the value `15`; check the **Sliding window** box and enter `150` as the value. Then, click **Detect Outliers** to build the remainder of the search:

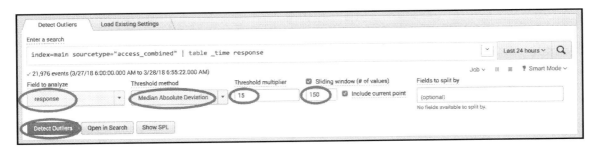

7. The Splunk Machine Learning Toolkit application will now build the search and return a **Data and Outliers** visualization:

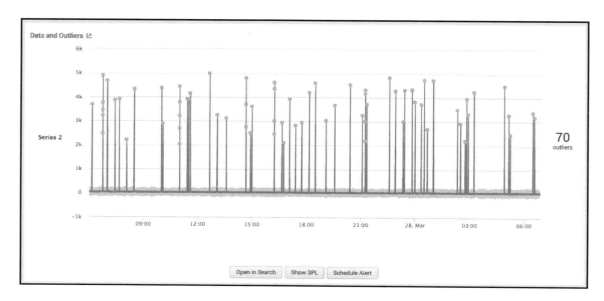

8. The search that has now been built by the Splunk Machine Learning Toolkit is what will be used in the Operational Intelligence application. Below the **Data and Outliers** visualization, click on the **Show SPL** button:

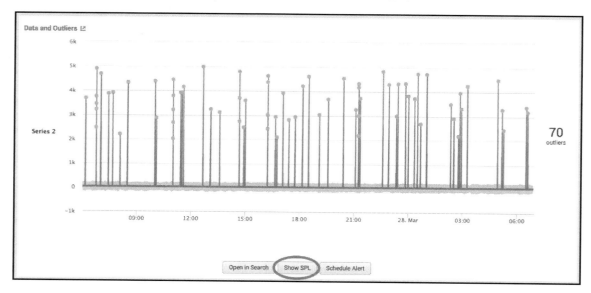

9. The search that has been built will be presented within the window that now appears:

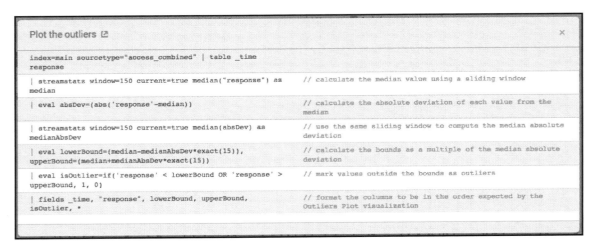

10. Copy the search from within this window as it will be used in a step to come. If the search cannot be copied from within this window, the same search will be referenced within the step to allow for you to manually input it.

11. Next, select the **Operational Intelligence** application:

12. Ensure the time range picker is set to **Last 24 Hours** and enter the search copied in step 9. Then, click on the search button or hit *Enter*:

```
index=main sourcetype="access_combined" | table _time response |
streamstats window=150 current=true median("response") as median |
eval absDev=(abs('response'-median)) | streamstats window=150
current=true median(absDev) as medianAbsDev | eval
lowerBound=(median-medianAbsDev*exact(15)),
upperBound=(median+medianAbsDev*exact(15)) | eval
isOutlier=if('response' < lowerBound OR 'response' > upperBound,
1, 0) | fields _time, "response", lowerBound, upperBound,
isOutlier, *
```

13. Splunk will return the resulting calculations in a tabulated format.
14. Click on the **Visualization** tab.
15. Since there are a number of visualizations within Splunk, the outliers chart visualization might not be displayed by default within the **Visualization** tab. Click on the dropdown listing the visualization types and select **Outliers Chart**:

16. You should now see the value represented as an Outlier Chart visualization:

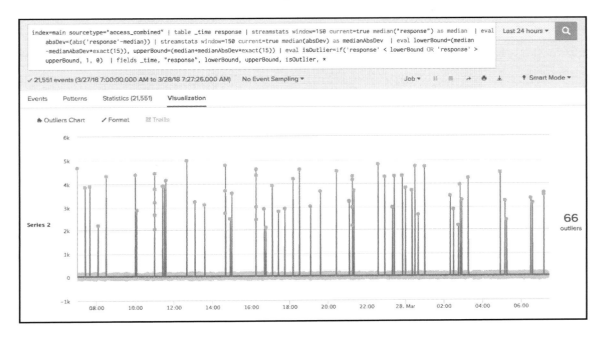

17. Let's save this search as a report. Click on **Save As** and choose **Report** from the drop-down menu:

18. In the pop-up box that appears, enter `cp06_response_time_outliers` in the **Title** field and then click on **Save**:

19. You will receive a confirmation that your report has been created. Now, let's add this report to a dashboard. In the next window, click on **Add to Dashboard**:

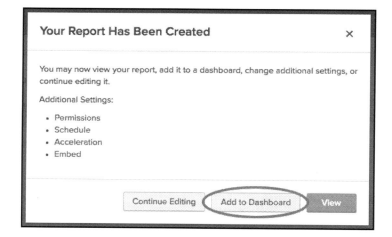

20. You add this report to the Session Monitoring dashboard that was created in an earlier recipe. In the **Save As Dashboard Panel** pop-up box, click on the **Existing** button beside the **Dashboard** label. From the drop-down menu that appears, select **Session Monitoring**. Enter `Response Time Outliers` in the **Panel Title** field and ensure the panel is powered by a **Report**. Then, click on **Save**:

21. You can now click on **View Dashboard** to see the panel on your Session Monitoring dashboard.

How it works...

Let's break down the search piece by piece:

Search fragment	Description
`index=main` `    sourcetype=access_combined`	You should be familiar with this search from the earlier recipes in this chapter. It is used to return events from the website access log.

`| table _time response`	Using the `table` command, we simplify the dataset into a tabulated view of the `_time` of the event and the value of the `response` field for the given event.
`| streamstats window=150    current=true median("response") as median`	Using the `streamstats` command, we calculate the median value of `response` using a sliding window value of `150`. This effectively calculates the running total for the `response` field for every event processed.
`| eval absDev=(abs('response'-median))`	Using the `eval` command, we calculate the absolute deviation of each value from the `median` field calculated using the `streamstats` command.
`| streamstats window=150    current=true median(absDev) as medianAbsDev`	We again use the `streamstats` command to use the same sliding window to compute the median absolute deviation value from the `absDev` field previously calculated.
`| eval lowerBound = (median-medianAbsDev * exact(15)), upperBound = (median+medianAbsDev * exact(15))`	Using the `eval` command, we calculate the bounds, as the `lowerBound` and `upperBound` fields, which are a multiple of the median absolute deviation and median values calculated previously. The median absolute deviation and median are represented by the `medianAbsDev` and `median` fields. The value `15` represents the `Threshold multiplier`.
`| eval isOutlier=if('response'    < lowerBound OR 'response' > upperBound, 1, 0)`	Using the `eval` command, we mark the values that are outside the bounds represented by the `lowerBound` and `upperBound` fields previously calculated as outliers in the `isOutlier` field.
`| fields _time, "response", lowerBound, upperBound, isOutlier, *`	Finally, the `fields` command is used to format the columns to be in the order expected by the `Outliers Chart` visualization, which will be used to display the results.

For more information on the Splunk Machine Learning Toolkit, visit `https://docs.splunk.com/Documentation/MLApp/latest/User`.

Forecasting weekly sales

In this recipe, you will write a Splunk search with the assistance of the Splunk Machine Learning Toolkit to forecast weekly sales based upon previous sales totals. The results will be visualized and added to a dashboard.

Getting ready

To step through this recipe, you will need a running Splunk Enterprise server, with the sample data loaded from `Chapter 11`, *Play Time - Getting Data In*, as well as have installed the Splunk Machine Learning Toolkit application. You should also complete the earlier recipes in this chapter and be familiar with navigating the Splunk user interface.

How to do it...

Follow the steps in this recipe to identify potential session spoofing activity:

1. Log in to your Splunk server.
2. Select the **Splunk Machine Learning Toolkit** application.
3. Click on the **Assistants** dropdown menu and select **Forecast Time Series**:

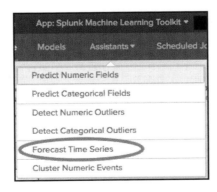

4. Ensure the time range picker is set to **Last 90 Days** and type the following search into the search bar. Then, click on the search button or hit *Enter*:

```
index=main sourcetype=log4j requestType="checkout" | timechart
sum(total) AS total span=1week
```

5. The Splunk Machine Learning Toolkit will now return a **Raw Data Preview** of the results:

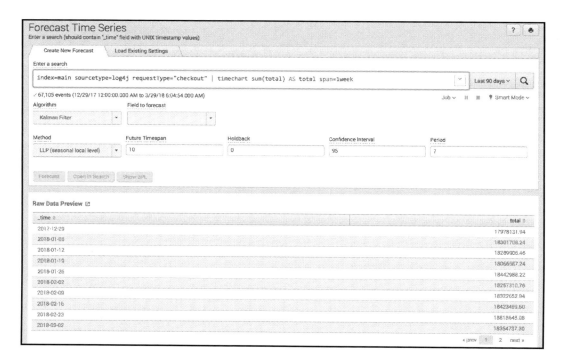

6. Now, let's choose the appropriate options to perform the forecasting. From the **Algorithm** dropdown, select Kalman Filter, which is generally the best starter algorithm for forecasting; from the **Field to forecast** dropdown, select total as this field represents the total weekly sales; from the **Method** dropdown, select LLP (season local level), which selects the forecasting algorithm option to use; in the **Future Timespan** input box, enter the value 10 as this instructs how many weeks in the future to forecast; in the **Holdback** input box, enter the value 0 as we do not wish to withhold values; in the **Confidence Interval** input box, enter the value 95, which represents how confident the algorithm is in its forecast; and in the **Period** input box, enter the value 7 to represent a period of one week.

Then, click **Forecast** to build the remainder of the search:

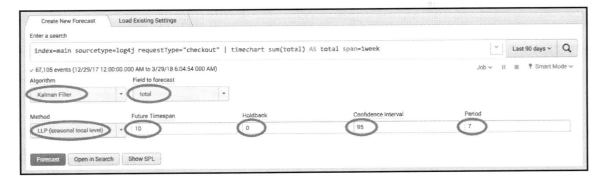

7. The Splunk Machine Learning Toolkit application will now build the search and return a **Forecast** visualization:

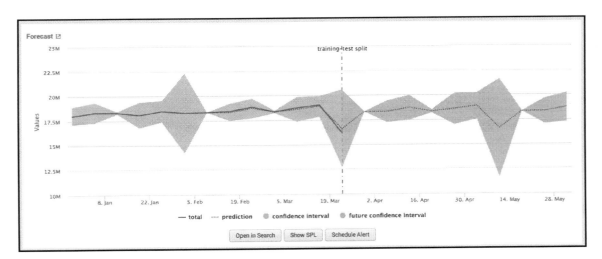

8. The search that has now been built by the Splunk Machine Learning Toolkit is what will be used in the Operational Intelligence application. Below the **Forecast** visualization, click on the **Show SPL** button:

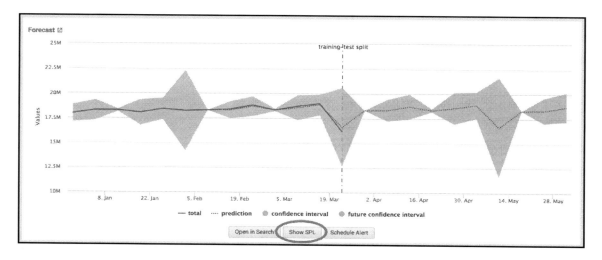

9. The search that has been built will be presented within the window that now appears:

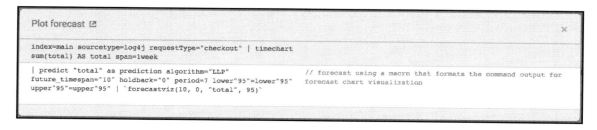

10. Copy the search from within this window as it will be used in a step to come. In case the search cannot be copied from within this window, the same search will be referenced within the step to allow for you to manually input it.

11. Next, select the **Operational Intelligence** application:

12. The search copied in step 9 includes a macro to format the forecast visualization, which is not currently present in our Operational Intelligence application; therefore, we need to first create this macro so that the search executes properly. Click on the **Settings** menu and then click on **Advanced Search** from the menu options that appear:

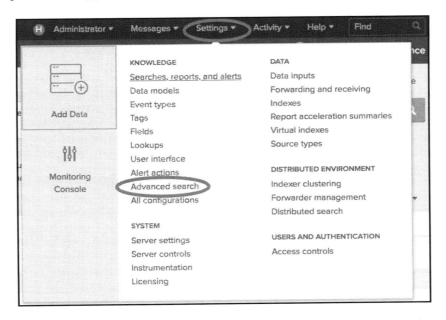

13. On the Advanced Search page, click on **+Add New** to the right of **Search macros:**

14. On the resulting Add new page, enter the following values:
    Name: **forecastviz(4)**
    Definition: **eval _ft=ft, _hb=hb, _var="v", _ci=ci**
    Arguments: **ft, hb, v, ci**
    And finally, click on **Save** to create the new macro.

15. Next, update the permissions on the macro so that it is no longer private. Click on **Permissions** and in the new window, select the **This app only** radio button and click **Save**.

16. Navigate back to the Search page by clicking on **Search** in the menu bar.

17. Ensure the time range picker is set to **Last 90 Days** and enter the search copied in step 9. Then, click on the search button or hit *Enter*:

```
index=main sourcetype=log4j requestType="checkout" | timechart
sum(total) AS total span=1week | predict "total" as prediction
algorithm="LLP" future_timespan="10" holdback="0" period=7
lower"95"=lower"95" upper"95"=upper"95" | `forecastviz(10, 0,
"total", 95)`
```

18. Splunk will return the resulting calculations in a tabulated format.

19. Click on the **Visualization** tab.

20. Since there are a number of visualizations within Splunk, the outliers chart visualization might not be displayed by default within the **Visualization** tab. Click on the dropdown listing the visualization types and select **Forecast Chart**:

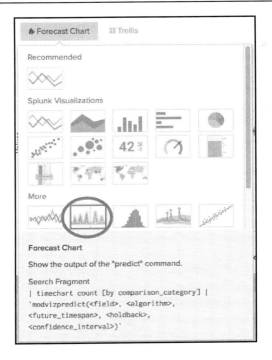

21. You should now see the value represented as an Forecast Chart visualization:

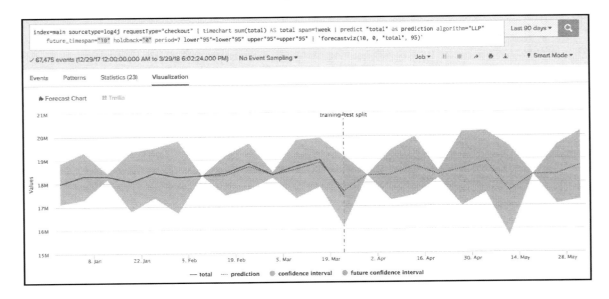

22. Let's save this search as a report. Click on **Save As** and choose **Report** from the drop-down menu:

23. In the pop-up box that appears, enter `cp06_weekly_sales_forecast` in the **Title** field and then click on **Save**:

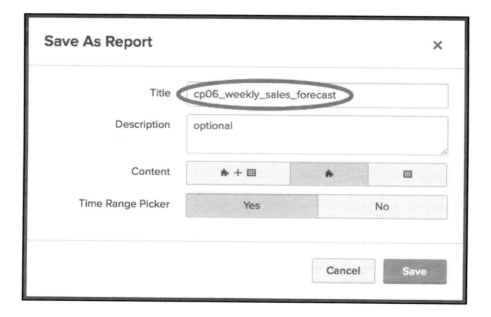

24. You will receive a confirmation that your report has been created. Now, let's add this report to a dashboard. In the next window, click on **Add to Dashboard**:

25. You add this report to the Product Monitoring dashboard that was created in an earlier recipe. In the **Save As Dashboard Panel** pop-up box, click on the **Existing** button beside the **Dashboard** label. From the drop-down menu that appears, select **Product Monitoring**. Enter `Weekly Sales Forecast` in the **Panel Title** field and ensure the panel is powered by a **Report**. Then, click on **Save**:

26. You can now click on **View Dashboard** to see the panel on your Product Monitoring dashboard.

How it works...

Let's break down the search piece by piece:

Search fragment	Description
`index=main sourcetype=log4j requestType="checkout"`	You should be familiar with this search from the earlier recipes in this chapter. It is used to return events from the website access log. The search contains a field value filter, `requestType="checkout"`, so that the returned results only include those events that are checkout requests, effectively representing a completed transaction.
`| timechart sum(total) AS total    span=1week`	Using the `table` command, we simplify the dataset into a tabulated view of the `_time` of the event and the value of the `response` field for the given event.
`| predict "total" as prediction algorithm="LLP" future_timespan="10" holdback="0"    period=7 lower"95"=lower"95" upper"95"=upper"95"`	The `predict` command is used to look back over the given data set and generates three new fields: `prediction`, which is the predicted future value of total sales; `upper95`, which is the upper confidence interval; and `lower95`; which is the lower confidence interval. Parameters are specified when executing the predict command to instruct it to use the LLP algorithm for forecasting, to forecast 10 weeks in the future, not to hold back any values during forecasting (0), that the periodicity of the time series is one week (7), and to have a 95% confidence interval to represent how confident the algorithm is in its forecast.
`| `forecastviz(10, 0, "total", 95)``	The `forecastviz` macro that was created in this recipe formats the values into their proper fields for use with the forecast chart visualization to display the results properly.

For more information on time series forecasting, visit `https://docs.splunk.com/Documentation/Splunk/latest/Search/Aboutpredictiveanalytics`.

14
Speeding Up Intelligence – Data Summarization

In this chapter, we will cover the methods that exist within Splunk to speed up intelligence. You will learn about:

- Calculating an hourly count of sessions versus completed transactions
- Backfilling the number of purchases by city
- Displaying the maximum number of concurrent sessions over time

Introduction

We learned all about data models and how they can be accelerated to facilitate faster Pivot reporting. Data model acceleration works by leveraging data summarization behind the scenes. In this chapter, we will take a look at two more data summarization methods in Splunk: summary indexing and report acceleration. These methods enable you to speed up reports or preserve focused statistics over long periods of time. You will learn how to populate summary indexes, use report acceleration, backfill summary indexes with historical data, and more.

Data summarization

Big data is just that, big, and even with the best infrastructure, it can be extremely time consuming to search or report over large datasets and/or very costly to store for long periods of time. Splunk has data summarization features that simplify and speed up reporting over large sets of data. Data summarization essentially allows for raw event data to be summarized into much smaller (usually statistical) sets of data, which can then be searched to facilitate significantly faster reporting.

The following diagram helps to illustrate how data summarization works. In the example, we start with a large raw set of data on the left, and then create a statistical summary from it, capturing the key information. The statistical summary will be much faster to report on than the raw log data as it represents a lot less data. This summarized data can either be written into a new index or automatically captured alongside the raw event data behind the scenes by Splunk:

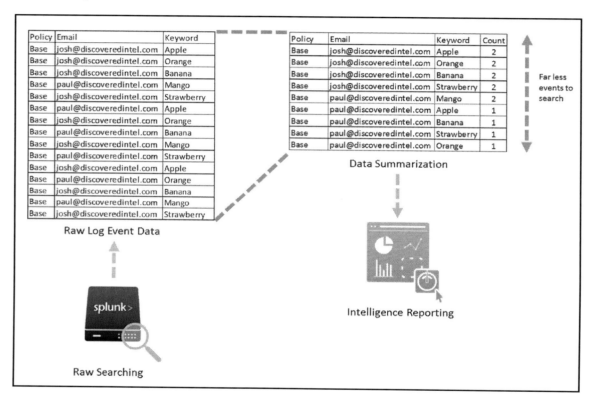

From an Operational Intelligence perspective, data summarization allows you to unlock the ability to quickly calculate and report on key, focused metrics, while also reducing the underlying data storage footprint.

Data summarization methods

At the time of writing this book, there are three data summarization methods in Splunk, which are listed in the following table:

Data summarization method	Description
Summary indexing	Summary indexing involves the creation of separate indexes to hold summarized event data. These indexes, instead of the index containing the raw event data, can be searched and reported on.
Report acceleration	Report acceleration creates automated summaries behind the scenes, alongside the raw event data, to facilitate faster execution of reports that have been accelerated.
Data model acceleration	Data model acceleration is similar to report acceleration in that automated summaries are created behind the scenes. However, this summarization is performed on an entire modeled set of data, rather than individual reports, and the acceleration is only realized when using Pivot.

In this chapter, we will focus on summary indexing and report acceleration.

About summary indexing

Summary indexing is a simple but very useful feature in Splunk, which allows you to summarize large amounts of data into smaller subsets, based on defined search criteria. This summarized data is usually stored in a separate index from where the original data exists and is typically a lot smaller in size. Reporting over the smaller summary index rather than the original data will be a lot faster. Additionally, as the summary index is smaller, you will be able to retain data for longer periods of time, which is key for long-term trending and predictive analytics. Summary indexing is the only method to keep data longer than the retention time of the index that stores the raw events; the other summarization methods need raw events to be present.

How summary indexing helps

One of the more common operational intelligence use cases is around the generation of metrics. For example, say we want to find the average execution time of a web request for the past month. This data might come from multiple web servers and millions of events per day. So, running a report over an entire month's raw event data will likely take a long period of time simply due to the event volume.

With summary indexing, a search can be scheduled to run each day to compute the average execution time for the day, and the results can be stored in a summary index. This will result in a summary index containing roughly 30 events for a given month-a lot less than the millions of raw event records! The following month, when this same report is run, the report is merely run against the summary index, which is inherently much smaller than the raw event data, resulting in a report that is computed at an exponentially faster rate than what was observed previously.

Summary indexing of data does not count against your Splunk license, as data being used for summary indexing is almost always already indexed into Splunk.

About report acceleration

When it comes to operational intelligence, detection and response times can be critical, with delays adding to costs and potential severity. Therefore, it is likely that you will want to get to your intelligence data as fast as possible. Report acceleration allows you to speed up the time it takes to execute operational intelligence reports. Report acceleration can be thought of as a form of summary indexing, without the need to create a separate index as the summary data is stored alongside ordinary indexes.

The big difference between report acceleration and summary indexing is the way in which data is computed. Summary indexing is based on the execution of scheduled searches over a given time frame that populates summary indexes with their search results. However, report acceleration is based on the execution of acceleration-enabled scheduled searches over a given timeframe, which results in Splunk executing background processes to automatically manage the summary of data related to the search. In addition, report acceleration is self-repairing after any data interruption, whereas summary indexing is unaware if the data over a time frame is incomplete in any way or has gaps.

The words search and report are used interchangeably in Splunk, but are essentially the same thing. In legacy versions of Splunk, searches that were saved and/or scheduled were known as *saved searches*; however, in Version 6 and above, they are known as *reports*.

The simplicity of report acceleration

We earlier outlined that the one key difference between report acceleration and summary indexing is in the way in which report acceleration automatically handles the data summarization behind the scenes. Not only is this automatically computed, but Splunk also automatically identifies when searches are run that might benefit from the already accelerated report data and make this data available to the searches; all of this is performed by the click of a button.

Calculating an hourly count of sessions versus completed transactions

From an operational intelligence standpoint, it is interesting to understand how many visitors we have to our online store and how many of these people actually purchase something. For example, if we have 1,000 people visiting a day, and only 10 people actually purchase something, this might indicate something is not quite right. Perhaps the prices of our products are too high, or the site might be difficult to use and thus needs a redesign. This information can also be used to indicate peak purchasing times.

In this first recipe, we will leverage summary indexing to understand how many sessions we have per hour versus how many actual completed purchase transactions there have been. We will plot these on a line graph going back the last 24 hours.

Getting ready

To step through this recipe, you will need a running Splunk Enterprise server, with the sample data loaded from `Chapter 11`, *Play Time - Getting Data In*. You should be familiar with navigating the Splunk user interface and using the Splunk search language.

How to do it...

Follow these steps to leverage summary indexing in calculating an hourly count of sessions versus the completed transactions:

1. Log in to your Splunk server.
2. Select the **Operational Intelligence** application.
3. From the search bar, enter the following search and select to run over **Last 60 Minutes**:

```
index=main sourcetype=log4j | stats dc(sessionId) AS
  Sessions, count(eval(requestType="checkout")) AS
  Completed_Transactions
```

4. Splunk should now display results similar to the following:

5. Click on the **Save As** dropdown and select **Report** from the list:

6. In the pop-up box that gets displayed, enter
   `cp09_sessions_transactions_summary` as the title of the report and select
   No in the **Time Range Picker** field; then, click on **Save**:

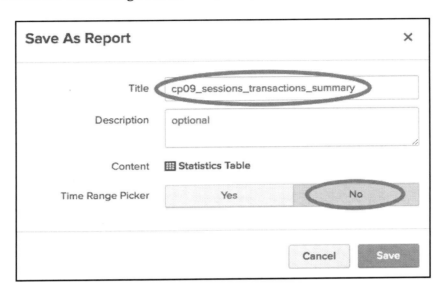

7. On the next screen, click on **Schedule** from the list of additional settings:

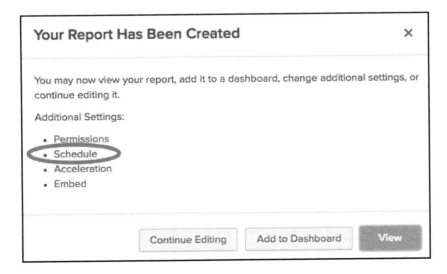

8. Select the **Schedule Report** checkbox, **Run every hour** in the **Schedule** field, and a time range of **Last 60 minutes**. Then, simply click on **Save**:

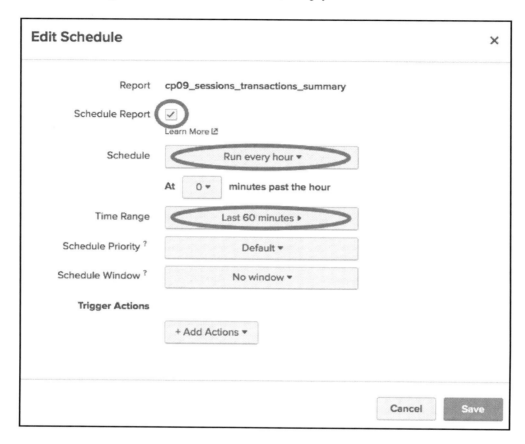

9. In order to activate summary indexing on the report that you just saved, you will need to edit the search manually. Click on the **Settings** menu at the top right-hand side and select **Searches, reports, and alerts**:

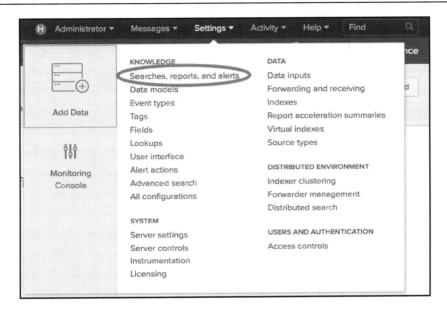

10. A list of all the saved searches will be displayed. Locate the search named
cp09_sessions_transactions_summary; underneath **Actions** click on the **Edit**
button; and in the menu, click on **Edit Summary Indexing**:

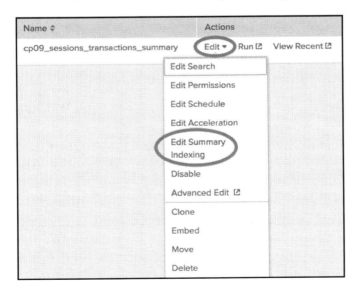

11. The Edit Summary Index screen will be displayed. Select the **Enable Summary Indexing** checkbox. Ensure the default summary index called **summary** is selected and then click on **Save**:

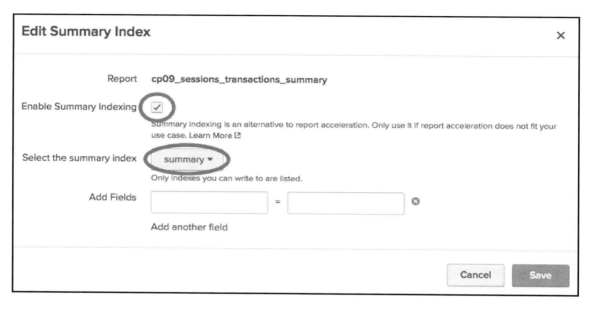

12. The search is now scheduled to run every hour, and the results are scheduled to be written to a summary index named **summary**. After 24 hours have passed, run the following search from the search bar in the **Operational Intelligence** application, with a time range set to **Last 24 hours**:

```
index=summary source="cp09_sessions_transactions_summary"
| table _time Sessions Completed_Transactions
```

13. The search will complete very fast and list 24 events, one for each hour. Select the **Visualization** tab to see the data presented as a line chart representing sessions versus completed transactions:

14. Let's save this as a report and then add the report to a dashboard panel. Click on the **Save As** dropdown and select **Report**.

15. Enter `cp09_sessions_vs_transactions` in the **Title** field of the report, and ensure the **Content** field is set to **Line Chart**; then, click on **Save**:

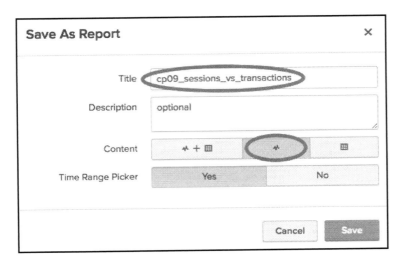

16. On the next screen, click on the **Add to Dashboard** button.

17. In the pop-up box that appears, select **New** to add a new dashboard and give it a title of `Session and Purchase Trends`. Ensure permissions are set to **Shared in App** and give the panel we are adding a title of `Hourly Sessions vs Completed Transactions`. Ensure the panel is powered by **Report** and the panel content is set to **Line Chart**, and then click on **Save** to create the new dashboard with the line chart panel:

How it works...

In this recipe, you created a scheduled search that will take hourly snapshots, counting the number of unique sessions and the sessions that resulted in completed purchase transactions. Every hour the search runs, a single line item with two values is created and the results are written to a summary index named **summary**. Returning to the search 24 hours later, you are able to run a report on the summary index to instantly see the activity over the past day in terms of sessions versus purchases. There were 24 events in the summary, one for each hour. Reporting off the summary data is a lot more efficient and faster than attempting to search across the raw data. If you wait longer, say 30 days, then you can run the report again and plot the results across an entire month. This information might then be able to provide predictive insight into the sales forecast for the next month.

There were two searches that you used for this recipe. The first search was used to generate the summary data and ran hourly. The second search was used to search and report against the summary data directly. Let's break down each search piece by piece:

Search 1 - Summary index generating search

Search fragment	Description
`index=main sourcetype=log4j`	You first select to search the application data in the main index over the past hour.
`| stats dc(sessionId) AS Sessions, count(eval (requestType="checkout")) AS Completed_Transactions`	Using the `stats` command with the distinct count (`dc`) function, you obtain the number of unique sessions in the past hour. You then select `count` to count the checkout requests. A checkout request indicates that a sale has gone through.

Search 2 - Reporting off the summary index

Search fragment	Description

`index=summary`
`source="cp09_sessions_`
`    transactions_summary"`
	You first select to search the summary index. Then, within this index, you look for data with a source of `cp09_sessions_transactions_summary`. This is the name of our saved search and is used as the source field by Splunk when writing to a summary index.

`| table _time   Sessions` `Completed_Transactions`	You tabulate the data by time, number of sessions, and number of completed transactions.

If you search the summary data directly, you will notice that Splunk gives the summary data a `sourcetype` field value of `stash` by default. However, the source field value for the data will be the name of the saved search. Therefore, searching by source rather than `sourcetype` is likely to be your preferred approach.

There's more...

As you can see, summary indexing is a great way to shrink our raw data into just the valuable data that we need to report on, and because the raw data still exists, we can create many summaries off the same data if we want to do so.

As with many of the key concepts in Splunk, there are some best practices to consider when using summary indexing.

Generating the summary more frequently

In this recipe, the summary-generating search was set to run hourly and look back over the past hour. This results in a single event being generated per hour and written to the summary. If more granularity is required, the search can be set to run every 15 minutes; look back over the past 15 minutes, and four events per hour will be generated. As the search is now only looking back over the past 15 minutes, instead of the past hour, it will likely execute faster as there is less data to search over. For some data sources, generating the summary index data more frequently over smaller chunks of time can be more efficient.

Avoiding summary index overlaps and gaps

Care needs to be taken when creating summary index generating searches to avoid both gaps in your summary and overlaps in the data being searched.

For example, you schedule a summary index generating search to run every 5 minutes and look back over the past 5 minutes, but the search actually takes 10 minutes to run. This will result in the search not executing again until its previous run is complete, which means it will run every 10 minutes, but only look back over the past 5 minutes. Therefore, there will be data gaps in your summary. This can be avoided by ensuring adequate search testing is performed before scheduling the search.

In another example, you schedule a summary index generating search to run every 5 minutes and look back over the past 10 minutes. This will result in the search looking back over 5 minutes of data that the previous run also looked back over. Therefore, there will be data overlaps in your summary. This can be avoided by ensuring there are no overlaps in time when scheduling the search.

Additionally, gaps can occur if you take the search head down for an extended period of time and then bring it back up. Backfilling can be used to fill in past gaps in the data, and this is discussed in the next recipe.

See also

- The *Backfilling the number of purchases by city* recipe
- The *Displaying the maximum number of concurrent sessions over time* recipe

Backfilling the number of purchases by city

In the previous recipe, you generated an hourly summary and then, after waiting for 24 hours, you were able to report on the summary data over a 24-hour period. However, what if you wanted to report over the past 30 days or even 3 months? You would have to wait a long time for your summary data to build up over time. A better way is to backfill the summary data over an earlier time period, assuming you have raw data for this time period in Splunk.

In this recipe, you will create a search that identifies the number of purchases by city on a given day, and write this search to a summary index. You will leverage the IP location database built into Splunk to obtain the city based on the IP address in the results. You will then execute a script that comes bundled with Splunk in order to backfill the summary for the previous 30 days. Following this, you will use the generated summary data to quickly report on the number of purchases by city for the past month.

Getting ready

To step through this recipe, you will need a running Splunk Enterprise server, with the sample data loaded from `Chapter 11`, *Play Time - Getting Data In*. You should be familiar with navigating the Splunk user interface and using the Splunk search language.

How to do it...

Follow the steps in this recipe to leverage summary indexing and to backfill the number of purchases by city:

1. Log in to your Splunk server.
2. Select the **Operational Intelligence** application.
3. From the search bar, enter the following search and select to run over **Last 24 hours**:

```
index=main sourcetype=log4j requestType="checkout"
| iplocation ipAddress | fillnull value="Unknown" City
| replace "" with "Unknown" in City
| stats count AS Purchases by City
```

4. Splunk should now display the results of the search, similar to the results shown in the following screenshot:

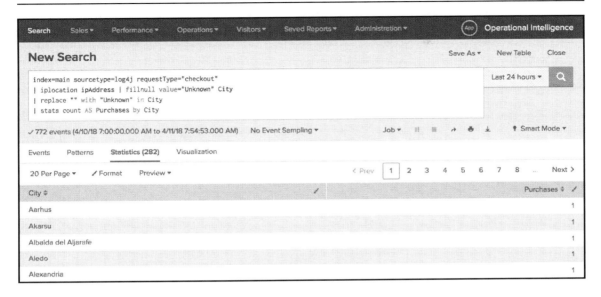

5. Click on the **Save As** dropdown and select **Report** from the list:

6. In the pop-up box that gets displayed, enter `cp09_backfill_purchases_city` as the title of the report and select **No** in the **Time Range Picker** field. Then, click on **Save**:

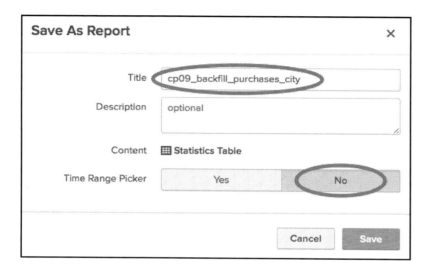

7. On the next screen, select **Schedule** from the list of additional settings:

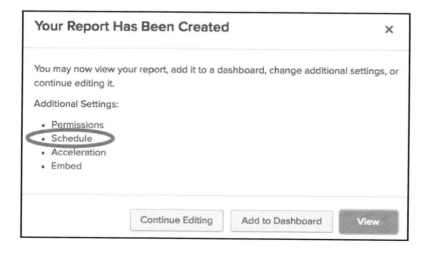

8. Select the **Schedule Report** checkbox, and set **Schedule** to **Run every day** and **Time Range** to **Last 24 hours**. Then, simply click on **Save**:

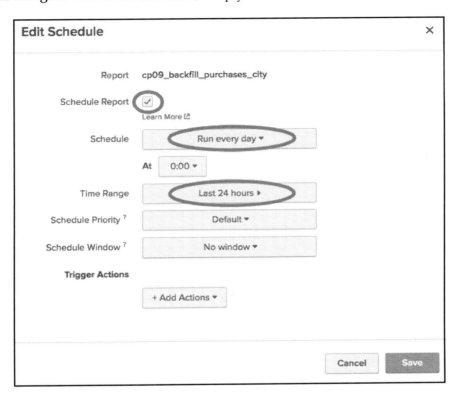

9. You will be taken back to the report you just saved. Select the **Edit** dropdown and then select **Edit Permissions** from the list:

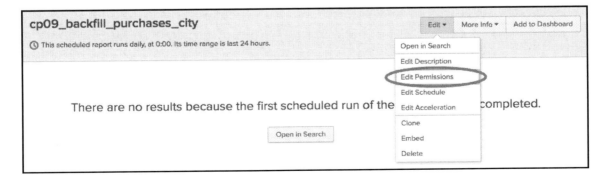

10. In the Edit Permissions pop-up box that is displayed, select the **App** option against **Display For** and then click on **Save**:

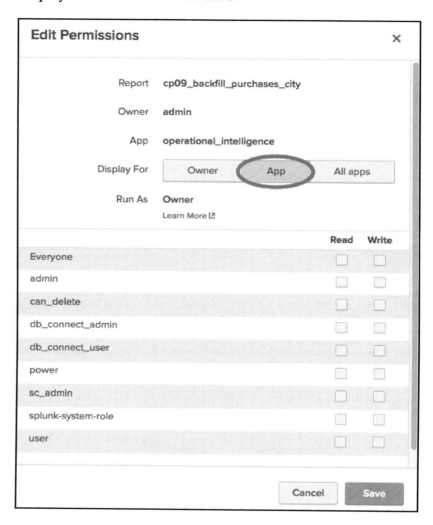

11. In order to activate summary indexing on the report that you just saved, you will need to edit the search manually. Click on the **Settings** menu at the top right-hand side and select **Searches, reports, and alerts**:

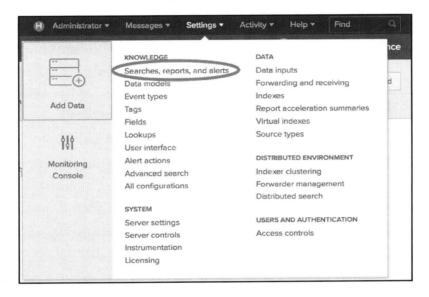

12. A list of all the saved searches will be displayed. Locate the search named **cp09_backfill_purchases_city;** underneath **Actions** click on the **Edit** button; and in the menu, click on **Edit Summary Indexing**:

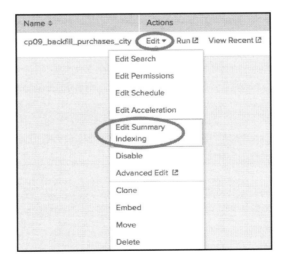

13. The Edit Summary Index screen will be displayed. Select the **Enable Summary Indexing** checkbox. Ensure the default summary index called **summary** is selected and then click on **Save**:

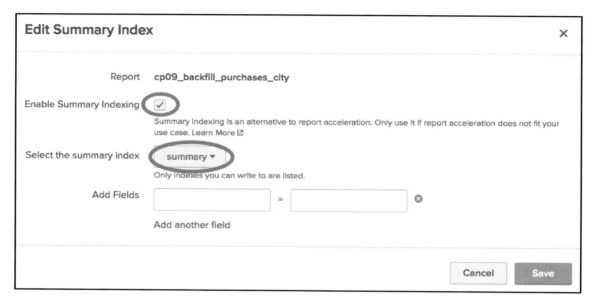

14. The search is now scheduled to run every day, and the results are written to a summary index named **summary**. Now, you will leverage a script to backfill the summary. Bring up a terminal window in Linux or open a command window in Windows.

15. From within your terminal or command window, change your working directory to `$SPLUNK_HOME/bin`.

16. From the command line, tell Splunk to backfill the summary index by executing the `fill_summary_index.py` script and supplying the required parameters. Execute the following command and change the values for `admin:changeme` to the `username:password` combination of the user who populates the summary index in Splunk; an administrative login can be used here to ensure proper access to populate the summary index:

```
./splunk cmd python fill_summary_index.py -app
operational_intelligence -name cp09_backfill_purchases_city
-et -30day@day -lt now -j 8 -auth admin:changeme
```

17. In Windows, omit the . / at the start of the command.

18. Once the script has completed executing, run the following search from the search bar in the **Operational Intelligence** application with a time range set to **Last 30 days**:

```
index=summary source=cp09_backfill_purchases_city
 City!="Unknown"
| timechart span=1d useother=F sum(Purchases) by City
```

19. The search will complete very fast and list one result per day for the last 30 days. Select the **Visualization** tab to see the data presented as a line chart (change the visualization type if required) representing the total purchases by day for each city over the past month:

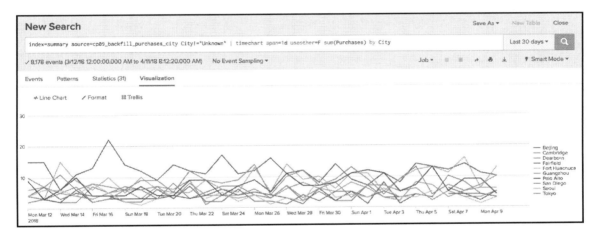

20. Let's save this chart to our **Session and Purchase Trends** dashboard that we created in the previous recipe. Click on the **Save As** dropdown and select **Report**.

21. In the pop-up box that appears, enter cp09_purchases_city_trend in the **Title** field and ensure **Visualization** is set to **Line**; then, click on **Save**.

22. On the next screen, select **Add to Dashboard**.

23. On the **Save As Dashboard Panel** screen, select **Existing** as the dashboard and then select the **Session and Purchase Trends** dashboard. Give the panel the title of `Purchases by City – Last 30 Days`, ensure the panel is powered by **Report**, and the content is set to **Line Chart**. Then, click on **Save** to save the chart to the dashboard:

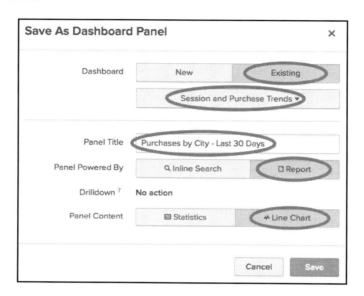

How it works...

This recipe started off by taking a similar approach to the first recipe in this chapter. You first created a search to look back over the past day for purchases by city and wrote the summarized results to a summary index. You then scheduled this search to run on a daily basis. However, rather than waiting 30 days for data to be populated, you executed a script to backfill the summary with the previous 30 days' worth of data.

The bundled Splunk script inputs a number of variables, including the saved search name (`cp09_backfill_purchases_city`), the time frame that the search runs over (**Last 24 hours**), and the period of time that you wish to backfill (**Last 30 days**). Using this information, the script essentially executes the search 30 times, once for each of the 30 days, and the results of each day are written to the summary. Once the script is successfully executed, you are able to run a report across the summary index over the past 30 days to quickly see the daily purchases by city over time.

There are two searches that you used for this recipe, in addition to a script. The first search was used to generate the summary data and was run daily. The script used the first search to backfill the summary with 30 days of data. The second search was used to search and report against the summary data directly. Let's break down each search piece by piece:

Search 1 - Summary index generating search

Search fragment	Description
`index=main sourcetype=log4j requestType="checkout"`	You first select to search the application data in the main index over the past day. You select to search for only events with a `requestType` of checkout.
`| iplocation ipAddress`	Using the built-in `iplocation` command, you deduce the geolocational city information from the `ipAddress` field in the data.
`| fillnull value="Unknown" City | replace "" with "Unknown" in City`	The `fillnull` command is used to fill in the blanks with a value of `"Unknown"`, where the `iplocation` command is unable to match a city to the IP address. The `replace` command replaces all `""` values with a value of `"Unknown"`.
`| stats count AS Purchases by City`	Using the `stats` command, you do a simple count to count the number of purchases by city.

fill_summary_index.py - Backfilling the summary index

`./splunk cmd python fill_summary_index.py`	This is the actual command execution telling Splunk that you wish to run a command (`cmd`) ensuring the various Splunk environment variables are set prior to execution. Next, the command you wish to execute is specified (`python`). Finally, you tell Python what you wish to do; in this case, we execute the backfill script provided with Splunk, which is named `fill_summary_index.py`.
`-app operational_intelligence`	This parameter tells the script the name of the application under which the saved search resides. For our purposes, it will be the `operational_intelligence` application.
`-name cp09_backfill_purchases_city`	This parameter tells the script the name of the saved search to run. For this execution, it will be the name of the search saved in the `cp09_backfill_purchases_city` recipe.
`-et -30day@day`	This parameter tells the script the earliest time for which results are to be returned. For our purposes, it will be 30 days.

`-lt now`	This parameter tells the script the latest time for which it should return results. For our purposes, it will be the current time of execution.
`-j 8`	This parameter tells the script the maximum number of concurrent searches to run, which will be `8`.
`-auth    admin:changeme`	This parameter specifies the user how to authenticate to Splunk as. In this case, it will be Splunk's default credentials, `admin:changeme`.

Search 2 - Reporting off the summary index

Search fragment	Description

`index=summary`
`source=cp09_backfill_purchases_city`
`City!="Unknown"`
	Firstly, you select to search the summary index. Then, you look for data with a source of `cp09_backfill_purchases_city` in this index. This is the name of our saved search and is used as the source field by Splunk when writing to a summary index. You also filter out cities with a value of `"Unknown"` to focus on the cities that you do know about.

`| timechart    span=1d useother=F` `sum(Purchases) by City`	Using the `timechart` command and spanning across a single day, you sum the purchases by city over 30 days. By specifying `useother=F`, you ensure that cities are not grouped together and listed as `"Other"`. This data is then perfect to use on a line chart, with each line representing a different city.

There's more...

In this recipe, you leveraged a script to help backfill the index automatically in Splunk. However, in many cases, access to the command line to execute scripts might not be permitted and/or you won't mind doing a little bit more work to backfill a summary, if it means you can do it directly from the search bar within Splunk.

Backfilling a summary index from within a search directly

Splunk provides a way to write to a summary index directly from the search using the `addinfo` and `collect` commands. For example, using the summary-generating search in this recipe, you can modify the search to directly write to the summary index, as follows:

```
index=main sourcetype=log4j requestType="checkout" earliest=-2d@d
latest=-1d@d
| iplocation ipAddress | fillnull value="Unknown" City
| replace "" with "Unknown" in City
| stats count AS Purchases by City| addinfo | collect index=summary
source="cp09_backfill_purchases_city" addtime=t
```

The `earliest` and `latest` field values are used to set the time range that the search should run over. In this case, you run the search over the previous day, starting 2 days ago and ending 1 day ago. You also add the `addinfo` command, which adds information that Splunk needs for summary indexing. Additionally, you use the `collect` command and specify the summary index, as well as the value for the source field that is written to the summary. The source field value you use is the name of the saved search. If you execute this search, it will write a day's worth of data to the summary index. You can repeat this search, modifying the `earliest` and `latest` field values back a day each time, until you run the search 30 times and backfill the entire month. You can also use the `append` command to append 30 searches together, each with a different `earliest` and `latest` time. It is a bit uglier than the script method used in the recipe and more prone to user error, but it works.

With summary indexing, it is very easy to write data to an index that you don't want. Perhaps you duplicate the data, or tweak your generating search to correct the results. Splunk has a `delete` command that can be used to clean out bad data from any index. However, you will likely need to have your Splunk administrator delete the data for you.

See also

- The *Calculating an hourly count of sessions versus completed transactions* recipe
- The *Displaying the maximum number of concurrent sessions over time* recipe

Displaying the maximum number of concurrent sessions over time

In the past two recipes of this chapter, you leveraged a method of data summarization called *summary indexing* to summarize data into a new index, which you then reported on. In this recipe, you will use another method of data summarization known as *report acceleration* to speed up your report times.

In this recipe, you will create a report to look for the maximum number of concurrent sessions over a time period of 30 days. This report will then be accelerated to reduce the time taken to execute the search.

Getting ready

To step through this recipe, you will need a running Splunk Enterprise server, with the sample data loaded from Chapter 11, *Play Time - Getting Data In*. You should be familiar with navigating the Splunk user interface and using the Splunk search language.

How to do it...

Follow the steps in this recipe to leverage report acceleration to display the maximum number of concurrent sessions over time:

1. Log in to your Splunk server.
2. Select the **Operational Intelligence** application.

3. From the search bar, enter the following search and select to run over **Last 7 days**:

```
index=main sourcetype=log4j
| timechart span=1m dc(sessionId) AS concurrent_sessions
| timechart span=30m max(concurrent_sessions) AS
 max_concurrent_sessions
```

4. You might find that the search takes about 2-3 minutes to run if you have 7 days of generated data. Splunk should now display the results of the search, similar to the results shown here:

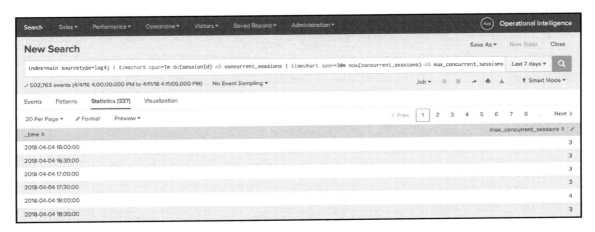

5. Click on the **Save As** dropdown and select **Report** from the list:

6. In the pop-up box that gets displayed, enter
   `cp09_maximum_concurrent_sessions` as the title of the report and select **No**
   in the **Time Range Picker** field. Then, click on **Save**:

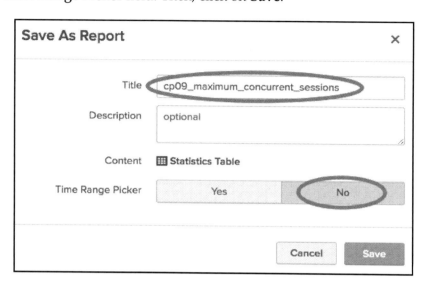

7. On the next screen, select **Acceleration** from the list of additional settings:

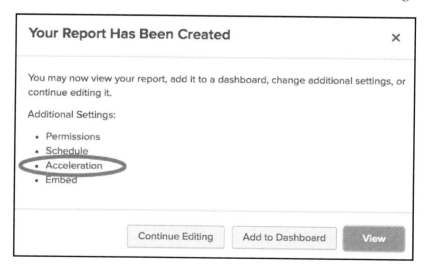

8. In the Edit Acceleration window that appears, select the **Accelerate Report** checkbox, set a summary range of **1 Month**, and then click on **Save**. If you see a warning about running in verbose mode, it is OK to ignore it:

9. The report is now saved and Splunk builds the accelerated summary behind the scenes. There is no need to schedule the search. To check on the status of the summary building, click on the **Settings** menu and select **Report acceleration summaries**:

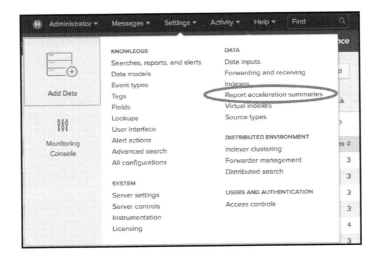

10. The list of report acceleration summaries will be displayed, and you will see the report that you just created with **Summary Status** of **Building Summary**:

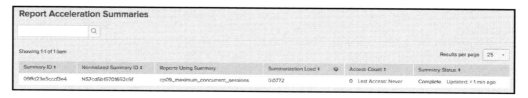

11. If you do not see the summary building, try hitting refresh in the browser. Sometimes, you have to wait a bit. If you are impatient, click on **Summary ID** value that you are monitoring and you will be taken to a screen where you can force a build by clicking on **Rebuild**. A Summary Status of Pending is normal, as it is telling you that an update to the summary is pending. If you see **Not enough data to summarize**, it is letting you know that there is not enough data yet to summarize properly and it will wait until there is. If that occurs, consider updating the **Summary Range** in the acceleration configuration to a smaller window:

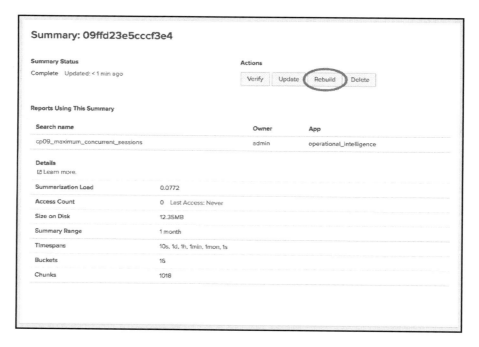

12. Eventually, the report will complete the building of the summary. When it is complete, click on the **Apps** menu and select the **Operational Intelligence** app.

13. Once back in the app, click on **Saved Reports** in the menu bar, then click on Chapter 9 - Speed Up Intelligence:

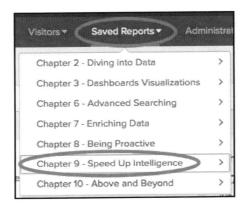

14. The menu now dynamically adjusts based on the clicked value; now, click on the **Open in Search** icon next to the **cp09_maximum_concurrent_sessions** report:

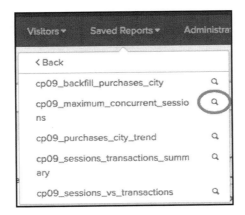

15. The report will now load in seconds. Select the **Visualization** tab to see the data presented as a line chart representing the maximum number of concurrent sessions, and select a time range of **Last 7 days**:

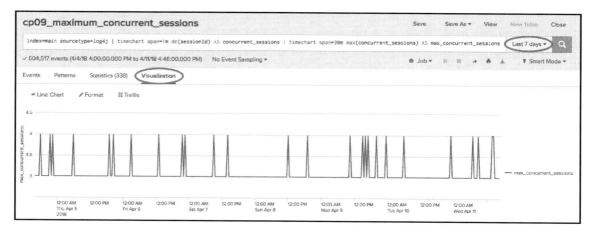

16. Let's save this chart to our **Session and Purchase Trends** dashboard that we created in the first recipe. Click on the **Save As** dropdown and select **Dashboard Panel**.

17. In the pop-up box that appears, select **Existing** in the **Dashboard** field, and then select the **Session and Purchase Trends** dashboard. Enter `Maximum Concurrent Sessions` as the title of the panel, ensure the panel is set to be powered by **Report**, ensure the panel content is set to **Line Chart**, and click on **Save** to save the chart to the dashboard:

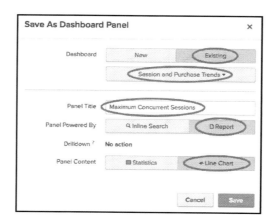

How it works...

In this recipe, you first created a search to look for concurrent sessions over time. The search has two `timechart` components to it. Let's break down the search piece by piece:

Search fragment	Description
`index=main sourcetype=log4j`	Select to search the application data in the main index.
`| timechart span=1m dc(sessionId) AS concurrent_sessions`	The first `timechart` command identifies the number of distinct (or unique) sessions in each 1-minute period.
`| timechart span=30m max(concurrent_sessions) AS max_concurrent_sessions`	The second `timechart` command takes the number of concurrent sessions that have been calculated for each minute and identifies the highest (or maximum) number in any 30-minute period.

This search is actually fairly resource intensive when searched for over an extended period of time. Running the non-accelerated search over 7 days will likely take several minutes, mostly because Splunk performs a calculation for every minute of data for the past week. Once the report is created, you select to accelerate it over a 1-month period. Behind the scenes, Splunk creates an internal summary in line with the data itself. Once the summary is built, you return to the report and rerun it; it completes in seconds, thanks to the new acceleration. As the report is accelerated for an entire month, you can look back up to a month in the past and it will still run fast. Going forward, Splunk will periodically refresh the internal summary every 10 minutes to summarize and accelerate any new event data.

Report acceleration will only work with searches or reports that contain what is known as a **transforming** command. Examples of commonly used transforming commands are `stats`, `timechart`, `chart`, and `top`.

There's more...

Report acceleration does add some overhead, as the CPU has to run searches in the background to generate the summaries and disk space is used to store the internal summary data.

You can view the detailed information that Splunk provides on the health of the various reports that are accelerated and how they are being used, in order to determine if they are healthy or not.

Viewing the status of an accelerated report and how

To investigate the details of an accelerated report, first click on the **Settings** menu and then select **Report acceleration summaries**. A list of all the accelerated reports will load, together with a high-level build status. Click on the report we accelerated in this recipe to drill into the details. The **Summary Details** screen provides some good insight into the accelerated report, including information such as how many times the report has been accessed, the range the report is set at, and how much data is being used by the summary:

See also

- The *Calculating an hourly count of sessions versus completed transactions* recipe
- The *Backfilling the number of purchases by city* recipe

15
Above and Beyond – Customization, Web Framework, HTTP Event Collector, REST API, and SDKs

In this chapter, we will learn how to customize a Splunk application and use advanced features of Splunk, Splunk SDKs, and APIs to work with data in Splunk. You will learn about:

- Customizing the application navigation
- Adding a Sankey diagram of web hits
- Developing a tag cloud of purchases by country
- Adding Cell Icons to Highlight Average Product Price
- Remotely querying Splunk's REST API for unique page views
- Creating a Python application to return unique IP addresses
- Creating a custom search command to format product names
- Collecting data from remote scanning devices

Introduction

Throughout all of the chapters so far, we have been dealing directly with the core functionality found in Splunk Enterprise. In this chapter, we will dive into functionality that lets us create an even more powerful interactive experience with Splunk. By leveraging the latest technology in Splunk Enterprise, we can customize the look and feel, expose our users to richer visualizations, extract knowledge and data from Splunk into our own internal applications, or build completely new applications that leverage Splunk.

Taking your Splunk experience to the next level breaks out into four areas: the web framework, the REST API, **software development kits** (**SDKs**), and the HTTP Event Collector (HEC).

Web framework

The web framework is a core component of the Splunk platform. The framework extends the abilities of Splunk to allow for more extensible development. In this framework, you don't have to restart Splunk to see your changes, can write custom handlers and URL routing, and can create custom templates that can be used to generate client-side components. On the client side, you can leverage a custom Splunk JavaScript stack combined with HTML-based dashboards. You no longer need to do everything in SimpleXML! The SplunkJS Stack can even be downloaded as a set of libraries to be included in your applications outside of Splunk.

The full power of these technologies can be used to create the types of dashboard and report that will meet your exact needs.

REST API

The backbone of Splunk has always been the underlying REST API. The REST API allows access to everything from searching, to configuration, to ingesting data. Whether it's running one-off scripts to extract some data or automating a workflow with a third-party system, it can all be done with simple web requests to the API.

As with most of Splunk, the REST API is also very flexible and can many parameters that you can manipulate to change the output types (JSON, XML, and so on) or filter the results. Long before Splunk had the web framework, the REST API was the workhorse of integrating with Splunk and still plays a big part in this.

Software development kits (SDKs)

Over the past few years, the Splunk development team has been creating SDKs to assist developers with the creation of their own Operational Intelligence applications.

Using the SDKs, developers can easily:

- Manage and execute searches and saved searches
- Manage configuration details and user access
- Log data directly into Splunk
- And many other features

The SDKs are written to interact with the REST API and abstract the various details away to let you focus on getting the operational intelligence you need. Splunk currently has SDKs for Python, Java, JavaScript, PHP, Ruby, and C#.

HTTP Event Collector (HEC)

The HTTP Event Collector is a highly efficient and secure way to get data into Splunk over HTTP/HTTPS from devices that don't need, or are unable to run, the Splunk Universal Forwarder. This is especially relevant to the growing Internet of Things (IoT) market.

The HTTP Event Collector is easy to configure and can run on any Splunk instance. It utilizes tokens for authentication, which means you will never need to put credentials into the sending application.

OK, let's get a hands-on experience of this exciting technology!

Customizing the application navigation

As you come to the end of this book, it is a good time to look at the Operational Intelligence application you developed and add some simple customization to pull the app together from a presentation standpoint.

In this recipe, you will add custom navigation to your application to better organize the reports and dashboards.

Getting ready

To step through this recipe, you will need a running Splunk Enterprise server, with the sample data loaded from Chapter 11, *Play Time - Getting Data In*. Ideally, you should have completed all the earlier recipes in this book so that you have an Operational Intelligence application with a number of dashboards and reports contained within it. By now, you should be familiar with navigating the Splunk user interface and using the Splunk search language.

How to do it...

Follow the steps in this recipe to add some custom navigation and design tweaks:

1. Log in to your Splunk server.
2. Select the **Operational Intelligence** application:

3. Click on **Settings** and then on **User interface:**

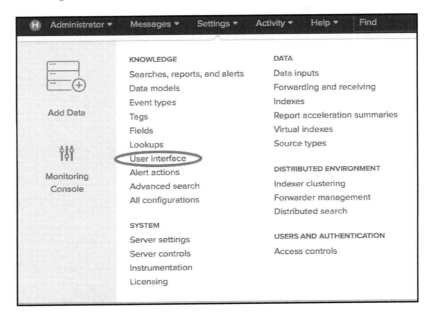

4. Click on **Navigation menus:**

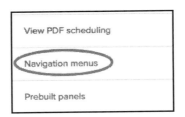

5. You should see one item in the list named **default**. Click on it.
6. You should see some existing code as follows:

```
<nav search_view="search" color="#65A637">
<view name="search" default='true' />
<view name="datasets" />
<view name="reports" />
<view name="alerts" />
<view name="dashboards" />
</nav>
```

7. Modify the code as follows:

```
<nav search_view="search" color="#0E3677">
  <view name="search" default='true' />
<!--
  <view name="data_models" />
  <view name="reports" />
  <view name="alerts" />
-->
  <collection label="Sales">
    <view name="product_monitoring" />
    <view name="purchase_volumes" />
  </collection>
  <collection label="Performance">
    <view name="operational_monitoring" />
    <view name="website_monitoring" />
    <view name="session_monitoring" />
    <view name="predictive_analytics" />
  </collection>
    <collection label="Operations">
    <view name="session_and_purchase_trends" />
    <view name="web_hits" />
  </collection>
  <collection label="Visitors">
    <view name="visitor_monitoring" />
  </collection>
  <collection label="Saved Reports">
    <collection label="Chapter 1 - Play Time">
        <saved source="unclassified" match="cp01" />
     </collection>
    <collection label="Chapter 2 - Diving into Data">
        <saved source="unclassified" match="cp02" />
     </collection>
        <collection label="Chapter 3 - Dashboards
          Visualizations">
        <saved source="unclassified" match="cp03" />
  </collection>
    <collection label="Chapter 4 - Building an App">
        <saved source="unclassified" match="cp04" />
     </collection>
    <collection label="Chapter 5 - Extending Intelligence">
        <saved source="unclassified" match="cp05" />
     </collection>
     <collection label="Chapter 6 - Advanced Searching">
        <saved source="unclassified" match="cp06" />
     </collection>
    <collection label="Chapter 7 - Enriching Data">
        <saved source="unclassified" match="cp07" />
```

```
      </collection>
      <collection label="Chapter 8 - Being Proactive">
          <saved source="unclassified" match="cp08" />
      </collection>
      <collection label="Chapter 9 - Speed Up Intelligence">
          <saved source="unclassified" match="cp09" />
      </collection>
      <collection label="Chapter 10 - Above and Beyond">
          <saved source="unclassified" match="cp10" />
      </collection>
      </collection>
      <collection label="Administration">
          <a href="http://docs.splunk.com">Splunk
              Documentation</a>
          <a href="http://apps.splunk.com">Splunk Apps</a>
          <a href="http://discoveredintelligence.ca/
      getting-started-with-splunk/">Splunk Help</a>
      <view name="dashboards" />
          </collection>
      </nav>
```

You can also view this file outside of the Splunk GUI, and it can be found in `$SPLUNK_HOME/etc/apps/operational_intelligence/default/data/ui/nav/default.xml`.

8. Once the edits have been made, click on **Save** and then select the **Operational Intelligence** app as you did in step 2. You should now see that you have fully customized the menus of the application and changed the navigation toolbar highlight color to blue (the colored bar under the selected menu item):

How it works...

In this recipe, you edited the navigation of the **Operational Intelligence** application to better organize the dashboards and reports. You also changed the color of the navigation bar from the default green to gray. Let's break down the code a bit to explain a few things.

XML fragment	Description
```<nav search_view="search" color="#0E3677">```	This is where the color of the navigation highlight was changed using the HEX color value for blue.
```<!-- <view name="data_models" /> <view name="reports" /> <view name="alerts" /> -->```	These default views were commented out so that they do not display in the application. You can also simply delete the lines instead.
```<collection label="Sales"> <view name="product_monitoring" /> <view name="purchase_volumes" /> </collection>```	Next, you added a series of collection elements that group the various views (dashboards) into categories such as sales, performance, and so on.
```<collection label="Saved Reports"> <collection label="Chapter 1 - Play Time"> <saved source= "unclassified" match="cp01" /> </collection> ... </collection>```	You then added a series of nested collection elements, which allow for grouping within a common group. In this case, we list all of the reports that you saved during the recipes in this book. Using the `match` parameter, we are able to match the searches by chapter name into their respective collections. Note that to display searches, we use the `saved` parameter, and earlier we used the `view` parameter.

| <pre><collection
    label="Administration">
<a   href="http://
         docs.splunk.com">
         Splunk
         Documentation</a>
<a   href="http://
         apps.splunk.com">
         Splunk Apps</a>
<a   href="http://
         discovered
         intelligence.ca/
         getting-started-
         with-splunk/">
         Splunk Help</a><view
    name="dashboards" />
</collection></pre> | Finally, you added an admin menu that lists a number of resources. To do this, you simply added the familiar HTML `href` code. We also retain the dashboards menu item for easy access to a centralized listing of all dashboards. |

There's more...

This just skims the surface of some of the customization that can be applied to a Splunk application. For example, you can implement your own CSS for the app, or even use your own icons and graphics.

 Splunk has a detailed manual on advanced development, including how to modify the CSS for an app, how to change the icons and images, and how to package your application to upload it to the Splunk app store. For more information, see the documentation at https://docs.splunk.com/Documentation/Splunk/latest/AdvancedDev.

Adding a Sankey diagram of web hits

As you have seen from the other recipes throughout the book, you have used many of the normal everyday visualizations commonly seen in spreadsheets and presentations. As data intelligence tools such as Splunk push the boundaries of getting data into a user's hands, there is a need to deliver and represent data using new and unique visualizations.

This recipe will show you how to install the Sankey diagram visualization add-on and create a custom visualization of relationships between web page hits and average bytes transferred, which will be populated as a new dashboard in the Operational Intelligence application.

Getting ready

To step through this recipe, you will need a running Splunk Enterprise server, with the sample data loaded from Chapter 1, *Play Time - Getting Data In*. You should be familiar with navigating the Splunk user interface and using the Splunk search language. Some basic knowledge of JavaScript is recommended.

You will also need to download the Sankey Diagram Visualization add-on app from Splunkbase. This app can be found at `https://splunkbase.splunk.com/app/3112/`.

How to do it...

Follow the steps in this recipe to add a Sankey diagram:

1. Log in to your Splunk server.
2. From the **Apps** menu in the upper left-hand corner of the home screen, click on the gear icon:

3. The Apps settings page will load. Then, click on the **Install App from file** button.
4. Click the **Choose File** button and select the app file that was previously downloaded from Splunkbase, then click the **Upload** button:

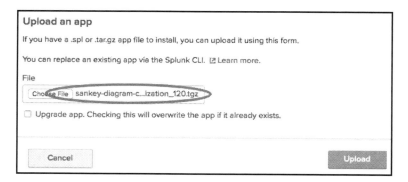

5. After the app has been installed, select the **Operational Intelligence** application from the **Apps** menu:

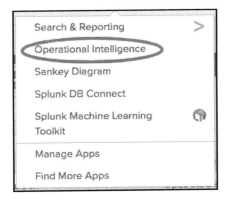

6. Click on the **Administration** menu and then click the **Dashboards** menu item.
7. Click on the **Create New Dashboard** button.
8. In the **Create New Dashboard** window, enter `Web Hits` in the **Title** field and select **Shared in App** in the **Permissions** field.
9. Click on **Create Dashboard:**

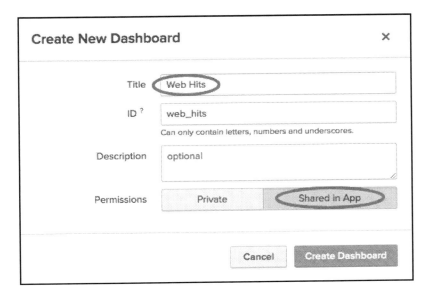

10. Click on the **+ Add Panel** button:

11. In the Add Panel flyout menu, select Sankey Diagram and enter the following **Search String**:

```
index=main sourcetype=access_combined | rex field=referer
"https?://.*(?<referer_path>/.*)" | stats count, avg(bytes) by
referer_path uri_path
```

The following is a screenshot of how the screen will look:

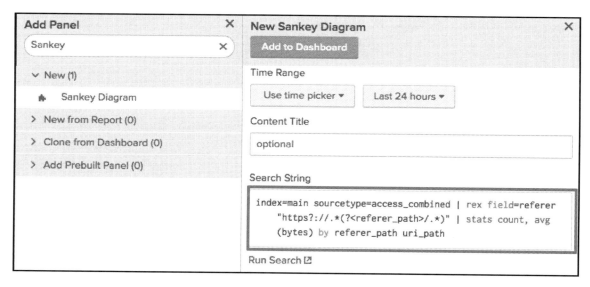

12. Click **Add to Dashboard**, then click **Save**.

13. After a short while, you should see the Sankey diagram load on your dashboard. This shows the relationships between pages and bytes transferred:

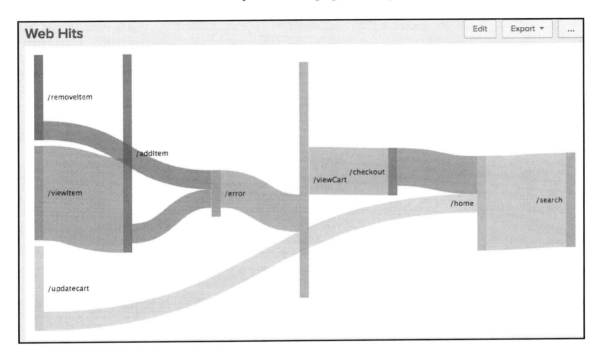

How it works...

Before the custom visualization framework was available in Splunk, you would have needed to acquire the custom code or create your visualization code and modify your dashboard using JavaScript. Now that visualizations can be properly packaged, you can simply select them from the same visualization picker that the built-in visualizations use.

To use a custom visualization, you first download the app that contains the visualization and then install the app in your Splunk instance. From there, you create your dashboards as you normally would and can select the right visualization for your data.

For our Web Hits dashboard, you took the web logs data over the past 24 hours and using the requested page (uri_path) and the page the request came from (referer_path), you created a source-target relationship between pages, using a simple statistical count-driven search. The Sankey Diagram visualization expects the source and target data fields to be the first two columns in your statistics table. The count field in your statistics becomes the field used to provide the weight of the Sankey lines. The average bytes transferred column then becomes additional data that is displayed when you mouse over the line.

The custom visualization framework has been a very popular feature that has seen many new visualizations, such as the Sankey diagram, developed that leverage D3.js JavaScript library. The D3.js library helps create dynamic and interactive data visualizations.

To find more custom visualizations that have been created by Splunk and the Splunk community, visit `https://splunkbase.com`.

For more details on the D3.js library, visit `https://d3js.org`.

There's more...

Splunk is very flexible, and there are a few tweaks you can make to improve or modify the behavior of the dashboard.

Changing the Sankey diagram options

As with most visualizations, there are usually parameters that can be changed to alter its behavior. These parameters could affect anything from the way the visualization is rendered on the screen to how it processes the data it receives.

The developer of the custom visualization decides which options they want to expose to the user, unlike the built-in dashboards that come with Splunk. To access the options, put the dashboard in Edit mode by clicking the **Edit** button on the dashboard and then click on the paintbrush icon of the visualization. From there, you can go through the different options and update as necessary. When you're finished, you can click the X in the upper-right corner of the menu:

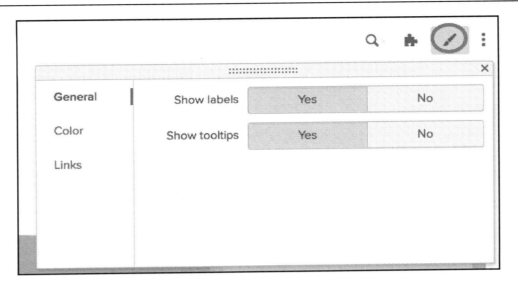

See also

- The *Developing a tag cloud of purchases by country* recipe
- The *Remotely querying Splunk's REST API for unique page views* recipe
- The *Creating a Python application to return unique IP addresses* recipe

Developing a tag cloud of purchases by country

As you saw in the *Adding a Sankey diagram of web hits* recipe, using custom visualizations allows for more creative and unique representations of your data.

This recipe will show you how to develop a tag cloud custom visualization from scratch and add it to a new dashboard in the **Operational Intelligence** application. The tag cloud will allow you to visualize purchases by country for the past week.

Getting ready

To step through this recipe, you will need a running Splunk Enterprise server, with the sample data loaded from Chapter 1, *Play Time - Getting Data In*. You should be familiar with navigating the Splunk user interface and using the Splunk search language. Some basic knowledge of JavaScript and CSS is recommended.

This recipe requires that you have NodeJS and the Node Package Manager (NPM) already installed and working on the Splunk server. NodeJS is a server-side JavaScript runtime environment.

 For more information on NodeJS and instructions for installing it and NPM, visit https://nodejs.org.

How to do it...

Follow the steps in this recipe to create a new dashboard that contains a tag cloud of purchase countries:

1. Log in to your Splunk server.
2. Select the **Operational Intelligence** application:

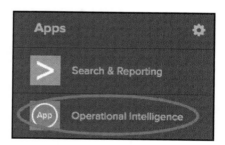

3. Click on the **Administration** menu and then click the **Dashboards** menu item.
4. Click on the **Create New Dashboard** button.
5. In the **Create New Dashboard** window, enter `Purchase Volumes` in the **Title** field and select **Shared in App** in the **Permissions** field.

6. Click on **Create Dashboard:**

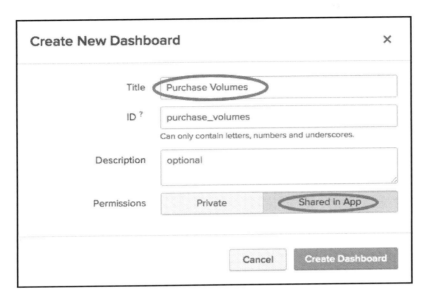

7. Click on Source:

8. Replace the source with the following SimpleXML and click **Save:**

```
<dashboard>
<label>Purchase Volume</label>
<row>
<table>
<title>Table</title>
<search>
<query>index=main sourcetype=log4j requestType=checkout |
iplocation ipAddress | stats sum(total) as "Total Purchases($)"
by Country | sort - "Total Purchases($)"
</query>
<earliest>-7d</earliest>
<latest>now</latest>
</search>
</table>
```

```
<viz type="operational_intelligence.tag_cloud">
<search>
<query>index=main sourcetype=log4j requestType=checkout |
iplocation ipAddress | stats sum(total) as "Total Purchases($)"
by Country | sort limit=20 - "Total Purchases($)"</query>
<earliest>0</earliest>
<latest></latest>
</search>
<option name="drilldown">true</option>
<option
name="operational_intelligence.tag_cloud.maxFontSize">48</optio
n>
<option
name="operational_intelligence.tag_cloud.minFontSize">12</optio
n>
<option
name="operational_intelligence.tag_cloud.valueField">Total
Purchases($)</option>
<option
name="operational_intelligence.tag_cloud.labelField">Country</o
ption>
</viz>
</row>
</dashboard>
```

9. In the `$SPLUNK_HOME/etc/apps/operational_intelligence/` **directory, create the following directories if they do not already exist:**

```
appserver
appserver/static
appserver/static/visualizations
appserver/static/visualizations/tag_cloud
appserver/static/visualizations/tag_cloud/src
```

10. In the `$SPLUNK_HOME/etc/apps/`
`operational_intelligence/appserver/static/visualizations/tag_cl`
oud **directory, create a** `package.json` **file and add the following to it:**

```
{
  "name": "tag_cloud",
  "version": "1.0.0",
  "description": "Splunk Operational Cookbook Tag Cloud
Recipe",
  "main": "visualization.js",
  "scripts": {
    "build": "$SPLUNK_HOME/bin/splunk cmd node
./node_modules/webpack/bin/webpack.js",
    "devbuild": "$SPLUNK_HOME/bin/splunk cmd node
```

```
./node_modules/webpack/bin/webpack.js --progress",
    "watch": "$SPLUNK_HOME/bin/splunk cmd node
./node_modules/webpack/bin/webpack.js -d --watch --progress"
    },
    "author": "Splunk",
    "license": "MIT",
    "devDependencies": {
      "webpack": "^1.12.6"
    },
    "dependencies": {
      "jquery": "^2.2.0",
      "underscore": "^1.8.3"
    }
}
```

11. In the
    $SPLUNK_HOME/etc/apps/operational_intelligence/appserver/static
    /visualizations/tag_cloud **directory, create a** webpack.config.js **file and
    add the following to it:**

```
var webpack = require('webpack');
var path = require('path');

module.exports = {
    entry: 'visualization_source',
    resolve: {
        root: [
            path.join(__dirname, 'src'),
        ]
    },
    output: {
        filename: 'visualization.js',
        libraryTarget: 'amd'
    },
    externals: [
        'api/SplunkVisualizationBase',
        'api/SplunkVisualizationUtils'
    ]
};
```

12. In the
$SPLUNK_HOME/etc/apps/operational_intelligence/appserver/static
/visualizations/tag_cloud **directory, create a** visualization.css **file and**
add the following to it:

```
.tagcloud-viz {
    text-align: center;
    margin: 20px auto;
    max-width: 60%;
    line-height: 18px;
}

.tagcloud-viz .link {
    padding: 2px 3px;
    display: inline-block;
    vertical-align: middle;
}
```

13. In the
$SPLUNK_HOME/etc/apps/operational_intelligence/appserver/static
/ visualizations/tag_cloud/src **directory, create a**
visualization_source.js **file and add the following to it:**

```
define([
    'jquery',
    'underscore',
    'api/SplunkVisualizationBase'
], function($, _, SplunkVisualizationBase) {
    return SplunkVisualizationBase.extend({

        initialize: function() {
SplunkVisualizationBase.prototype.initialize.apply(this,
arguments);
            this.$el = $(this.el);
            this.$el.addClass("tagcloud-viz");
        },

        getInitialDataParams: function() {
            return ({
                outputMode:
SplunkVisualizationBase.ROW_MAJOR_OUTPUT_MODE,
                count: 200
            });
        },

        updateView: function(data, config) {
            var labelField =
```

```
config['display.visualizations.custom.operational_intelligence.
tag_cloud.labelField'];
            var valueField =
config['display.visualizations.custom.operational_intelligence.
tag_cloud.valueField'];
            var minFontSize =
parseFloat(config['display.visualizations.custom.operational_in
telligence.tag_cloud.minFontSize']);
            var maxFontSize =
parseFloat(config['display.visualizations.custom.operational_in
telligence.tag_cloud.maxFontSize']);

            var el = this.$el.empty().css('line-height',
Math.ceil(maxFontSize * 0.55) + 'px');
            var minMagnitude = Infinity, maxMagnitude = -
Infinity;
            var fieldNames = _.pluck(data.fields, 'name');
            var labelFieldIdx = fieldNames.indexOf(labelField);
            var valueFieldIdx = fieldNames.indexOf(valueField);
            _(data.rows).chain().map(function(result) {
                var magnitude =
parseFloat(result[valueFieldIdx]);
                minMagnitude = magnitude < minMagnitude ?
magnitude: minMagnitude;
                maxMagnitude = magnitude > maxMagnitude ?
magnitude: maxMagnitude;
                return {
                    label: result[labelFieldIdx],
                    magnitude: magnitude
                };
            }).each(function(result) {
                var size = minFontSize + ((result.magnitude -
minMagnitude) / maxMagnitude * (maxFontSize - minFontSize));
                $('<a class="link" href="#" />
').text(result.label + ' ').css({
                    'font-size': size
                }).appendTo(el).click(function(e) {
                    e.preventDefault();
                    var payload = {
                        action:
SplunkVisualizationBase.FIELD_VALUE_DRILLDOWN,
                        data: {}
                    };
                    payload.data[labelField] =
$.trim($(e.target).text());
                    this.drilldown(payload);
                }.bind(this));
            }, this);
```

```
                    }
            });
        });
```

14. In the `$SPLUNK_HOME/etc/apps/operational_intelligence/local` directory, create a `visualizations.conf` file and add the following to it:

    ```
    [tag_cloud]
    label = Tag Cloud
    description = Visualize text frequency as a tag cloud
    ```

15. From the `$SPLUNK_HOME/etc/apps/operational_intelligence/appserver/static/visualizations/tag_cloud` directory, run the `npm run build` command, which will build the visualization and make it available to your dashboard.

16. Restart Splunk.

17. Log in to your Splunk server.

18. Select the **Operational Intelligence** application and return to the Purchase Volume dashboard.

19. You should now see both a table and a tag cloud of the top purchasing countries:

How it works...

The tag cloud visualization is a way to represent and render the magnitude of data values as they relate to each other. In this case, you represented the total number of purchases by country over the past 7 days. You then used this data to visualize the top purchasing country and the next highest purchasing countries.

Like the Sankey visualization recipe, the tag cloud is a built using the Splunk visualization framework, which allows for the creation and distribution of reusable visualizations.

The visualization framework leverages NodeJS and NPM as build tools on the Splunk server to bundle the code that renders the visualization in a way that can be easily portable and viewed in a dashboard, without worrying about module dependencies with other parts of the dashboard. NodeJS and NPM do not become part of the visualization.

The `package.json` file tells NPM when you run `npm init`, which third-party JavaScript modules you want to use in your visualization, as well as Webpack. Webpack is the tool that performs the JavaScript bundling and needs a `webpack.config.js` configuration file to define which JavaScript files to input, what to do with the JavaScript code, and where to output it.

When all the files are ready to be bundled, you run the `npm run build` command. This command runs a NodeJS process and bundles the JavaScript files together. The `visualizations.conf` file lets Splunk know about the visualization so that it can be used in the dashboard.

Most of the visualization's functionality comes from JavaScript and CSS and can be made to create a visualization that meets your exact needs.

Let's break down the JavaScript:

JavaScript fragment	Description

<pre>define([
    'jquery',
    'underscore',
    'api/SplunkVisualizationBase'
], function($,   _, SplunkVisualizationBase) {
    return   SplunkVisualizationBase.extend({</pre>
	This code tells JavaScript which modules to load and the objects in which to make them available within the script.

<pre>initialize: function() {
SplunkVisualizationBase.prototype.initialize.apply(this,   arguments);
    this.$el = $(this.el);
    this.$el.addClass("tagcloud-viz");
},</pre>
	The initialize function sets up a reference to the main DOM element that the visualization will be tied to and adds a custom CSS class to it.

<pre>getInitialDataParams: function() {
    return ({
        outputMode: SplunkVisualizationBase.ROW_MAJOR_OUTPUT_MODE,
        count: 200
    });
},</pre>
	The getInitialDataParams function tells Splunk what the output format of your data should be and how many results the search is limited to.

```
updateView:   function(data, config) {
    var   labelField =
config['display.visualizations.custom.operational_intelligence.tag_cloud.labelField'];
    var   valueField =
config['display.visualizations.custom.operational_intelligence.tag_cloud.valueField'];
    var   minFontSize =
parseFloat(config['display.visualizations.custom.operational_intelligence.tag_cloud.minFontSize']);
    var   maxFontSize =
parseFloat(config['display.visualizations.custom.operational_intelligence.tag_cloud.maxFontSize']);
    var el =    this.$el.empty().css('line-height', Math.ceil(maxFontSize * 0.55) + 'px');
    var   minMagnitude = Infinity, maxMagnitude = -Infinity;
    var   fieldNames = _.pluck(data.fields, 'name');
    var labelFieldIdx   = fieldNames.indexOf(labelField);
    var   valueFieldIdx = fieldNames.indexOf(valueField);
    _(data.rows).chain().map(function(result) {
        var   magnitude = parseFloat(result[valueFieldIdx]);
        minMagnitude = magnitude < minMagnitude ? magnitude: minMagnitude;
        maxMagnitude = magnitude > maxMagnitude ? magnitude: maxMagnitude;
        return {
            label: result[labelFieldIdx],
            magnitude: magnitude
        };
    }).each(function(result) {
        var size   = minFontSize + ((result.magnitude - minMagnitude) / maxMagnitude *
(maxFontSize - minFontSize));
        $('<a    class="link" href="#" /> ').text(result.label + ' ').css({
            'font-size':   size
        }).appendTo(el).click(function(e) {
            e.preventDefault();
            var   payload = {
                action: SplunkVisualizationBase.FIELD_VALUE_DRILLDOWN,
                data: {}
            };
            payload.data[labelField] = $.trim($(e.target).text());
            this.drilldown(payload);
        }.bind(this));
    }, this);
}
```

The updateView function is where you define the main code that creates and updates the visualization. In the tag cloud, the custom parameters from the SimpleXML configuration are retrieved, then the remaining code processes each of the rows of the data passed to it and determines and updates the size of the text, based on the relative sizes of the other data the visualization already has. A drilldown option is also applied to the resulting HTML so that users can click on the data points properly.

For the tag cloud visualization, you set custom parameters in the SimpleXML that were passed to the visualization so that certain values do not have to be hardcoded into the JavaScript.

For more details on how to create custom visualizations, visit
https://docs.splunk.com/Documentation/Splunk/latest/AdvancedDev/
CustomVizDevOverview.

There's More...

If you would like your custom visualization to be usable in other apps on your Splunk server, you must make the visualization global.

To enable the visualization to be global, in the $SPLUNK_HOME/etc/apps/
operational_intelligence/metadata directory create or update the local.meta file
with:

```
[visualizations/tag_cloud]
export = system
```

The export = system setting tells Splunk that the tag_cloud visualization should be
made available to all other apps on the server.

See also

- The *Adding a Sankey diagram of web hits* recipe
- The *Remotely querying Splunk's REST API for unique page views* recipe
- The *Creating a Python application to return unique IP addresses* recipe

Adding Cell Icons to Highlight Average Product Price

As you saw in the *Adding a Sankey diagram of web hits* and *Developing a tag cloud of purchases
by country* recipes, visualizing data with charts can be a great way to gain visibility into
meaning of your data. However, some types of data are best visualized using a table. In this
case, you can get some added benefit by highlighting specific cells based on some logic that
we can control.

This recipe will show you how to create a new dashboard panel containing a table of
purchase locations for the past week. You will then add icons to cells within the table, to
better highlight and visualize the average purchase price.

Getting ready

To step through this recipe, you will need a running Splunk Enterprise server, with the sample data loaded from Chapter 1, *Play Time - Getting Data In*. You should be familiar with navigating the Splunk user interface and using the Splunk search language. Some basic knowledge of JavaScript, CSS, and HTML is recommended.

How to do it...

Follow the steps in this recipe to create a new panel in the Product Monitoring dashboard with tabular cell highlighting:

1. Log in to your Splunk server.
2. Select the **Operational Intelligence** application.
3. From the search bar, enter the following search and select to run over **Last 60 Minutes**:

```
index=main sourcetype=log4j requestType="checkout" | eval
avg_price=round(total/numberOfItems,2) | table customerId
orderId numberOfItems total avg_price
```

4. Click on the **Save As** dropdown and select **Report** from the list, as shown in the following snapshot:

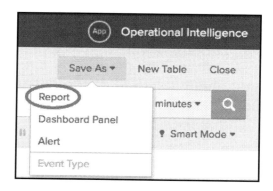

5. In the pop-up box that gets displayed, enter
   `cp10_average_checkout_product_price` as the title of the report and select
   No in the **Time Range Picker** field; then, click on **Save**:

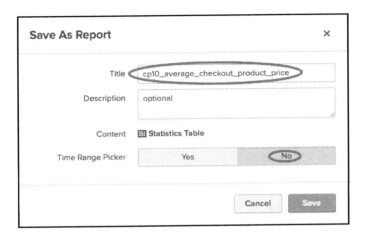

6. On the next screen, click on the **Add to Dashboard** button.
7. In the pop-up box that appears, select **Existing** and select **Product Monitoring**.
   Give the panel we are adding a title of `Average Checkout Product Price`.
   Ensure the panel is powered by **Report** and then click on **Save** to create the new
   dashboard with the statistics table:

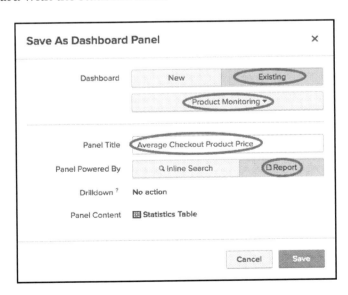

8. Click on **View Dashboard** to see the panel that's been added to your Product Monitoring dashboard.

9. Click on the **Edit** button and then click **Source**:

10. In the opting `<dashboard>` tag, update it with a `script` and `stylesheet` attributes:

```
<dashboard script="cp_10_table_cell_icon.js"
stylesheet="cp_10_table_cell_icon.css">
```

11. Locate the `<table>` tag of the panel that was just added and update the tag with an `id` attribute:

```
<table id="cp10_highlight">
<title>Average Checkout Product Price</title>
<search ref="cp10_average_checkout_product_price"></search>
</table>
```

12. Click **Save**.

13. From a console window or a file explorer window, go to the `$SPLUNK_HOME/etc/apps/operational_intelligence` directory and create an `appserver` folder, and then a `static` folder (if not already created), so that the complete path is now `$SPLUNK_HOME/etc/apps/operational_intelligence/appserver/static`.

14. In the `$SPLUNK_HOME/etc/apps/operational_intelligence/appserver/static` directory, create a `cp_10_table_cell_icon.js` file and add the following to it:

```
require([
    'underscore',
    'jquery',
    'splunkjs/mvc',
    'splunkjs/mvc/tableview',
    'splunkjs/mvc/simplexml/ready!'
], function(_, $, mvc, TableView) {
```

```
            var RangeMapIconRenderer =
TableView.BaseCellRenderer.extend({
        canRender: function(cell) {
                // Only use the cell renderer for the range field
                return cell.field === 'avg_price';
        },
        render: function($td, cell) {
        var value = parseFloat(cell.value);
                var icon = 'error';
                var range = 'severe';

                if (value > 1000) {
                        icon = "check-circle";
                        range = "low";
                }
                else if (value > 200) {
                        icon = "alert";
                        range = "elevated";
                }

                $td.addClass('icon').html(_.template('<%- value %>
<i class="icon-<%-icon%> <%- range %>" title="<%- range
%>"></i>', {
                        icon: icon,
                        range: range,
                        value: value.toFixed(2)
                }));
                $td.addClass('numeric');
        }
    });
mvc.Components.get('cp10_highlight').getVisualization(function(
tableView){
        // Register custom cell renderer, the table will re-
render automatically
        tableView.addCellRenderer(new RangeMapIconRenderer());
    });
});
```

15. In the `$SPLUNK_HOME/etc/apps/operational_intelligence/appserver/static` directory, create a `cp_10_table_cell_icon.css` file and add the following to it:

```
td.icon i {
    font-size: 22px;
}
td.icon .severe {
```

```
            color: red;
        }
        td.icon .elevated {
            color: orangered;
        }
        td.icon .low {
            color: #006400;
        }
```

16. Restart Splunk.
17. Log in to your Splunk server.
18. Select the **Operational Intelligence** application and return to the Product Monitoring dashboard.
19. You should now see the cells of the `avg_price` column highlighted based on the amount.

How it works...

First, you created a search. Let's break down the search piece by piece:

Search fragment	Description
`index=main    sourcetype=log4j requestType="checkout"`	You should be familiar with this search from the recipes in previous chapters. It is used to return events from the application logs. For this search, you just want the checkout requests.
`| eval avg_price=round(total/numberOfItems,2)`	Using the `eval` command, you calculate the average price per product by taking the total amount spent over the total number of items purchased. You then round the average to two significant digits.
`| table   customerId orderId numberOfItems total avg_price`	Using the `table` command, you return just the fields you want to see in your table and the order in which you want to see them.

You added this search as a report and then added to a dashboard panel, so you can add your custom icons. To add the icons, you included a custom JavaScript file in the app. This file contains all the custom logic for adding your cell icons.

Let's break down the JavaScript:

JavaScript fragment	Description
```require(['underscore', 'jquery', 'splunkjs/mvc', 'splunkjs/mvc/tableview', 'splunkjs/mvc/simplexml/ready!'], function(_, $, mvc, TableView) {```	This code tells JavaScript which modules to load and the objects in which to make them available within the script.
```var CustomRangeRenderer = TableView.BaseCellRenderer.extend({ canRender: function(cell) { return _(['avg_price']).contains(cell.field); },```	You then create the custom table renderer by extending the base cell renderer object. You then implement a canRender function that only returns on the avg_price column that you want to add highlighting to.
```render: function($td, cell) {var value = parseFloat(cell.value);var icon = 'error';var range = 'severe';if (value > 1000) {icon = "check-circle";range = "low";}else if (value > 200) {icon = "alert";range = "elevated";}$td.addClass('icon').html(_.template('<%- value %> <i class="icon-<%-icon%> <%- range %>" title="<%- range %>"></i>', {icon: icon,range: range,value: value.toFixed(2)}));$td.addClass('numeric');}});```	You create a render function that is called when the correct column is rendered. This function contains the main logic and uses the value of the cell to determine which icon and CSS style to add to the cell. You then ensure that the column remains with the numeric style so that it will be sorted properly.

`mvc.Components.get('cp10_highlight').getVisualization(function(tableView)`
`{`
`        tableView.addCellRenderer(new CustomRangeRenderer());`
`    });`
	Finally, you tell JavaScript which Id to bind this custom table renderer to and pass it the reference to your custom object.

The following CSS styles were applied to the icon highlighting:

CSS fragment	Description

`td.icon i {`
`    font-size:    22px;`
`}`
	This CSS sets the font size for an icon cell with an icon tag to 22 pixels. This allows the icon image to be a bit larger than the text size.

`td.icon    .severe {`
`    color:    red;`
`}`
`td.icon    .elevated {`
`    color:`
`orangered;`
`}`
`td.icon .low {`
`    color:    #006400;`
`}`
	This CSS sets the background color of the icon depending on the severity level that is applied in the JavaScript.

Splunk allows you to include and reference custom JavaScript and CSS with Simple XML dashboards. This allows you to tap into the full power of the Web Framework and SplunkJS without having to use custom HTML dashboards.

See also

- The *Adding a Sankey diagram of web hits* recipe
- The *Remotely querying Splunk's REST API for unique page views* recipe
- The *Creating a Python application to return unique IP addresses* recipe

Remotely querying Splunk's REST API for unique page views

Web services have become the technology of choice for most of the applications that we use daily. By leveraging the connections that we use for regular web browsing, we can transfer data in a more programmatic fashion; this allows for easy integration between applications.

In this recipe, you will learn how to use Splunk's REST API to return unique IP addresses from the web server logs of our application.

Getting ready

To step through this recipe, you will need a running Splunk Enterprise server, with the sample data loaded from Chapter 1, *Play Time - Getting Data In*. You should be familiar with navigating the Splunk user interface and using the Splunk search language. This recipe will use the open source command-line tool **curl**. There are other command-line tools available, such as **wget**. The curl tool is usually installed by default on most Mac and Linux systems, but can be downloaded for Windows systems as well.

> For more information on curl, visit `http://curl.haxx.se/`.

How to do it...

Follow the steps in this recipe to remotely query Splunk for unique page views using the REST API. Note that you will need to change admin and changeme throughout this recipe to the Splunk username and password you have configured:

1. Open a console or command-line window on your Splunk server.
2. Create an initial request to ensure that the authentication works correctly. If it is successful, it will return a list of Splunk apps installed in XML format:

```
curl -k -u admin:changeme
  https://localhost:8089/servicesNS/admin
```

3. Update the REST endpoint in the request. This will return a fatal error as we have not defined a search:

```
curl -k -u admin:changeme
https://localhost:8089/servicesNS/admin/search/search/jobs/
export
```

4. Add the search to be executed to the request. This will return the results of the search in XML over the past 7 days, as we are including the earliest field value:

```
curl -k -u admin:changeme --data-urlencode search="search
 index=main sourcetype=access_combined earliest=-7d status=200
 |
 dedup clientip uri_path | stats count by uri_path"
https://localhost:8089/servicesNS/admin/search/search/jobs/
export
```

In all these curl examples, the username admin and password changeme were used. This is the default username and password set in a new installation of Splunk, and it is recommended that you update it with a more secure password.

How it works...

In this recipe, you executed a Splunk search using the REST API to look for unique page views over the past 7 days. On every Splunk installation, Splunk opens port 8089 by default to listen for REST requests. The requests can be sent using command-line tools such as curl, as seen in our examples, or they can be called using the browser directly.

Splunk supports GET, POST, and DELETE requests. You use a GET request to retrieve or view data, a POST request to update data, and a DELETE request to remove data. Also, results can be returned in various formats, such as XML, JSON, and CSV.

The type of operation you are looking to perform will change the value of the URL you are accessing. In this recipe, you are using an endpoint that allows for an export job, and as such, the URL included search/jobs/export.

As is expected, the access controls and permissions that you set up in Splunk are enforced in the REST API as well. This ensures that your users can't get around any security restrictions using lower-level tools than the normal web interface. All requests to the REST API are also encrypted using SSL. Self-signed certificates are created by default, but can also be replaced with the ones signed by your own certificate authority.

 Even the Splunk Web GUI uses the Splunk REST API behind the scenes when performing operations such as searching. For more information on REST, check out the REST Wikipedia page at
https://en.wikipedia.org/wiki/Representational_State_Transfer.

There's more...

The REST API in Splunk is very flexible, and there are a few tweaks you can make to improve or modify the behavior of the API calls.

Authenticating with a session token

Instead of having to pass the username and password on every request to the API, as you saw by setting the -u parameter, you can create a session token and then pass this on subsequent requests. The advantage of this is that it reduces the load on your Splunk server, as it does not require the caller to authenticate every request.

First, create the session token by calling the auth/login endpoint:

```
curl -k https://localhost:8089/servicesNS/admin/search/auth/login/ -d
'username=admin&password=changeme'
```

This will return a token such as the following:

```
<response>
 <sessionKey>XzcmjvXT4SKL6loDHx6dsGxFCrQNENwlWoKraskF_yQbvDyQ47zIl9
 icR1VUzA6dX8tGbKiCMghnhKfbPslKuzSaV4eXLioKwo</sessionKey>
</response>
```

Then, use the value contained in the session key tags as an authentication header in subsequent requests:

```
curl -k --data-urlencode search="search index=main
sourcetype=access_combined status=200 latest=now earliest=-15m | dedup
clientip uri_path | stats count by uri_path" -H "Authorization: Splunk
XzcmjvXT4SKL6loDHx6dsGxFCrQNENwlWoKraskF_yQbvDyQ47zIl9icR1VUzA6dX8tGb
 KiCMghnhKfbPslKuzSaV4eXLioKwo"
https://localhost:8089/servicesNS/admin/search/search/jobs/export
```

See also

- The *Developing a tag cloud of purchases by country* recipe
- The *Creating a Python application to return unique IP addresses* recipe
- The *Creating a custom search command to format product names* recipe

Creating a Python application to return unique IP addresses

The Splunk Python SDK was one of the first SDKs that Splunk developed and has since been used to integrate Splunk's ability to process and analyze large streams of data into custom applications. By leveraging the ability to integrate directly with your applications, you can see immediate results and fully leverage your operational intelligence capabilities.

In this recipe, you will learn how to use Splunk's Python SDK to create a custom Python application that will return unique IP addresses from the web server logs of our application.

Getting ready

To step through this recipe, you will need a running Splunk Enterprise server, with the sample data loaded from Chapter 1, *Play Time - Getting Data In*. You should be familiar with navigating the Splunk user interface and using the Splunk search language.

Some basic knowledge of Python is recommended. The Splunk Python SDK should also be downloaded and available on your Splunk Enterprise server. This recipe expects that the user has Python 2.7+ installed on their Splunk server. This example will not run under Python 3+.

 The Splunk Python SDK can be downloaded from
`https://dev.splunk.com`.

How to do it...

Follow the steps in this recipe to create a Python application that returns unique IP addresses:

1. Open a terminal window on your Splunk server.
2. Execute the following command to export the Python SDK directory location as an environment variable. Update the value of PYTHONPATH with the actual path where you have installed the SDK:

   ```
   export PYTHONPATH=~/splunk-sdk-python
   ```

3. Create a new file called `uniqueip.py` and open it for editing.
4. To the `uniqueip.py` file, add the import statements that are needed to load the correct Splunk libraries that we will be using:

   ```
   import splunklib.client as client
   import splunklib.results as results
   ```

5. Add constants to hold the values of the Splunk server you are connecting to and the credentials you are connecting with. You will likely need to change the Splunk username and password credentials from the default ones:

   ```
   HOST     = "localhost"
   PORT     = 8089
   USERNAME = "admin"
   PASSWORD = "changeme"
   ```

6. Define the service instance you will be using to connect and communicate with your Splunk Enterprise server:

```
service = client.connect(
    host=HOST,
    port=PORT,
    username=USERNAME,
    password=PASSWORD)
```

7. Define a dictionary of search arguments that will be used with your search and will modify its behavior:

```
kwargs = {"earliest_time": "-15m",
          "latest_time": "now",
          "search_mode": "normal",
          "exec_mode": "blocking"}
```

8. Add a variable to hold the search query you will be using to return a list of unique IP addresses. Any double quotes in the search query need to be escaped:

```
searchquery = "search index=main
 sourcetype="access_combined" | stats count by clientip"
```

9. Create the job request and print out to the console when it has been completed:

```
job = service.jobs.create(searchquery, **kwargs)
print "Job completed...printing results!n"
```

10. Create a reference to the search results as follows:

```
search_results = job.results()
```

11. Add a ResultsReader, iterate through the results, and print out the IP address and the associated count:

```
reader = results.ResultsReader(search_results)
for result in reader:
    print "Result: %s => %s" %
(result['clientip'],result['count'])
```

12. The completed program code should look as follows:

```
import splunklib.client as client
import splunklib.results as results

HOST     = "localhost"
PORT     = 8089
USERNAME = "admin"
PASSWORD = "changeme"

service = client.connect(
    host=HOST,
    port=PORT,
    username=USERNAME,
    password=PASSWORD)

kwargs = {"earliest_time": "-15m",
          "latest_time": "now",
          "search_mode": "normal",
          "exec_mode": "blocking"}

searchquery = "search index=main sourcetype="access_combined" |
stats count by clientip"

job = service.jobs.create(searchquery, **kwargs)
print "Job completed...printing results!n"

search_results = job.results()

reader = results.ResultsReader(search_results)
for result in reader:
    print "Result: %s => %s" %
(result['clientip'],result['count'])
```

13. To execute your program, run this:

```
python uniqueip.py
```

The output of the program should look like this:

```
Result: 106.207.151.69 => 1
Result: 107.220.112.174 => 12
Result: 12.181.33.129 => 12
Result: 120.76.179.40 => 1
Result: 128.180.195.184 => 10
```

The program output details the number of events in the web access logs by the client IP over the last 15-minute timeframe specified in the Python code.

 In all the curl examples, the username `admin` and password `changeme` were used. This is the default username and password set in the new installation of Splunk and it is recommended that you update it with a more secure password.

How it works...

The REST API is a core part of Splunk and is used to do everything from authenticating, to searching, to configuration management. As you have seen in another recipe of this chapter, you can interact with the REST API very easily with simple command-line tools.

Organizations that maintain their own line of business applications and are looking to integrate the operational intelligence they can get out of Splunk can do so by leveraging the SDK for the language that their application is written in. Splunk has created SDKs for many of the mainstream programming languages. Python was the first one developed and released, since a large amount of Splunk is developed using Python.

The SDK is a wrapper around calls to the REST API and helps abstract the details by providing easy-to-use objects that can be interacted with. Most of the same REST endpoints available natively can be created as objects from the SDK.

As seen in the recipe, the majority of functionality that is used is assisting with the creation of a connection and management of the authentication, creation of a search job, and processing of the results. There are also objects that can be created to manage users and roles, getting data into Splunk, and working with saved searches.

There's more...

In this recipe, you begin to scratch the surface of utilizing the Python SDK. You also saw how you can extend your own applications to leverage Splunk data. As with most of Splunk, there are many ways to manipulate and view your data.

Paginating the results of your search

Leveraging the program created in this recipe, you can modify it as follows to paginate through your results:

```
job = service.jobs.create(searchquery, **kwargs)
print "Job completed...printing results!n"

total  = job["resultCount"]
offset = 0;
count  = 10;

while (offset < int(total)):
    page_args = {"count": count,
                 "offset": offset}

    search_results = job.results(**page_args)
    reader = results.ResultsReader(search_results)
    for result in reader:
        print "Result: %s => %s" % (result['clientip'],result['count'])
    offset += count
```

Paging your results from the server is a more efficient approach to retrieving the results for searches with many results as the Splunk server doesn't have to try and put all of the data into one response back to the client.

See also

- The *Remotely querying Splunk's REST API for unique page views* recipe
- The *Developing a tag cloud of purchases by country* recipe
- The *Creating a custom search command to format product names* recipe

Creating a custom search command to format product names

Sometimes, you just need that extra bit of logic or custom processing of data that might be unique to your line of business. You might also simply be in a position where you have picky executives who like to see their data formatted in a very specific manner.

In this recipe, you will learn how to use Splunk's Python SDK to create a custom search command that you can use to apply consistent formatting to product names, or any other string field, by capitalizing the first letter of each word in the string.

Getting ready

To step through this recipe, you will need a running Splunk Enterprise server, with the sample data loaded from Chapter 1, *Play Time - Getting Data In*. You should be familiar with navigating the Splunk user interface and using the Splunk search language. Some basic knowledge of Python is recommended. The Splunk Python SDK should also be downloaded and available on your Splunk Enterprise server.

The Splunk Python SDK can be downloaded from `https://dev.splunk.com`.

How to do it...

Perform the steps in this recipe to create a custom search command to format product names:

1. Open a console terminal on your Splunk server.
2. Change to the directory where you downloaded the Splunk Python SDK.
3. Expand the ZIP file using an appropriate tool located on your Splunk server.
4. Copy the `splunk-sdk-python-X.X.X/splunklib` (replace the Xes with your correct SDK version) directory into `$SPLUNK_HOME/etc/apps/operational_intelligence/bin`.

5. Create and add the following code to `commands.conf` located in the `$SPLUNK_HOME/etc/apps/operational_intelligence/local` **directory:**

```
[fixname]
filename = fixname.py
supports_getinfo = true
supports_rawargs = true
outputheader = true
requires_srinfo = true
```

6. In `$SPLUNK_HOME/etc/apps/operational_intelligence/bin`, **create** `fixname.py` **and add the following code:**

```
#!/usr/bin/env python

import sys

from splunklib.searchcommands import
    dispatch, StreamingCommand, Configuration, Option,
validators

@Configuration()
class FixNameCommand(StreamingCommand):
    """ Takes the first letter of each word in the field
     and capitalizes it
    ##Syntax

    .. code-block::
        fixname fieldname=<field>

    ##Description

    Takes the first letter of each word in the field and
     capitalizes it

    ##Example

    Uppercase the first letter of each word in the message
     field in the _internal
    index

    .. code-block::
        index=_internal | head 20 | fixname
         fieldname=message

    """
    fieldname = Option(
        doc='''
```

```
**Syntax:** **fieldname=***<fieldname>*
**Description:** Name of the field that will be
 capitalized''',
require=True, validate=validators.Fieldname())

    def stream(self, records):
        self.logger.debug('FixNameCommand: %s' % self)  # logs
command line
        for record in records:
            record[self.fieldname] =
             record[self.fieldname].title()
            yield record

dispatch(FixNameCommand, sys.argv, sys.stdin, sys.stdout,
 __name__)
```

7. Restart Splunk.
8. Log in to Splunk.
9. Select the **Operational Intelligence** application.
10. In the search bar, enter the following search over **Last 24 hours**:

```
index=main sourcetype=log4j ProductName=* | eval
ProductName=lower(ProductName) | fixname
fieldname=ProductName
```

- You should see that despite forcing the `ProductName` field values to be all lowercase, the `fixname` command has now capitalized each value.

How it works...

The Splunk Python SDK can allow you to not only get information out of Splunk in an easy, programmatic way, but also manipulate the processing of events as they move through your search.

Originally, custom search commands could be created using Python and added to Splunk, but they were difficult to debug and had no logging mechanism. With the Python SDK, you can now create your own custom search commands in a quicker and easier way, with better tools for troubleshooting.

Custom search commands come in three different flavors.The three commands and their descriptions are as follows:

Command	Description
Generating commands	This type of command generates new events that are inserted into the results. Examples include commands that read from lookup files, such as `inputcsv`.
Reporting commands	This type of command takes incoming events and generates a new set of outgoing events, usually based on some sort of processing or analysis. Examples include commands that do statistics, such as `stats` and `top`.
Streaming commands	This type of command takes incoming events and modifies or filters the outgoing events. Examples include commands that add or replace fields, or eliminate events based on some calculation, such as `eval`, `rename`, and `where`.

Let's review how the `fixname.py` script works:

Script fragment	Description

`#!/usr/bin/env python`
`import sys`
`from splunklib.searchcommands`
`   import dispatch,`
`StreamingCommand,`
`   Configuration, Option,`
`   validators`
	Import the necessary modules and libraries. This includes the Splunk library that has to be copied into the `bin` directory of the Splunk app.

`@Configuration()`	Here, you apply any configuration options that need to be specified to Splunk when the command is executed.
`class FixNameCommand` `   (StreamingCommand):`	This line defines the class name of the command, as well as any inheritance that might be required. In this command, the `StreamingCommand` class is to be inherited from.

``
""" Takes the   first letter of each
    word in the field and capitalizes
    it
    ##Syntax
    .. code-block::
        fixname   fieldname=<field>
    ##Description
    Takes the   first letter of each
        word in the field and
        capitalizes it
    ##Example
    Uppercase the   first letter of
        each word in the message field
        in the _internal
    index
    .. code-block::
        index=_internal
	head 20 |
	        fixname fieldname=message
	    """
	``
		Here, you are outlining all of the information that Splunk will present through the Splunk Web interface in the search bar help.

``
fieldname =   Option(
        doc='''
        Syntax:
fieldname=*<fieldname>*
Description: Name of
        the field that will be
        capitalized''',
require=True, validate=
        validators.Fieldname())
``
	This section defines the various options that the custom command will accept or is required to accept. The format, as well as any validation that is required, is also specified here.

``
def stream(self,   records):
        self.logger.debug
        ('FixNameCommand: %s'
        % self) # logs
        command line
    for   record in records:
        record[self.fieldname]
=
    record[self.fieldname].title()
        yield record
``
	This section implements the stream function. The stream function is called when records are to be processed. In this example, you are iterating through each of the records, and depending on the field that was defined in the options, you execute the title method on that value.

``
dispatch(FixNameCommand,   sys.argv,
    sys.stdin, sys.stdout,
    __name__)
``
	Finally, you dispatch the command, passing in the required arguments.

The `fixname` command is a straightforward command that leverages the title operation, available within the `String` object in Python, to uppercase the string that is in the requested field. It is a streaming command, as it is manipulating a field within an event as it moves through the command.

By leveraging the SDK, any number of commands can be developed that integrate with third-party systems, or apply proprietary algorithms or logic, to implement business rules that give organizations better visibility into their operations.

 For more information on how to create custom search commands, check out the documentation at `https://dev.splunk.com`.

See also

- The *Remotely querying Splunk's REST API for unique page views* recipe
- The *Creating a Python application to return unique IP addresses* recipe

Collecting data from remote scanning devices

It seems that every device being created and sold today can be "smart" and sit on your network, sending data about what it has been doing. The ability to capture this data in real time and integrate it into other business data is a critical step to enhancing your operational intelligence.

In this recipe, you will learn how to use the Splunk HTTP Event Collector to receive data from a remote scanning device that collects the inventory levels of products from your warehouse. The scanning device has been configured to send HTTP requests with a custom JSON object indicating what it has just scanned, versus the traditional process of waiting until the end of the day to download its data.

Getting ready

To step through this recipe, you will need a running Splunk Enterprise server, with the sample data loaded and configurations done from Chapter 1, *Play Time - Getting Data In*. You should be familiar with navigating the Splunk user interface and using the Splunk search language. This recipe will use the open source command-line tool **curl**. There are other command-line tools available, such as **wget**. The curl tool is usually installed by default on most Mac and Linux systems, but can be downloaded for Windows systems as well.

 For more information on curl, visit `http://curl.haxx.se/`.

How to do it...

Perform the steps in this recipe to create a custom search command to format product names:

1. Open a console or command-line window on your Splunk server.
2. Simulate your scanner sending data by create an HTTP request from the command-line, using the token for authentication that was created in Chapter 1, *Play Time - Getting Data In*:

   ```
   curl -k https://localhost:8088/services/collector/raw -H
   "Authorization: Splunk 8e958bb5-73fd-4cd2-b186-3c233f23168e " -
   d '{ "itemId": "1000016", "count": "120" }'
   ```

3. You should receive a success message back if the request was processed correctly:

   ```
   {"text":"Success","code":0}
   ```

4. Log in to Splunk.
5. Select the **Operational Intelligence** application.
6. In the search bar, enter the following search over **Last 24 hours**:

   ```
   index=main sourcetype=inventory:scanner
   ```

7. You should now see your simulated scanner entries as JSON events:

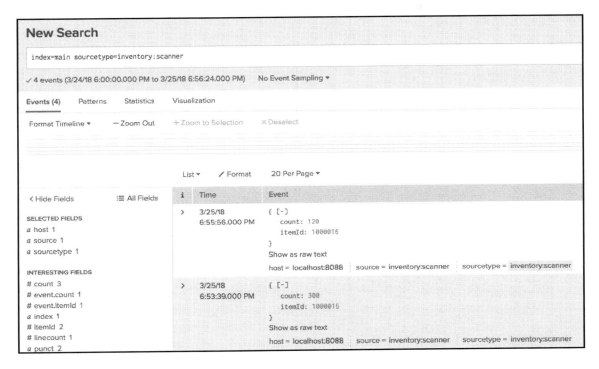

How it works...

To get the HTTP Event Collector to work, you first needed to configure the global settings. This defines the HTTP endpoint it will listen on - typically port 8088. This single port can receive multiple different types of data, since it is all differentiated by the token that is passed with it and by interpreting the data within the payload of the request. Other global defaults can be set, such as the index and sourcetype.

To set up the HTTP Event Collector for a specific data input, you needed to create a token. When setting up the token, you defined a default index and default sourcetype. These values will be used unless the data itself contains the values to use. The set of indexes that can be used by that token also have to be specified, so that someone cannot craft a custom event that could be routed into the wrong index.

Finally, you simulated the sending of an event using the Linux curl utility. You specified the token in an authorization header and the data to be posted as a JSON object. The data passed in the JSON object is what Splunk will interpret as the data for the event.

The HTTP Event Collector (HEC) can collect data at extremely high volumes from many devices and data sources. Taking advantage of the HEC for these additional data sources can help to drive better visibility into your data and increase your operational intelligence capabilities.

For more information on how to use the HTTP Event Collector, check out the documentation at
https://dev.splunk.com/view/event-collector/SP-CAAAE6M.

See also

- The *Remotely querying Splunk's REST API for unique page views* recipe
- The *Creating a Python application to return unique IP addresses* recipe

Other Books You May Enjoy

If you enjoyed this book, you may be interested in these other books by Packt:

Mastering Splunk Administration
Somesh Soni

ISBN: 9781785887734

- From installation to monitoring, best practices, and configuration details, get to know everything you need to know to become Splunk admin certified
- Design an environment to work in and analyze machine generated data with the Splunk base and apps
- Evaluate when to cluster a Splunk indexer
- Set up and utilize forwarders to retrieve data from your system
- Use the Splunk deployment server to host and deploy apps to various components within the infrastructure
- Improve your Splunk environment's security by seeing how to limit access and configure various areas of your Splunk infrastructure
- Improve your knowledge of search performance methodology

Splunk 7 Essentials - Third Edition

J-P Contreras, Erickson Delgado, Betsy Page Sigman

ISBN: 9781788839112

- Install and configure Splunk for personal use
- Store event data in Splunk indexes, classify events into sources, and add data fields
- Learn essential Splunk Search Processing Language commands and best practices
- Create powerful real-time or user-input dashboards
- Be proactive by implementing alerts and scheduled reports
- Tips from the Fez: Best practices using Splunk features and add-ons
- Understand security and deployment considerations for taking Splunk to an organizational level

Leave a review - let other readers know what you think

Please share your thoughts on this book with others by leaving a review on the site that you bought it from. If you purchased the book from Amazon, please leave us an honest review on this book's Amazon page. This is vital so that other potential readers can see and use your unbiased opinion to make purchasing decisions, we can understand what our customers think about our products, and our authors can see your feedback on the title that they have worked with Packt to create. It will only take a few minutes of your time, but is valuable to other potential customers, our authors, and Packt. Thank you!

Index